THE SPHINX ON
THE TABLE

THE SPHINX ON THE TABLE

Sigmund Freud's Art Collection and the Development of Psychoanalysis

Janine Burke

Walker & Company
New York

Published by Walker Publishing Company, Inc., New York
Distributed to the trade by Holtzbrinck Publishers

All papers used by Walker & Company are natural, recyclable products made from
wood grown in well-managed forests. The manufacturing processes conform to the
environmental regulations of the country of origin.

Library of Congress Cataloging-in-Publication Data has been applied for.

ISBN-10: 0-8027-1503-6
ISBN-13: 978-0-8027-1503-6

Published in Australia by Random House, Australia, 2006
as a Knopf book entitled *The Gods of Freud*

First U.S. edition 2006

Visit Walker & Company's Web site at www.walkerbooks.com

1 3 5 7 9 10 8 6 4 2

Printed in the United States of America by Quebecor World Fairfield

To Gabrielle Pizzi

All artefacts referred to are in the Freud Museum London,
unless otherwise noted.

CONTENTS

❧

Introduction

*I may say at once that I am no connoisseur in art, but simply a
layman . . . Nevertheless, works of art do exercise a powerful effect on me.*
SIGMUND FREUD[1]

A normal man with no complexes is unlikely to become a great collector.
MAURICE RHEIMS[2]

FREUD WAS NOT ALONE WHEN he entered the sea of dreams. His
companions were the gods of Egypt, Greece and Rome.

In the late 1890s, while writing *The Interpretation of Dreams*,
Sigmund Freud became an art collector, developing an obsession
with antiquity, beauty, myth and archaeology that led him to amass
a brilliant private museum of over two thousand statues, vases,

{ 1 }

reliefs, busts, fragments of papyrus, rings, precious stones and prints. In Freud's study at Berggasse 19, Vienna, every available surface was so crowded with antiquities, he barely had room to move.

Despite Freud's modest assertion that he was 'simply a layman', his taste was precise and discerning. His collection is an intriguing catalogue of world civilisations where objects rare and sacred, useful and arcane, ravaged and lovely are on display: Neolithic tools, delicate Sumerian seals, a great goddess of the Middle Bronze Age, Egyptian mummy bandages inscribed with magical spells and stained with embalming ointment, superb Greek Hellenistic statues, images of the Sphinx, erotic Roman charms, luxurious Persian carpets and Chinese jade lions no bigger than a baby's fist.

The popular image of Freud as austere, remote and forbidding is contradicted by the collection, which reveals a very different personality: an impulsive, hedonistic spender, an informed and finicky aesthete, a tomb raider complicit in the often illegal trade in antiquities, a tourist who revelled in sensual, Mediterranean journeys, a generous fellow who lavished exquisite gifts on his family and friends, and a tough negotiator for a bargain. Though Freud prescribed the intense, inner journey of psychoanalysis for his patients, his own therapy was shopping. Arranging choice items on his desk, Freud confessed to Jung, 'I must always have an object to love'.[3]

The collection offers multiple readings: as the embodiment of Freud's theories; as an investigation and celebration of past cultures; as an exercise in aesthetics; as a quest for excellence; as a memento of real and imagined journeys; as a catalogue of desires; and as a self-portrait.

Freud bought his first artworks in 1896, shortly after his father, Jacob (pl. 31), died. He was shaken by the event. 'In [my] inner self,' he reflected, '. . . I now feel quite uprooted.'[4] Jacob's death provoked a crisis during which Freud plunged into his own unconscious, the underground recesses of his buried self. *The Interpretation of Dreams* was the result of that painful and exhilarating journey of self-analysis, the foundation stone of his life's work. For Freud, mourning and art were aligned at this crucial transition.

Patients were taken by surprise the first time they were ushered into his rooms. Sergei Pankejeff, the Wolf Man, felt he was not in a doctor's office but an archaeologist's study, surrounded by 'all kinds of statuettes and other unusual objects, which even the layman recognised as archaeological finds from ancient Egypt'. A Russian aristocrat, Pankejeff had recounted to Freud his dream about a tree filled with white wolves. Writing about the case, Freud gave Pankejeff the pseudonym of the Wolf Man. To Pankejeff the artworks from 'long-vanished epochs' created a sense of sanctuary, a 'feeling of sacred peace and quiet . . . Everything here contributed to one's feeling of leaving the haste of modern life behind, of being sheltered from one's daily cares.'[5]

Hilda Doolittle, the poet known as H.D., was stunned.

> I cannot speak. I look around the room. A lover of Greek art, I am automatically taking stock of the room's contents. Priceless lovely objects here on the shelves to right, to left of me . . . I was to greet the Old Man of the Sea, but no one had told me of the treasures he had salvaged from the sea depth.

H.D. felt that Freud 'is at home here. He is part and parcel of these treasures.'[6]

Freud built his collection during the grand era of archaeological discoveries. His hero was Heinrich Schliemann, the buccaneering amateur who unearthed the site of Troy in 1871. In 1900, Arthur Evans began excavating the Palace of Minos at Knossos on Crete; twenty-two years later Howard Carter discovered Tutankhamun's tomb. Freud was eager to compare the process of psychoanalysis to archaeology, telling Pankejeff, 'the psychoanalyst, like the archaeologist, must uncover layer after layer of the patient's psyche, before coming to the deepest, most valuable treasures'.[7]

Max Pollak's 1914 etching (pl. 32) reveals the psychoanalyst's relationship with his art collection. Freud pauses while writing to gaze at the statues assembled on his desk. Perhaps he is completing *The Moses of Michelangelo*, published the same year. Freud focuses on the central figure, *Head of Osiris* (Third Intermediate Period, 1075–716 B.C. or later; pl. 21), Egypt's major deity, the god of life, death and transformation. Murdered by his brother Seth, cut into pieces and scattered, Osiris was restored to life by the magical intervention of Isis, his sister-wife. The myth suggests the narratives of recovery and healing integral to psychoanalysis. Pollak's dramatic study in light and dark links Freud's creative process as a thinker and writer to the contemplation of art. The statues are cast in shadow, symbolising the past; Freud, the triumphant excavator of the modern mind, is dramatically illuminated. The gods bear witness as divine counsellors, providing inspiration, cultural tradition, historical context and aesthetic stimulus for Freud's investigations.

Freud was justifiably proud of his collection. He protested when his friend Stefan Zweig, the prolific Viennese writer, neglected to mention it in an essay on Freud: 'I have sacrificed a great deal for my collection of Greek, Roman and Egyptian antiquities, have actually read more archaeology than psychology.'[8] In a frantic schedule that involved teaching at the University of Vienna, running a private practice, writing and translating, developing a network of international connections, travel and the demands of a large family, Freud also made the time to haunt antiquities shops in Vienna, Florence, Salzburg and Rome. Home with a new prize, Freud would bring it with him to the dinner table, 'placing it in front of him as a companion during the meal'.[9] Nor could he bear to be parted from the collection, even on holidays. Finishing 'the dream book' in the mountains near Berchtesgaden in 1899, Freud told a friend he was accompanied by '[m]y old and grubby gods . . . [who] take part in the work as paperweights for my manuscripts'.[10] As time went by, travelling with the gods became a necessity. During the 1930s, most of the collection would be packed by his wife Martha and Paula Fichtl, the maid, and transported to his summer residences near Vienna.

In his study, Freud created a private gallery kept aloof from the mundane world: none of his artworks was permitted anywhere else in the apartment he shared with Martha, their six children and Minna Bernays, Martha's sister. Freud's study was opulent, exotic and idiosyncratic; the rest of the apartment's decor was comfortable, bourgeois and unremarkable.

It was a contradiction that typified Freud. Describing himself as 'a godless Jew', his writings dismiss the consolations of religion yet he was enthralled by magical and sacred objects. Regarding the occult, Freud wrote 'if I were at the beginning rather than at the end of a scientific career . . . I might possibly choose just this field of research, in spite of all difficulties'.[11] Freud relished dichotomies and proposed dualistic theories about human behaviour and culture. Eros (the libido) struggled against the death drive. Statues of Eros, the god of love and desire, are well represented in Freud's collection. Though Freud developed revolutionary theories about powerful, instinctual sexual urges that determined the destiny both of civilisation and the individual, he was a traditionalist regarding women's role and cynical about social change.

Freud disdained modern art. When his friend Oscar Pfister published a book discussing Expressionism from a psychoanalytic view, Freud read it with 'interest as much as aversion', confiding 'I am terribly intolerant of cranks, that I only see the harmful side of them and that so far as these "artists" are concerned I am almost one of those whom you castigate as philistines and low-brows.' He congratulated Pfister for explaining 'why these people lack the right to claim the name of artist'.[12] The Surrealists insisted Freud was their patron saint, while he regarded them as 'complete fools'. But when Salvador Dalí visited Freud in 1938 and sketched his portrait, he was impressed by 'the young Spaniard . . . with his candid fanatical eyes and his undeniable technical mastery'.[13]

For Freud, the great enterprise of psychoanalysis and his art collection developed simultaneously, a symbiotic, nourishing relationship, each informing and enriching the other. Freud was never a wealthy man. In his early years of collecting, he had a growing family, as well as an extended family who often required financial assistance. Nor was his practice, given his controversial theories, thriving. After the First World War, it was often patients from England and America who were making their way to Berggasse 19, not the Viennese. When Freud received an inquiry from the taxation office expressing their doubts about his tax return 'since it is well known that your fame attracts patients who are able to pay high fees from foreign countries', he replied dryly, 'I note with pleasure this first official recognition which my work has found in Austria.'[14]

Freud did not allow privation to limit his compulsion to be

surrounded by beautiful things. He was the collector par excellence. Enough was never enough. 'The taste for collecting,' writes Maurice Rheims, 'is like a game played with utter passion.'[15] Collecting can also be an aggressive and compulsive urge, about competition and possession, the need to be first, to snatch the prize from beneath a rival's nose. Freud was a combative individual, as his long, sustained battle to secure the credibility of psychoanalysis shows. 'I am by nature nothing but a conquistador,' he declared, 'an adventurer, if you wish to translate the term, with all the inquisitiveness, daring and tenacity capable of such a man.'[16] His collection was also a retreat, a world designed for himself alone, his 'personal microcosm'.[17]

Curiously, Freud did not analyse his reasons for collecting. Nor did he, in a long and productive publishing career, write more than a few sentences at a time about his 'old and grubby gods'. Like Freud's other intriguing omissions in his writing – regarding his mother, his sexuality and his marriage – his obsession for collecting also involved love, desire, pleasure and possession. The collection highlights his contradictory attitude towards women. Freud was surrounded by women in his home, his practice and his professional life, as well as in the collection with its images of Isis, Athena, Artemis and Venus. But in Freud's version of the origins of religion and the development of civilisation, women's power was erased: males dominated and their battles for supremacy brought society into being. His treasured goddesses were unable to influence his opinion.

When Freud fled Vienna for London in 1938, near death from cancer, he declared 'a collection to which there are no new additions is really dead'.[18] Through grace and good fortune, Freud was able to whisk all the antiquities away from the Nazi invaders.

Today the collection is on display at 20 Maresfield Gardens, Hampstead – now the Freud Museum London – where he died on 23 September 1939.[19] In 1971, a selection of antiquities was given by his daughter Anna Freud to celebrate the opening of the Sigmund Freud Museum Vienna at Berggasse 19. Freud chose to die in his study, surrounded, as Lynn Gamwell has written, by 'his ancestors of choice, his most faithful colleagues, and the embodiments of his excavated truths of psychoanalysis'.[20]

Nature Boy

*I read that every known superstition in the world is gathered into the horseshoe of
the Carpathians, as if it were the centre of some sort of imaginative whirlpool.*
BRAM STOKER, DRACULA[1]

*To leave one's beloved home, fond relatives — the most beautiful
surroundings — ruins in the immediate neighbourhood — I must stop or I shall
become as sad as you!*
SIGMUND FREUD TO EMIL FLUSS, 16 JUNE, 1873[2]

FREUD BUILT THE ENTIRE edifice of psychoanalysis on childhood
memories: by the age of three the compass was set. When it came
to telling the story of his own childhood, Freud created a fairy
tale.

Once upon a time, he played happily in the forest near the small town of Freiberg in Moravia, then part of Austria-Hungary, now Příbor, Czech Republic, where he was born on 6 May 1856 (pl. 1). Freud loved the forest and escaped from his father to lose himself in its depths. Freiberg is ringed by the magnificent snow-capped Beskydy mountains, part of the Carpathians, that stretch across Central and Eastern Europe for over 1500 kilometres. A landscape of spectacular beauty and Gothic folklore, Bram Stoker set *Dracula* in the section of the Carpathians where they cloak Transylvania, now part of Romania. Published in 1897, *Dracula* was a purely imaginary endeavour: Stoker never visited Transylvania.

When Freud was three, this idyllic existence ended. Freud explained: 'the branch of the industry [textiles] in which my father was concerned met with a catastrophe. He lost all his means and we were forced to leave.' The family moved first to Leipzig, then to Vienna, where Freud grew up in a series of overcrowded apartments in the Jewish quarter of the Leopoldstadt. Freud drew a veil across that time. As far as he was concerned, the long and difficult years that followed were simply not worth remembering. Leaving Freiberg was such a shock it gave Freud a kind of amnesia and there were gaps when he tried to recall his early years in Vienna. 'I never felt really comfortable' in Vienna, Freud complained, and he ached for 'the beautiful woods near our home'.[3]

Freiberg, meaning 'free mountain', is a thirteenth-century market town built on a hill above the shallow Lubina River. Today its town square is named after Freud. Surrounded by arches and covered with cobblestones, it has changed little since Freud's time, aside from the addition of a bleak 1930s town hall. The family lived in a network of narrow streets a stone's throw from the square

in a rented room above a blacksmith's at Schlossergasse 117 (pl. 2).
From his upstairs window, Freud had a panoramic view of the
Beskydy mountains, shimmering, green and alluring. In 1931,
when a bronze plaque was unveiled honouring his birthplace,
Freud, then seventy-five, wrote to the town's mayor that deep
within him remained 'the happy child from Freiberg' who
'received the first indelible impressions from this air, from this soil'.[4]

Freud returned to the beautiful woods in the summer of
1872, when he was sixteen. They were his first holidays in the
country since the move to Vienna. He developed a crush on
Gisela Fluss, the twelve-year-old sister of his schoolfriend Emil.
It was a miserable experience. Not only did Freud lack the
courage to flirt with Gisela but he observed, with no small
degree of envy, how the Fluss family's fortunes had risen. 'I could
compare the comfort reigning there with our own style of living
at home in the town.' It was especially grating since Ignaz Fluss
was a textile merchant, like Jacob Freud. When Gisela departed
for school, she left Freud with his emotions at a high pitch. He
rediscovered the woods where he had played as a child and
consoled himself by wandering in his solitary 'little paradise',
building castles in the air.[5] If only Jacob's business had not gone
bust, Freud mused, he could have stayed in Freiberg, won Gisela's
heart and lived happily ever after.

Freud's forest remains an enchanting place, a vivid contrast of
sunlight and shadow, rivered with paths, where copses of slender
silver birch give way to the engulfing dark of pine trees (pl. 3).
The ground is covered with a tangle of grasses, wildflowers and
thick pine needles. The air is alive with birdsong. It is a wonderful place for a child to play. Less than two kilometres from Freiberg,
Jacob could have carried his small son there. Further afield are

more strenuous treks, to the commanding views of Hukvaldy Castle and the Stramberk Tower.

In the forest it seems that Freud discovered not only a sanctuary of solace and freedom but an appreciation of beauty that would remain with him all his life. Nature was a key factor in awakening his aesthetic sense. The exquisite pleasure of being surrounded by the natural world encouraged him to duplicate the experience by creating a personal environment of rare and lovely things. Nostalgia saturated Freud's memories of Freiberg, creating a sentimental hankering for the past, one that led him to collect treasures from ancient history and buried eras, souvenirs from the childhood of civilisation. Freud cast that time as an 'undisturbed golden age'.[6]

Nature taught, inspired and directed Freud, providing him with a rich vocabulary of metaphor, and training his eye and mind in the skills of perception and observation. His first memory was of picking dandelions in a 'steeply sloping piece of meadow-land, green and thickly grown', a recollection where lush natural beauty provides a theatre for play: 'the very recollection', Freud noted, that 'proves to be the most important, the very one that holds the key to the secret pages of [a person's] mind'.[7]

Decades later, as Freud's own family grew, summer holidays were taken at a variety of spectacular mountain retreats in Austria and South Tyrol where the forest became, once again, a playground, not only for himself but for his children, too. Going to the mountains with his brood was 'the greatest fun' for Freud.[8] These breaks also provided him with the time and opportunity to haunt antiquities shops. Whenever he walked through the streets of a strange town on holidays 'I read every shop sign that resembles the word . . . "Antiquities". This betrays the questing spirit of the collector.'[9] While holidaying at Innsbruck in 1898, Freud bought one of his first antiquities, a small Roman statue described by his three-year-old-daughter, Anna, as 'an old child'.[10] His passion for the past also took him on journeys to Italy and Greece.

Immersing himself in nature gave Freud the chance to mentally and physically renew himself. Martin, his eldest son, observed the change on holidays from the driven, workaholic doctor and his regular programme of eighteen-hour days, to the relaxed, playful father with *ein fröliches Herz*, a happy heart. The Austrians, like the Germans, were enthusiastic proponents of the therapeutic benefits of 'healthy' mountain air and shared a semi-mystical reverence for the mountains.

When Freud's mother, Amalia, felt ill (she suffered from a bout of tuberculosis) or debilitated, she 'took the waters' at a sanatorium at Roznau, not far from Freiberg. Freud admitted he was 'always longing for fresh air and always anxious to open windows'.[11] He told his fiancée, Martha Bernays, that he intended to 'ramble about on the Semmering for at least three days', explaining that 'alone, without you, it cannot be beautiful; in fact, it is not meant to be a pleasure, simply a medicine'.[12] The Semmering is a wild and romantic area about fifty kilometres south-east of Vienna. Its combination of imposing limestone cliffs, craggy rocks and wide, deeply forested valleys, plus its proximity to Vienna, made it a favourite resort.

Freud was fit. He enjoyed the rigours of mountain climbing and, much to the admiration of his eldest son, had made a solo trek across the Dachstein in central Austria, a massive, snow-crested peak that rose to nearly three thousand metres. He also enjoyed strenuous walks that could exhaust his younger companions.

Hanns Sachs, a member of Freud's inner circle, accompanied the sixty-one-year-old Freud on a walking tour through the Tatra mountains, part of the Carpathians, in 1917. While the group took a break after a three-hour march, Freud wandered off alone, discovering unexpected views or unusual plants that interested him. An ardent amateur botanist, Freud was always on the hunt for rare plants and flower specimens. He was an expert on varieties of grasses and herbs and even enjoyed eating them, a habit begun in the Freiberg forest. Admitting it was a somewhat odd request, in 1873 Freud asked his friend Eduard Silberstein, who was staying at Roznau, to find a type of local cypress because its twigs and needles were delicious but 'you have to be a seasoned eater of leaves and branches like myself to detect it'.[13]

On his birthdays friends and colleagues deluged him with orchids. When H.D. gave him gardenias, he was touched, telling her they were the flowers 'I most admire'.[14] There were always fresh flowers in his study, offering 'the illusion of splendour and glowing sunshine'.[15] On hiking expeditions, he was especially keen to search for mushrooms, organising competitions to find the best and tastiest examples, prizes he always won. It was on holiday in 1895 in the Kahlenberg region on the outskirts of Vienna, with its vineyards and its views of the Carpathians, that Freud had the momentous dream leading him to the conclusion that all dreams were wish-fulfilment. Following another summer holiday two years later, Freud developed the theory of the Oedipus complex.

The sudden loss at age three of a personal territory of beauty, release and pleasure that nature provided was the foundation of Freud's lifelong hostility to Vienna. Holidays in the mountains exacerbated his feelings and on his return 'all the bad humour of Viennadom' would descend, wounding his soul, laying bare

'everything that had begun to heal'. The place was 'almost physically repulsive'.[16] Something precious had been snatched from
him and he yearned to regain it. Integral to the forest's magic was
solitude: it was an environment he did not have to share, it was
his alone.

In Freud's reminiscence, the forest was a profoundly comforting emotional landscape. For the child, it signalled adventure and
freedom where he could escape paternal restraint. For the lovesick
teenager, it was the sanctuary to contemplate the twin losses of
Gisela and his former home, where his imagination could have
full rein. When Emil Fluss had to leave Freiberg in 1873, Freud's
despairing litany of what he must relinquish – 'beloved home,
fond relatives', 'beautiful surroundings', as well as 'ruins in the
immediate neighbourhood' – was too awful to contemplate. 'I
shall become as sad as you!' By listing Freiberg's pleasures, Freud
was enumerating his continuing sense of loss.

The journey into the forest, especially by children such as
Hansel and Gretel or Little Red Riding Hood, is enshrined in
European folklore as a metaphor for self-knowledge and sexual
maturity. It involves danger, tests of character and, finally, the
triumphant return home. Freud's 'beautiful forest' is Eden: not a
threatening place, but an enchanted realm, a lost domain, the place
to which he longed to return. It is the earth as bountiful mother,
beautiful, nurturing, encompassing, a womb of safety and healing.
But Freud also recognised the dark side of Mother Earth, the
inescapable 'silent Goddess of Death'.[17] His own mother had introduced him to the concept of death by gloomily assuring him,
when he was six, that humans were made of earth and must return
to it. When Sigmund refused to believe her, Amalia rubbed her
hands together, showing him dark fragments of her skin that had

come off. The trick worked and, for the first time, Freud was chilled by a sense of mortality.

For Freud, the mother symbolised a constellation of nature's forces that could be kindly and aggressive, maternal and destructive, protective and unpredictable. Freud described himself escaping from his father into the freedom and wildness of the forest, almost before he had learned to walk. Confident and impetuous, even as a child, Freud relished calling himself reckless.

Though Freud did not admit it, Freiberg was an excellent place for his family to leave. In a population of around 4500, only 130 were Jewish, leaving the family stranded in a sea of Christianity, mistrust and anti-Semitism. Moravia might have been at the very heart of Europe, where, as one nineteenth-century writer noted, 'castles, estates and provinces of its most distinguished families are crowded together in great numbers' but it was also virulently racist.[18] In 1844, the editor of *The Prague News* warned, 'We must regard [the Jews] as a separate Semitic nation who lives only incidentally in our midst . . . He who wants to be a Czech must cease to be a Jew.'[19] Hiking through the Carpathians with her husband early in the twentieth century, English travel writer Lion Phillimore was told by resentful peasants that 'Jews got the best of everything'.[20]

Folklore also had its part to play in prejudice. As late as 1929, belief in apparitions and supernatural beings, as well as the power of sorcerers and magical ceremonies, was still alive among the peasants of the Carpathians. Local people were convinced that relatives or acquaintances had seen this or that supernatural being – 'a vampire, a spirit of the night, a sorcerer or a witch'.[21] Often such demons took the form of the peasants' Jewish neighbours.

Moravia was an especially devout Christian region, famous for pilgrimages and shrine churches devoted to the Virgin. Its major historical legacy to the region was the introduction of Christianity in the ninth century. Though not large, Freiberg has four churches, and statues of saints and the Virgin Mary adorn its square. The town is dominated by the tower of the Church of The Nativity of Our Lady. The church's interior has a dramatic altar-piece with baroque wooden sculptures celebrating Mary as queen of heaven, flanked by angels and saints, and an impressive pulpit. Freud attended Sunday Mass with his Czech nanny, dipping his fingers in the holy-water font and genuflecting before taking his seat. Goodness knows what the congregation made of the little Jewish boy attending their services. Perhaps they hoped he would convert, like many Jews keen to rise in gentile society. Not cele-brating Catholic holy days and festivals made the Freuds outsiders to the rhythm of the town's life. At least Freiberg, unlike other towns in the Czech provinces, had no ghetto so the Freuds lived in freedom.

Jews in Moravia also faced a hostile political environment. In 1798, Emperor Francis II had confined Jews to fifty-two areas that excluded them from living in the royal cities and he also restricted their numbers to 5400 families. Only the eldest son of a Jewish family was allowed to marry and then only after his father's death. Further, the rise of Czech nationalism during the nineteenth century led to the emergence of a Czech middle class who sought to replace Jews in the rural economy and provided tough compe-tition for Jewish traders. Czechs regarded Jews as pro-German because they spoke German and voted for the German parties, at least before those parties became anti-Semitic. Tomas Masaryk, president of Czechoslavakia in 1920, recalled that, as a child, he heard 'frequent warnings about Jews in sermons as well as in schools . . . Every little Moravian Slovak was raised to be anti-Semitic.'[22] Jews in Moravia were not allowed to own land. It is no wonder that after the revolution of 1848, when the decrees governing Moravian Jews were annulled, they flooded into Vienna. In the 1860s, fifty per cent of all Jewish immigrants in Vienna came from Moravia or Bohemia. The Freud family was part of that exodus.

Freud was proudly and defiantly Jewish, hostile to any hint of anti-Semitism and all his life chose Jewish people as his closest friends and associates. When Freud told the story of his childhood, he ignored Freiberg's intolerant and restrictive environment, though it could offer him little in the way of education or intellectual and professional advancement. He could not have been educated at a Catholic school but would have been forced to attend a less equipped and less prestigious Jewish school. Even if Jacob Freud's business had not failed, Sigmund would have had to leave home and seek his fortune elsewhere, unless he chose to become a local burgher. Gisela Fluss' mother, whom Freud admired, wryly observed that in provincial Freiberg 'one can unlearn everything and learn nothing new'.[23] Yet Freud continued to laud Freiberg as the ideal, the lost and longed-for home.

Freud blamed Jacob for the move that ruptured his connection with nature and took him to the infinitely less interesting, man-made city. But Amalia had lived most of her life in bustling, fashionable Vienna. It was where Jacob had met and courted her. Perhaps she wanted to return there and find a measure of security surrounded by her own family. Living in one room above the blacksmith's must have been cramped and unpleasant. The house, while charming, is tiny, with low ceilings and small rooms. No wonder Jacob escaped with his son to the forest. Amalia had had two more babies in Freiberg: Julius, who lived less than a year, was born in 1857 and Anna in 1858. But Freud cherished the memory of his first home. 'The dwelling-house [is] a substitute for the mother's womb, the first lodging, for which in all likelihood man still longs, and in which he was safe and felt at ease.'[24]

Another reason Freud brooded on the move to Vienna was because it did not achieve its goal: prosperity for the family. Jacob was a hapless businessman and never managed to establish himself professionally or earn a good income. Financial support came from Emmanuel and Philipp, the two sons from Jacob's first marriage, and also from Amalia's family. At times, Freud characterised his father as a feckless child who could be 'the greatest optimist of all us young people' when he wasn't 'grouchy, which alas is very often the case'. When the Jewish businessmen of Freiberg were asked to contribute to the town purse, Jacob recklessly offered ten gulden; the canny Ignaz Fluss, who made his fortune there, gave two. Meeting his dreamy, improvident father by chance in the streets of Vienna, Freud observed that Jacob, who was sixty-eight at the time, was 'still full of projects, still hoping'.[25]

Jacob was a disappointment, as Freud clearly illustrates in *The Interpretation of Dreams*, yet he provided a foil, a figure to contest and best, the son's aggressive rival in the triangle of the Oedipus complex. When Freud was a child, Jacob told him a story about life in Freiberg but it was not a fairy tale. It was a harsh, factual account of anti-Semitism. Jacob was assaulted by a Christian who, with a single blow, knocked his new fur cap into the mud, shouting, 'Jew! Get off the pavement!' Freud asked his father, 'And what did you do?' Jacob's answer unnerved his son. 'I went into the roadway and picked up my cap.' Freud seethed at Jacob's humble behaviour. It struck him as 'unheroic conduct'.[26] His father's cowardice roused dreams of glory in Freud, of Hannibal, the Semitic general who valiantly took on the Roman empire.

Jacob told the story years after the event, in the comparative freedom and safety of Vienna where the family lived in a Jewish neighbourhood and where it was unlikely a gentile would behave in such a manner. It was easy enough for Freud to be outraged there. But if he had stayed in Freiberg, it was the very kind of situation he would have faced. Jacob's way of dealing with anti-Semitism seemed obsequious, yet it was a diplomatic strategy for a man with a family, who could have been injured by the belligerent Czech, and would have had small chance of redress. It was a parable, Jacob's gentle method of explaining why it was necessary for the family to leave Freiberg, an explanation Freud refused to understand.

Freud was evasive about his mother, perhaps because the Oedipus complex sexualised family relations. Though he believed that 'for each of us, destiny takes the form of a woman', he remained secretive about his intimate relationships with them.[27] Despite being trenchantly conservative regarding women's role in society, Freud was attracted to intelligent, independent women. Ambivalent and contradictory, his attitude towards women mirrors his response to Vienna.

After leaving Freiberg, Amalia had four girls in rapid succession — Rosa, Marie, Adolfine and Paula — followed by her youngest child, Alexander, who was born when Freud was ten. Amalia had a strong personality: attractive, lively and sociable, and, aside from the tuberculosis, radiantly healthy, she lived until she was ninety-five. Amalia adored her eldest boy, her 'golden Sigi'. Freud observed 'if a man has been his mother's undisputed darling he retains throughout life the triumphant feeling, the confidence in success, which not seldom brings actual success along with it'.[28]

Ernest Jones, Freud's authorised biographer, recalls the close attachment between mother and eldest son and compliments Amalia on her 'gaiety, alertness and sharp-witted intelligence'.[29] But her grandson Martin was not smitten. Amalia was uncontrollable, 'a tornado'.[30] None of the family envied Adolfine, 'Aunt Dolfi', whose job it was to care for her. By the time Amalia died, Dolfi was completely broken and left without any real interest or purpose in life. Amalia disrupted family gatherings, creating an atmosphere of growing crisis that focused on Sigmund's arrival. If he were late, Amalia would start running up and down the stairs to check for him, having fits of rising anxiety that could last an hour. None of the family dared try to calm her because it would 'produce an outburst of anger which it was better to avoid'.[31] Freud used to suffer indigestion before his regular Sunday morning visits to his mother, a standing joke in the family. Amalia's powerful emotional dependence on Sigmund sent a message to the rest of the family that, without him, any gathering was incomplete.

Slender, with dark, deeply-lidded eyes, Amalia has a rather delicate, melancholic air in the photograph taken with Freud in 1872 (pl. 33), the year of his return visit to Freiberg. Mother and son, stiffly posed, seem distant. That summer, while Freud loitered lovesick in the forest, Amalia was at Roznau for her health. In a photograph (pl. 34) taken four years later, Amalia's youthfulness has ebbed. The matriarch, seated at the centre of her family, gazes directly at the camera. Perhaps it is Amalia's irregularly shaped eyes that make her expression seem troubled, moody, unsettled.

Jacob's open, sensitive, kindly face is easier to read. Freud stands behind his mother, straight-backed as her chair. Handsome and sleekly bearded, he has grown in height and confidence and, at twenty, gives the impression of being a man of the world.

Like Jacob, Amalia appears in *The Interpretation of Dreams*. Freud dreams of his mother's death, a 'true anxiety-dream' that he had when he was seven or eight, when he saw 'my beloved mother, with a peculiarly peaceful, sleeping expression on her features, being carried into the room by two (or three) people with birds' beaks and laid upon the bed'. He awoke 'in tears and screaming'. Freud recognised the beaked figures as gods with falcons' heads from an ancient Egyptian funerary relief that he had seen in the illustrated family Bible.[32] By the time he published the dream, his knowledge of Egyptian mythology told him that Horus was the falcon-headed god, the son of Isis and Osiris, and special protector of kings.

If every dream were a wish-fulfilment, as Freud believed, what did he have to gain from Amalia's death? In the dream she is treated like an Egyptian queen, carried by gods, by Horus, the son, to her funeral bed. Her expression is 'peculiarly peaceful'. Death means silence, the end of struggle – to 'rest in peace'. Freud dispatches his mother with honour, as befits a good son. Nonetheless, she is dead and he is the witness at her funeral.

Around 1931, Freud bought a *Falcon-headed Figure* (19th century A.D.; pl. 4) from Robert Lustig, his favourite antiquities dealer in Vienna. Unfortunately, it is a fake, a rare thing in Freud's collection, and was made not several centuries B.C., but during Freud's lifetime. There was a huge market in fakes, emanating from Egypt, churned out for the unwary buyer. If Freud found he had a forgery, he usually dispatched it with speed. But in this case his keen eye deserted him and he was convinced it was the real thing. A strange, ungainly work made of gessoed and painted wood, *Falcon-headed Figure* looks less a work of art and more a child's ancient, ugly, cherished toy.

Freud had many Egyptian painted wooden figures in his collection, including two other bird figures, *Mummified Falcon* (716–332 B.C. or later [Late Period]) and *Human-headed Bird* (332–30 B.C. [Ptolemaic Period]; pl. 5), which have a distinctive style and charm *Falcon-headed Figure* lacks. *Mummified Falcon* is not the mummy of a bird but a painted figure which would have been placed on a coffin. It is an image of the underworld god Sokar, not Horus, a much more magnificent deity in the Egyptian pantheon. *Human-headed Bird* shows a cheeky-faced *ba*, the personality of the deceased, who, unimpeded by mortality, could fly from the grave, return to the land of the living and indulge in its pleasures. Such abilities may account for its chirpy expression.

The *Falcon-headed Figure* of Horus is depicted striding forward, wrapped in a white kilt. Horus, the avenger of his murdered father, Osiris, is the ultimate good son in the family drama and the child of the kind of incestuous marriage between brother and sister that Egyptian royalty and religion took for granted. Such myths intrigued Freud, fashioner of the Oedipus complex. Horus was a valiant warrior, who went to war against his father's killer, Seth, staging a classic battle between good and evil. After vanquishing Seth, Horus was rewarded for his efforts by becoming king of Egypt, from whom all pharaohs were descended. Seth was a symbol of anarchy and chaos: the very act of cutting Osiris into pieces indicates his divisive nature. Disorder horrified the disciplined Egyptian mind: its art bears witness, over thousands of years, to the desire for stability and resistance to change.

In his dream about Amalia's death, Freud organised a team of noble sons, Horus lookalikes, as her pall bearers. No wonder he could recall the dream so vividly three decades later. He had arranged a royal Egyptian funeral for his mother. He killed her, but in great style. Freud said he lost his memory when he moved to Vienna. But his first post-Freiberg memory on record is the dream of Amalia's death. Consciously, Freud blamed Jacob for the loss of his home. Unconsciously, he blamed Amalia too. He bought *Falcon-headed Figure* around 1931, nearly seventy years after he had the dream, proving the god with the falcon's head remained a powerful, attractive and mysterious force, connecting Freud, through art and myth, to buried losses and ancient longings. Amalia had died the previous year: Freud did not attend her funeral.

Aside from Ernest Jones' comments about the bond between mother and son, few first-hand references remain to illustrate Freud's relations with Amalia. But from Freud's comments on Jacob in 'Screen Memories', *The Interpretation of Dreams* and in letters, a complex, interesting picture emerges regarding his feelings about his father. In 'Screen Memories', published in 1899, Freud disguises his identity to write a mini-autobiography. He describes his first memories, followed by the 'catastrophe' of Jacob's business failure, the traumatic shift to Vienna and Freud's return to Freiberg in 1873. He uses his memories to suggest that the fragmentary visual images of early childhood are not pictures of reality but distortions or screens that allow us to avoid facing what actually happened. His idea, that conscious recollections are distorted by a person's wishes, desires, and unconscious conflicts, became a core assumption of psychoanalysis.

The relentless investigator of the mind's deepest secrets, Freud did not wish to be similarly dissected. In 1885, Freud gleefully informed his fiancée, Martha, that 'I have destroyed all my notes of the past 14 years, as well as letters, scientific excerpts and manuscripts of my papers.' It amused him that he had frustrated 'a number of as yet unborn and unfortunate people . . . my biographers . . . Let them worry, we have no desire to make it too easy for them.' Otherwise he would be suffocated because 'the stuff settles round me like sand-drifts round the Sphinx; soon nothing but my nostrils would have been visible above the paper'.[33]

It was another death, a real one, that offers clues about Freud's attitude towards Amalia. In January 1920, he wrote to his mother telling her of the death of his daughter Sophie. Pregnant with her third child, Sophie had succumbed to the influenza pandemic raging after the First World War. Freud ends the letter by writing, 'I hope you will take it calmly; tragedy, after all, has to be accepted. But to mourn this splendid, vital girl who was so happy with her husband and children is of course permissible.'[34] *Permissible?* In Freud's first shock of grief, he distances himself from his mother, accomplished by instructing her in the etiquette of bereavement. Freud assumed his professional role: he was the doctor, the therapist, not the grieving father or the stricken son but sufficiently in control to behave responsibly and to monitor others' behaviour. His letter is an exercise in alienation.

Grief is a time of loss, not only of the beloved but of decorum and formality, as strong emotions disrupt the masks and patterns of daily life. Freud refused to break down in front of his mother or to share his feelings with her. Sharing implies need and vulnerability, a democracy of feeling, the warm messiness of intimacy. Freud's cool letter suggests old boundaries, where Amalia must be reminded to stay calm. It is a doubly sad letter, both because of its literal contents and its deeper message, that he did not feel he could trust her. Not prepared to burden Amalia with his grief, Freud certainly did not wish to deal with hers.

The following day, writing to Oscar Pfister, the Swiss pastor who was committed to the cause of psychoanalysis, Freud felt free to open his heart. 'Sweet Sophie' had been 'snatched away in the midst of glowing health, from a full and active life as a competent and loving wife, all in four or five days, as though she had never existed'. The 'undisguised brutality of our time' – post-war Europe – meant Sigmund and Martha could not travel to Hamburg for the funeral; there were no trains. 'Tomorrow she is to be cremated, our poor Sunday child!'[35] Freud could not share such sentiments with Amalia.

In Freud's dream about his mother, only in death could she achieve the control he urges in his letter about Sophie. It seems Freud found both his parents lacking, and for similar reasons: they were childlike, over-emotional and irresponsible. It was his task to manage them. He was still 'managing' his mother when she was eighty-four. Of course, that does not mean he did not love and respect his parents. But to achieve his emotional sanctuary, the tranquil, beautiful place that the forest had represented and that his art collection would mean to him, Freud needed to distance himself from an incompetent father and a turbulent, domineering mother.

Freud had an excellent Greek terracotta *Sphinx* (South Italian, late 5th–early 4th century B.C.; pl. 6), as well as a print of Ingres' *Oedipus and the Sphinx* (Louvre, 1808). In the myth of Oedipus, the Sphinx is a trickster, a fabulous creature often depicted with the face and breasts of a woman, the body of a lion and the wings of a bird. Oedipus must solve her riddle, or be devoured. Once an Egyptian symbol of justice and protection, and an emblem of the pharaoh, in Greek mythology the Sphinx is associated with fatal combat and death, and decorates tombs. As both woman and beast, Bruno Bettelheim has described the Sphinx as 'a symbol of the good, nurturing mother and the bad, destructive mother'.[36] Cunning and seductive, she must be answered and outwitted; she is the powerful and troublesome feminine, whom man needs to govern or who will destroy him. By choosing this myth on which to base a central theory of psychoanalysis, Freud, who identified with Oedipus, hints at the strategies he believed were necessary to control female energy.

Freud was determined to remain in mourning for Freiberg his entire life. Weakened by age and illness in 1931, he was unable to return for the unveiling of the plaque at his birthplace but perhaps the only way to retain the fantasy of the 'beautiful woods' was never to revisit them. Freud delighted in masterminding long, elaborate summer holidays for himself and his family, choosing a variety of picturesque retreats, but he never chose Freiberg. With it safely buried in the past, he could contemplate its beauty without subjecting it to the critical gaze of the present, the vicissitudes of time and the changes it brings. Freiberg was a charmed mirror in which Freud saw only what he wanted to: the happy child at play in an enchanted forest. Freiberg was the dream and Vienna was the reality where Freud's 'thirst for grandeur' was made manifest.[37] But Freud never forgave Vienna for the loss of Freiberg, always finding reason to criticise and blame the city.

When the Freuds arrived in 1860, Vienna was in the throes of transforming itself from a medieval city into a self-consciously grand, modern metropolis. The upwardly mobile Jewish immigrants made themselves part of the new Vienna and by doing so shaped its character. Pressure had been mounting for decades to tear down the old city walls and allow Vienna the freedom to be reimagined and redesigned. In 1843, a consortium of prominent bankers had commissioned architect Ludwig Förster to draw up plans for a modern city and, tired of asking Emperor Ferdinand I to take the initiative, they were preparing to bankroll the venture themselves. Inside the city walls was a claustrophobic and 'extravagant maze of buildings... The streets are narrow, the houses six, seven and eight stories high' and 'buildings whose grandeur demands a great public square ... are stuck into narrow alleys, and lost in a forest of houses.'[38] Carriages careened down the narrow streets to the terror of pedestrians.

The revolution of 1848 altered the political landscape and prompted important reforms (including the repeal of the laws restricting Jews). Ferdinand abdicated in favour of his son Franz Josef, who acquiesced to the populist mood and, in 1857, announced Vienna's transformation. The Ringstrasse, the great boulevard that encircles the old city, was the most ambitious urban development since Baron Haussmann's reconstruction of Paris. The walls of the city were razed and the *glacis*, a swathe of green common land, was redeveloped for public, commercial and housing use. An international competition was launched and eighty-five European architects vied for the top honour: the winning development was a combination of designs submitted by the first- and second-prize winners, Friedrich Starcke and Ludwig Förster.

In 1860, the design for the Ringstrasse was made public and work began. The new Vienna was trumpeted as an aesthetic masterpiece, a city 'bedecked by art'. Magnificent buildings were constructed along the Ringstrasse — university, national theatre, city hall, parliament, stock exchange, opera house, art and natural history museums — as well as a series of enormous parks and lavish apartment buildings. Though the Ring was declared open in 1873, building continued and the Kunsthistorisches, the Art Museum, was not completed until 1891. For thirty years, the slow growth of the sumptuous Ringstrasse was a key part of Freud's visual landscape. When he was twelve, Jacob began taking him on long walks through Vienna, making Freud an 'indefatigable walker'.[39] The Ringstrasse itself became one of his favourite terrains and he regularly covered its five-kilometre length at a cracking pace.

The slums of the Leopoldstadt where Freud was learning bitter, frustrating lessons about the 'limitations' of poverty were worlds away.[40] The Leopoldstadt, across the Danube canal from the rest of the city, had been the site of a Jewish ghetto before the Jews were expelled from the city in 1670. Another, more hideous pogrom had taken place in 1421, when over three hundred men and women belonging to wealthy Jewish families had been publicly burned at the stake and the rest of the Jewish population herded onto boats bound for Hungary. Until 1848, only select Jews who could afford to pay an exorbitant annual fee to the government were legally allowed to live in Vienna, but a thriving trade in bribes meant thousands stayed in the city for years.

Though many Jews lived in its poorer tenements, the Leopoldstadt was a diverse, populous neighbourhood which also included wealthy, stylish areas where prosperous Jewish families chose to live. Playwright and doctor Arthur Schnitzler, whose work Freud admired, was part of Vienna's *fin-de-siècle* renaissance. He was born in the Leopoldstadt where his father had a medical practice and home on a stately boulevard. Schnitzler recalled that the Leopoldstadt's main street 'managed to preserve some of its festiveness even during the quieter hours when an elegant and carefree world came tearing back from the races or flower shows in their equipages and fiacres'.[41]

The Leopoldstadt also contained the Prater, a vast 800-hectare park, the playground of Vienna and one of the oldest leisure parks in Europe. Once a private hunting domain for the aristocracy, Emperor Josef II had opened it to the public in 1766 and it proved an immediate success. By the nineteenth century, it had been divided into the Grüner Prater (the green Prater) with its 'expanse of wild, magnificently timbered marshland' that extended to the banks of the Danube, and the People's Prater where the world's biggest ferris wheel stood at the head of a gigantic permanent fairground with a circus, sideshows, concerts, dances, cafés and a racetrack.[42] Strauss waltzes filled the air. The Prater was the fashion and culinary hub of Vienna, a place of spectacle and display, constantly crowded with all sections of society. One evening at a restaurant there, a wandering poet announced to Amalia and Jacob that twelve-year-old Sigmund was destined to be a cabinet minister.

Such pleasant memories were rare. There were other green areas in which Freud could roam, such as the Vienna Woods to the city's west or the formal splendour of the Augarten or the new parks that were part of the Ringstrasse, but none, apparently, could compare with the forest near Freiberg. Freud disliked the Vienna Woods in particular and his children could not drag him there. In fact, although Freud lived in a big city, he was surrounded by large stretches of open country. In the Grüner Prater he developed an interest in botany, enthusiastically collecting plants and flowers. He could also study a variety of birds, including kingfishers, woodpeckers and golden orioles, and watch the park's herd of red deer. But it was not a territory that was wholly his; he had to share it with the rest of Vienna. Nor was it wild: these were safe, tamed areas. There was no thrill of exploration, or of solitude. He had to rub shoulders with the common crowd. It gave Freud, always sensitive to physical charms, or the lack of them, another reason to dislike Vienna: its inhabitants had 'grotesque and animal-like faces . . . deformed skulls and potato noses'.[43]

Loathing Vienna was a piquant pastime for its intellectuals. Karl Kraus, acerbic editor of *Die Fackel* (The Torch), wrote, 'My hatred of this city is not love gone astray; rather I have discovered a completely new way of finding it intolerable.'[44] But Kraus chose not to leave (and Freud did so only when forced in 1938). Freud rejected Vienna's charming, genial public face: the Prater, the theatres and concerts held little attraction for him. He had his coffee house, Café Landtmann, but he could not be classed as an habitué, like so many Viennese. The world that he constructed through the development of psychoanalysis and his art collection was determinedly interior.

Freud's love of nature determined his choice of profession and his future. He proved a brilliant student when he entered the local high school, or *Gymnasium*, staying at the top of his class until he graduated when he was seventeen. The *Gymnasium* provided a rigorous training in Greek and Latin classics, preparing the boys for university and high-status careers. It was the ideal education for a collector of antiquities. Latin and Greek grammar were believed essential for developing logical thought, the study of classical literature shaped the taste for beauty, and ancient history and philosophy were meant to arouse noble and heroic sentiments.

It was at school that Freud's love of art and archaeology originated with his first glimpses into the ancient civilisations that were to bring him 'unsurpassed consolation in the struggles of life'.[45] Freud read *The Iliad* and *The Odyssey* in Greek. When he was nine, he began studying Latin, including Virgil's *The Aeneid* and Ovid's *Metamorphoses*. *The Aeneid* provided the motto for *The Interpretation of Dreams* – 'If I cannot bend the higher powers, I will move the infernal regions' – and *Metamorphoses* was a source book of mythology with magical transformation as its theme. Freud also studied mathematics and science, learnt English and French and, with his gift for languages, taught himself Spanish and Italian. Religion was also on the curriculum.

In his final year at school, Freud was planning to study law, the path to entering politics, following the destiny suggested by the poet in the Prater, when he attended a lecture at which Goethe's essay 'On Nature' was read. It begins:

Nature! We are surrounded and embraced by her; powerless to separate ourselves from her, and powerless to penetrate beyond her. Without asking or warning, she snatches us up into her circling dance, and whirls us on until we are tired, and drop from her arms. She is ever shaping new forms. She is complete but never finished . . . She hides under a thousand names and phrases, and is always the same.[46]

This effusive, animistic ode appealed to the young Freud of the forest, the child who worshipped nature and who longed to re-establish his rich, intense contact with it. Goethe pictured nature as a maenad, an uninhibited, inspiring and shamelessly seductive feminine force, enacting an eternal cycle of destruction and renewal. The earth itself is imagined as the body of the goddess, enchanting and irresistible. Freud responded to these sentiments in May 1873. His return visit to Freiberg had taken place the summer before, a time when his feelings about the natural world were particularly sensitive. It was also, due to his crush on Gisela Fluss, a period of sexual arousal, of first love, heartbreak and longing. He announced to her brother Emil, 'I have decided to be a Natural Scientist and herewith release you from the promise to let me conduct all your law suits. It is no longer needed. I shall gain insight into the age-old dossiers of Nature, perhaps even eavesdrop on her eternal processes, and share my findings with anyone who wants to learn.'[47] He might not have been able to return to the forest but he could find a path back through study.

Interestingly, during Freud's attacks on religion in works such as *Totem and Taboo* and *The Future of an Illusion*, animism was spared the same scorn. Freud praised animism as civilisation's mythopoetic foundation: the first of the 'three great pictures of the universe', followed by religion and science. It was 'the most consistent and exhaustive' of the three, giving 'a truly complete explanation of the universe'. Animism appealed to Freud because it was 'a *psychological* theory'.[48] Tribal people believed spirits existed independently of material existence and could inhabit one individual and/or migrate to another. To Freud animism was a dualistic system, incorporating unsettled spirits that, like the emotions and the neuroses, were powerful, independent agents, potent symbols not only worthy of analysis but capable of being apprehended by the modern mind and recast in his own picture of the universe. Animism also explained the origins of art: 'There is no doubt that art did not begin as art for art's sake.'[49] Instead, it was first used by palaeolithic tribes in the service of magic, animism's technique to invoke the gods.

Goethe, as author of 'On Nature', attracted Freud too. Goethe was a 'great universal personality' whom Freud compared with Leonardo da Vinci, another renaissance man and one of his heroes.[50] Freud did not know the essay had been written by Swiss theologian Georg Christoph Tobler and attributed to Goethe. But it cast a spell, convincing Freud it was by listening, or 'eaves-dropping', that nature's secrets would be revealed to him, an apt metaphor for psychoanalysis. Twenty-five years later, Freud had lost none of his enthusiasm for the essay, which he described as 'incomparably beautiful'.[51]

Goethe may not have been the only influence acting on Freud's choice of a career. His experiences of anti-Semitism growing up in Vienna must have made him aware that a Jewish man, no matter how brilliant, would find great difficulty in rising to the exalted position of a cabinet minister. It was at the *Gymnasium* that he learned 'what it meant to belong to an alien race'.[52] As Schnitzler recalled, 'a certain separation of Gentile and Jew into groups that were not kept strictly apart . . . could be felt always and everywhere, also therefore in school'. In those days, the term 'anti-Semitism' had not been invented. 'One was satisfied to call those who were particularly inimical towards Jews, almost contemptuously *Judenfresser* or Jew devourers.'[53]

During Freud's schooldays, Vienna was a liberal city, one of the reasons Jewish people were keen to live there. The Habsburg monarchy, which had made Vienna the headquarters of its empire since the thirteenth century, publicly disdained anti-Semitism, as did the rest of the aristocracy. But that did not impress Freud, who boasted that he refused to doff his hat to the Emperor. He also loathed Catholicism and cursed 'that detestable tower' of St Stephen's, the Gothic cathedral that stands at the city centre, an emblem for the forces of religion and conservatism that excluded Freud from Vienna's elite.[54] Another hurdle for Jews was an upper crust known as Austria's twenty families, who throttled public initiatives. Hanns Sachs observed that this group 'had none of the brutality of the warrior caste, but a good deal of graceful and complacent callousness'.[55] Beneath the surface of liberalism undercurrents of anti-Semitism swirled.

Like many bourgeois Jewish families in Vienna, the Freuds sought assimilation by largely dispensing with religious customs and observances. The sabbath was not celebrated and Arthur Schnitzler recalled the younger generation 'tended to display indifference to the spirit of Jewish religion, and opposition, and sometimes even a sarcastic attitude to its formalities'.[56] Freud, who did not have a bar mitzvah but was circumcised, told Eduard Silberstein that 'our festivals have outlived our dogma, like the funeral meal that has outlived the dead'.[57] Freud makes the point by referring to the ancient Egyptian custom of placing a feast in the deceased's tomb, meant to stave off hunger on the journey to the afterlife.

Freud declared himself to be 'completely estranged from the religion of his fathers' and made sure his wife and children followed suit.[58] But the profound and persistent interest in spiritual relics that directed his collection, the emphasis in his writings on the relationship between religion and culture and the recent discovery that he owned several sacred Jewish objects mean Freud's remarks should not be taken at face value.[59] His attitude to his Jewish identity, and to spirituality, remained as complex and as dualistic as other aspects of his thought.

2

Love Object

Love is the great educator.
Sigmund Freud[1]

THE FIRST OBJECTS FREUD collected were not artworks but books. As a university student, he began creating a library that became a magnificent companion to his art collection. Though he lacked both the space and money to indulge his passion, he allowed neither limitation to curb him. He zealously furnished his study with books and, short of cash, went into debt to buy more.

In 1875, Jacob had moved his family for the last time: their fortunes had inexplicably risen and the new apartment in Kaiser Josefstrasse was more spacious than previous abodes. But it was hardly luxurious: six children and two adults crammed into three bedrooms. There was also 'a cabinet' that Freud occupied. The family did not have the comforts of a bathroom and when the children were small they made do with one bath a fortnight: a wooden tub, accompanied by kegs of hot and cold water, would be carted into the flat and removed the following day. When the children were older, Amalia took them to the local public baths.

But no matter how straitened their circumstances, 'golden Sigi' always had his own room – and his own way. When his sister Anna began to learn the piano, Freud, deaf to music's charms, told his parents the noise interrupted his studies. He was ten at the time. The instrument had to go. None of Freud's children learned music and when Minna, Martha's sister, who was fond of playing her gramophone, moved into Berggasse 19, Freud made sure her room was as far from his study as possible. Silence was Freud's favourite sound.

Anna recalled that Freud's study in Kaiser Josefstrasse was a long, narrow room separated from the rest of the flat, with a bed, chairs, bookshelves, a desk, and a window looking onto the street. 'All through the years of his school and university life, the only thing that changed in his room was the increasing number of crowded bookcases.'[2] He had an oil lamp while the rest of the household made do with candles in their bedrooms, although Freud, with his taste for finery, regarded it as a 'miserable, eye destroying paraffin lamp'.[3] Freud's youthful retreat was the precursor for his study-art museum at Berggasse 19, the beautiful realm reserved for him alone. As a student, Freud even ate his evening meal in his cabinet, away from the family. This was where he entertained his friends and, even after he left home to live at the university as a young doctor, he returned there on weekends.

Immersed in his study, Freud was like a child at play, creating a world of his own, the kind of activity that he described as a continuation of, and a substitute for, the play of childhood.[4] Together with specialist books for his course, Freud avidly collected volumes by his favourite authors, including Goethe, Schiller, Heine, E. T. A. Hoffmann, the Brothers Grimm, Milton, Zola, Dickens and Twain. 'He read everything . . . He never forgot what he read. He had a photographic memory.'[5] Freud's interests were encyclopaedic, covering history, philosophy, anthropology, biography, fiction and poetry, making his library a repository for learning, a cultural reference centre and 'a treasure-house of myths, legends and fairy tales'.[6]

Freud's books 'certainly made some demands on his pocket money', as Ernest Jones puts it diplomatically.[7] Freud got into the habit of borrowing sums from less impecunious friends and, by 1884, his debt had increased to the considerable amount of 2300 gulden, several thousand dollars by today's reckoning. Freud admitted 'the filthy lucre runs through my fingers at such frightening speed'.[8] He did not receive a proper salary until he became an aspirant, a kind of clinical assistant, at the General Hospital of Vienna in 1882, and the amount was a pittance. By then, he was twenty-six. As a young man, Freud seemed as profligate as Jacob had been throughout his life. He boasted that Braumuller's, Vienna's largest bookstore, was 'at my unlimited disposal'.[9]

Freud's introduction to the love of books was occasioned by destruction. When he was five, Jacob gave Anna and him a travel book about Persia, mischievously suggesting they amuse themselves by tearing out the colour plates, a task the children completed with alacrity. Freud also enjoyed looking at the family Bible's illustrations, some of which provided the setting for his dream about Amalia. Ludwig Philippson's edition of *Die israelitische Bibel* is a kind of encyclopaedia, lavishly illustrated with romantic views of Egypt, examples of Egyptian and classical art, together with birds, plants and scenes of everyday life in the ancient world. Later, Jacob gave the book to his son, noting 'It was in the seventh year of your age that the spirit of God began to move you to learning.'[10] Freud became engrossed in the biblical stories as soon as he learned to read. At eight, he was reading Shakespeare, another lifelong hero whose work he would quote liberally in his own writings. For Freud, Hamlet's prevarications led inevitably to repressed feelings for his mother, making him the perfect examplar of the Oedipus complex.

Freud entered university with all the confidence of a young prince. He announced he would devote his first year to 'purely humanistic studies, which have nothing to do with my later field but will not be unprofitable for all that'. His main interest was in philosophy, not science, and he was excited by Franz Brentano's lectures on the existence of God. Freud had no intention of following the path of humble academic toil, as befitted the lot of the indigent boy from the Leopoldstadt. His vision of his education was much grander. He told schoolfriend Eduard Silberstein that 'being a student means being master of your own time . . . Use your time for your own good; youth is but the close season in which destiny allows us to gain strength so that we may amuse her by our resistance if she later decides to hunt us down.'

When Silberstein, who also struggled financially, canvassed the prospect of teaching to supplement his income, Freud scoffed at the idea: such a scheme was beneath his dignity. 'If you sell your time, spending several hours a day in slavery, you will be left with few opportunities and little desire to enjoy your freedom, the less so as you also want to study and, what is more, without constraint and at your leisure.' As for attending lectures 'for six hours at a stretch', as Silberstein did at the University of Leipzig, Freud could no more do that 'than breathe fire or walk a tightrope for six hours . . . Have you never heard that we live only once?'

As far as Freud was concerned, university life was designed for his enjoyment, especially as it included the 'infinite pleasure' of increasing his library. He did have some pangs, however, recognising that 'were I a little more diligent I should be a fairly contented fellow'. Freud was generous: he insisted on making gifts of books to Silberstein who, knowing the Freud family's parlous circumstances, did his best to refuse. 'To consider the cost is absurd,' Freud replied.[11]

Though Freud's love of nature had inspired his choice of a career, once embraced, he seemed incapable of making good his decision. He was something of a dilettante, recalling 'in my circle of acquaintances I was regarded as an idler and it was doubted whether I should ever get through'.[12] He had difficulty in selecting subjects that could advance his career and for years he floundered, unclear whether to concentrate on zoology (nature) or medicine (human nature). Freud's inclination was to pursue the pure research of the laboratory and shy away from the direct contact involved in clinical practice. In 1875, he was keen to follow Brentano's influence and take his doctorate in philosophy and zoology, but three years later he joked that he was still preparing himself for his real profession: would it be flaying animals or torturing human beings? Though he started his medical degree in 1873, at the early age of seventeen, he did not gain a position with a salary until eight years later.

What had happened to the brilliant schoolboy who topped his class? Describing his early professional life in *An Autobiographical Study*, he excised his dilatory behaviour and blamed Jacob for the loss of a promising career, just as his father was blamed for the happy childhood lost in Freiberg.

In 1882, Freud was working in the laboratory of Ernst Brücke, the first of his elected father figures, a man who was all Jacob was not: professionally distinguished, commanding, successful and prosperous. Freud was in awe of him. In the habit of arriving late for work, one morning he was confronted by Brücke, whose Medusa-like gaze from terrible blue eyes made Freud feel reduced to nothing. Brücke was also something of a renaissance man, which Freud especially admired and strove to emulate. As well as specialising in the nervous system of animals, Brücke had taught anatomy at the Academy of Art in Berlin and in his book *Beauty and Imperfection in the Human Form* he compared modern art with antiquity – and found it lacking.

As Freud told it, he was working productively in the laboratory completing research on the nervous structures of fish when Brücke took him aside and 'corrected my father's generous improvidence by strongly advising me, in view of my bad financial position, to abandon my theoretical career'.[13] Wisely, Brücke advised Freud to seek employment where he could make money and a name for himself, rather than spend his time fruitlessly waiting for a senior research position. After all, Freud had already been in the laboratory for six years and Brücke, keenly aware of Freud's financial situation, had once recommended his assistant for a job in the provinces, describing him as 'a very poor Jew'.[14]

But that was not the whole story about Freud's change of direction. He had fallen in love. His passion for the almost equally poor Martha Bernays ended the dithering, giving him the incentive he needed to specialise in medicine, get a job with a future, earn money and leave home – in short, become an adult. It was when he advised Brücke of his engagement to Martha that the older man suggested Freud change his career. 'I followed [Brücke's] advice, left the physiological laboratory and entered the General Hospital.'[15] Freud added as a rider that neither then nor at any other time in his life did he feel any desire to be a doctor.

Freud omits the determining factor behind quitting the laboratory. Neglecting to address the realities of the situation was not his father's fault but his own. Jacob, now in his sixties, was struggling to maintain his large, second family, including his elder son's extravagant tastes. He had borne with good grace Freud's lack of direction and apparently unending term of study, plus his mounting bills. Poverty did not allay Freud's desires: in Brücke's laboratory he made a new and generous friend, Josef Breuer, from whom he borrowed more money. It was behaviour learned from Jacob, who accepted loans and gifts from Amalia's family, and from Philipp and Emmanuel, his sons from his first marriage, who had migrated to England and prospered in the textile industry. At one point, Jacob had hoped Sigmund might follow in their footsteps but Philipp and Emmanuel persuaded their father to desist and allow their gifted half-brother to continue his studies.

Blaming Jacob is a screen memory: it was Freud who was prodigal about his prospects. Immured in Brücke's laboratory, he seemed unable to determine he was in a dead-end situation. Much of his energy was devoted to acquiring and reading books. Though in awe of Brücke, he did not imitate the great man's ambition and determination. The model for Freud's professional passivity and casual, spendthrift ways was his father, and he seemed incapable of breaking his dependence on him. Brücke, another father figure, had to take the initiative for him.

It was not only Jacob on whom Freud relied. His role as
Amalia's adored son had kept him by her side and he remained in
thrall to the mother. The smartly dressed and confident young
fellow standing behind Amalia in the family photograph of 1876
is something of an illusion. Aside from his crush on Gisela Fluss,
there were no girlfriends, no experiments with the hot, sweet
pleasures of courting, flirting or sex. 'Not another has taken
[Gisela's] place,' Freud said at seventeen, 'indeed that place can
remain empty.'[16] Until he met Martha, so it did. Articulate, witty,
even bossy with male friends such as Eduard Silberstein, Freud
was shy and hopelessly tongue-tied with women his own age.
Without any firm evidence to the contrary, it is safe to assume
that Freud remained a virgin until his marriage at thirty. Although
by no means unusual for a young man of his time, it is curious
simply because Freud was Freud.

Meanwhile, Arthur Schnitzler, also studying under Brücke at
the University of Vienna, was entering the realm of the senses,
enjoying evening trysts, 'embracing and kissing on the dusky paths
of the Rathaus or the Volksgarten'. Schnitzler, a dedicated liber-
tine and bohemian, soon graduated from these innocent pleasures
to prowling the red-light district around Kärntnerstrasse, where
'rouged and seductively winking ladies' became the targets of his
attention.[17]

The spectacle of sexual display and the public nature of prostitution aroused anxieties in Freud. One hot summer afternoon,
Freud recalled, as he was walking through the deserted streets of
a provincial Italian town, he found himself 'in a quarter whose
character I could not long remain in doubt. Nothing but painted
women were seen at the windows of the small houses, and I
hastened to leave the narrow street at the next turning.'[18] The

episode unfolds comically as Freud attempts to flee but, to his embarrassment, finds himself back in the same street where his presence had begun to attract attention.

Paul Ferris wonders if this recollection was based on a visit to Trieste in 1876 where Freud was involved, as part of his zoology studies, in a research project that involved dissecting the gonads of eels.[19] Freud's initial contact with Mediterranean culture was sensual and disturbing. On his first day in Trieste, he felt overwhelmed. It was not only because he had been 'transplanted suddenly to the shores of one of the most beautiful seas' (the Adriatic) but because the city was inhabited by 'Italian goddesses' who filled him with apprehension. They were 'slim, tall, slender-faced'. But the following day they had vanished, replaced by women who adorned themselves with a lock of hair dangling over one eye, meaning they belonged to 'the most dubious classes of society'.[20] The goddesses had become whores. To make the point, Freud included in a letter to Eduard Silberstein a whimsical, child-like drawing of a face with a lock of hair covering one eye.

Freud had already lectured Silberstein on dangerous liaisons. When Silberstein confided a flirtation, Freud railed at him like an Old Testament god, telling him it was 'very wrong . . . to encourage the imprudent affections of a sixteen-year-old girl'. Not only did it harm Silberstein, it upset Freud. 'A thinking man,' Freud went on, 'is his own legislator, confessor and absolver. But a woman, let alone a girl, has no inherent ethical standard: she can act correctly only if she keeps within the bounds of convention . . . She is never forgiven if she rebels against convention – perhaps rightly so; all her dignity and worth rest in general on one point.' Freud draws a cruel but accurate portrait of nineteenth-century morality: once a girl had lost her honour, she became a fallen woman, little better than a prostitute. Freud showed himself an adherent of that morality. He also warned his friend that girls were silly creatures and 'you do harm to the poor things when you accustom them to flattery and gallantries that they quickly come to consider as necessities'.[21]

In Trieste, Freud could not take his eyes off them. Even when he took a boat trip to nearby Muggia, 'the local beauties were out promenading on the *molo* [jetty] inspecting and laughing at the strangers'.[22] When he averted his gaze from the women of Trieste, there was much for the budding collector to see, including the remains of a Roman theatre built facing the sea on the side of a hill, like an ancient Greek theatre. Freud also knew of the death of Johann Joachim Winckelmann, the influential German art historian, who, after visiting Vienna, was murdered in Trieste in 1768. Though it has been conjectured that Winckelmann's stabbing by a local lad was an adventure in rough trade gone horribly wrong, simple thievery is the more likely answer. Winckelmann, whose *History of the Art of Antiquity* popularised the taste for classical art, is regarded as the first modern archaeologist for his studies of Pompeii, which Freud visited in 1902, and Herculaneum.

At Muggia, there was more to explore. In the main square, Freud found a fifteenth-century 'weatherbeaten beast hewn in stone' that he guessed was a lion and beneath it an inscription in Latin which he translated as: 'To this place the praetor ordered the Jews to emigrate under the command of Venetus and forbade them to depart from here'. More evidence of ghettos and tyranny. Freud made no comment on his find. Amid Muggia's ancient ruins, Freud sighted girls and children who were '*assai belle* [pretty enough], half of them rustic beauties, and even the women were pleasing to behold'. He now regarded the temptresses of Trieste as '*brutta, brutta* [ugly]'.[23]

When Freud fell in love it was pure romance: intense, irrevocable and instantaneous. 'You must love me irrationally as other people love,' he told Martha, 'just because I love you, and you don't have to be ashamed of it.'[24] Freud believed in life-changing flashes of intuition, momentous, spontaneous decisions and love at first sight. 'In vital matters . . . such as the choice of a mate or a profession the decision should come from the unconscious, from somewhere within ourselves. In the important decisions of our personal life, we should be governed, I think, by the deep inner needs of our nature.'[25] Passion for him was real, *l'amour fou*, and it was embodied in the pale, sweet-faced girl with the soulful emerald eyes on whom he lavished his affections and who conformed to his ideal of femininity. Freud felt that 'one is very crazy when one is in love'.[26] As soon as he saw Martha, he had to have her: she was his treasure, his prized possession, 'my most ardently worshipped Martha'. She was 'like a jewel that I have pawned and that I am going to redeem as soon as I am rich'.[27]

Freud's sisters were used to seeing their brother bustle in and out of his 'cabinet', often in the company of male friends from university whose acquaintance they longed to make. One evening in April 1882, hurrying into his room, Freud saw 'a little girl, sitting at a well-known long table, talking so cleverly while peeling an apple with her delicate fingers'.[28] The 'little girl' was Martha Bernays, twenty years old, slender and serious, and a recent friend of Freud's sisters. Within a short time, Freud had won his suit, and Martha was passionately in love too. 'Oh my beloved sweet Sigi, why can't we be together? I could not sleep half the night . . . your dear and noble image was before me and my longing for you was so intense.'[29]

Martha's widowed mother was displeased at the thought of her daughter marrying the penniless doctor, so Freud and Martha contrived a secret engagement. To thwart the lovers Emmeline Bernays had, within the year, whisked her daughter off to Wandsbek, near Hamburg, but it only made their commitment stronger. Freud and Martha's separation and their long, four-year courtship was a boon for posterity: they exchanged hundreds of letters that, as Peter Gay observes, add up to a veritable autobiography of Freud in the early 1880s.[30] The letters also provide a diary of Freud's art and literary interests, as well as a moving portrait of Freud the lover who was, by turn, tempestuous, anguished, tender and demanding. In his letters to Eduard Silberstein, Freud self-consciously displayed himself as a clever and confident young chap. His letters to Martha come from the heart: for the first time he exposes his vulnerabilities as a man, and reveals himself as a writer who can plumb the depths of feeling. Just as Jacob's death uprooted Freud and helped generate his art collection, so the profound feelings aroused by Martha tore him open and made him responsive to new subtleties.

Freud had several statues of Eros, winged messenger of desire and representative of the life-force. Apart from Osiris, he is the best represented deity in the collection. Given Freud's attitude towards love, it seems he understood the god well. Nearly fifty years after falling for Martha, he declared that 'language has carried out an entirely justifiable piece of unification in creating the word "love" with its numerous uses . . . In its origin, function and relations to sexual love, the "Eros" of the philosopher Plato coincides exactly with the love-force, the libido of psychoanaly-sis'.[31] H. D. F. Kitto remarks that, in Greek, 'eros has different asso-ciations: it means something like "passionate joy" . . . [h]e is something which makes every nerve tingle'.[32]

Eros, a superb Greek terracotta (c.150–100 b.c. [Hellenistic period]; pl. 7), is one of the major works in Freud's collection. The youthful god is shown with one foot lightly touching the earth and without his trademark bow and arrows, weapons he used to strike the hearts of gods and mortals and inflame them with love.[33] But Eros was not just a playful sprite engaged on a series of reckless missions to cause passion and mayhem. Mythologically, he was an ancient figure, a powerful and mysterious force, arising at the formation of the world, though it took centuries before a specific cult to him evolved.[34] Plato's *Symposium*, written in the fourth century b.c., is both a debate between Socrates and his friends about the nature of love and a sign of how deeply Greek culture was seeking to understand love's complexities.

Freud took his cue from Plato's frank and intelligent exposi-tion. Eros can mean 'love' or 'sexual desire'. It can lead to 'the most potent experience of overwhelming pleasure and thereby set a pattern for our quest for happiness'.[35] It can be a civilising force, igniting the spark between lovers that can result in steady rela-tionships, marriage, children and a sense of community, as well as unleashing turbulent and unbridled emotions. Freud experienced both aspects of Eros in his love for Martha.

Freud's *Eros* is depicted as a handsome adolescent, with the same sublime, enigmatic smile that attracted Freud to Leonardo's angelic studies of youths and madonnas. Eros' charm is seductive, referring to love's illusions, its blindness. But his joyful vitality, conveyed by his light stance, raised arms and wings stretched in full flight, symbolises the rapture and energy of love's awakening. Freud respected Eros, 'the preserver of all things', though recognising he was also a mischief-maker.[36] Eros aroused desire, for people and for objects. Plato suggested love and desire are directed at 'what you don't have, what isn't there, and what you need'.[37] Freud, lover of beautiful things, recognised the urge. The statue of *Eros* was an object of desire he had to possess. Not only did it epitomise classical civilisation and the brave new ideas Freud developed in relation to it but, equally, *Eros* was an item of pure aesthetic pleasure.

Eros comes from the ancient city of Myrina (near present-day Aliaga on Turkey's Aegean coast). In the late nineteenth century, many treasures were excavated from a necropolis on the site. The haul by the French School at Athens found its way to the Louvre while many other antiquities, pillaged by the locals, surfaced in the marketplaces of Athens and Paris. Freud's *Eros* is better than similar examples in the Louvre. He bought it in September 1934, four years after publishing *Civilization and its Discontents*, his final essay testifying to Eros' power. Two other statues of *Eros* in his collection, also Greek Hellenistic, show him as a child, the cute Cupid who remains familiar today as a figure on Valentine's Day cards. These *Eros* are no bigger than a thumb, the god of love as a naughty little boy, made a century or so after Plato wrote his *Symposium*. Interestingly, Freud's statues of Eros have lost their weapons. In his apartment at Berggasse 19, Freud arranged them together, a small battalion of the god of love unarmed: Eros idealised, his destructive potential removed.

After their engagement, Martha sent Freud her photograph. He had established a little gallery in his 'cabinet' and wanted to give her photograph 'a place among my household gods'. These were 'the severe faces of the men I revere', which hung above his desk, but he felt unable to include Martha's 'lovely face' among them: he had to hide away her image.[38] Then, after closing his door (the engagement was still secret), he would take out her photograph, to refresh his memory.

Freud was an ardent hero-worshipper. As a child, he idolised the sons of Mars, warlike men including Alexander the Great, Hannibal, Napoleon and his general Marshal Masséna. Even Horus, the falcon-headed god, was a warrior. As Freud grew older, the severe men included Brücke and the physiologist and philosopher Hermann Hemholtz. Dismissive of the transcendent, pantheistic approach to nature proposed by Goethe and the philosopher Frederick Schelling, Hemholtz's universe was mechanistic and deterministic. Hemholtz, whose lectures in Berlin Freud had longed to attend, was another universal man: his writings encompassed optics, colour and music, as well as mathematics and science. Freud named his youngest son after Ernst Brücke and his second son after the austere English Protestant leader, Oliver Cromwell. Freud needed to surround himself with beautiful things but also with images of masculine greatness to inspire and encourage him. It also made him aware of the gap between the hero he longed to be and the less-than-confident man he was.

'I have often felt as though I had inherited all the defiance and all the passions with which our ancestors defended their Temple and could gladly sacrifice my life for one great moment in history,' he told Martha. 'And at the same time I always felt so helpless and incapable of expressing these ardent passions even by a word or a poem. So I have always restrained myself, and it is this, I think, which people must see in me.'[39]

It is significant that Freud did not include Martha's photograph in his 'hero' gallery, just as later he kept his art collection separate from the domestic arena. Perhaps it was no accident that he first spied Martha in the dining room, helping serve the evening meal, even if she was peeling apples, the fruit of temptation.

But with Martha, he could plan his future and that meant his ideal home, a bourgeois haven adorned with the feminine fripperies and furbelows that he conjured with the eye of a novelist.

> We would need two or three little rooms to live and eat in and to receive a guest, and a stove in which the fire for our meals never goes out. And just think of all the things that have got to go into the rooms! Tables and chairs, beds, mirrors, a clock to remind the happy couple of the passage of time, an armchair for an hour's pleasant daydreaming, carpets to help the housewife keep the floors clean, linen tied with pretty ribbons in the cupboard and dresses of the latest fashion and hats with artificial flowers, pictures on the walls, glasses for everyday and others for wine and festive occasions, plates and dishes, a small larder in case we are suddenly attacked by hunger or a guest ... And there will be so much to enjoy, the books and the sewing table and the cosy lamp, and everything must be kept in good order or else the housewife ... will begin to fret.

Keeping the household together was not financial security but something far more important, 'a feeling for beauty'. But Freud had to admit that this 'small world of happiness' was in the future. 'Not even the foundation of the house has been laid, there is nothing but two poor human creatures who love each other to distraction.'[40]

Though Freud lived on a knife edge regarding money, he was always prepared to cast caution to the wind for another shopping spree. After bemoaning their mutual lack of cash, he encouraged Martha to buy a new jacket. 'Don't deny yourself, my precious, any little luxury; I don't.' Freud's attitudes towards love and money were linked: 'One must not be mean with affection; what is spent of the funds is renewed by the spending itself. If they are left untouched for too long, they diminish imperceptibly.' Books were objects of beauty, too. Freud revelled in a gift of Cervantes' *Don Quixote* with Gustave Doré's flamboyant, grotesque, highly detailed illustrations, which were superb, 'enough to make one die with laughter'.[41] Poring over the book was far more compelling than Freud's research into brain anatomy. Largesse and impetuosity, key elements in Freud's personality, helped to shape him as a collector.

Freud was fastidious about his appearance. A distinguished countenance could signify a fortunate destiny and Freud felt 'aggrieved that nature had not, in one of her benevolent moods, stamped my face with that mark of genius which now and again she bestows on men'.[42] He was also sensitive to the appearance of others, especially women. Martha, his 'pale princess', represented his preferred type: slim, youthful and rather ethereal, an ultra-feminine woman who emphasised Freud's masculinity. In his letters he worries she will age before they have married and lose the bloom of youth. In a photograph (pl. 35) taken during their engagement, Martha stands next to Freud, one hand resting uncertainly on his shoulder. Freud, seated in his chair, emanates vigour and repressed energy while Martha, in her well-upholstered gown, seems diffident, watchful, unsure.

When Freud came to collect art, he chose Egypt. He collected Greek and Roman art as well, but much of his collection favours the schematised, elegant style that was the hallmark of Egyptian civilisation's ideal human form. Classical art's robust, humanist representation of the body, replete with emotive expressions, vigorous movement and flowing robes, shown in Freud's statuettes of *Artemis* (2nd century B.C.; pl. 9) and *Eros*, contrast with the calm beauty of *Isis Suckling the Infant Horus*, a small bronze from the Late Period (664–525 B.C. [26th Dynasty]; pl. 8).[43]

Bought from Robert Lustig in 1935, the statuette of *Isis* was a high point of Freud's collection and given an honoured place on his desk. The canny Lustig had spotted it in a country shop where he bought it for the price of its weight in metal. The goddess as madonna is as svelte as a girl: her clinging shift reveals pert breasts, trim hips, graceful, elongated legs and feet. It is a modern body, thinness qualifying as a factor in beauty's equation. *Isis'* features are exquisitely neat and symmetrical. Offering her breast to her son, she is a study in harmony and balance. Restrained, composed, girlish and slim, Egypt's all-powerful female deity provides an image of femininity that attracted Freud and that he found echoed in Martha's features and demeanour. Because Isis brought Osiris back to life, she was regarded as 'the highest type of a faithful wife and mother and it was in this capacity the Egyptians honoured and worshipped her most'.[44] As the symbol of the annual Nile flood, which promised prosperity and growth, she also represented fertility. Isis was a mother goddess, emblematic of fecundity and renewal. Freud knew that mother goddesses had once reigned supreme. 'The male deities appear first as sons beside the great mothers.' But matriarchy was overthrown and 'a patriarchal order' was established.[45]

Around the time Freud fell in love with Martha, he began to look closely at art, and it was images of women, specifically madonnas, that attracted him. Visiting Dresden's Zwinger Museum in December 1883, he had an aesthetic breakthrough. Until then, he had suspected that it was 'a silent understanding among people who don't have much to do, to rave about pictures painted by the famous masters'. But he challenged his own 'barbaric' philistinism and 'began to admire'.[46]

Madonnas by Hans Holbein and Raphael caught his attention. Initially Holbein's *The Virgin and Child with the Family of the Burgomaster Meyer* (1528, Schlosssmuseum, Darmstadt) annoyed Freud because of 'the ordinary ugly human faces' of the mayor and his family who had commissioned the altar painting and were included in it. Freud loathed ugliness and it blinded him, at that point, to the wonderfully characterised, warmly human portraits of the Meyer family, who looked too ordinary to him to rate a divine audience. Freud judged Holbein's Madonna as 'not exactly beautiful' but her aura of 'sacred humility' made her a 'true queen of heaven such as the pious German mind dreams of'. Although Raphael's *Sistine Madonna* (c.1513–14, Gemäldegalerie, Dresden) had 'a magic beauty that is inescapable', this madonna disturbed Freud. She looked too earthly. She gazed out at the world with such a fresh and innocent expression that she suggested 'a charming, sympathetic nursemaid, not from the celestial world but from ours'. Raphael contrasts Mary's role as virgin and triumphant queen of heaven by representing her as a handsome, sloe-eyed, flesh and blood young woman on the brink of movement in flowing robes. Freud found Holbein's dignified madonna a more acceptable image of the sacred feminine. Another work to catch his eye, Titian's *The Tribute Money* (c.1518, Gemäldegalerie, Dresden), with its 'noble human countenance' of Christ, made Freud covetous. 'I would love to have gone away with it, but there were too many people about.'[47]

The look of things, the world of appearances, of taste and style, was becoming increasingly important to Freud. He was fashionable, though not a dandy, and most particular about his attire, insisting on the best, down to the details. 'I am considering a reckless purchase,' he told Martha. It was 'a decent silver watch . . . it has the value of a scientific instrument, and my old wreck of a thing never keeps proper time. Without a watch, I am not really a civilised person.'[48] Martin Freud remembered that there was never a hair out of place on his father's head, and his clothing, 'rigidly conventional', was cut from the best materials and tailored to perfection.[49] 'All the things that a person does with his clothing,' Freud noted, '. . . [are] intended to express something which the wearer of the clothes does not want to say straight out and for which the most part he is unaware of.'[50]

When Freud visited an exhibition by Jaray, Vienna's top furniture store, it made him 'lose all my philosophy . . . I was in ecstasy'. He imagined Martha's delight at the furnishings. 'Though,' he reflected, 'the wife should always be the most beautiful ornament in the house.' In the late nineteenth century, the domestic interior became what Walter Benjamin described as 'the universe of the private citizen'. In that universe, Freud was adamant about Martha's place. 'It seems a completely unrealistic notion to send women into the struggle for existence in the same way as men. Am I to think of my delicate sweet girl as a competitor? . . . No, in that respect I adhere to the old ways.'[51]

Though Freud identified the three forms taken by the figure of the mother in the course of a man's life as 'the mother herself, the beloved one who is chosen after her pattern and lastly the

Mother Earth who receives him once more', he chose to marry a very different kind of woman to Amalia and organised a different emotional economy than the one in which he had grown up.[52] Firstly, he would be the master of the house, unlike his irresponsible father. He had no desire to live with 'a tornado' and he made sure at the outset that he challenged Martha's will on a key matter, religious observance, and broke it. Martha was an Orthodox Jew and the grandddaughter of a rabbi. Once they were married, Freud forbade her to observe Jewish customs. Unwillingly, she obeyed. It was only after Freud died that, once more, Martha could light the Sabbath candles. 'I want to be the way you want me to be,' Martha dutifully told him.[53] Whereas Amalia was explosive and domineering, Martha was calm, tractable and quietly dignified.

But she was no pushover, as Freud discovered in the early days of their courtship. 'You admitted,' Freud reminded Martha, that 'I had no influence over you. I found you so fully matured and every corner in you occupied, and you were hard and reserved and I had no power over you.' Wearing down her resistance only made her more precious, though the effort made him miserable. Ever the anxious swain, he complained, 'I have always loved you much more than you me.' Freud meant to possess Martha's heart and soul: he challenged and hectored her, and rarely apologised for his explosive moods. He explained that 'when I am angry with you nowadays . . . it is gone as soon as I have spoken my mind, and I don't like to leave it unspoken, for it all burrows its way into me and cannot be cauterised away'. Several times he confessed to 'the tyrannical temperament that makes little girls afraid of me' and that 'could not be subdued'.[54]

Characteristically, he refused flattery. 'I would rather you didn't make me out so good-natured. I can hardly contain myself for silent savagery, and your latest letters are so tame; if you weren't such a very sweet angel, I would love to have a good squabble with you.'[55] Sex before marriage, of course, was out of the question. When the couple met on Freud's visits to Hamburg, petting had to suffice. 'You kiss so wonderfully,' Martha told Freud. 'Cover me with love.'[56] Freud's frustrated lust may have motivated some of his 'silent savagery' and 'a good squabble' may stand for a desired act more carnal and satisfying. He had to take the advice he later gave to his students: 'Be abstinent but under protest.'[57]

Martha was Freud's beloved but she was not his intellectual companion: that role was later assigned to women friends like Lou Andreas-Salomé, Princess Marie Bonaparte and his youngest daughter, Anna. As a teenager, he had glimpsed the kind of woman she might be. Though he'd had a crush on Gisela Fluss, it was her worldly, sophisticated mother who commanded his admiration. Widely read in contemporary literature and the classics, Frau Fluss was even knowledgeable about politics. But 'don't take her for a frustrated bluestocking,' Freud advised Eduard Silberstein. Frau Fluss was active in local affairs, as well as being an excellent hostess and a firm but benevolent mother. She also took a decisive hand in running the family textile business. 'I have never seen such superiority before,' Freud sighed.[58] But he was not inclined to choose a similarly accomplished, worldly woman – an equal – to share his home but a girl he could rule. 'Just you wait,' he told Martha, during one of their regular disagreements. 'When I come you will soon get used to having a master again.'[59]

As the essay 'On Nature' had inspired Freud to begin his career in science, so the feminine roused him from his languor in 1882. Freud was Sleeping Beauty when he met Martha; she awoke him to a new life. Though he presents his departure from Brücke's laboratory as a misadventure, it presaged his career in neurology which would lead to the foundation of psychoanalysis. Like the hero in a fairytale, to win Martha, Freud had to confront the dragon — tackle those aspects of himself of which he was ashamed or unsure. He lacked the confidence to make an impression on the world and by becoming a doctor he had to address that fear by entering the hurly-burly of a general hospital, treating patients, working in the wards and assuming new responsibilities. Freud was a dreamer forced to manifest his ideals in a practical form. He quit the ivory tower of the laboratory to gain an object worth having — Martha in marriage — and it transformed him from an irresolute youth into an alert and focused individual, fired with ambition.

A year after their engagement, Freud told Martha that 'you give me not only aim and direction, but so much happiness as well ... You give me hope and certainty of success ... It is your doing that I have become a self-confident, courageous man.' Freud recognised 'the great turning point in my life' was a combination of 'our love and my choice of profession'.[60]

3

Paris

I am under the full impact of Paris and, waxing very poetical, could compare it to a vast overdressed Sphinx who gobbles up every foreigner unable to solve her riddles.

SIGMUND FREUD TO MINNA BERNAYS, PARIS, 3 DECEMBER 1885[1]

In the last decades of the nineteenth century, the Salpêtrière was what it had always been . . . a nightmare in the midst of Paris's Belle Epoque.

GEORGES DIDI-HUBERMAN, INVENTION OF HYSTERIA: CHARCOT AND THE PHOTOGRAPHIC ICONOGRAPHY OF THE SALPÊTRIÈRE[2]

FREUD HAD BEEN LONGING TO visit Paris for years. His opportunity came in October 1885, when he arrived to study under Europe's most highly regarded and flamboyant neurologist, Jean-Martin Charcot. On a grant from the University of Vienna that Ernst Brücke helped secure for him, Freud stayed in France until February 1886.

He was bewitched, provoked and inspired by Paris. At first, he was overwhelmed by its sheer spectacle, the 'brilliant exterior, the swarming crowds, the infinite variety of attractively displayed goods, the streets stretching for miles', but he resisted seduction, declaring 'my heart is German provincial'.[3] On his first day, if he had not been consoled by his beard and his silk hat, he confessed he would have wept. Freud, like many nineteenth-century visitors, was stunned by what Balzac described as 'the rapid whirl of life in Paris'.[4] It was the rhythm Balzac captured in *Lost Illusions*, in which Lucien de Rubempré, the ambitious provincial boy, is subjected to a very urban rite of passage. At a rapid rate, Paris deflowers him, disencumbering him of his ideals and reshaping his character. Balzac, himself a compulsive collector, understood precisely the catalogue of desires the city offered. Freud's initiation was not quite as extreme as Lucien's but, on his return to Vienna, he concluded that 'Paris meant the beginning of a new existence for me'.[5]

Initially, Freud found the French bewildering: they struck him as 'uncanny', they seemed like 'a different species'. He also encountered the frustrations of language, the humiliation of a proud, educated man who could not make himself understood. 'I can't speak enough to ask for bread in a café,' he admitted to Minna Bernays, his future sister-in-law. 'When I said "du pain" to the garçon, I have no idea what he made of it: he just shook his head till I got so annoyed I refused to go to any café.' He was also miserably homesick. 'Paris is simply one long confused dream, and I shall be very glad to wake up.'[6]

Even cheerful moments were tinged with melancholy. Years later, Freud recalled how 'on the Boulevard [St] Michel, a group of young men and girls walked in front of me. Every now and then they stopped walking and fell spontaneously into a few dance steps without any apparent cause or motive, just because they were young and in Paris'.[7] It is an image of youthful *joie de vivre* worthy of an Impressionist painting, but it is offset by the figure of Freud, the lonely voyeur to the happiness of others.

Paris is a city traditionally associated with art, bohemianism and romance: feminine, sophisticated, sensuous and stimulating. Described by Walter Benjamin as 'the capital of the nineteenth century', it was also the site of modernity, of change, speed and movement.[8] Freud, the 'indefatigable walker', must have approved of Baron Haussmann's judicious urban planning that had transformed Paris into a modern metropolis: the architects of the Ringstrasse had taken their cues from him. Commissioned by Napoleon III, Haussmann created spacious *grands boulevards* and elegant architecture that delighted the eye and made walking its streets a pleasurable and satisfying excursion. Paris also offered Freud the opportunity to visit the Louvre, as well as Notre-Dame, the Cluny Museum, the theatre, bookshops and cafés.

Freud uses the word 'provincial' to describe his heart. He is the innocent abroad, gauche visitor to the dazzling metropolis. Vienna might have been the third largest city in Europe, with a paramount reputation for music, but Paris was undisputed international centre for fashion and art. Freud recognised the dangers of being entranced by this alluring city. Beneath its surface charms, there lurked the yawning maw of a destructive feminine force ready to consume the unwary male, the 'overdressed Sphinx who gobbles up every foreigner unable to solve her riddles'.

Freud did allow Paris to seduce him, but it was only when Charcot, his commanding mentor, brought him in from the cold. Warmed by the fire of Charcot's approval and hospitality, Freud's confidence buoyed. Then he suddenly discovered 'what a magic city this Paris is!'[9] Entering Charcot's home was also to be privy to an impressive and luxurious environment: the neurologist was a collector. It gave Freud a vision of his ideal home and workplace, one that advertised individuality, learning, taste and power.

Freud settled himself at the Hotel de la Paix, a cheap *pension* in the student quarter near the Luxembourg Gardens, then set off to discover the city. At Place de la Concorde, he was thrilled to see 'a real obelisk from Luxor' which stands in its centre. 'Imagine,' he wrote to Martha, 'a genuine obelisk, scribbled all over with the most beautiful birds' heads, little seated men and other hiero-glyphs, at least 3000 years older than the vulgar crowd around it, built in honour of a king whose name today only a few people can read and who, but for this monument, might be forgotten!'[10] Dating from the thirteenth century BC, the obelisk's inscriptions describe the deeds of that inveterate builder of monuments to himself, Ramesses II. The obelisk was a gift from Mohammed Ali, viceroy of the Ottoman Sultan, to Charles X, and had arrived in Paris four years later, in 1833. Transporting it from the Temple of Luxor to the centre of Paris was not an easy task: a canal to the Nile had to be dug, then it was carried first by sea, then by a special boat along the Seine.

Freud headed for the antiquities wing at the Louvre. This was
not his first encounter with ancient art and making it a priority
shows his interest. For centuries, the Habsburgs had been enthusiastic collectors. From 1776, their treasure trove of Egyptian
and classical art, together with their collections of medieval,
Renaissance and baroque painting, were displayed to the public,
free of charge, in the sumptuous rooms of the Belvedere, an
eighteenth-century palace, surrounded by gardens, in the suburbs
of Vienna. It was an enlightened gesture, making the Belvedere
one of the first public museums devoted to visual art. In 1891, the
collection was relocated to the new Kunsthistorisches Museum
on the Ringstrasse.

But the glories of the Habsburg collection paled beside those
of the Louvre. The museum's vast and seemingly endless exposi-
tion of world cultures can be a daunting experience. After seeing
the range of classical and preclassical art, it is no wonder Freud
promised himself, 'I must visit again several times.' He paced
himself. On his first visit, he saw the Roman and Greek antiquities and paid 'a fleeting visit' to the Egyptian and Assyrian
galleries. He was astonished by 'the incredible number of Greek
and Roman statues, gravestones, inscriptions and relics'. He saw
'a few wonderful things, ancient gods represented over and over
again, as well as the famous armless Venus de Milo to whom I paid
the traditional compliment'.[11]

The tale of Venus' arrival in Paris has the quality of a myth.
As soon as it was discovered on the Aegean island of Melos in
1820, the Hellenistic statue became an object of desire. The avari-
cious peasant who found it hid it in his cowshed, eager to sell to
the highest bidder. Jules Dumont d'Urville, a French naval officer
who later led three voyages of exploration to the Pacific, was

impressed by Venus' charms, and he had a tussle with local authorities to remove her. He enlisted the help of the Marquis de Rivière,
the French ambassador to Constantinople. Rivière escorted Venus
to France, where she arrived amid great fanfare and was presented
to Louis XVIII. A debate then ensued about whether Venus' arms
should be restored: fortunately, the consensus was in the negative.
In 1821, Louis presented the work to the Louvre. Since then she
has, as Kenneth Clark writes, 'held her place in popular imagery
as a symbol, or trademark, of Beauty'.[12]

Goddess of love, pleasure and beauty, Aphrodite (Venus is her
later Roman name) is shown seductively half naked, her robes
sliding down her thighs at her moment of triumph when Paris
chose her as the winner of a beauty contest with Athena and Hera.
The prize was a golden apple. The judgement of Paris was a subject
attracting artists from Botticelli to Rubens: it offered the opportunity to reveal the goddesses' charms, as well as to portray an
ominous event. To secure her win, Aphrodite had not only
loosened her robes for Paris but offered him the love of Helen, the
world's most beautiful woman. Paris' affair with Helen led to
the Trojan War. The golden apple was the fruit of discord and
Aphrodite's gift of Helen left a bitter legacy: the destruction of
Troy by the Greeks.

Though Freud paid Venus 'the traditional compliment' – that
she was beautiful without her arms – the statue, celebrated as an
archetype of femininity, does not depict Aphrodite as a delicate
nymph. Her face seems masculine with its distinctive chin, firm
lips and broad brow. Her torso is strong and muscled. From behind,
she has the thickset frame of a man of action, perhaps fitting for a
goddess who so recklessly pursued the games of love. Freud, whose
ideal of feminine beauty was slender and girlish, was not

captivated by such a robust and imposing creature. Rather primly, he informed Martha that 'the beauty of the statue was not discovered till later, and that it has become fashionable to think so. For me these things have more historical than aesthetic interest.'[13]

First encounters with great works of art can be disconcerting. Expectations falter, reputations are not confirmed. The work may appear less attractive in the original than it did in reproduction. Freud hints Venus' reputation has been contrived, 'discovered later', and perhaps is merely a fad. He is too uncertain to offer a critique. Instead, he retreats to a neutral position: he is not a connoisseur or an art lover, his concerns are objective and 'historical'. A collection is built on an individual's taste, a process informed by negative as well as positive responses. Freud did not like the *Venus de Milo*. She was not his kind of girl. But he lacked the confidence to say so.

He was impressed with 'the large number of emperors' busts, some of them excellent characterisations'. Freud, the hero-worshipper, with his home portrait gallery arrayed with 'the severe faces of the men I revere', delighted in the noble austerity of the Louvre's Roman emperors including Septimus Severus, Constantine and Hadrian. With his eye for physiognomy, he noted 'most of them are represented several times and don't look in the least alike'.

But Freud's major discovery was Egyptian art. He felt he had entered 'a dreamlike world' when he came upon the Egyptian collection with its 'bas-reliefs decorated in fiery colours, veritable colossi of kings' and 'real sphinxes'.[14] Though the *Sphinx of Wah-ib-re* (380–362 B.C.), which Freud had seen in the Habsburg collection, is a graceful work, it could not compare with the antiquity, expert craftsmanship and impressive bulk of the Louvre's major

Sphinx, found at Tanis, which is nearly two metres high and five metres long. Perhaps it was the sheer impact that made Freud describe the work, displayed in its own court in the Salle de Colonnade, as 'real'. Carved from a single block of red granite, the *Sphinx* has powerfully articulated legs and paws and the calm visage of the pharaoh, possibly Amenemhat II (1929–1985 B.C.), though the work could be even older. In Egypt the Sphinx was a guardian, a benevolent protector of entrances and passages in palaces and temples, not the enigmatic temptress of Greek myth. The lion's body symbolised strength and valour; the face was the pharaoh's. The Egyptians regarded monarchs as gods, so the sphinx represented both worldly and divine protection.

Freud had many representations of the Sphinx in his collection including a tiny Egyptian amulet (716–332 B.C.), a sturdy compact terracotta figure from the late 5th century B.C., a Greek vase from the Classical Period (c.380–360 B.C.) showing Oedipus grappling with the Sphinx's riddle and a fragment of a Roman wall painting (1st century B.C.–1st century A.D) where the Sphinx is depicted as a tamed creature, playful as a kitten, against a decorative pink-orange ground. Freud also hung Heinrich Ulbrich's print of Egypt's most famous Sphinx in his consulting room – the *Great Sphinx at Giza*, one of the oldest known sculptures (probably 2722–2563 B.C.) and certainly one of the largest. In 1905, it was dug out of the sands of the Sahara that periodically rose to its nose, and Ulbrich's print celebrated its liberation.

The Louvre's department of Egyptian antiquities, founded by Jean-François Champollion, who is best known for using the Rosetta Stone to crack the code of the Egyptian hieroglyphs, had opened in 1827. Champollion had excellent taste, recommending the obelisk which found its way to Place de la

Concorde. After establishing the world's first Egyptian museum in Turin, Champollion was invited to Paris to create the collection at the Louvre. Aside from the British Museum, it is the best Egyptian collection outside Cairo. The story of its development mirrors complex colonial attitudes towards the cultures of the East – a mixture of respectful scholarship, arrogance, paternalism, looting and a genuine desire for preservation. Egypt's glories were in the past and its citizens were deemed incapable by their colonial masters of managing the treasures of that past, and must be relieved of them. The Europeans justified the wholesale removal of antiquities by contrasting the splendours of the ancient world with present squalor, oriental 'barbarism' with European enlightenment.[15] Given a large acquisitions budget, Champollion was able to assemble an impressive body of nine thousand works in a short time, mainly from buying the collections of the English and French consuls in Egypt. His own travels in Egypt also garnered some excellent finds including the Tanis *Sphinx*.

More acquisitions came via Auguste Mariette, who arrived in Egypt in 1850 to buy Coptic manuscripts for the Louvre. Instead, he abandoned his mission and began excavating the necropolis of Memphis (now Saqqara) at the Nile delta.[16] The Louvre was so impressed with Mariette's discoveries that more funds were arranged. Between 1852 and 1856, Mariette sent around six thousand objects to the museum including the compelling *Seated Scribe* (c.2620–2350 B.C.), found at Saqqara.

New to Freud were original examples of Assyrian art and he was impressed by the Louvre's spectacular holdings. 'There were Assyrian kings tall as trees, holding lions for lapdogs in their arms,' Freud told Martha, 'winged human animals with beautifully dressed hair', as well as 'cuneiform inscriptions clear as if they had been done yesterday.'[17]

Hero Holding a Small Lion is a monumental work, over five metres tall, and made of alabaster, as is *Winged Assyrian Bulls*. Both were discovered in 1843 by French consul Paul-Emile Botta when he excavated the palace of King Sargon II at Khorsabad, near Nineveh (now Mosul, Iraq). Sargon II, who died in battle in 705 B.C., captured both Babylon and Israel during his reign and was an able representative of the ruthless and efficient Assyrian empire. His three-year siege at Samaria, which ended in 722 B.C., led to the destruction of the kingdom of Israel and the exile of its Ten Tribes. 'Israel was exiled from their own land to Assyria until this day,' the Bible notes. Inscriptions on the palace walls at Khorsabad boast that Sargon deported nearly thirty thousand people. When the Assyrian monuments arrived in Paris in 1846, they were enthusiastically welcomed by the French public, and most major European newspapers devoted an unprecedented amount of space to them. Such a find from one of Mesopotamia's ancient civilisations was rare. These remains received greater coverage than any archaeological subject until Carter's discovery of the tomb of Tutankhamun.

Among the Assyrian monuments were 'lamassu', bulls with human heads and eagles' wings, that guarded the palace gates. Like Egyptian sphinxes, which they resemble, they were powerful and benevolent spirits, good genii, protectors against chaos and misfortune, and of the palace itself. The *Hero*, like the lamassu, adorned the palace's throne room and was an emblem of the king, a mighty warrior who could deal with a lion as if it were no more trouble than a pet dog, as Freud noted. Assyrian art's abstracted, schematised treatment of the body, reminiscent of Egyptian art, especially the rhythmic, decorative modelling of hair, made it attractive to Freud.

It was the beginning of Freud's interest in Mesopotamian culture and language. He began to follow the archaeological discoveries in the region and tried to master the language of its cuneiform script. Later he acquired several exquisite Sumerian and Babylonian cylinder seals for his collection (pl. 10). Made of stone and patterned with tiny, elegant figures, these pictographs were used to authenticate documents and mark ownership: essentially, they are signatures, similar to but more abstract than Egyptian hieroglyphics. They are also among the oldest works in his collection.[18]

Napoleon's invasion of Egypt in 1798 had made Paris a focal point for the trade in antiquities. Dominique Vivant Denon, artist, writer and courtier and the first director of the Napoleon Museum, later renamed the Louvre, had helped to promote the international fascination for Egypt. Invited by Napoleon to join the team of 170 scientists, scholars and artists who accompanied the campaign, Denon was commissioned to draw the monuments of Egypt. His magnificently detailed, two-volume *Voyages dans la basse et la haute Egypte* was published in 1802, and translated into English and German the following year. It created a vogue for Egypt that led to scientific expeditions and unbridled looting. As Edward Said has observed, Denon's book 'staged' Egypt for Europe: it was ancient Egypt as reflected through the imperial eye.[19]

Tomb-robbing had been practised for centuries. Local people used materials from temples to build their homes and burned temple stones to produce lime, as well as trading objects for cash, and tourists and professional looters conducted their own souvenir hunts. In Freud's time, the legitimate and the illegal trade in foreign antiquities combined to become an international business with Paris as its headquarters. When Freud began buying art in the 1890s, many of the artefacts he acquired had made their journey from Egypt (or Greece or Rome) to Paris before being bought by Viennese dealers. Despite the English wresting power in Egypt from the French in 1882, the flow of artefacts to the French capital did not stop. Paris might have been 'the capital of the nineteenth century' but it was also the marketplace. It was no accident that Bon Marché, the world's first department store, opened there.

Freud was poor on his first visit to Paris: the grant afforded him little aside from his accommodation, and once again he was reliant on loans. However, that was not the reason he did not commence buying antiquities then. Being broke rarely stopped him buying anything. In 1885, Freud had not encountered the emotional changes, and the new spectrum of desires, that attuned him to the collection of art. Art was experienced at a distance, observed and appreciated in public galleries such as the Louvre and the Belvedere, not acquired for his personal posses- sion. Freud the art collector, like Freud the doctor, was immature, a student: he did not have the confidence to make what he saw his own.

His most intense visual experience in Paris was not the art of antiquity but the Gothic cathedral at the city's heart. Prior to the construction of the Eiffel Tower in 1889, Notre-Dame, in the Ile de la Cité, was Paris' most famous image and remains a symbol of its spirit and history. 'The platform of Notre-Dame was my favourite resort in Paris,' Freud reminisced. 'Every free afternoon I used to clamber about there on the towers of the church between the monsters and the devils.'[20] His first impression on entering Notre-Dame gave him 'a sensation I have never had before: "This is a church".' It was the first time a Christian monument had left Freud awestruck. He had never seen anything 'so movingly serious and sombre' and it offered him 'an entirely new idea about perfection'. Prompted to read Victor Hugo's popular novel *Notre-Dame de Paris*, he announced to Minna Bernays shortly afterwards, 'To understand Paris this is the novel you must read; although everything in it is fiction, one is convinced of its truth. But don't read it till you are in a perfectly calm frame of mind and in Paris.'[21]

Begun around 1163 and completed nearly two centuries later, Notre-Dame is a grand expression of French Gothic. The interior's soaring columns, its ceiling of delicately interlocking transverse arches and slender nave create an impression that is feminine and beautiful, 'unadorned and very narrow', as Freud observed, a fitting homage to the Christian madonna it celebrates. The magnificent rose window on the west façade provides another symbol of Mary, who was *super rosam rosida*, the rose of roses. Outside a plenitude of carved saints, gargoyles and flying buttresses creates rhythms that are energetic, romantic and extravagant — 'a vast symphony in stone', Hugo extolled.[22]

Hugo's prose mirrors the great medieval cathedral. Goethe may have sneered that Hugo's characters were little more than marionettes but the public embraced the book, a curious mix of impassioned argument about the cathedral's need for conservation and the tragic tale of the hunchback Quasimodo, and his colleagues in misery, La Esmeralda and Frollo. Hugo heaped praise upon the 'sublime and majestic building', one of architecture's 'social creations' in which 'each stone . . . is a page . . . of our country's history . . . Time is the architect, the nation the builder.'[23] Hugo's concern for Notre-Dame's deterioration led to a government committee, on which Hugo served, and finally to restoration projects completed, most famously, by Viollet-le-Duc.

For the wretched Quasimodo, 'the gnarled cathedral was his carapace'. Clambering about on the 'maternal edifice' offered Quasimodo freedom, sensuality and and satisfaction, 'the consubstantial coupling of a man and a building . . . This abode was his.'[24] Freud found exploring the cathedral similarly exhilarating and comforting. It was the place he could escape to, like the Freiberg forest, and 'clamber about' to his heart's content.

Notre-Dame was more than a building to Freud, more than an object to be coolly appraised, like the *Venus de Milo*. He became emotionally enmeshed. The cathedral offered a refuge and a new standard of excellence, and Hugo's book was both a key to understanding the uncanny and bewildering French, as well as a guide to the church itself. When Freud contemplated his departure, it was 'Notre-Dame looking so beautiful in the sunlight' that made it a wrench.[25]

How did a Jewish man of science fall in love with a Catholic church? Freud was always prepared to be seduced by beauty and he responded to forms that were elegant, slender and feminine, like the frame of Notre-Dame, 'unadorned and very narrow', like the body of *Isis Suckling the Infant Horus* or like slim and yearned-for Martha, in far-off Wandsbek. Hugo wrote evocatively of architecture as an image of civilisation, comparing a nation's literature with its buildings, the equal strands in the country's consciousness and identity: 'In the Egyptian East, poetry, like the buildings, has a grandeur and tranquillity of line; in ancient Greece, beauty, serenity and calm.' Hugo constructed Notre-Dame's personality from its archaeology, a history that, in his hands, was intimate and partisan. Quasimodo was made of the same metaphors. Not only his body but also his mind 'seemed to have been fashioned to fit the cathedral' and if a light were shone on Quasimodo's 'unhappy psyche', a 'wretchedly stunted' creature would appear.[26] Freud made use of archaeological metaphors and comparisons with architecture to explain the processes of psycho-analysis.

There were plenty of churches in Vienna that might have dazzled Freud, including the Votivkirche and the imposing Karlskirche. St Stephen's, Vienna's Gothic cathedral, which had commanding views of the city, he regarded as 'detestable'. Freud's dislike of Vienna blinded him to the difference between its successful monuments and its failures. His experience in Notre-Dame – 'This is a church' – meant none of the others could compare. Notre-Dame conveyed to Freud a sense of the sacred, of reverence and worship, balance and harmony. Though he had experienced bliss in nature, he had never tasted such emotions in architecture, let alone in a church. He categorised himself as godless but his developing aesthetic sense gave him a feeling for the sublime and the transcendent.

Paris also had plenty of contemporary art to offer Freud. In 1881, Renoir summarised the Impressionist spirit and style in *The Luncheon of the Boating Party* (Phillips Collection, Washington D.C.), its mood of genial festivity underscored by the frisson of his brush-strokes creating rippling effects of light and movement. By then, the Impressionists were no longer the wild ones of French art. The group, including Monet and Pissarro, socialised at regular dinners but it was in memory of the past, a sentimental way of keeping in touch, rather than to plan strategies *épater le bourgeois*. In 1885, Monet was painting and gardening at Giverny, art dealer Paul Durand-Ruel was organising an Impressionist exhibition bound for New York, and Emile Zola, friend of the Impressionists and of Cézanne, whose novels Freud admired, had just published *Germinal*, which had been hailed as a masterpiece.

Freud's hostility to modern art meant he had no interest in Impressionism. In antiquity, Freud sought form, definition and clarity; the Impressionists dissolved the world into swirling, incandescent sensations. For Freud, art existed in the hallowed security of the past, not the fluid, indeterminate present. He shared his antagonism with Charcot, also an admirer of antiquity and medieval art. Charcot 'had no use for the paintings of the impressionists and symbolists; he did not understand them. He said he did not like the vague and the imprecise.'[27]

Determinedly anti-modern in their response to art, Charcot and Freud were innovative in the exposition and treatment of neurosis. At the Salpêtrière, Charcot was staging a different spectacle of modernity, one that inspired Freud. It dealt not with Paris' 'brilliant exterior' but with a compelling inner world, in which Charcot created bizarre and disturbing tableaux for an enthralled audience.

From 1863, Charcot was the director of one of the biggest madhouses on earth, at the Salpêtrière Hospital, situated in an enormous enclosure east of the city centre, near the Seine and Jardins des Plantes. Between five and eight thousand people, mostly women, were incarcerated there. The population of Paris at the time was around half a million. Charcot aptly termed the hospital 'the great emporium of misery'. His friend, writer Jules Clarétie, was more specific. 'Behind those walls, a particular population lives, swarms, and drags itself around: old people, poor women, *reposantes* awaiting death on a bench, lunatics howling their fury or weeping their sorrow in the insanity wards or the solitude of the cells ... It is the Versailles of pain.'[28] Michel Foucault observed that the creation of the Salpêtrière, and similar institutions in major European cities during the Enlightenment, indicated 'a sensibility ... which had drawn a line and laid a cornerstone and which chose – only to banish'.[29]

When Charcot arrived at the Salpêtrière as professor of clinical diseases of the nervous system, there was one doctor for every five hundred patients and three to four patients sometimes shared a bed. It was an asylum for the poor, for beggars, the disabled, the aged and children. It was also the general hospital for women as well as for unmarried mothers, prostitutes and the insane.

One of Charcot's first initiatives was to set up a laboratory to conduct investigations into the nervous system. Many of the women inmates had been diagnosed as hysterics. (The Greek word *hysterikos* means suffering in the uterus.) The conventional method of treating a woman suffering from hysteria had been to perform a clitorectomy. But Charcot believed it could be treated with hypnosis, a largely discredited technique that was regarded as the tool of charlatans. Charcot's research also proved that hysteria was not only the province of women, but that men, too, were its victims. He charted and, more notoriously, displayed hysteria, courtesy of his patients, in his Tuesday morning lectures, some of which Freud attended and translated into German.

Freud gives a vivid sketch of his first impression of Charcot. He was:

a tall man of fifty-eight, wearing a top hat, with dark, strangely soft eyes (or rather, one is; the other is expressionless and has an inward cast), long wisps of hair stuck behind his ears, clean shaven, very expressive features with full protruding lips – in short, like a worldly priest from whom one expects a ready wit and an appreciation of good living.

Freud observed Charcot treating outpatients and was 'very impressed by his brilliant diagnosis and the lively interest he took in everything, so unlike what we are accustomed to from our great men with their veneer of distinguished superficiality'. Afterwards, Freud was introduced to Charcot, who took him on a tour of the Salpêtrière which included the laboratory where Freud would work, the lecture hall and several wards. He made the young doctor feel 'very much at ease, and I realised that in the most inconspicuous fashion he was showing me a great deal of consideration'.[30]

Freud planned to continue neurological experiments at the Salpêtrière where his task was to dissect the brains of children. But the financial restraints that forced him out of Brücke's physiological laboratory were still operating. 'With an eye to pecuniary considerations, I began to study nervous diseases.'[31] It was Charcot who illuminated Freud's path. 'No other human being has ever affected me in the same way,' Freud declared. Charcot was 'one of the greatest of physicians and a man whose common sense borders on genius'. In a short time, Freud realised that Charcot was 'simply wrecking all my aims and opinions'.[32]

Charcot's lectures were a profound experience for Freud, similar to the intense emotions aroused by Notre-Dame, and they gave him 'an entirely new idea about perfection'. The French neurologist was transforming Freud's ideas and ambitions and the process was both exhilarating and exhausting. '[W]hen I come away from him I no longer have any desire to work at my own silly things … and I have no feelings of guilt.'[33] Freud regarded each lecture of Charcot's as 'a little work of art in construction and composition'. They were 'perfect in form'.[34] Ruminating on Charcot's effect on him, Freud wondered 'Am I under the influence of this magically attractive and repulsive city?'[35]

How did Charcot enchant Freud? André Brouillet's painting *Une Leçon Clinique à la Salpêtrière* (1887, National Library of Medicine, Maryland; pl. 36) illustrates Charcot's theatrical methods and charismatic personality. Freud bought Eugène-Louis Pirodon's lithograph of the painting to hang in his consulting room. The painting caused a sensation at the 1887 *Salon* and was viewed by half a million people. Charcot is shown at his Tuesday morning lecture, surrounded by students. He has hypnotised Blanche Wittmann, his most famous patient, the 'Queen of the Hysterics', and she is swooning in the arms of Charcot's assistant, Joseph Babinski.[36] Wittmann's clothes are loosened, sliding down her body like the *Venus de Milo*'s, and her bared breast, catching the light, provides the painting's focus. Her head is thrown back in a kind of ecstasy, her hand is clenched, her eyes are closed, she seems to smile. Charcot's lesson is demonstrating that hysteria can be controlled – literally turned off and on – by hypnosis, but the painting's message is flagrantly erotic and dramatic. Wittmann offers an image of abject and available femininity for a male audience, with Charcot as the director of the spectacle. In her unconscious state, she is the creature of Charcot's will. Though Babinski seems to support Wittmann, his hand strays so close to her breast it seems like a covert caress, emphasised by his tender, amorous expression. Female madness is depicted as a live sex act, in which the woman revels in her violation, witnessed by an audience of voyeurs. Brouillet's painting is pornography dressed up as scientific experiment.

No wonder Freud was aroused. 'I found to my astonishment that here were occurrences plain before one's eyes, which it was quite impossible to doubt, but which were nevertheless strange enough not to be believed unless they were experienced at first hand.'[37] Charcot was a kind of magician, changing his appearance at will. Usually good-humoured, on these occasions he became solemn and serious, 'indeed he even seems to have grown older'. His voice sounded subdued. It made Freud understand how 'ill-disposed strangers could reproach the whole lecture with being theatrical'.[38]

'Behold the truth,' said Charcot. 'I've never said anything else; I'm not in the habit of advancing things that aren't experimentally demonstrable . . . I am nothing more than a photographer; I inscribe what I see.'[39] Charcot's insistence on the close examination of hysterical symptoms impressed Freud. He never grew tired of looking at the same phenomenon, till his repeated efforts allowed him to reach a good diagnosis. Freud believed Charcot had 'the nature of an artist – he was, as he himself said, a "*visuel*", a man who sees'.[40]

In fact, Charcot aspired to be an artist. At home, he had a studio where he painted on porcelain and enamel. While travelling, he sketched constantly. He was a keen photographer who installed both a museum and a photographic studio at the Salpêtrière. Freud described the hospital as 'the museum of clinical facts'. Charcot published two art books with Paul Richer, *The Demoniacs in Art* (1887) and *The Deformed and the Ill in Art* (1889) that Freud admired. He hailed Charcot as the foremost author to identify hysteria in works of art.[41]

Hysteria was traditionally thought to be the result of demonic possession and, for centuries, such a conclusion had contributed to the torture and death of women as witches. In *Demonaics*, Charcot explored the representation of hysteria in medieval and Renaissance art, as well as in drawings by his patients. To Charcot, his book demonstrated that 'hysteria is in no way, as some claim, a sickness typical of our century and that in the archives of the past there is also proof it attacks the male as well as the female'.[42] Freud's longstanding interest in witchcraft may have been generated by Charcot's investigations. *The Deformed* is a gruesome catalogue: lepers, the blind, the crippled and sufferers of syphilis are illustrated by examples culled from Egyptian art in the Louvre, plus Velasquez, Tiepolo and Leonardo da Vinci (one of Freud's favourite artists).

What was Freud's impression of Charcot's office at the Salpêtrière? The entire room and all its furnishings were painted black. A single window shed light and the walls were decorated with engravings of works by Raphael and Rubens. Such Gothic gloom must have inspired some anxiety in his patients and curiosity in his colleagues, but Charcot was a master of effects.

Freud was eager to have a closer relationship with his mentor. He effected this by asking Charcot's permission to translate the third volume of his Tuesday lectures into German. 'For the past two months,' Freud wrote to Charcot, 'I have been fascinated by your eloquence.'[43] Charcot granted the request with good grace, and soon after, Freud was invited to Charcot's home, first to discuss the translation and then to attend a soirée.

That evening Freud dressed in his best. 'My appearance was immaculate,' he told Martha. He bought a 'beautiful' black tie, a new shirt and white gloves. 'I had my hair set and my rather wild

beard trimmed in the French style . . . As a result I looked very
fine and made a favourable impression on myself.' He completed
his toilette with a dose of cocaine. 'I had reasons to fear making a
blunder.' Freud regarded cocaine as a miracle drug and he had
been experimenting with its use in treating heart disease, fatigue,
digestive upsets, anaemia and asthma. He often used cocaine to
deal with his recurrent migraines and to calm his nerves, and he
enthusiastically recommended it to Martha, as well as to friends
and colleagues. '[A] small dose lifted me to the heights in a
wonderful fashion.'[44]

Freud had every reason to be anxious about an evening at
Charcot's. Charcot was a social lion and his Tuesday evening recep-
tions, held during winter and spring, were attended by the cream
of high society, including top-ranking doctors, politicians, the best
known painters and sculptors of the day, writers, art collectors,
police chiefs, even cardinals. The guest list could include an
emperor of Brazil, the son of the bey of Tunisia and the grand
dukes of Russia, together with many of Charcot's students. The
gatherings took place at his palatial residence at 217 Boulevard
Saint-Germain with its coffered ceilings, fabulous tapestries,
sculpted wood furniture, gilded chandeliers and stained-glass
windows.

In breathless detail, Freud described Charcot's study to Martha.

It is as big as the whole of our future apartment, a room worthy
of the magic castle in which he lives. It is divided in two, of
which the bigger section is dedicated to science, the other to
comfort. Two projections from the wall separate the two
sections. As one enters one looks through a triple window to
the garden; the ordinary panes are separated by pieces of

stained glass. Along the side walls of the larger section stands
his enormous library on two levels, each with steps to reach
the one above. On the left of the door is an immensely long
table covered with periodicals and odd books; in front of the
window are smaller tables with portfolios on them. On the
right of the door is a smaller stained-glass window, and in front
of it stands Charcot's writing table, quite flat and covered with
manuscripts and books; his armchair and several other chairs.
The other section has a fireplace, a table, and cases containing
Indian and Chinese antiques. The walls are covered with
Gobelins [tapestries] and pictures; the walls themselves are
painted terracotta. The little I saw of the other rooms on
Sunday contained the same wealth of pictures, Gobelins,
carpets and curios – in short, a museum.[45]

Charcot's study had been built in 1880 and occupied a new wing
at the front of the house. It was dark, the stained-glass windows
giving a rather mystical appearance and the lighting effects resembling a church. At the end of the room, Charcot sat behind his
large desk and received his patients. He had an illustrious clientele of private patients who travelled across Europe to be treated
by him. Even Charcot's bookcases had been designed in the grand
manner, copied from Michelangelo's Laurentian library for the
Medicis in Florence.

Charcot's taste was not unusual for the time. Interior decorators and furniture makers favoured dark woods such as ebony and
rosewood and Viollet-le-Duc had created an enthusiasm for
medieval stained-glass windows. Since the sixteenth century,
Gobelins, the state-run tapestry works in Paris, had been producing magnificent works that were eagerly collected. Freud was

overwhelmed by Charcot's house. Most visitors were. But he seems the only one to have noted the Indian and Chinese antiques.

Although collecting Asian art was not unusual in Paris, the taste for Chinese and Indian art was less common. In 1885, Edmond de Goncourt's literary salon, frequented by Zola, was held every Sunday in rooms that 'looked more like an exhibition space for the Orientalia he collected than an agreeable environment for social discourse'. Guests remembered it as the writer's 'private museum'.[46] When Japan opened its doors to the West, a craze began for all things Japanese which, in 1876, critic Philippe Burty dubbed *japonisme*. Samuel Bing, the Parisian dealer and orientalist, had helped establish the fashion. The Impressionists were influenced, too. Not only did they quote the decorative qualities of Japanese screens and prints in their paintings but they incorporated several of Japanese art's formal imperatives – sinuous black lines to gird form, negative space and flat areas of colour – bringing Japanese art within the vocabulary of modernism.

In the eighteenth century, the enthusiasm for Chinese objects had swept Europe, affecting nearly every decorative art – interiors, furniture, pottery, tapestries and clothes – creating the vogue for chinoiserie. Subsequently, the export of Chinese porcelain to Europe, and its popularity, had declined. But its consummate elegance must have appealed to Charcot. The long centuries of experience Chinese potters had in the use of clay, the understanding of shape and the techniques of production and decoration initially gave them an advantage over their European counterparts.

There is no record of exactly what Freud saw at Charcot's. Like the works Freud would collect, the antiques, displayed in glass cases, were not large. Charcot was interested in ceramics and porcelain and there was a profusion of painted crockery and enamels in his home. He also had his own studio where he worked with his wife and daughter. Charcot's Chinese antiques probably included examples of fine porcelain, as well as lacquer and jade. Freud followed his example, collecting Chinese and Japanese art and acquiring many pieces of jade: he was particularly fond of precious stones. Charcot's Indian antiques could have included bronze statues of popular Hindu deities such as Siva and Ganesha, statues of the Buddha and miniatures from the Moghul period, all readily available in Paris at the time.

As he waited to meet Charcot's guests, Freud cooled his heels, 'admiring the wonderful salons'. Freud had been invited to arrive after dinner: he received the honour of attending a meal the following month. That first evening, guests included writer Léon Daudet, 'an unattractive youth', in Freud's opinion. Freud was an admirer of Léon's father, Alphonse, referring to the latter's day-dreaming protagonist Monsieur Joyeuse in *The Interpretation of Dreams*. A number of distinguished doctors whose acquaintance Freud was keen to make were also present, as was an Italian artist, Emile Toffano.

After the introductions, Freud 'drank beer, smoked like a chimney and felt very much at ease without a mishap occurring' – for which he praised cocaine. He also paid court to Charcot's wife and daughter. The daughter, Freud told Martha, was 'small, rather buxom . . . very natural and amiable' with an 'almost ridiculous resemblance to her father'. It made Freud ponder that 'if I were not in love already and were something of an adventurer, it would be a strong temptation to court her, for nothing is more dangerous than a young girl bearing the features of a man whom one admires'.[47] The fantasy of seducing Charcot's daughter symbolises Freud's yearning for intimacy with his mentor. But it was an ungallant sentiment to convey to Martha in Wandsbek, who was probably anxious about the spell Paris might cast on her fiancé. Freud had already been quizzed by John Philipp, Martha's cousin, whether he had a mistress in Paris. He replied in the negative.

Léon Daudet described Charcot's hospitality as 'sumptuous . . . he wanted everything to be perfect: the food, the wine, the conversation, the gowns of the ladies, the service . . . One could write a captivating story just by recording the conversations that were held at the table and in the study.'[48] Dining at Charcot's the following month, Freud was not as impressed by his host's table, commenting 'We were not given very much to eat, but each dish was exquisite and accompanied by different wines'. By then, Freud had relaxed and did not need cocaine to boost his confidence. 'I enjoyed myself very much and talked a lot more with Charcot himself.' The following day, Freud 'couldn't help thinking what an ass I am to be leaving Paris now that spring is coming. Notre-Dame looking so beautiful in the sunlight, and I have only to say one word to Charcot and I can do whatever I like with the patients. But I feel neither courageous nor reckless enough to stay any longer.'[49]

Charcot provided a decisive influence on Freud's career, inspiring him to follow a new path: the study of neurosis. Before Freud went to Paris, he admitted 'About the neuroses I understood nothing'.[50] Paris marked the end of Freud's life in the laboratory. Charcot's insistence on close visual examination of cases, of trusting his eyes to lead him to revelation and diagnosis, was excellent training for an art collector as well as a psychiatrist. Charcot had taught Freud to use the same skills, to rely on his intution, his hunches.

Charcot had also created a distinctive home and work environment, one that displayed to full advantage his art collections, as well as his impressive library. It was an environment that acted as a stage for his personality. No wonder Charcot did not enjoy the light and pleasure-saturated canvases of the Impressionists. His taste, and Freud followed suit, was for a crowded, dimly lit interior, systematically arranged with beautiful and precious objects – an atmosphere that suggested not the pace of modernity but a sense of eternity evoked by the contemplation of the past.

Second Empire taste, like that of Victorian England, was ornate, ostentatious and eclectic, and the bourgeoisie, like Charcot, used *horror vacui* to great effect to display their wealth, revealing the home as a cornucopia of possessions. There was an enormous demand for luxury articles, a delight in patterns and fabrics, rugs and tapestries, in the glittering surfaces of glass, china and brass. It was not only a blatant show of materialism: sentimental objects, mementos and treasures were also on show. The exotic and the local, the precious and the manufactured, were combined in a visual panoply.

Freud would not have been unfamiliar with examples of such aspirational middle-class taste. His own home in the Leopoldstadt may have emulated it. But, until he visited Charcot's, he had not seen it orchestrated to such effect. Charcot created a house-museum, a respository of cultures, a layering of media, styles, periods, textures and colours that amounted to a complex and idiosyncratic self-portrait. 'Here, indeed,' comments Jean Baudrillard, 'lies the whole miracle of collecting. For it is invariably *oneself* that one collects.'[51] Entering Charcot's study was to be privy to a marvellous inner world, a spectacle as astonishing as his Tuesday lectures.

In Paris, Freud also visited the Cluny Museum, off Boulevard St Michel. Built on the site of Roman thermal baths, the fifteenth-century monastery was bought by Alexandre du Sommerard in 1833. He filled it to the brim with his vast collection of medieval artefacts: tapestries, including *The Lady and the Unicorn* series, the crowns of Visigoth kings, armour, tools, jewellery, stained glass, costumes and everyday utensils. After Sommerard's death in 1842, his house and collection were bought by the state and opened as a museum. Sommerard had created a home that literally turned into a museum, one that may have influenced Charcot, who lived nearby and had a taste for the medieval.

Charcot was the renaissance man Freud desired to be, 'like Goethe, Montaigne . . . men who radiate an interest in everything', with a 'gift for observation and ellipsis' and a loathing of 'banalities and the commonplace'.[52] He was a wealthy, respected and influential doctor who pioneered revolutionary methods of treatment, a commanding personality who could attract the best and brightest minds to his circle, a married man at the centre of a harmonious and stable family life, and a collector of inimitable taste and style. When Freud came to start his collection a decade later, Charcot offered a potent model.

Leaving Paris for Berlin in February 1886 to complete the research programme set out in his grant, Freud was dispirited. There was 'no adventure, no thrill, no éclat, as we used to have in Paris. Just quiet work.'[53] Freud was translating Charcot's lectures, which perhaps added to his melancholy.

Art cheered Freud and he roused himself to visit Berlin's Altes Museum, then known as the Royal Museum. Karl Friedrich Schinkel's design for Europe's first purpose-built, public art museum, constructed to display the royal collections, had been completed in 1830. Freud's brief look at the antique fragments filled him with 'deep regret at not being able to understand more about them and with nostalgic memories of the Louvre, which is so much more magnificent and substantial'. He was impressed by the museum's major work, the enormous Pergamon Altar with its frieze dedicated to Zeus, depicting a battle between the gods and the giants, created for King Eumenes II around 180 B.C. to celebrate Greek military victories. It is over 120 metres long and two metres tall. The frieze, with its writhing bodies and fluttering drapery, was the Hellenistic style par excellence and Freud rightly selected it as the museum's best item, appreciating its full-bodied depiction of tension and drama.

But he missed Paris. '"How different it was in France!" I sighed like Maria Stuart among the neuropathologists.' Nor did he long to return home. 'Vienna weighs upon me,' he complained. 'If I had had to travel from Paris to Vienna, I think I would have died en route.' Freud believed he owed Paris – and Charcot – a great deal. 'I feel I have experienced something precious that cannot be taken away from me. I feel increasingly self-confident, more urbane, more adroit in dealing with colleagues.' Like Balzac's Lucien de Rubempré, he was a changed man. It also gave him a rosier view of the future. 'A new era is beginning,' he told Martha. 'A good one, I hope.'[54]

4

At Home

The whole Ring Boulevard had a magic effect upon me, as if it were a scene from
The Thousand-and-One-Nights.

ADOLF HITLER[1]

*I am not angered to learn that the greatest psychologist of this age lives in a
commonplace house in an out-of-the-way quarter of Vienna.*

ANDRÉ BRETON[2]

FREUD'S FIRST PROFESSIONAL ROOMS and own home indicated his
ambitions. Bolstered by Charcot's inspiration, Freud had quit the
general hospital and set up private practice as a neurologist. In
April 1886, he moved to the Ringstrasse, the most prestigious
address in Vienna. Since he was a child, Freud had watched the

slow completion of the vast boulevard, arrayed with sumptuous buildings, parks and statues, advertising Vienna's wealth, grace and pre-eminence in dazzling, theatrical style. The Ringstrasse was the desired destination for the upwardly mobile and Freud joined the club. In Paris, he had strolled the tree-lined boulevards – Charcot's home stood on one – prime locations of wealth and prestige. The Ringstrasse united new aristocracy with old, money with birth, ability with rank, the arts and scholarship with politics and administration. For the smart set, it was the 'ideal location'.[3] Freud couldn't afford it. But that didn't matter. He wanted to arrive.

Freud lived in a luxurious new apartment building, just behind the town hall. From his upstairs window at Rathausstrasse 7, he could gaze at the town hall's immense, neo-Gothic façade, festooned with arches and statues. Further down the street was the Ringstrasse itself. The entrance to Freud's building, glowing with marble and brass, was as classy as a five-star hotel. It was the best professional quarter in Vienna.[4] Freud felt nervous about his finances, as usual, complaining to a friend he had settled at his new address 'rather desperately' and his 'small fortune' was rapidly dwindling away.[5] But Freud's patients were no doubt impressed, as they were meant to be. It was a long way from the poverty and overcrowding of the Leopoldstadt – and from its intimacy and neighbourliness, its sense of a close-knit Jewish community. The windswept plazas of the Ringstrasse can be inhuman places, dwarfing the individual. No wonder Hitler admired them: his taste for spectacle and triumphalist architecture was nurtured there.

Freud's serviced suite was already elegantly furnished. He divided one room with a curtain to create his bedroom, bought a medical couch for the other room and installed his library. The family rallied round and helped him settle in, bringing lavish bouquets, home-made cakes, family photographs and accessories for his study. Martha sent an evergreen plant. A friend supplied the doctor's plaques and Dr Freud's practice was open. Freud revelled in the attention and good wishes, though in the early days appointments were spasmodic, a fact probably not helped by the bizarre decision to open on Easter Sunday. Starting his independent professional life, Freud veered between optimism and anxiety. As usual, the problems were blamed on Vienna and he had 'very little hope of being able to make my way'. Anyway, he didn't care where he lived, it could be Australia or America, as long as Martha was beside him, 'waking me up with a kiss'.[6] The couple still did not have enough money to marry.

The cost of keeping up appearances in Vienna was not only exorbitant but rigorously exact. Viennese society was built on rules that had to be obeyed visually, as well as literally, otherwise loss of face, and, worse still, loss of income and position were guaranteed. For example, Freud had to pay for a carriage to visit his patients. The fiacre, or carriage and pair of horses, advertised his place in the world. As Martin, Freud's eldest son, observed, 'an *Einspanner*, drawn by only one horse, would have been much cheaper; but no respectable doctor in those days would have visited a patient in an *Einspanner*. To use a bus or tram would show eccentricity, or even lunacy' and would 'kill the reputation of a doctor'.[7] So a fiacre it had to be. 'What I saved on suppers during the past three days had to be spent on [the carriage],' Freud complained.[8]

It was the creative principle that governed the Ringstrasse. The look of things was paramount and, though it was an attitude that infuriated Freud, it also influenced him. With its neo-Gothic town hall, Italian Renaissance-style university and neoclassical parliament, the Ringstrasse is a gigantic collection of objects, a museum of styles, a fabricated history, an arrangement of architectural forms bearing little relation to the organic growth of the city. Meant to be experienced as a total work of art, Vienna, from the perspective of the Ringstrasse, appears as an artificial display, a series of splendid curios staged for the spectator, as if a proud collector had laid out their treasures for all to see. In the dying decades of the Habsburg monarchy, Vienna took the aesthetic attitude to an extreme: appearance mattered more than meaning, symbol more than sense, style more than substance and extravagance certainly more than any budget. On the Ringstrasse, Vienna attempted to consolidate its identity and, instead, magnificently displayed its insecurity, vanity, folly and ambition.

Freud, like many Viennese, invested a great deal in the Ringstrasse, both personally and communally. He needed to live and work there to prove that he was another bright, successful young Jewish man, who was making it out of the ghetto and into the highest strata of bourgeois society – and he was paying for it, with carriages and a high rent. It was one of the reasons Freud felt harassed by Vienna: the city made him measure up to nearly impossible standards. Nor did he choose another way: for all his mutterings about emigrating, he made no plans to leave, nor did he reject Vienna's siren song of beauty and glamour. He imbibed its values. The aesthetic attitude was not foreign to him, he had been fostering it for years. As Freud's refined and expensive tastes developed, so did the Ringstrasse, growing grander all the time. Its chronology parallels Freud's life: the design was made public in 1860, the year his family moved to Vienna. In 1902, when the enormous statue of Athena was erected in front of the parliament, Freud could celebrate, too. He was emerging from years of struggle and isolation to receive the success he had longed for.

Athena was the crowning glory, the Greek goddess of wisdom, war and the arts whom the city fathers had chosen as the city's symbol and protector, borrowing her, like everything else on the Ringstrasse, from someone else's history. Freud's statuette of *Athena* (pl. 11) was his favourite piece. When it seemed he would lose his entire collection as the Nazis took over Vienna in 1938, he selected two works to be smuggled out, to represent all that his collection meant to him. One of those was *Athena*, the other a tiny *Jade Screen* (Qing Dynasty, 19th century). When *Athena* was restored to Freud in Paris, when he was en route to London, he felt beholden to her agency. He told the enterprising Princess Marie Bonaparte, who had spirited the little statue out of Vienna, that he felt 'proud and rich under the protection of Athene'.[9]

When Freud bought *Athena*, sometime after 1914, he positioned her in pride of place in the centre of the antiquities on his desk, just as she was positioned at the forefront of the Austrian parliament. Freud did not treat his artworks as sacrosanct. During the analysis of H.D., he picked up *Athena* and handed it to her. 'This is my favourite,' he said. 'She is perfect . . . only she has lost her spear.'[10] *Athena* is far from perfect. Some of Freud's major artworks, such as *Isis Suckling the Infant Horus*, made their journey from the ancient world to his apartment relatively unscathed but *Athena* seems to have had a rough ride. A Roman bronze from around the first century A.D., she has been copied from a fifth-century B.C. Greek original. Her surface is pitted and scored. Nor is she especially elegant: her eyes are expressionless pits, she tilts forward and her terrifying attribute – Medusa's head on her breastplate – is crudely drawn. She is so small, only ten centimetres high, that she can almost be overlooked among the pantheon on Freud's desk.

Athena is a masculine goddess. As the protector of Athens, the Parthenon was her temple. Despite the fact that in ancient Greece, women were treated as little better than slaves, Greek culture had no trouble in conjuring authentic images of feminine power and authority. Athena is the most compelling. She was the daughter of Zeus, his favourite child, born fully formed from his head. She was a fierce warrior who, with her enormous bronze-tipped spear, helped the Greeks fight the Trojans. When Perseus fought Medusa, the snake-haired monster, Athena assisted, advising him to use her great shield like a mirror because those who gazed into Medusa's eyes were turned to stone. On her breast, Athena wore Medusa's image, an emblem of a vanquished force she had turned to her own advantage. Like most of the gods, she had a range of characteristics: in times of peace, she was benevolent and inspiring, a patron of the arts and a wise, civilising influence.

On the Ringstrasse, where Athena was the final artwork, Vienna showed itself off in three-dimensional style, offering an intense education in sculpture, architecture and decoration. When Freud explained how art exercised 'a powerful effect' on him, it was works of 'literature and sculpture, less often of painting' that gripped him and he would spend a long time trying to apprehend them 'in my own way'. Subject matter, rather than formal and technical qualities, was the strong attraction.[11] The Ringstrasse's six-kilometre length was Freud's constitutional, giving him ample time to study it on a daily basis. Freud had walked the Ring for years, first in the company of Jacob and then, as his children grew, he took them along, amusing them with jokes and fairytales he invented. One was about the devil's grandmother. Once upon a time, when she was flying over Vienna, she dropped her tea set and it fell on the rooftops, which explained the city's oddly styled chimney pots. Despite the fairytales, these were not leisurely promenades as Freud stormed around the Ringstrasse with the small detachment of his offspring following in his tracks though at 'a much slower pace and with less determination': he marched at such terrific speed that he reminded his son Martin of a soldier.[12]

Though impressive, the Ringstrasse can be an overwhelming experience, a display that can appear kitsch, phoney and slightly ridiculous. Was that why Freud declared Vienna was 'almost physically repulsive'?[13] When he came to collect art, he valued authenticity and strived to rid himself of fakes and forgeries. But *Athena* was a copy of an earlier original. The Romans copied the masterpieces of Greek art and, even in the first century A.D, Greek antiquities were prized. The Romans also accepted Greek deities as their own: in Roman mythology, Athena became Minerva. What Freud learned on the Ringstrasse was that, in terms of embellishment and decoration, enough was never enough. He could also see how the past could be regained, re-arranged and re-presented in a contemporary manner. It would be his project in psychoanalysis, to bring a patient's traumatic childhood memories into the conscious realm of the present and thereby effect a cure.

Athena was one of the many illustrious personages decorating the Ringstrasse. A sculpture of Empress Maria Theresa, between the art and natural history museums, stares across at Heldenplatz, or Heroes' Plaza, where huge monuments to Archduke Charles and Prince Eugene of Savoy face each other. It was in Heldenplatz in 1938 that the Viennese gathered in their cheering thousands to welcome Hitler, the new conquering hero. Statues of Mozart and Goethe are positioned elsewhere on the Ringstrasse, and every building is dripping with mythological or historical statues. It meant that Freud was used to seeing sculptures in relation to one another, telling stories, illustrating the past with a series of symbols, competing for attention by virtue of style, beauty and scale. In Vienna, art wrote history.

Unlike Freud's *Athena*, the goddess of the Ringstrasse was complete. Not only does she have her spear but she is also adorned with a glittering helmet and breastplate, as well as holding a winged victory. The Greek-style parliament building behind her, designed by Danish architect Theophil Hansen, is the Ringstrasse's central point where the viewer contemplates a past Austria had only recently enjoyed: liberal parliamentary democracy. Vienna had to borrow Athena because, as Carl Schorske observes, myth had to step in where history failed to serve.[14]

Austria was a monarchy, and democracy a latter-day addition. The Habsburgs, who had established Vienna as the capital of their empire in 1282, were one of Europe's most enduring royal houses. They had never been vanquished or deposed, like English or French monarchies: they held on by diplomacy rather than force, by remaining flexible and attentive to public opinion, and adding the pomp and circumstance expected of royalty. There was no empire in a deep, cohesive, national sense. There was no common, unifying language either: Austrians spoke German and the colonies, such as Moravia, fought to retain sovereignty by speaking their local tongue. It was one of the reasons the Czechs mistrusted the Jews: they spoke German, the language of the rulers. At the height of its reign, the Habsburg empire extended to Hungary, Bohemia, Moravia, Croatia and parts of Poland, Romania,

Bulgaria, Italy, the Netherlands and Spain. It was a collection of real estate the Habsburgs cannily acquired and managed. 'For seven hundred years the Habsburg line appears to have been intent on only one thing, the accumulation of property, the aggrandisement of its private estates.'[15] As A. J. P. Taylor caustically remarks, the Habsburgs were landlords, not rulers.[16]

But the Habsburgs knew how to conduct themselves in the grand manner, setting the tone for the whole town. For the annual Corpus Christi Day procession, which began at St Stephen's cathedral, the emperor, in a white tunic and a green feathered hat, rode in a carriage drawn by six horses, followed by archdukes in glass and gold-embellished wagons drawn by Spanish-bred white horses. The archbishop carried the consecrated host in a monstrance beneath a gold-embroidered canopy called 'Heaven' by the Viennese. Behind him, organised strictly according to social rank, came the aristocrats, the mayor and city councillors, clergy, guilds and professional groups. Thousands of Viennese filled the grandstands and lined the streets, kneeling when the host passed them and cheering the emperor. Aristocrats were celebrities and the Freud children were thrilled by their appearances. In Vienna, everything was made an occasion for celebration, Stefan Zweig recalled. Even funerals found enthusiastic audiences.[17]

When Franz Josef ascended the throne in 1848, he was eighteen. It was the year revolution swept Europe, galvanising many countries and awakening national consciousness. Franz Josef listened to the burghers of Vienna who had been clamouring for urban change, and he approved and encouraged the plans for the Ringstrasse. The subsequent frenzy of construction provided employment for architects, tradesmen, decorators and other craftspeople who flooded into the city. The Habsburgs also starred on the Ringstrasse where massive monuments to various family members, as well as a new wing for the Hofburg, their palace in the centre of town, gave them an even more conspicuous role in Viennese life. Hitler was 'disgusted by the grovelling way in which the Vienna Press played lackey to the Court. Scarcely a move took place at the Hofburg which was not presented in glorified colours to the readers.'[18] But the Ringstrasse was not only a glittering advertisement for the monarchy: it was designed as an artery for the deployment of soldiers and weapons. The unrest of 1848 had taught the nobility another lesson: when the masses rise, they must be routed swiftly.

If the Ringstrasse's development parallels Freud's early years, it also chronicles Franz Josef's reign. As it grew, so the empire crumbled and by the time Austria-Hungary was defeated in the First World War, the monarchy was lame and dispirited, ossified by increasingly elaborate and meaningless ritual. But the Ringstrasse was a magnificent swansong. Like the empire itself, there was no common language: each building was created in a different style that aped the glories of the past, whether Greek, Italian or Gothic. Though Athena was chosen for the parliament, she did not represent an Austrian tradition and foreshadowed not triumphant continuity but the Habsburgs' demise. She may be perfect but, towering above the street on her pedestal, she seems cold, distant and lifeless, a hollow symbol. Freud's *Athena* is a more humble goddess. She is small, plain and damaged. Without her spear, she is tamed, too. She claims the quiet centre on Freud's desk, indicating that wisdom does not need to be bold or beautiful to command attention and respect.

Freud was concerned with style and appearance, down to the tiniest and most exquisite detail. A quietly vain man, he visited his barber every morning to have his beard trimmed (foppish even by Viennese standards) and aspired to wear the best suits money could buy, even if it did mean his tailor got paid much later. Freud's new apartment, too, was a statement about comfort and position.

The apartment houses (known as *Wohnpalast*, which roughly translates as 'apartment palace') were as much part of the Ringstrasse as the opera house or the parliament, domestic equivalents of public grandeur. Freud rented until he moved to London in 1938, shortly before his death. His art collection was his most valuable asset. But living well was crucial. His six-storey Italian neo-Renaissance style apartment building was in 'the classic zone of the *Grossburgertum*, the Rathaus Quarter. Here dwelt the strongest social pillars of ascendant liberalism', and statistics confirm that 'financial and business leaders, *rentiers*, university professors, and the largest number of high officials of government and business to be found in any quarter lived here'.[19] A good client base, no doubt, and Freud was treating the wives of doctors and professors, as well as two police officials, with hypnotism learned from Charcot. Another patient was 'the beautiful and interesting' wife of an American doctor. This woman's effect was disturbing. 'It seemed weird to me,' Freud told Martha, 'that on both occasions she was here your photograph, which has otherwise never budged, fell off the writing table.' Superstitious Freud assured Martha that 'such hints' were not needed.[20]

Below the apartments on the *Wohnpalast*'s ground floors were discreetly designed shops. The higher up the flat was, the less prestigious, the cheaper the rent and the less external decoration it earned. The lower storeys of Freud's building are heavily rusticated and ornamented with masks of demonic-looking, laughing, long-haired men – whose origin may be Pan, the god of the forest – alternating with those of pretty, smiling girls. Above that are balconies, both real and *faux*. Marble columns grace the entrance. With such buildings, the Rathaus Quarter achieved the sense of opulent dignity to which the elite aspired. It was a fitting environmental setting for such public edifices, the jewels in liberal Vienna's Ringstrasse.[21]

Home alone, Freud didn't bother about cooking, instead regularly eating out at restaurants and cafés. Café Landtmann is on the Ringstrasse, just a short walk from his apartment. His chosen seat, at the rear of the restaurant's main room, offered him excellent views of the boulevard, theatre and town hall. After meetings of the Vienna Psychoanalytic Sociey, Freud took the group to the Landtmann. It remains one of Vienna's most splendid cafés.

Everyone in Vienna had their café. Some people virtually lived in them. They sipped coffee while reading the freely supplied newspapers, art and literary journals from all over Europe, conducted business and love affairs, even had their mail delivered. The Viennese café, Stefan Zweig recalled, 'is a particular institution which is not comparable to any other in the world . . . it is a sort of democratic club to which admission costs the price of a cup of coffee'. They were largely male preserves. Once the patrons had received their coffee – in Freud's case *eine kleine Braunen* (an espresso or a short black) – the waiters left them alone. There was no pressure to order more, or to leave. Indeed, to down a coffee and demand the bill was akin to bad manners. In the warm, dreamlike environment of the café, time drifts by. When Zweig was a lad, he knew practically nothing of Vienna's surrounding countryside because summertime meant 'the city was empty, we got more papers and magazines in the cafés, and we got them more quickly'.[22]

Landtmann was not a bohemian haunt like the famous Café Griensteidl, where the literary set including Arthur Schnitzler and Karl Kraus met, or Café Central, sometimes frequented by Freud but more often by Trotsky before the First World War. Trotsky sat beneath the arched ceiling of Café Central for hours, drinking coffee, playing chess and plotting the revolution. Freud, in the splendid environment of Café Landtmann, was restless. He had already alarmed the Ringstrasse strollers with his frantic gait: it was deemed uncouth to rush in Vienna. Landtmann is larger and more opulent than the cosy Café Central, more bourgeois, too. Its vestibule has carved wooden columns, and neoclassical friezes decorate the walls, making it rather like an art gallery. Its ambience is stylish, low-key and comfortable. From Freud's discreet position, where he could see but not be seen, he observed the class he treated: the haut bourgeois, the new Vienna, represented by the Ring-strasse. It was another reminder that he had arrived or, at least, that he was trying to. But Vienna's frivolous attitude towards time, epitomised by the café with its conviviality and its smiling surface of manners, did not suit Freud. Up-and-coming young Viennese men used the cafés to further their careers. Charismatic personal-ities, such as Schnitzler and Kraus, became the admired centres of cultural groups. When Freud created his circle, however, it would be in the realm he designed: at home.

Bachelor life did not agree with Freud. The shock of leaving the warm nest of the Leopoldstadt, the lonely evenings at Rathausstrasse 7 and the expensive, solo meals in cafés took their toll. Within months, he was arguing strenuously to set the wedding date. He had to overcome the objections of Emmeline,

Martha's strong-willed mother, who regarded the plan as reckless because of the couple's lack of money. The income from Freud's practice remained unstable. But he was tired of waiting and forged ahead, with Martha's approval, fixing the date for September 13.

First, Freud needed to find a new, larger apartment to begin married life. Again he chose the Ringstrasse. Finding accommodation proved a difficult enterprise: because of his schedule, he could only search in the evenings, there were the usual dilemmas about money and, with Martha in Wandsbek, discussions had to be conducted by letter. Freud soon set his heart on one of the newest apartment palaces, close to the new University of Vienna and its school of medicine, where he lectured. It had been designed by Friedrich Schmidt, the architect for the town hall Freud had been able to admire from his Rathausstrasse window. For Freud's apartment house, Schmidt created another neo-Gothic fantasy, complete with a giant stained-glass rose window, rather like Notre-Dame's. Freud was thrilled, describing his 'large apartment' as being in 'the most beautiful house in Vienna'.[23] A police headquarters now stands on the site.

The building had a macabre history. It was on the site of a theatre that had burned down in 1881, taking the lives of six hundred of the audience. Franz Josef had ordered a building erected there, presumably to cast aside the gloom and bad luck associated with it: revenue earned went to the families of the dead. But the public were hesitant about moving in and Freud found he could easily secure an apartment. Officially, it was known as Kaiserliches Stiftunghaus (literally, Imperial Donation House) but more popularly as Sühnhaus, the House of Atonement. At Maria Theresienstrasse 5 (Freud's entrance was in the block behind the Ringstrasse), it was near the new Stock Exchange and not far from the Votivkirche. In true Viennese style, the Stock Exchange is as elaborate as an Italian palazzo, and the Votivkirche, commissioned by Franz Josef in gratitude for his lucky escape from a knife-wielding assassin, rises in neo-Gothic splendour. Today the park outside the Votivkirche is dedicated to Freud. It is ironic that Freud, who loathed Catholicism, should have his memorial there.

Unlike other Viennese, Freud and Martha were not nervous about the Sühnhaus. Money was the issue. Martha had misgivings about the high rent and on that score Freud managed to allay her fears. Because she was in Wandsbek, he was in charge of furnishing the apartment. She firmly rejected his suggestion to buy furniture on hire purchase, perceiving that it was a wasteful idea, creating long-term debt. Trying to organise everything, and borrow more money to finance the wedding, Freud was growing anxious and impatient. As soon as he was married, he promised, he would 'willingly let myself be once more harassed and economise, and if we sometimes have to rack our brains to know where this or that is coming from, what will it matter?'[24] Not only were his words designed to quell Martha's concerns, they reveal Freud's fundamental attitude towards the bothersome business of money and desire. Essentially, Eros came first.

Since their engagement four years earlier, Freud had been planning the dream home with its tables and chairs, beds and mirrors, 'a clock to remind the happy couple of the passage of time, an armchair for an hour's pleasant daydreaming . . . pictures on the walls, plates and dishes . . . books and the sewing table and the cosy lamp'.[25]

Shopping in Vienna was a time-consuming activity. After the crash of 1873, the economy remained shaky and, to protect local shopkeepers, the city council prohibited department stores, like the glorious Bon Marché and Printemps that Freud could have sampled in Paris. The law required most shops to sell a narrow speciality, so one shop sold gloves, the next sheet music, and so on. Freud bustled from shop to shop, exactly the sort of expedition he usually relished, but now under pressure of time. His good taste meant he was attracted to quality materials and good design. A 'splendid sofa' made him 'lose all my philosophy . . . I was in ecstasy'.[26] Vienna offered a plenitude of excellent handcrafted objects and fine furniture to choose from.

Freud wrote to Martha detailing the purchases and asking her advice. He told her he missed her help deciding the delicate problems of colour schemes and curtains. He enlisted his sister Rosa's aid. Rosa was his favourite sister, the beautiful one, in Freud's opinion, and the most artistic. Expert with needle and thread, Rosa had kept herself 'terribly busy' making clothes for Freud while he was in Paris, sewing shirts and a winter coat.[27] But Martha was keen to be involved and there was so much talk of furniture that Freud commented, 'I have the impression that the dearest woman in the world is mortal on one point and that regards a husband as a supplement – a necessary one, it is true – to a beautiful home.'[28]

Freud was, literally and figuratively, the designer of their new life, their 'little home' of 'quiet contentment'. He was clear about their roles, about the space each would occupy and govern. 'I will let you rule the house as much as you wish,' he told Martha, 'and you will reward me with your sweet love and by rising above all those weaknesses for which women are so often despised.'[29] Once Freud had created the domestic environment, he intended to retreat to his study to create another world. Freud's Athenas, the independent intellectuals he cultivated, such as Princess Marie

Bonaparte, belonged to the other realm of study and work. Martha, punctual, calm and organised, was the angel of the house, a role she fulfilled superbly. Each day at the stroke of one, lunch was served: as the door opened for the maid to enter with the soup, Freud emerged from his study. His favourite meal was *Rindfleisch* (boiled beef) and Martha made sure it was cooked to perfection and served with different sauces several times a week. Freud adored globe artichokes, loathed chicken and never ate cauliflower. Dessert, often *Apfelstrudel*, was 'always a work of supreme culinary art'.[30]

But, once settled in the Sühnhaus, Freud was not convinced he lived up to its grandeur, telling a friend, 'My little wife, helped by her dowry and wedding presents, has created a charming home which, however, looks too modest for the noble and splendid rooms of Master Schmidt.'[31]

In 1938, Edmund Engelman photographed the Freud home at Berggasse 19, the only thorough record of the Freuds' domestic style. When Martha escorted Engelman through the living quarters, he observed 'typical massive, upper middle-class furniture', together with mementos, photographs of children and decorative crystal and china.[32] The apartment was a hotchpotch of furniture, patterned wallpaper and heavy drapes. The rooms reminded Hanns Sachs of middle-class homes in the 1880s, like his own. 'There was nothing modern or strikingly personal about them.'[33]

Progressive changes in interior design, advertised by the sinuous swirls of Art Nouveau and the Modern Movement's cool minimalism, were ignored. The Freuds did collect some Biedermeier furniture, including the table in the middle of their sitting room, but its intricate marquetry and honey-coloured wood were disguised by a thick lace cloth. Popular in Vienna in the early nineteenth century, the Biedermeier style with its light, French, neoclassical curves and colours, underwent a revival around the turn of the century, when the Freuds may have bought their table. Other French touches are provided by a Louis XV-style gilded tapestry chair and an empire table. The dining room was dominated by a large table and leather-backed, brass-studded chairs made of dark wood. The overall effect is comfortable, heavy and plain.

Freud kept the same furniture all his life, creating a domestic environment of worthy objects that promised stability and continuity, embodied good bourgeois values and represented his expectations of Martha and family life. His study, crowded with antiquities, is one kind of museum; his living quarters are another. Whereas the latter suggest absence — Freud's retreat from the domestic realm into the highly personalised zone of his study — the rooms were also a memorial to the era of his marriage: passionate hopes symbolised by sturdy, unglamorous, functional and durable objects.

After his wedding, Freud drew a curtain across his private life. Whether the sex, after so much ardent waiting, was good or disappointing is unknown. The following year Martha gave birth to Mathilde, the first of six children born between 1887 and 1895. Mathilde was followed by Martin, Oliver, Ernst, Sophie and Anna. By the time of Anna's birth, Martha was exhausted. A family photograph from around 1898 (pl. 37) shows her surrounded by five of the children, together with her sister Minna, and Freud. In her late thirties, Martha is no longer Freud's slender princess. Her features are puffy and sag with age. As she holds on to Sophie and Anna in an attempt to stop them wriggling – the early camera's long exposure time meant any movement resulted in a blur – her expression is tired and patient. While the others stare into the camera, engaging the viewer, Martha's eyes are averted and her mouth set, giving her an appearance of resignation and withdrawal. Behind her, Freud looks cheerful, stocky and robust, the commanding presence in the family group.

Freud's contraception of choice was abstinence, a state all too familiar from his long engagement. Given the rapid arrival of their children, it would not seem a particularly successful strategy. Freud developed theories about the psychological dangers of condoms and coitus interruptus, the main types of contraception then practised. In 1894, between the births of Sophie and Anna, Freud declared it struck him with 'certainty' that 'coitus interruptus practiced on a woman leads to anxiety neurosis'; further, 'the use of a condom is evidence of weak potency; being something analogous to masturbation' and could also cause depression.[34] Freud's theories arose from observing his patients' problems, but they suggest such forms of contraception made sex less satisfying for him. He was concerned for Martha. 'Since child followed child,' there had been 'little room for change and relaxation in her life'.[35]

A proud father, Freud was delighted at Mathilde's birth and loved his new daughter 'very much'. He told his mother-in-law that he 'never ceased' congratulating himself on having proposed to Martha and 'treasured the priceless possession' he had acquired.[36] Franz Josef was also pleased with the good omen of the Sühnhaus' first birth. He sent a courtier to hand-deliver a letter of congratulation and, as Freud's sister Anna recalled, the

Freuds were presented with a handsome vase from the Imperial Porcelain Factory.[37]

By 1891, when Martin was born, the four-room apartment at the Sühnhaus, which also catered for Freud's practice, was filled to bursting. One afternoon, after finishing his rounds, Freud dismissed his carriage and began to walk through the city, apparently at random. Unexpectedly, he found himself outside a building where an apartment was to let. He 'suddenly experienced a great attraction' towards the place, inspected the apartment and signed the lease on the spot.[38] When he took Martha there that evening, she was appalled: the neighbourhood, where no reputable physician had his rooms, was less than salubrious, plus the stair-well was dark, steep and uncarpeted, and the flat itself quite small. But she did not desist: she recognised her husband had set his heart on the place. Freud had snapped it up with a collector's verve.

Others shared Martha's initial disappointment with Berggasse 19 (pl. 38). André Breton expressed his disdain for Freud's 'commonplace' abode while Bruno Bettelheim was equally dismayed by the 'dull and undistinguished street in a nondescript part of the ninth district'. As a young man in the 1920s, Bettelheim used to walk the 'hilly unattractive street . . . only because Freud lived there'. Looking up at Freud's flat, he wondered why 'the great man chose to live there, when Vienna had so many other streets that were more attractive in themselves, had more beautiful buildings, or at least offered charming or historically interesting vistas'.[39]

In fact, Freud had done his research, choosing *the* neighbour-hood for young Jewish professionals. Between 1870 and 1910, the ninth district, or Alsergrund, emerged as Vienna's most populous new Jewish community. Here lived Jewish doctors, lawyers, writers and other ambitious professionals, the group who were helping to transform Vienna's cultural life. 'Jews in Vienna did not simply leave their homey immigrant enclave in the Leopoldstadt to move randomly to middle-class areas.'[40] They went to the Alsergrund. Berggasse was its heartland, and almost all the local middle-class Jews lived in the streets surrounding it. There they clustered more compactly than they did in either the Leopoldstadt or the inner city. After Freud settled in, he suggested his parents move in around the corner. Then his sister Rosa took the flat next door. Jewish organisations rented offices in Berggasse: the Union of Austrian Jews and the Society for Jewish Assistance were at number 4, and the Jewish Humanitarian Society at 33. Later, Freud established a clinic and a publishing press a few doors down at number 7. Nearby in Müllnergasse was a synagogue.

Berggasse was not as glamorous as the Ringstrasse but, with his rapidly growing family, Freud had to concede he could no longer afford life on the grand boulevard. Though still within a short walk of Café Landtmann and the university, Freud opted for community, the one he had left behind in the Leopoldstadt and that he had not found in the apartment palaces. The Ringstrasse lacked soul. Freud's retreat from it, which seems a kind of failure of enterprise and resilience, can also be read as a corrective, a necessary disillusionment about the glittering prizes Vienna offered. His observation, just after moving into the Sühnhaus, that despite his home's charm it was 'too modest for the noble and splendid rooms' of Schmidt's architecture, indicates his reservations.

Freud was a little too serious for the Ringstrasse: his domestic routines were simple and his home life a private affair. There were no lavish dinner parties, *à la* Charcot, at Berggasse 19. When Freud entertained, his guests were family members and close friends, all

Jewish. He joked about his wild Saturday evenings spent playing taroc, his favourite card game. Quitting the Ringstrasse, Freud defined himself against Vienna's charming surface. His personality, which he claimed was easily misunderstood because its 'surface of timidity' hid 'a bold oppositionist' and 'an extremely daring and fearless human being', and its contradictions and sensitivities were perhaps better served in the quieter reaches of Berggasse.[41] For Freud, home was a retreat and a sense of Jewish community was vital. The move suggests the geography of psychoanalysis where the inner life offers discovery and innovation, while its outer manifestation can be a mask.

Berggasse, meaning Mountain Street, though quite flat in the section where Freud lived, starts on a rise some blocks from the Votivkirche and ends at the Danube canal. The raffish Tandelmarkt stood there, a 'disgrace' according to Martin Freud.[42] A flea market where anything from birdcages to military decorations changed hands, it was also a treasure-seeker's paradise, another reason Freud knew the area. The Tandelmarkt (market to browse or dally in) was a specifically Jewish enterprise and had existed in a variety of locations around Vienna since the fifteenth century. When the Ringstrasse development reorganised the city, a group of stallholders decided to create a permanent home: they bought a block of land between Berggasse and Turkengasse and asked architect Emil Förster to design a single-storey building for two hundred shops. It lasted until the Second World War, when it was bombed.

Designed by architect Alfred Stierlin, Berggasse 19's lower storeys are in the dignified, handsome, Italian Renaissance style, and its upper floors are decorated in classical revival. Though it is one of the most decorated buildings in the street, its appearance is heavy and sombre. The Freud family apartment was on the first floor, directly above the entrance. Inside, a shared courtyard was graced by a chestnut tree.

Bettelheim's response indicates how the Viennese valued adornment and a smart address: Berggasse was not sufficiently endowed and it raised questions about Freud's taste and status. But Freud had identified what made him feel at home: Jewish family and friends. Big, beautiful and pompous, the Ringstrasse had not lived up to its promise of wealth and prestige: Freud was still struggling to make his name and a good living. Berggasse has no splendid vistas, no monuments in sight. It shows itself for what it is. Solid and worthwhile, without glamour or pretension, Berggasse 19 proved as durable as its furniture. It was Freud's home for nearly fifty years. Today the area remains sedate and suburban: aside from the restaurants, shops close at five on Saturday and do not reopen on Sunday, when the loudest noise in the streets is the sound of children playing. Most roads are narrow and there is little traffic, making it hard to credit Vienna's bustling centre is only a stroll away.

During the early, busy years of raising a family, Freud's career slowed. He seemed uncertain of his direction and more harassed than ever by his 'unsatisfactory wretched practice'.[43] Between 1886 and 1891, he did 'little scientific work and published scarcely anything', although an ongoing project was to translate Charcot's lectures. He felt distracted from any larger purpose because he was 'occupied with establishing myself in my new profession and with assuring my own material existence as well as that of a rapidly increasing family'.[44] That also included assisting his parents and his unmarried sisters. In fact, Freud's career was faltering. Though he blamed his colleagues in Vienna's neurological community for the difficulties he experienced in attracting patients and gaining reception for his ideas, it was not the whole picture.

Freud had returned from Paris brimming with admiration for Charcot's theories and for the man himself. He made this clear when reporting on his Paris sojourn to his professors at the University of Vienna, declaring himself a follower of Charcot's *grand hypnotism*, which he was surprised had 'so little credence'. Freud's description, which reads like a justification, of Charcot's interest in the bizarre, the unexplored and the unexplained in human behaviour, sounds like a defence of the same aspects of Freud's work and personality that came under fire when he began to chart the significance of dreams and of sexuality. 'I saw no sign, however, that Charcot showed any special preference for rare and strange material,' he insisted.[45] On the contrary, Charcot submitted his theories to rigorous scientific research. Freud, always tantalised by strong and complex characters, seemed to think that by enumerating Charcot's personal qualities, he would convince his professors of the French neurologist's worth as an innovative doctor. But they were unimpressed, and Freud's lecture on male hysteria, a favourite theory of Charcot's, met with disdain.

In his rooms, Freud hung his hero's image, the lithograph of Brouillet's *Une Leçon Clinique à la Salpêtrière* that encapsulated the reservations of conservative medical men about the theatrical Parisian. But Freud's admiration for Charcot was unswerving and the image took pride of place in Freud's study for the rest of his life. When his daughter Mathilde asked what was the matter with the woman in the picture, Freud replied that her corset was too tight. At Berggasse 19, Freud positioned it so both he and his patients could see it. Perhaps it was meant to be instructive for doctor and patient alike, though goodness knows what concerns it aroused in women about their forthcoming treatment. Like so many objects in Freud's collection, it was a visual souvenir, an item packed with nostalgia, pleasure and information, which both recalled the past and explained it.

Next came the ghastly muddle of the cocaine episode. Freud had been experimenting with the drug's benefits, as well as using it to treat his own nerves and migraines. He was disappointed when two other doctors, including his friend Carl Koller ('Coca Koller', as Freud dubbed him), preceded him in publishing reports on its benefits. Undeterred, Freud continued to espouse the drug's value, especially during the withdrawal of morphine. But in 1886 when cases of cocaine intoxication and addiction began being reported internationally, there was general alarm and Freud was named as a proponent of a dangerously addictive substance. It was the moment for a decisive rebuttal, yet Freud took nearly a year, and the response was equivocal. Then his book published in 1891, *On the Conception of Aphasias: A Critical Study*, which examined the impaired ability to speak or comprehend words, attracted little regard. Freud, who sometimes needed to blame someone for his professional bungles, began to feel antagonism for Josef Breuer, his long-time supporter and co-researcher, who was unable to embrace Freud's desire for scientific adventures with a similar brio.

In these years, Freud was unaided by flashes of original insight. He stumbled. He was also assailed by resentment, close to paranoia, about the disaffection of his Viennese colleagues. The figure he cut was of an isolated, slightly eccentric and not particularly successful fellow. His self-image was not much happier. 'I consider hanging up my photograph in the waiting room with the inscription: *Enfin seul* [finally alone]', he wrote gloomily to Minna. 'Unfortunately it wouldn't find any admirers there.' One solution was to escape to the blissful countryside at nearby Reichenau because in Vienna 'things are really too stupid'.[46]

5

Renaissance Man

Every collector is a substitute for a Don Juan Tenorio, and so too is the
mountaineer, the sportsman, and such people. These are erotic equivalents.
SIGMUND FREUD[1]

It is men in their forties who seem most prone to the passion [of collecting].
JEAN BAUDRILLARD[2]

WHEN FREUD BEGAN TO collect art in 1896, the year he turned
forty, it was during the most intense and creatively fertile period
of his life. The death of his father provoked a turbulent journey
of self-analysis, while a growing friendship with Wilhelm Fliess
(pl. 39), a Berlin ear, nose and throat specialist, offered him the
muse with whom he could share the initial discoveries of psycho-

analysis. The year before, Freud had had the significant dream that led him to conclude that all dreams were wish-fulfilment, and undertaken his first visit to Florence. *The Interpretation of Dreams* was published in 1900. In Vienna important cultural events were taking place, including the opening of the Kunsthistorisches and the Jewish museums, and the birth of the Secession, the city's own controversial modern art movement. It was a personally testing time: Freud continued to feel isolated and ignored, and he was assailed by an array of health problems. 'At that time [1896],' he recalled, 'I was at the nadir of desolation, had lost all my old friends and had not acquired any new ones; no one cared about me, and the only thing that kept me going was a bit of defiance and the beginning of *The Interpretation of Dreams*.'[3]

Martha was right about the size of the apartment at Berggasse 19. It was tight for the family's needs, especially following the births of Ernst, Sophie and Anna – and after Freud had squeezed his practice into the living quarters. When the watchmaker's directly below became vacant, Freud took possession of the property, which was the largest his practice had thus far occupied. In December 1896, just two weeks after he had moved in, Freud bought his first artworks. 'I have now adorned my room with plaster casts of Florentine statues,' he announced to Fliess. The purchases were inspired by a visit to Florence in September, which Freud cherished as 'a source of extraordinary invigoration for me; I am thinking of getting rich, in order to be able to repeat these trips'.[4]

Freud had travelled to Florence with his younger brother Alexander, single at the time and chosen companion for Freud's Mediterranean journeys. There had been a few trips with the family to northern Italy and would be more in later years with his daughter Anna and sister-in-law Minna. Freud liked to travel in comfort. When the family set off on holidays, Martha made sure that she and the children travelled second class while Freud travelled alone in first. Otherwise it was all too much of 'an ordeal' for him.[5]

Alexander was Freud's choice for longer and more robust southern journeys. Of all Jacob's children, Alexander resembled him most: they shared the same broad forehead and almond-shaped eyes, as well as a gift for storytelling. The brothers provided a foil for each other. Whereas Freud told stories with a laconic air, Alexander waxed lyrical. No matter whether the incident was minor or significant, Alexander bestowed upon it 'the same glowing and elastic treatment . . . All the people came alive.'[6] His stories enthralled Freud's children. But unlike Jacob, Alexander was practical and successful. He was employed by the Ministry of Freight, Transport and Tariff Affairs (making him an ideal travelling companion) and lectured at the Consular Academy.

One of the reasons Freud invited Alexander along was to provide his overworked brother with a break. Alexander was the family's other breadwinner, helping Freud carry the responsibility for their parents 'and so many women and children'.[7] He was always anxious about being swindled. He was notorious among the cab drivers of Vienna for insisting on the basic fare, which the cab drivers, used to dealing with the easy-going locals, found disconcerting. Once, when given poor-quality fruit after a meal, Alexander exclaimed that it was only fit for swine: *pro porci*. 'Not *pro porci*,' Freud replied calmly, '*pro pesci*,' and threw the rotten apples into the sea.[8] Alexander was also the family photographer, a good-natured fellow who loved music and fine food and, like his brother, was addicted to cigars.

Freud may have needed a confident sidekick: he suffered from travel anxiety for which he blamed the move from Freiberg. When the family left Freiberg in 1859, they went to Leipzig for a few months, before settling in Vienna.[9] Freud told Fliess that passing through the station of Breslau on the way to Leipzig, 'the gas flames which I saw for the first time reminded me of spirits burning in hell . . . My travel anxiety . . . is bound up with this.'[10] Freud's condition did not prevent him from travelling – it was not a phobia – but to calm his nerves, he arrived at least half an hour early at his point of departure. Though he insisted to Fliess that he had overcome his fear, Martin recalled his father's continuing 'horror' about missing trains.[11] Even hearing about train accidents set him on edge. What did the flames of hell mean to Freud? Hell is a Christian symbol, familiar to Freud from his church visits in Freiberg, a place of eternal loss, mourning and suffering where flames torture the damned. The gas flames of Breslau provided a terrifying symbol of Freud's lost Eden, an image of banishment that continued to haunt him.

The trip to Florence established a pattern Freud followed for some years. After a period spent with his family at a mountain resort, he would depart for Italy, exploring galleries, museums, ruins, gardens and, of course, shops selling antiquities. In this way, Freud satisfied two tastes: one for the splendid peaks and refreshing climate of the mountains, and the other for the sensual beauty and artistic treasures of the south. The geographic divide between north and south was also deemed cultural and temperamental. The north, especially Germany, was austere, intellectual and analytical; the south was characterised as warm, spontaneous and sensual. The former realm was conventionally 'masculine', the latter feminine. Freud needed both.

On this occasion, he left Martha and the children at Aussee, in one of Austria's most spectacular regions. Freud masterminded that part of the holiday, too. Aussee was a favourite destination for many of Vienna's middle-class Jewish families. In the late nineteenth century there were no hotels, just a few inns, and the Freuds followed the custom and rented a cottage for the summer. Freud took his summer break seriously and, as with the selection of furniture for the apartment, he was the designer, developing his skills 'like a fine art', becoming 'a kind of pioneer, ranging about the mountains until he found what he believed would be popular with the family'. The Freuds' cottage at Aussee was excellently sited: it had a magnificent view of the mountains while nearby were the pine forests that Freud's children regarded as 'our summer playgrounds' and the transparent, dark green waters of the lake.[12]

Then Freud headed for Italy, returning two weeks later, after a whirlwind tour of Tuscany that included Bologna, Ravenna and Faenza. Martin noted that 'when father's financial position gradually improved, the difference was marked during holidays: we went farther afield, travelled more comfortably and stayed at more expensive hotels'.[13] Freud also splurged on himself, booking swank hotels in Rome when finances permitted.

Freud planned his trip to Florence carefully, consulting his Baedeker, the best contemporary guidebook. Karl Baedeker began publishing tourist guides in 1829. They rapidly became the most popular and reliable tool for the middle-class traveller and exploited the huge growth in tourism spawned by the expansion of the nineteenth-century railway system. Europe was no longer an adventure playground for the leisurely 'Grand Tour', under-taken by aristocrats and others who had the time and the money to be ferried in carriages from one sublime spot to another. It was tracked by the middle classes, eager to take advantage of the speed and ease with which trains delivered them to their desired desti-nations during limited summer holidays. John Ruskin might have mourned that 'all travelling becomes dull in exact proportion to its rapidity', but it was not the view of the culture-hungry bour-geoisie, like Freud, who set off in their thousands to slake an appetite that a classical education had aroused: first-hand experience of great works of art.

After Baedeker's death in 1859, his son continued to produce the lucrative guidebook series. With their distinctive red binding and stamped gilt lettering, the little books provided comprehen-sive information on accommodation and food, as well as useful maps, transportation routes and timetables. Museums and other cultural sites were described in detail, and addresses of bookshops, reading rooms and artists' studios were supplied. Freud could even find where to buy Havana cigars. Baedeker also provided a section on 'intercourse' with Italians, warning that not only were the trains often late but 'the pernicious custom of demanding consid-erably more than will ultimately be accepted has long been preva-lent'.[14] The books became synonomous with the tourist. When Lucy Honeychurch, heroine of E.M. Forster's *Room with a View*, was bereft of her Baedeker, she was almost reduced to tears. Wandering disconsolate in a chilly Florentine church, she observed fellow tourists whose 'noses were as red as their Baedekers'.[15] But not everything lived up to expectations: Freud complained one cloudy night that 'the evenings are long, the moon is missed and the stars are in the Baedeker'.[16]

Freud's first impressions of Florence were ecstatic. The city had 'an amazing magic. The treasures are standing in the streets . . . One swims in art.'[17] He had booked a *pensione* in the very centre of town, opposite the Duomo. Florence in September was hot and Freud slaked his thirst with ice cream, slices of melon and coffee, religiously following Baedeker's injunction to avoid drinking the water. But the heat did not stop him from exploring the city in a brisk and organised fashion. Alexander found his brother's pace daunting. Later, it led to the cancellation of a holiday, Freud ruminating it was 'a kind of punishment for the complaints [Alexander] used to make that I was in the habit of overtiring him on such trips . . . by insisting upon moving too rapidly from place to place and seeing too many beautiful things in a single day'.[18] Freud explained to Martha that because his excursions were 'terribly hectic', they were unsuitable 'for a lady'.[19] Perhaps they were. Freud refused to slow down. When Alexander was unable to keep up, and voiced criticism, he was temporarily dismissed. In the mountains, Freud was quiet, content, relaxed. As soon as he went south, his pace increased with the temperature.

The division of Freud's holidays into a period spent with the family in the mountains and another revelling in the singular, sybaritic joys of the south is similar to the separation between his conventional domestic environment and the exotic zone of his study where the art collection was housed. Though when he was abroad he maintained daily contact with Martha and the children in a stream of postcards, letters and telegrams, which were precise, amusing and affectionate, they were rarely invited to accompany him, even as the children grew older. Freud enjoyed holidays with his children, and they adored going on holidays with him. It was the time they felt that he 'came down from his Olympian heights' because they 'saw nothing at all of him' in Vienna.[20]

But in Italy, Freud became a single man again, in the company of his young, single brother. It was a carefully constructed period of renewal, gained through a separation from his duties as father and husband. The birth of six children in rapid succession had been exhausting for Martha: Freud also seemed to need respite. After several weeks in the continuous company of his family, he required refreshment and remove.

Freud saturated himself with Florence's riches. His programme of viewing masterpieces in the Uffizi and Santa Croce and visiting the vast, formal spectacle of the Boboli Gardens behind the Pitti Palace meant he soon felt 'almost blasé'.[21] Freud compared the Boboli Gardens with those surrounding Schönbrunn, the Habsburgs' summer residence, a short distance from Vienna and built to rival Versailles. The Boboli Gardens were so extensive that even Freud, the intrepid walker, was forced to take a carriage. Santa Croce, a huge thirteenth-century basilica, has frescoes by Giotto and Cimbaue, as well as the Pazzi Chapel designed by Brunelleschi. The church is also the burial place of some of Florence's most illustrious citizens, including the tomb of Michelangelo, designed by Vasari, and that of Galileo. It made Madame de Stael declare, 'This church of Santa Croce contains the most brilliant assembly of corpses in perhaps the whole of Italy.'[22]

When Freud discovered Torre del Gallo, it not only provided him with 'an adventure' but welcome relief from Florence. Torre del Gallo, a tower offering panoramic views of Florence is the place where Galileo made his astronomical observations. To get there, Freud wandered through the surrounding hills, decked with olive trees and vineyards, making him pronounce them 'the most beautiful things in Florence'.[23] Torre del Gallo at Arcetri, just past San Miniato, is only three kilometres from the city centre, but its narrow country lanes, almost traffic-free, and enchanting vistas make it seem idyllically rustic. The tower, described by nineteenth-century novelist Ouida,

> stood amongst the hills, with sounds of dripping water on its court, and wild wood-flowers thrusting their bright heads through its stone ... [T]here were peach trees in all the beauty of their blossoms, and everywhere about them were close-set olive trees, with the ground between them scarlet with the tulips and the wild rose bushes.[24]

This countryside was in contrast to Florence which, Freud complained, 'oppresses and overwhelms'. The Florentines themselves created 'a hellish spectacle, screaming, cracking with their whips ... in short, it is unbearable. We have gained bags under our eyes and little sleep.' Florence was famous for its clamour, irritating other such sensitive souls as John Ruskin and Henry James on their first visits. By staying near the Duomo, Freud had selected the noisiest and busiest part of town. Though the 'newness and the beauty of the art' richly compensated, even the presence of the statues 'standing by the half dozen around the streets' was disturbing. Freud could not quantify his sensations: 'historical memories are everywhere so one can't separate them'.[25]

Freud, highly sensitive to new places, seems to have experienced culture shock – a state of disbelief in which, saturated with impressions, the traveller feels dazed and over-stimulated. It followed a similar pattern to Freud's intense, initial reaction to Paris, where, in awe of the 'brilliant exterior, the swarming crowds', he also felt threatened by the 'vast overdressed Sphinx' who gobbled up foreigners.[26] Freud believed the pleasures of travel compensated for 'the dissatisfaction with home and family' and were linked to 'the limitations and poverty' of his own youth. To have arrived at some fabled destination was to recognise 'We really *have* gone a long way!' The jostling feelings of unreality and delight that affected Freud in Paris, Florence and later in Athens derived from a sense of guilt for surpassing the father. 'It was something to do with a child's criticism of his father ... It seems as though the essence of success was to have got further than one's father, and as though to excel one's father was still something forbidden.'[27]

But in the hills at Arcetri, in nature's embrace, Freud was entranced and pacified by a 'paradise garden' that illustrated the 'whole myth and legend of the beautiful south'. When Freud and Alexander discovered they could rent rooms at Torre del Gallo, they promptly quit Florence and moved there.

Torre del Gallo's owner, Count Galetti, had restored the building in fourteenth-century style. Not only was the count a 'noticeably handsome man', who plied Freud and Alexander with the local wine together with delicious produce from his garden, including figs, apricots and almonds, he was also a collector.[28] Freud had found his way to a private museum whose variety nearly rivalled Charcot's. He and Alexander shared a commodious apartment, arranged with pictures and antique furniture. The tower contained one of Galileo's telescopes (now in the Museum of the History of Science, Florence) and Freud was impressed with Galetti's other treasures, especially those connected with his heroes, Michelangelo and Cromwell. In the room next to Freud's hung a self-portrait believed to be by Michelangelo. In fact, it was not an original, but a copy by Michelangelo's follower Jacopino del Conte, a sensitive drawing showing Michelangelo's battered, anguished face cast in shadow.[29] Galetti also had a letter from Oliver Cromwell to Charles I, which was displayed under glass. Galetti's other prizes included Justus Susterman's *Portrait of Galileo* (1636, Uffizi) plus an array of weapons, bronzes, hourglasses and an autograph by renowned Renaissance goldsmith Benvenuto Cellini.

Nearby was Villa Il Gioiello where Galileo had lived from 1631 until his death in 1642. Galileo was persecuted by the Inquisition and incarcerated at the villa for insisting that the earth revolved around the sun, a heretical view according to the Catholic Church. After publishing his theories in 1632 in a book that was banned, Galileo was subsequently tried in Rome and sentenced to life imprisonment. The terms were somewhat lenient and the sick, blind old man remained under house arrest at the villa. In 1640, John Milton was one of the few visitors he was permitted. The story tickled Freud, who felt he was in good company. At Arcetri, Freud basked in his paradise garden, surrounded by art and nature, paralysed by the 'godly beauty', taking siestas and dozing under the trees for hours.[30] It seems he had finally relaxed. It was not only Florence's public collections that impressed Freud and excited his desire to surround himself with art on his return to Vienna, it was the experience of Torre del Gallo.

Before he left town, Freud went shopping. Florence was a consumer's delight with the small studio-shops of skilled artisans displaying a range of local handicrafts, including ceramics, mosaics, jewellery and glasswork. Among Freud's purchases were photographic prints from Alinari's. Founded in 1852, Alinari is one of the oldest photographic firms and Freud continued to buy their high-quality reproductions in order to study Michelangelo's *Moses* and Leonardo's *Virgin, Child and St Anne* (c.1502–1516,

Musée du Louvre, Paris). Another memento was a print of Ottavio Leoni's 1624 portrait of Galileo which he had seen at Torre del Gallo. Perhaps Freud identified with the resolute, embattled scientist who had felt isolated and persecuted by the disrespect shown towards his research, too.

On his return to Vienna, Freud was faced with the prospect of his father's death. Jacob was eighty-one. In the months prior to his Florentine holiday, Freud considered cancelling trips that could take him far from home. In June, when Jacob was in 'a most shaky state, with heart failure [and] paralysis of the bladder', Freud felt 'a pall has been cast over me'. The following weeks saw no improvement, Freud writing to Fliess that he did not begrudge his father 'the well-deserved rest that he himself desires'. Tellingly, Freud described his father in the past tense: 'He was an interesting human being, very happy within himself.' In August, Jacob rallied, giving Freud the incentive to depart for his holidays. Jacob survived until 23 October, after his sons and grandchildren had returned to Vienna. It was, Freud reflected, 'quite an easy death'.[31] But it was not an easy funeral.

That morning, as usual, Freud went to the barber to have his beard trimmed. He was forced to wait and arrived 'a little late at the house of mourning'. Freud found his family fuming, not only because of his tardiness but 'because I had arranged for the funeral to be quiet and simple'.[32] Jewish funerals are meant to be simple: Jewish law mandates a plain pine box and to display wealth or status at such a time is viewed as undignified and immodest. Freud was abiding by tradition, as his family well knew. They were not annoyed because he had made them look cheap – that was a screen memory – they were shocked because he was late. The episode gave Freud a disturbing dream.

He was back at the barber's shop where a sign read, 'You are requested to close the eyes.' Freud interpreted the dream in terms of his family's displeasure: 'one should do one's duty to the dead (an apology as though I had not done it and were in need of leniency) and the actual duty'.[33] In Jewish funeral rites, the eyes and mouth are closed as soon as death occurs and the body is covered with a sheet. In other words, Freud's duty was to close his father's eyes, acknowledging his passing, but it was also his duty to honour his father and, in his family's eyes, he had failed to do this. Nor would the family have been impressed with Freud's excuse for lateness. According to Jewish tradition, during the initial period of mourning, shaving or cutting the hair is forbidden, as is any attention to personal appearance, even looking in a mirror.

Though Freud tried to justify himself, feelings of guilt and discomfort persisted. Revisiting the episode several years later in *The Interpretation of Dreams*, Freud rendered the dream vague and elliptical, deleting the stark message of admonishment it first offered. But retelling the dream gave him the opportunity to publicly chastise his family for a frivolous concern with appearances, though it was he who was culpable. Freud had chosen 'the simplest possible ritual for the funeral, for I knew my father's own views on such ceremonies', but other members of the family 'were not sympathetic to such puritanical simplicity and thought we should be disgraced in the eyes of those who attended the funeral'.[34]

All his life, Freud was loath to participate in the pomp and circumstance of ceremonies, especially if they involved his Jewish spiritual heritage. Such occasions proved stressful. But the matter seemed more personal and idiosyncratic than logical and prescriptive. He did not attend Amalia's funeral, though when his daughter Sophie died in Hamburg, he was distraught that he was unable to attend hers. Jacob was buried in the Jewish section of Vienna's Central Cemetery. Many Jewish graves were destroyed by the Nazis during Kristallnacht, the orgy of destruction against Jewish people and property that took place in November 1938, but Jacob's is among the sixty thousand that survived. In the tradition of Vienna's liberal Jewry, Jacob was assimilationist but he remained Jewish to the core. Judith Bernays Heller, his granddaughter, remembered how earnestly he studied the Talmud and read Hebrew literature. She was also 'greatly impressed' by the way he could recite the Passover Seder by heart.[35]

Jewish funerals tend to be short and simple, their length usually determined by the eulogy delivered by the rabbi. They are a community event and members of Vienna's Jewish community would have been present to console the family. An important moment in the ritual is the reading of Kaddish by the deceased's son. An Aramaic word meaning holy, Kaddish is a prayer traditionally recited at the cemetery after the burial. Freud declared himself to be 'completely estranged from the religion of his fathers'.[36] Could that mean he refused to read Kaddish, giving another reason for the family's reproachful glances and making Freud want to 'close the eyes'?

Eight months later, in June 1897, Freud returned to Jacob's grave and Alexander photographed the family there (pl. 40), effectively re-staging the funeral with its key players. Martha was away and Freud wrote that Alexander's first photograph was unsatisfactory and the family had to reassemble. Standing from left to right are Mitzi, Freud, Rosa, Dolfi and Amalia, gazing at the marble tablet inscribed with the words *Unser Vater Herr Jacob Freud*

(Our Father Mr Jacob Freud). In 1930, Amalia joined her husband in the same plot. Despite Freud's attitude towards ceremony and religion, the family appears to be enacting a Jewish ritual.

During the Avelut, the twelve-month period of mourning observed by those who have lost a parent, a *matzveivah*, or tombstone, is placed on the grave in a ceremony called the 'unveiling'. A cloth is removed from the stone in the presence of the immediate family. In Alexander's photograph, Freud and Rosa are standing on either side of a pole with a cloth attached. On the bottom of the stone can be read five Hebrew letters, *tuf, nun, tzadi, bet* and *hay* meaning may his/her soul 'be bound up in the bond of life eternal'.[37] Kaddish is also recited at memorial services four times a year. One of those festivals is Shavuot (Pentecost), celebrated in May or June, marking the occasion when Moses received the Torah on Mount Sinai.[38] Alexander's photograph, taken in June, may commemorate the festival. Dressed in their ornate, late nineteenth-century best, the family gather around Jacob's grave. Freud's hand is tucked in his breast pocket over his heart, a touching, unselfconscious gesture. Amalia's head is bowed: she wears reading glasses, clasps a book against her chest and her right hand is bare. Perhaps she has been turning the pages of a prayer book and reading Kaddish.

Freud canvassed his relentless criticism of religion in a number of works including *The Future of an Illusion, Civilization and its Discontents* and *Moses and Monotheism*. As Ana-María Rizzuto observes, in spite of Freud's compelling need to reject religion, he could not stop thinking about it.[39] By 1910, he had developed the theory that he would hammer until his life's end: 'a personal God is, psychologically, nothing other than an exalted father'.[40] It seemed 'incontrovertible' to Freud that 'the derivation of religious needs' arose from 'the infant's helplessness and the longing for the father'. The origin of the religious temperament 'can be traced in clear outlines' to infantile fears.[41] Though Freud refused to allow Martha to observe Jewish ritual, he was fascinated by religion's artefacts. Indeed, his collection fetishises religion through its obsessive accumulation of sacred objects. Jewish ceremonial objects, a Hanukkah lamp and two kiddush cups, were included in his antiquities collection.

Though the cups have disappeared, they were in Freud's study in 1938 when it was photographed by Edmund Engelman. The lamp remains in the Freud Museum London. Both cups and lamp play celebratory roles in Jewish ritual. Kiddush is recited at the weekly sabbath table, prior to the meal, usually by the male head of the family who holds the kiddush cup filled to the brim with wine. At Hanukkah, the festival of lights, candles in a special lamp are lit successively for eight nights. Freud would not have used the items for such purposes. His small, copper *Hanukkah Lamp* (Northern France or Germany, 13th century; pl. 41) is not only extremely rare but unusual: it was designed to hang on a wall and to hold oil rather than wax candles.[42] Freud's *Hanukkah Lamp* is by far the most valuable item in his collection.

Although Freud placed these objects on display, he sometimes obscured his knowledge of Judaism. Writing to Martha from Rome in 1907, he described a trip to the Christian and Jewish catacombs. It was 'cold, dark and not very pleasant down there'. He noted that in the Jewish catacombs, the inscriptions were in Greek and an image of 'the candelabrum – I think it's called Menorah' appeared on many clay tablets.[43] The seven-branched menorah is one of Judaism's most ancient and venerable symbols, representing Israel itself, and connotes illumination, knowledge and continuity. Freud's *Hanukkah Lamp* is patterned after it. Freud's forgetfulness about the name is curious. In *The Psychopathology of Everyday Life*, he wrote, 'there is a type of forgetting [about names] which is motivated by repression'.[44] Later Freud described repression as a 'primary mechanism of defence, comparable to an attempt at flight'.[45] Freud's vagueness about the menorah's name indicates a wish to obscure his connections to his spiritual past, to 'forget' the word's powerful cultural associations. But including a Hanukkah lamp in his collection indicates Freud's continued exploration of his Jewish heritage which sought resonant symbols in the world of objects.

Why did Freud not collect artefacts from ancient Israel? Susan L. Braunstein points out that when Freud began collecting, the number of archaeological objects from Palestine was quite small and only 'a handful of monuments' had been excavated.[46] Though the digs greatly increased in the 1920s and '30s, it did not encourage Freud to purchase in this area. Freud's attitude towards his homeland, which he referred to as 'this tragic and fantastic country', was hardly laudatory. To Arnold Zweig, who visited Palestine in 1932, Freud wrote:

> To think that this strip of our native earth is associated with no other progress, no discovery or invention – the Phoenicians are said to have invented glass and the alphabet (both doubtful!), the island of Crete is said to have given us Minoan art, Pergamon reminds us of parchment, Magnesia of the magnet and so on *ad infinitum* – but Palestine has produced nothing but religions, sacred frenzies, presumptuous attempts to conquer the outer world of appearances by the inner world of wishful thinking. And *we* hail fom there.[47]

Freud's self-analysis, his 'dark and not very pleasant' journey to the underworld, began to be conducted systematically in May 1897. At the time Alexander's photograph was taken, Freud was undergoing 'some kind of neurotic experience' with 'twilight thoughts, veiled doubts, barely a ray of light here or there'.[48] Freud's self-analysis, provoked by Jacob's death, led to *The Interpretation of Dreams*. Grief's effect on Freud was disturbing and potent. It took him by surprise, luring him down 'one of those dark pathways behind the official consciousness' into a deep, prolonged and highly productive period of mourning. 'In [my] inner self the whole past has been reawakened by this event', making him feel 'quite uprooted'.[49]

Jacob's death also helped him to consolidate his recent discoveries about the neuroses, motivating and liberating him. It was a rite of passage that conferred maturity on Freud, enabling him to unify aspects of his personality that he felt had lain buried, unappreciated and unacknowledged. In 1886, he had confided to Martha that, although he 'often felt as though I had inherited all the defiance and all the passions with which our ancestors defended their Temple', he felt 'helpless and incapable of expressing these ardent passions'.[50] After 1896, Freud surmounted his sense of inadequacy. As Didier Anzieu suggests, Freud's achievement at this time was not so much the discovery of a technique for treating neurosis as 'a self-initiation into a creative approach in the field of mental processes'.[51] In short, Freud transformed himself as a man and a thinker. His self-analysis also gave him the confidence to explore his visual taste with new conviction and embrace the role of an art collector.

Freud had not been idle. In 1895, he published *Studies on Hysteria*, the result of a collaborative effort not only with Josef

Breuer but, on a more inspiring level, with the women whom Freud treated. It was his women patients who enabled him to discover the meaning of dreams. It was also a woman patient, Elisabeth von R. (Ilona Weiss), who helped him to develop the crucial metaphor of psychoanalysis that directed his collection: archaeology. During her treatment, 'the first full-length analysis of a hysteria undertaken by me', Freud arrived at a procedure which he later developed into a regular method and employed deliberately. Together, he and his patient cleared away the 'psychical material layer by layer, and we liked to compare it with the technique of excavating a buried city'. By instructing Elisabeth von R. to 'lie down and keep her eyes shut', Freud used Charcot's method of hypnosis to penetrate into 'deeper layers of her memory'.[52]

As Elisabeth told Freud her life story, with all its longings, loneliness and disappointments, the source of her hysterical symptoms – frightful, paralysing pains in her legs – became apparent to him. She had fallen in love with her brother-in-law. 'The recovery of this repressed idea had a shattering effect' on Elisabeth, who 'cried aloud' when Freud presented the idea to her. Freud offered Elisabeth a very modern consolation: 'we are not responsible for our feelings'.[53] It was an astute and unorthodox explanation, unencumbered by the strictures of late nineteenth-century morality. First offered to Freud by another patient, Lucy R., a governess who had fallen in love with her employer, he not only repeated it to Elisabeth but used it as a tool to treat his patients' problems and to relieve them of their feelings of guilt and shame.

Freud admired his patients, a group of mostly cultured, middle-class women who included Fanny Moser, a wealthy salon hostess and connoisseur, and Anna von Lieben, who wrote 'poems of great perfection' and whom Freud called his teacher. Freud's sympathy for his women patients, his ability to learn from them and be inspired by them, make his case studies gripping reading. Later Freud would bestow on these women a new name: they were not merely 'patients' but 'analysands'. As Freud reflected, 'it strikes me myself as strange that the case histories I write should read like short stories and that, as one might say, they lack the serious stamp of science'. In Elisabeth's situation, there was even a happy ending. Having lost contact with his former patient, Freud made it his business to go to a ball he knew she would attend. There he observed Elisabeth 'whirl past in a lively dance', cured of her paralysis.[54] Soon after, she got married.

The problem with Freud's treatment – a combination of hypnosis, massage, hydrotherapy, electrotherapy and talking – was that it did not seem to work, at least not for long. Nor was Freud discreet. Elisabeth was furious when Freud took it upon himself to discuss her feelings for her brother-in-law with her mother. At that point, her symptoms had resumed and she refused further treatment by him. It was one of many failures that made Freud recognise the shortcomings of hypnosis: the personal relationship between doctor and patient superseded its efficacy, plus not all his patients could or would submit to the process. Subsequently, Freud abandoned it. But there was an important aspect he retained: he asked the patient to lie on the sofa 'while I sat behind him'.[55]

Freud's couch (pl. 12), the seductive symbol of psychoanalysis, of dreams, fantasies and memories, was given to him in 1891 by Mrs Benevisti, a grateful patient. It is a well-padded chaise longue, on which a patient could comfortably stretch at full length. Freud decorated it with an exquisite Persian rug and cushions, transforming the solid, plain and rather ugly sofa into a deliciously comfortable object, glowing with patterns and textures, which took pride of place in his rooms. Not only did Freud cover the couch with a rug but, when he moved his practice upstairs in 1908, he attached another rug next to it, creating a cocoon effect. To counter the bitter Viennese winter, Freud had a stove installed at the foot of the couch, and placed light wool rugs nearby, surrounding the patient with warmth and luxury. Freud, meanwhile, settled himself in a moss-green velvet chair and a footstool, and puffed his interminable cigars. It was unusual for a doctor's consulting rooms to display such splendid fittings.

The rug Freud chose was a Qashqai, woven by the women of a nomadic tribe from southern Iran. They are among the most highly regarded of Persian carpets. At the time Freud bought his, the Qashqai were producing rugs 'so fine it is difficult to believe they were made by human hand'.[56] The rug's deep, warm tones of madder red and ochre, and its intricate geometric patterns, represent the cultural continuity of a proud, independent minority group. Qashqai men are expert horsemen and herders; the women are renowned for their weaving and their brilliantly coloured clothes. The tribe's nomadic life, which they have fought fiercely to maintain, takes them on annual pilgrimages from the Persian Gulf, where they winter with their herds, to the Zagros mountains for the summer, a journey of about five hundred kilometres. Most rugs are not made to sell commercially. They are an important dowry item and the weaver's skill is highly regarded. Made of a very fine and lustrous wool from the tribe's sheep herds and coloured with natural vegetable and root dyes, each rug is unique and takes months to make. The weaver consults no patterns or designs: each rug is an artwork, a form of self-expression.

The rugs, items of beauty and necessity, are placed on the earthen floors of the tents as protection from the cold and are also used as mattresses, pillows, blankets, couches and curtains. Prized by local dealers, they were exported to major European cities and snapped up by eager buyers such as Freud.[57] Vienna was responsible for the revival of western interest in oriental rugs, which had waned during the sixteenth and seventeenth centuries. In 1891, a mammoth exhibition of carpets drawn from royal treasuries and various dealers took place at the imperial Austrian Trade Museum and it renewed enthusiasm for the rugs internationally. Freud was impressed, too. He bought several rugs, including large carpets for the floor. He placed smaller rugs on tables beneath the antiquities where their lustrous patterns created another visual layer, another reference to Freud's admiration for Middle Eastern artefacts.

Freud's rug, festooned with flowers and birds, depicts a garden in paradise. Its geometric patterns 'enclose' the flowers in the same way a garden is organised with borders, paths and fences. 'This vision of Paradise, this dream of a richly watered garden, of superabundant nature' is typical of the nomad rug.[58] The word 'paradise' comes from *pairdaeza*, Old Persian for enclosure. In some mythologies, heaven is depicted as a garden and in the arid Middle East 'gardens are so precious as to be truly paradise'.[59] Freud had described Torre del Gallo as a paradise garden. The Qashqai weavers, nomads without gardens, travelling through harsh, dry country, created images of longing, an ideal of lush beauty and pleasure, a parallel with Freud's Eden, the lost domain of the 'beautiful woods' of his childhood.

The Arabian Nights, first written in Persian and later translated into Arabic, is set in a walled garden where Scheherazade beguiled the emperor with her tales. Cuckolded by his wife, whom he then had beheaded, the emperor threatened to avenge his honour by executing another woman each dawn. For a thousand and one nights, Scheherazade's stories of flying carpets, genies and treasure-filled caves enchanted the emperor and deflected him from his purpose. On a rug created by women, Freud's patients, who were mostly women, captivated him with their tales, woven from the fabric of their dreams and fears. The roles of storyteller and audience, like those of Scheherazade and the emperor, involve a compact of trust and commitment. Freud regarded psychoanalysis as a shared endeavour: 'It is left to the patient in all essentials to determine the course of the analysis.'[60]

Deliberately, Freud faced his patients away from him and sat behind them, 'seeing . . . but not seen myself'. It was an arrangement reminiscent of Freud's favoured seat at Café Landtmann where he could observe without being observed. It meant he occupied the position of power at the head of the couch, invisible, upright and observant like an Old Testament god, while the patient lay supine and receptive beneath his gaze. But there was more to the politics of the room's design. Initially, Freud sat opposite his patients. But one woman, awaking from a hypnotic trance on the couch, threw her arms around him, causing him consternation. 'The unexpected entrance of a servant relieved us from a painful discussion,' he commented.[61] Freud's professional conduct was consistently chaste and meticulous, with never a hint of scandal. Controlling the proximity of doctor and patient was a means of assuring that. There were other reasons for being out of sight. 'I cannot put up with being stared at by other people for eight hours a day.'[62] Nor did he wish patients to read his facial expressions.

Though Freud aspired to present himself with decorum, the couch, with its lavish rugs, blankets and cushions, undermines his project: it is an erotic object as intimate and inviting as a bed. Not only is it deliciously soft but delicately textured, a delight to the touch. Among tribes such as the Qashqai, furnishing a tent with an abundance of rugs was tantamount to creating a boudoir. Firdausi, the tenth-century Persian poet, describes an ardent young woman whose tent was 'intended for pleasure . . . completely furnished with rich rugs in vibrant colours'.[63]

Freud wooed his patients, entertaining an educated and intelligent clientele in comfort and style, welcoming them to a tastefully appointed salon, an impression that would not have been lost on a connoisseur such as Fanny Moser, an expert in antique furniture. Struggling to make ends meet, especially in the difficult, early years of private practice, Freud needed his patients to be faithful, aware of 'the crowds of neurotics, whose number seemed further multiplied by the way which they hurried, with their troubles unsolved, from one physician to another'.[64] To keep them, it was necessary to create a setting where they felt relaxed and protected and that had the appearance that he was a successful doctor. 'There are two kinds of women patients,' Freud observed, 'one kind who are as loyal to their doctor as to their husband, and the other kind who change their doctors as often as their lovers.'[65]

The Qashqai followed the Islamic tradition and treated their guests with reverence: guests were offered the best of everything, including the most exquisite carpet on which to rest. Freud followed suit, treating his patients to a feast of the senses, providing a unique and luxurious environment where they felt cheered and privileged, just as he did, surrounded by his collection.

Freud's excavation of his patients' neuroses, the descent to the lost world of their childhood memories, began to shape his ideas and emerge in his writing.

In April 1896, when Freud lectured on 'The Aetiology of Hysteria' to his colleagues, he presented the controversial notion that sexual problems were at the root of hysteria. Even more shocking was his suggestion that, tracing the causes of hysterical symptoms, 'we arrive at the period of earliest childhood . . . as far back as a human memory is capable of reaching'.[66] The lecture, packed with metaphors of archaeology, geography and genealogy, displays Freud as a resolute and adventurous explorer, equipping himself with the tools to map and plumb the mind, and the hubris to announce his discoveries to the world. Aetiology means the study of origins. Freud's lecture is intensely visual with its references to family trees, children's jigsaw puzzles, 'chains of memories' and 'sexual scenes'.

The lecture begins with an imaginary tour through an ancient city where Freud, the archaeologist

> may content himself with inspecting what lies exposed to view or . . . he may start upon the ruins, clear away the rubbish . . . uncover what is buried. If his work is crowned with success, the discoveries are self-explanatory . . . the fragments of columns can be filled out into a temple; the numerous inscriptions . . . yield undreamed-of information about the events of the remote past . . . *Saxa loquuntur!*'[67]

Stones talk! Just as his patients did with the new method he employed, free association, where they said whatever came into their minds.

But the lecture was given 'an icy reception by the asses', as Freud complained to Fliess. Chairing the session was Richard Krafft-Ebing, eminent professor of Vienna University's medical faculty and the author of *Psychopathia Sexualis*. His comment, 'It sounds like a scientific fairy tale', made Freud fulminate that 'after one has demonstrated to them the solution of a more-than-thousand-year-old problem, *a caput* Nili [source of the Nile]! They can go to hell, euphemistically expressed.'[68]

Six months later, the grief-stricken Freud became the explorer of his own unconscious. Mourning was the journey, represented by hallowed objects from the past: Freud adorned his rooms with Florentine mementos, souvenirs that served both as the foundation of his art collection and emblems of healing. Later, after decades of collecting, Freud observed that 'People who are receptive to art cannot set too high a value on it as a source of pleasure and consolation in life'.[69]

None of the plaster casts Freud owned survive. A photograph (pl. 42) taken by his son Martin around 1905 shows Freud on the light-filled veranda at the rear of Berggasse 19. Dressed in a velvet smoking jacket and vest, cigar in hand, Freud is seated next to Michelangelo's *Dying Slave* (1513–1516), a work he saw not in Florence but in the Louvre. Behind him hang some unidentified medallions and a print of Masaccio and Masolino's fresco, *The Healing of the Paralytic and The Raising of Tabitha* (1426–1428), from Florence's Brancacci Chapel, which Freud may have bought from Alinari's. By 1905, Freud had deserted the Renaissance for antiquity, dispensed with copies in favour of originals and happily surrounded himself with 'old and grubby gods'.[70] But the photograph records Freud the budding collector: in the foreground is the art form he favoured – sculpture – but neither the period nor the scale (no later choices were as large as *Dying Slave*). Nor does the veranda typify the style of Freud's rooms, in which crowds of statues fight for space, cheek by jowl, creating an atmosphere of almost claustrophobic intensity. By contrast, the veranda is airy and minimal in its decoration.[71]

Why did Freud choose Michelangelo's *Dying Slave*? He was drawn to Michelangelo and that other sexually ambivalent High Renaissance genius Leonardo da Vinci, writing essays about both. On holiday in Rome in 1912, Freud paid a daily visit to San Pietro in Vincoli to see Michelangelo's majestic *Moses* 'on whom I may perhaps write a few words'.[72] The following year, he published a study on the work, returning to the biblical hero in *Moses and Monotheism*. 'No piece of statuary,' Freud declared, 'has ever made a stronger impression on me than this.'[73]

Moses and *Dying Slave* are fragments of the same design. In 1505, Michelangelo was summoned to Rome to design the tomb of his patron, Pope Julius II. Julius' hubris was evident in the grandiose plans for his mausoleum: 'in beauty and magnificence, wealth of ornamentation and richness of statuary' it was meant to surpass 'every ancient imperial tomb ever made', gushed Vasari.[74] The symbolic intent of the forty life-sized statues surrounding the proposed tomb remains unclear but they are best read as an ascent from bondage into salvation. The lower level was dedicated to humanity's spiritual struggle, the middle level to the active and contemplative lives represented by prophets and saints, and the top to the Last Judgement.[75] At the summit were two angels leading the pope from his tomb on Judgement Day. Michelangelo's initial sketches show the *Slaves* on the lower level (there were to be six of them) and *Moses* at the middle.[76]

Imperious and demanding, Julius clashed with Michelangelo over schedules and payment for the tomb, and they had one of their spectacular tiffs. Freud judged Julius and Michelangelo 'akin' because both 'attempted to realise great and mighty ends ... especially designs on a grand scale'.[77] That was part of the problem because Julius advanced an even grander idea: he asked Michelangelo to paint the Sistine Chapel, which the artist, who regarded himself as a sculptor and not a painter, was loath to do. Plans for the tomb were shelved and only completed decades after the pope's death, a process muddied by design changes and simplifications, as well as litigation with Julius' family, making Michelangelo reflect, 'I want to get out of this obligation [finishing the tomb] more than I want to go on living.'[78]

In 1545, a scaled-down version of the tomb was finally constructed in San Pietro in Vincoli, not at St Peter's as Julius had intended. The only major statue remaining from Michelangelo's original conception was *Moses*. *Dying Slave*, together with its companion piece, *Rebellious Slave*, was given by Michelangelo to Roberto Strozzi, who in turn offered them to François I. During the French Revolution, both works were seized and placed in the Louvre, where Freud saw them. In Florence, he also saw Michelangelo's quartet of magnificent but unfinished *Slaves*. Once they stood in the Boboli Gardens, but when Freud visited they had been replaced by copies and the originals moved to the Accademia Gallery to conserve them. Seeing such marvellous reproductions in Florence probably encouraged Freud to buy his own.

Dying Slave writhes in a voluptuous display of exquisite torment. He is a prisoner of the flesh: the *Slaves* were also known as the *Prisoners*. Erwin Panofsky suggests the *Slaves* 'personify the human soul enslaved by matter'.[79] Freud's *Slave* struggles with his fate, his imperfect humanity, the bonds of the flesh that tie him to the physical realm while he strains for transcendent release. Though the statue is upright, the slave's posture, and his sleepy, passive expression, make him appear as though he is lying down. His swooning stance is the best way Michelangelo can reveal the young man's charms: his lovely face, his flesh, his muscles and genitals. *Dying Slave* is a homoerotic pin-up boy. Camille Paglia describes him as 'postorgasmic'.[80]

Michelangelo's tortured dualism, his attraction to men combined with his avowed celibacy, is reflected in the sculpture's interior conflict: movement seems 'stifled from the start or paralysed before being completed' so 'terrific contortions and muscular tensions never seem to result in effective action, let alone locomotion'.[81] In Martin's veranda photograph, Freud stares at the camera, steady and serious, the very picture of a gentleman, while the statue beside him is caught in a shameless rapture of emotion, like the unfettered and uncensored unconscious Freud was charting, like the urgent and beautiful lure of art itself. Freud believed 'the concept of "beautiful" has its roots in sexual excitation'.[82]

Still grieving for Jacob, Freud chose a sculpture designed for the tomb of a pope, the 'great father' and head of a church, a work that incorporates the issues of sexuality and repression he was exploring. The Renaissance marked a rebirth, when Europe emerged from the spiritual fervour of the Dark Ages into the pagan brilliance of classical art, literature and learning. It was a humanistic and hedonistic era that glorified the human form's capacity for sensual power. Though the medieval period was not wholly 'dark', it was a truism of Freud's time that western culture had floundered until classicism's rediscovery in fourteenth-century

Florence, reaching its ultimate expression in the trio of High Renaissance geniuses, Leonardo, Michelangelo and Raphael. Jacob Burckhardt, the Swiss art historian who championed the Renaissance and who was eagerly read by Freud, claimed 'a new spirit entered into the painting of the West'.[83] In the Middle Ages 'human consciousness . . . lay dreaming or half awake beneath a common veil' but, during the Renaissance, 'man became a spiritual *individual* and recognised himself as such'.[84]

Dying Slave presages and configures Freud's rebirth: it was the companion of his mourning, an image of masculine suffering and defeat redeemed by art's liberating and invigorating force, providing the illumination of beauty during the darkness of grief. It was also a precious memento recalling his holiday in Florence just before Jacob's death. Freud could not imagine 'any need in childhood as strong as the need for a father's protection'.[85] Having lost his father, his need for consolation was immediately expressed by surrounding himself with sculptures that constituted 'a defence mechanism against anguish and the experience of loss, a bulwark against the fear of abandonment and the dread of being alone and defenceless'.[86] Not long before he acquired his first antiquities, Freud declared that the collector was engaged in a game of substitution, in which the objects involved – whether in the amorous adventures of a Don Juan or the daredevil exploits of a mountaineer – were 'erotic equivalents', items of conquest and desire offering relief, love tokens designed to soothe and heal.[87]

Freud regarded mourning as work. It was a slow process because its very duration prolonged 'the existence of the lost object'. Melancholia, or pathological mourning, meant 'the loss of capacity to adopt any new object of love' because it meant replacing the original love object. In that equation, Freud did not seem to have any problem replacing Jacob: he consoled himself with artworks. But the extent of his collection, his insatiable thirst for more and more, indicates that his grief was unassuaged and, in the 'economics of pain', he continued to pay.[88]

Freud's pursestrings were loosened after Jacob's death because he no longer had to maintain his father, but there remained many family members to support. Buying cheap multiples such as plaster casts indicates the small sums Freud could allocate to his new hobby. In the nineteenth century, plaster casts were popular as educational aids, thronging not only the rooms of impecunious aesthetes but art museums too. Freud was familiar with the sight of art students setting up their easels in major galleries and drawing from plaster copies of antique and Renaissance works: he quotes one such example in *The Psychopathology of Everyday Life* of a young art student extricating herself from her studies by a series of willed 'errors'.[89] Freud, too, chose plaster copies to learn from: they were his learning tools, the foundation of his private museum.

If Freud had wanted to see a copy of Michelangelo's sculpture, he could do so close to home. In 1806, the Liechtenstein princes welcomed the public to their fabulous seventeenth-century palace and art collection, just around the corner from Berggasse 19.[90]

Like the Habsburgs, the Liechtensteins were collectors in the grand manner. It seemed that anybody with money in Vienna wanted to behave like a Renaissance prince. It was not enough to hoard one's treasures: philanthropy in the form of public access, emphasising art's moral and didactic purpose, together with the glittering status that such a display guaranteed, was the goal of Austria's elite. Prince Johann II, active during Freud's time, was an art lover who renovated the palace galleries. A science patron, he also made substantial donations to the University of Vienna.

It was an earlier prince, Johann Adam Andreas, who planned the palace, including its lovely formal gardens and much of its collection. As well as choosing paintings by Rubens, Franz Hals and Artemisia Gentileschi, he also commissioned a copy of Michelangelo's *Bacchus* (1496–97, Bargello, Florence). Massimiliano Soldani-Benzi's copy was highly regarded in its own right and proudly exhibited. A short walk from home, the Liechtenstein palace provided Freud with a princely prototype for his own collection's humble beginnings.

Freud's self-analysis was partly conducted on the Ringstrasse during his rapid daily walks, the boulevard providing the backdrop to his 'inner work'. He felt 'gripped and pulled through ancient times . . . my moods change like the landscapes seen by a traveller from a train'. Though Freud recognised that self-analysis was always imperfect and that 'true self-analysis is impossible; otherwise there would be no [neurotic] illness', it was a period of revelation during which he explored, 'in my own case, too', the phenomenon of the Oedipus complex, 'a universal event in early childhood'.[91]

His walks took him to the Kunsthistorisches Museum. The last building erected on the Ringstrasse, its splendid galleries housed the greater part of the Habsburgs' collections. Though its cornerstone was laid in 1871, two decades passed before the building was completed and the Habsburg collections were removed from their previous home in the Belvedere Palace and installed in the new, luxurious, purpose-built galleries.[92] Completed in 1891, architect Gottfried Semper's enormous neo-Italian Renaissance-style building faces the equally large Natural

History Museum, the two separated by an imposing statue of Empress Maria Theresa. The art museum's architectural style was a tribute to the Habsburgs, the Medicis of Vienna.

The story of the Habsburg collection is one of continuity and largesse. During the seventeenth century, Emperor Rudolf II behaved with the aplomb of a great patron, collecting masterpieces by Dürer, Pieter Brueghel, Leonardo and Correggio, as well as creating a *Kunstkammer*, or art chamber, in his Prague palace that was stuffed with curiosities and 'marvels' of nature as well as art. Next, Archduke Leopold Wilhelm sent his agents scouring the countryside for Italian, German and Dutch art, amassing a trove of over fourteen hundred works. But it was Josef II, devotee of the Enlightenment, who decided to coordinate the imperial collections in one place – the Belvedere Palace – and, in 1781, threw open its doors to the public. He also changed the Prater from a royal hunting reserve to a people's park. Before the British Museum or the Altes Museum in Berlin, 'a public museum was created in Vienna that was devoted to a special category of visual art' with 'clearly enunciated historical principles'.[93] Curator Christian Mechel's chronological order provided an historical overview, meant for 'instruction rather than passing enjoyment', and the gallery resembled 'a well furnished library in which anyone who wishes to learn will find works of every period and kind'.[94]

The European collection was stronger in Renaissance and baroque paintings than sculpture. The rooms of Egyptian, Greek and Roman sculpture would attract and influence Freud more. But his eye was educated by first-rate paintings: Raphael's demure *Madonna in the Meadow* (c.1505), the voluptuous voyeurism of Tintoretto's *Susanna and the Elders* (c.1555–56), Caravaggio's disturbing exercise in castration and self-portrai-

ture, *David with the Head of Goliath* (1606–07), the luscious
textures of Rubens' *The Fur* (c.1635–40), Rembrandt's haunting
Self Portrait (1652) and Vermeer's meditation on the muse, *The
Artist's Studio* (c.1665–66). Courtesy of the Habsburgs, Freud was
offered a peerless example of taste, generosity, vision and dedi-
cation to the task of collecting itself. He was learning from the
royal family that, as far as the accumulation of objets d'art went,
enough was never enough.

Nearby was a small museum also dear to Freud's heart, but for
different reasons. In 1895 the world's first Jewish museum opened
in rented quarters at Rathausstrasse 13 before it found a permanent home in the Leopoldstadt.[95] Not only did it display and
document objects of Jewish life and religion, it acted as a
communal and cultural focus, with a prestigious council that
included rabbis, architects, orientalists, writers and lawyers.
Lectures, also part of its programme, emphasised Jewish contributions to art, natural history and medicine. Freud could observe
a specifically Jewish initiative focused on art, culture and philanthropy. One of the museum's chief attractions was the recreation
of an eighteenth-century Jewish home, complete with period
furnishings, typical of South Russia and Galicia; the latter region
was where both Amalia's and Jacob's families orginated.

Freud also joined B'nai B'rith, a Jewish men's professional
organisation, and began to attend meetings regularly. It was a
move consolidating his links with Jewish men and community, as
well as symbolising his lost connection with his father and his
isolation from his medical peers. With fine melodramatic flourish,
Freud told his B'nai B'rith brothers that 'at a time when no
one in Europe listened to me and I still had no disciples even in
Vienna . . . you were my first audience'.[96]

There was another reason to show solidarity with fellow Jews. In 1897, Karl Lueger, an avowed anti-Semite, had been elected mayor of Vienna. To his credit, Franz Josef initially refused to confirm Lueger's win and Freud celebrated by lighting a cigar. But when 'Handsome Karl' was elected for the third consecutive time, the emperor bowed to the inevitable. Freud's wrath was aroused by the man he sneeringly called 'the master of Vienna'.[97] Hitler revered Lueger, learning the populist, minority-baiting style of politics from him. The problem for Hitler was that Lueger simply did not go far enough. Lueger played it both ways, insisting that although Jews dominated Vienna to its detriment, he was prepared to admit them to his inner circle — as long as they converted to Christianity. 'I determine who's a Jew,' was his much-quoted remark.[98] In late nineteenth-century Vienna, shaped by Freud's ambitious generation, Lueger created a loud, brutal and effective voice for anti-Semitism. It proved that, despite appearances, the distrust and dislike of Jews rippled just beneath the surface. Their prominence as key patrons and participants in Viennese life had made them a target. Gustav Mahler understood the rules: to win the coveted post of director of the Opera, he converted to Catholicism.

Though Freud disliked modern art, there was no escaping the Secession, Vienna's home-grown contemporary art movement. It marked the entrance of Austria into the ranks of the avant-garde. The Secession artists were blessed with talent, as well as media acumen, and they made their presence felt in a publicity campaign that lured both the emperor and Karl Lueger to their exhibitions. Though Freud did not acquire any of their works, the secessionists' taste for classical art and mythology, plus their emphasis on sex, symbolism and psychological states, runs parallel with Freud's at a time when he was choosing his first artworks and developing his theories about the power of sex and the unconscious.

The Secession was born in 1897, partly from a loathing for the Ringstrasse. The young Turks, led by Gustav Klimt, had grown to hate its pomposity, its phoney historical references, its big, bold, macho presence. Though it is difficult today to locate an aesthetic gulf between the pretty, glittering surfaces of Klimt's *The Kiss* (1907/08, Österreichische Galerie Belvedere, Vienna) and nineteenth-century's Vienna's lust for decoration, the Secession artists regarded themselves as groundbreaking radicals. Klimt's cohorts, who included Josef Hoffman, Kolo Moser and Joseph Maria Olbrich, felt excluded by the art establishment of the day, which was represented by the Academy of Fine Arts. The Academy had its own great, bulky headquarters designed by Theophil Hansen, who was also responsible for the Parliament.

The Secession staked its claim as the city's new art movement in true Viennese fashion: by designing its own building, directly opposite the Academy. Olbrich's clean, white, determinedly modern monument looks like an Egyptian mausoleum – part from its golden headdress, meant to be a crowning sphere of laurel but irreverently dubbed 'the golden cabbage'. Freud's favourite newspaper, the liberal *Neue Freie Presse*, noted the building's eastern qualities and hailed it as 'the temple' of the Secession, 'the mysterious cult sanctuary for the new art'.[99] It was also one of the first buildings to break with the dominant baroque and historicist tradition of Viennese architecture.

In a sense, the secessionists were never outsiders, despite skirmishes over public standards of taste and morality in which Klimt later became embroiled: its artists were successful, prominent and accepted by mainstream culture almost immediately. Industrialist Karl Wittgenstein, uncle of the philosopher, was one of the movement's early patrons: he arranged the finance to build its temple. Mayor Lueger gave the land. Freud, like other curious Viennese, probably visited the building. The secessionists held exhibitions, grand events that were attended by thousands at which they not only promoted their own art but that of other important European modernists, including Rodin and Whistler. The Secession gave an avant-garde edge to Vienna's rich visual environment.

Though the style of Olbrich's Secession House is cool and restrained, prefiguring minimalist twentieth-century architecture, Klimt's art is crowded with sinuous and stylised figures, patterns, textures and colours, especially gold. He privileges the femmes fatales of late nineteenth-century symbolist art: his paintings and murals glide and seethe with their svelte forms and tangled tresses — beautiful, alluring, wicked women who smile lasciviously as they display themselves. Klimt also celebrated the castrating dominatrixes of the Bible: *Judith I* (1901, Österreichische Galerie Belvedere, Vienna) and *Salome* (1909, Ca' Pesaro, Venice).

Freud was familiar with Klimt's earlier, academic-style murals that decorate the foyer of the Kunsthistorisches. He, too, was disturbed by archetypal enchantresses, especially that most fecund siren of the dark side, the witch. 'The broomstick they ride is probably the great Lord Penis,' Freud theorised, and their 'secret gatherings, with dancing and entertainment, can be seen any day in the streets where children play'. He studied *Malleus maleficarum* (The witches' hammer), the notorious fifteenth-century handbook of the Inquisition, while dreaming of a 'primeval devil religion with rites that are carried on secretly'. The prospect of an uncontrollable feminine force made Freud 'understand the harsh therapy of the witches' judges'.[100] Freud was struck that his patients' stories resembled those of witches under torture, tales of rape and bizarre sexual acts.

It was such stories that led Freud to develop the seduction theory: that many children, especially girls, were sexually molested either by a parent (usually the father) or another adult close to them. Even Jacob was not exempt. 'Unfortunately, my own father was one of these perverts,' Freud told Fliess, accounting for 'the hysteria' of his brother Alexander, as well as several of his sisters.[101] Conveniently, Freud excluded himself from this explosive scenario. Late in 1897, after returning from a period of rest and reflection in Italy and the mountains, Freud abandoned the seduction theory, deciding the stories were 'only phantasies which my patients had made up or which I myself had perhaps forced on them'.[102]

But the turmoil caused by such speculations, together with the sheer intellectual ferment embroiling him – 'this abundance of visions' – manifested in a startling array of illnesses.[103] Freud suffered from migraines, depression, anxiety and irregular heartbeat, making the long walks around the Ringstrasse more necessary than ever to his health and well-being, especially given that some problems were due to his addiction to cigars. Freud's concerns about his health, especially his dark foreboding that he was shortly doomed to die, canvassed in letters to Fliess, together with the nervous origin of some of his complaints, make him appear as neurotic as his patients. No doubt Jacob's death had also raised issues of mortality, emphasising loss and life's fragility.

While migraine remained a chronic condition, Freud's other problems gradually abated after the publication of *The Interpretation of Dreams* in 1900.

Self-analysis, however, did not end, Freud confiding to Ernest Jones that he devoted half an hour at the end of each day to that purpose. It provided a fertile training ground for Freud the collector, with its programme of observation and reflection, its attention to details and fragments, its forensic study of small and apparently insignificant images and episodes that, after scrutiny, could appear as valuable as revelations. Self-analysis, like collecting, became an indispensable, ongoing quest.

Plate 1: View of Příbor (Freiberg). 2004. (Janine Burke)

Plate 2: Freud's home, Příbor (Freiberg). 2004. The house has been remodelled since Freud's day. The Freud family room was upstairs right. (Janine Burke)

Plate 3: Freud's forest, near Příbor. 2004. (Janine Burke)

Plate 4: *Falcon-headed Figure*. Forgery.
19th century A.D. Gessoed and painted
wood. H. 22 cm. Cat. no. 3124.
(Courtesy Freud Museum London.)

Plate 5: *Human-headed Bird*. Egyptian. Ptolemaic Period, 332—30 B.C. Gessoed and painted wood. H. 14 cm. Cat. no. 3286. (Courtesy Freud Museum London.)

Plate 6: *Sphinx*. Greek, South Italian. Late 5th—early 4th century B.C. Terracotta. H. 18.5 cm. Cat. no. 4387. (Courtesy Freud Museum London.)

Plate 7: *Eros*. Greek. Hellenistic Period, from Myrina. c.150—100 B.C.
Terracotta. H. 38 cm. Cat. no. 3880. (Courtesy Freud Museum London.)

Plate 8: *Isis Suckling the Infant Horus*. Egyptian. Late Period (26th
Dynasty) 664—525 B.C. Bronze. H. 21.5 cm. Cat. no. 3037.
(Courtesy Freud Museum London.)

Plate 9: *Artemis.* Greek. Hellenistic Period, from Myrina. 2nd century B.C. Terracotta. H. 25 cm. Cat. no. 3273. (Courtesy Freud Museum London.)

Plate 10: *Cylinder Seal*. Old Babylonian. C.19th—18th century B.C. Hematite. 2.6 × 1.5 cm. Cat. no. 4243. (Courtesy Freud Museum London.)

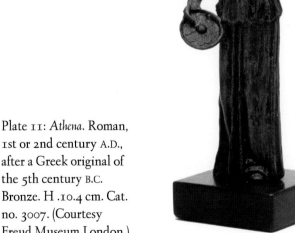

Plate 11: *Athena*. Roman, 1st or 2nd century A.D., after a Greek original of the 5th century B.C. Bronze. H .10.4 cm. Cat. no. 3007. (Courtesy Freud Museum London.)

Plate 12: Freud's couch, Freud Museum London. On the couch is the Qashqai rug. (Courtesy Freud Museum London.)

Plate 13: *Jar*. Roman. C.50 — 150 A.D. Glass. H. 19.5 cm. Cat. no. 4394. (Courtesy Freud Museum London.)

Plate 14: *Balsamarium*. Etruscan. 3rd century B.C. Bronze. H. 9.4 cm. Cat. no. 3029. (Courtesy Freud Museum London.)

Plate 15: *Phalluses*. (Courtesy Freud Museum London.)

Plate 16: *Engraved Mirror*. Etruscan, late 4th—early 3rd century B.C. Bronze. 24.5 × 16.6 cm. Cat. no. 3082. (Courtesy Freud Museum London.)

Plate 17: *Fragment From the Lid of a Sarcophagus*. Roman. 160—210 A.D. Marble. 25.4 × 94 cm. Cat. no. 4381. (Courtesy Freud Museum London.)

Plate 18: *Corinthian Black-figured Alabastron.* Greek. Archaic Period, c.600 B.C. Terracotta. H. 28.2 cm. Cat. no. 3699. (Courtesy Freud Museum London.)

Plate 19: *Antefix in the form of a Gorgon Head.* Roman. Terracotta. Second half of the first century B.C. —early 2nd century A.D. H. 18 cm; base 22 cm. Cat. no. 6416. (Courtesy Freud Museum London.)

Plate 20: *Baboon of Thoth*. Egyptian. Roman Period, 30 B.C.—A.D. 395. Marble. H. 21.5 cm. Cat. no. 3133. (Courtesy Freud Museum London.)

Plate 21: *Head of Osiris*. Egyptian. Third Intermediate Period, 1075—716 B.C. or later. Bronze. H. 18 cm. Cat. no. 3128. (Courtesy Freud Museum London.)

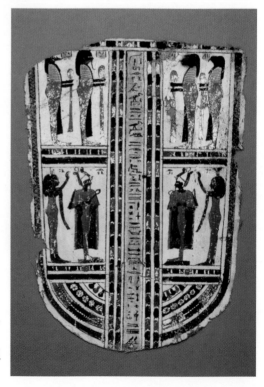

Plate 22: *Frontal Covering of a Mummy*. Egyptian. Ptolemaic Period, 332—30 B.C. Cartonnage. 38 × 24 cm. Cat. no. 4936. (Courtesy Freud Museum London.)

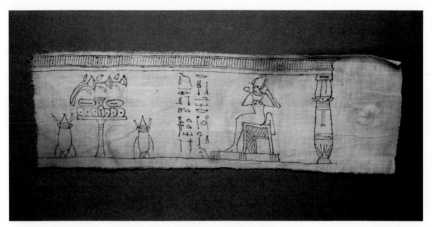

Plate 23: *Mummy Bandages with Vignettes from the Book of the Dead.* Egyptian. Ptolemaic-Roman Period, c.100 B.C. — 200 A.D. Linen. 11.5 × 38 cm. Cat. no. 3441. (Courtesy Freud Museum London.)

Plate 24: *Heart Scarab.* Eyptian. New Kingdom (18th — 19th Dynasty), 1540 — 1190 B.C. Serpentine. 2.4 × 4 × 5.6 cm. Cat. no. 4004. (Courtesy Freud Museum London.)

Plate 25: (far left) *Shabti of Imhotep Born of Bastetirdis.* Egyptian. Late Period (30th Dynasty), 380 — 342 B.C. Egyptian faience. H. 20.3 cm. Cat. no. 3351. Freud Museum London; (centre) *Shabti Figure of Senna,* Egyptian. New Kingdom (18th Dynasty), Tuthmosis III — Amenophis II, 1479 — 1400 B.C., Limestone, H. 23 cm. Cat. no. 3271. (Courtesy Freud Museum London.)

Plate 26: *Mummy Portrait* I. Egyptian. Roman Period, c. 250 — 300 A.D. Tempera on wood. 34 × 23 cm. Cat. no. 4946. (Courtesy Freud Museum London.)

Plate 27: *Female Figure (Ishtar)*. Syrian. Middle Bronze Age, c.2000—1750 B.C. Clay. H. 11.7 cm. Cat. no. 3725. (Courtesy Freud Museum London.)

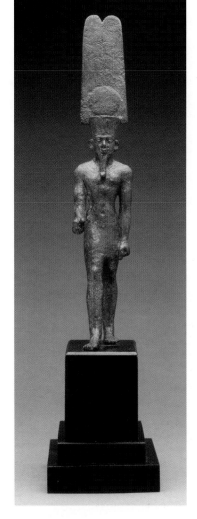

Plate 28: *Amon-Re*. Egyptian. Probably Late Period, 716—332 B.C. Bronze. H. 21.2 cm. Cat. no. 3138. (Courtesy Freud Museum London.)

Plate 29: *Table Screen.* Chinese. Qing Dynasty, 19th century. Wood and jade. Scren (without stand) 19 × 12.6 × 2.5 cm. Cat. no. 3001. (Courtesy Freud Museum London.)

Plate 30: 20 Maresfield Gardens, London. 2003. (Janine Burke)

6

Dream Collector

*At last I was able to realise the dream of my life, and to visit at my leisure
the scene of those events which had always had such an intense interest
for me, and the country of the heroes whose adventures had delighted and
comforted my childhood.*

HEINRICH SCHLIEMANN, ILIOS: THE CITY AND
COUNTRY OF THE TROJANS[1]

In dreams, to be sure, we hear nothing; but we see.

SIGMUND FREUD, 'THE ARCHITECTURE OF HYSTERIA'[2]

THE INTERPRETATION OF DREAMS is not only a catalogue of
dreams but of artworks and journeys. It is a distinctively modern
work, both in form and content, a book that marks a break with

the nineteenth century and helps introduce the twentieth. Aside from presenting a new theory about the mind, it gave Freud the opportunity to chronicle his interests in the pleasures of art and place, offering a mirror of Freud the aesthete. While writing it, Freud's love of art and confidence as a collector developed rapidly. He established Mediterranean antiquity as his favoured period and sculpture his favoured art form, he began acquiring works zealously, as well as forming the habit he retained for the rest of his life: taking his collection on holidays with him. Dreams themselves are images and Freud's dreams, memorably described by Peter Gay as 'opulent and pellucid', provide vivid, visual representations of his ideas.[3]

In the summer of 1895, on holiday with the family at Bellevue, on the outskirts of Vienna, surrounded by vineyards and with views of the Carpathians, Freud had a dream about one of his female patients. The dream of Irma's injection alerted Freud to the possibilities of the dream and the power of the unconscious. It was the first dream he analysed in depth and it takes pride of place in *The Interpretation of Dreams*, not only providing the basis of psychoanalytic dream theory but the subject for debate ever since. Freud dreams that Irma (probably his patient Emma Eckstein) complains of pains in her throat and abdomen. Upon examination, it transpires that Otto, a medical friend of Freud's, has given Irma an injection that is to blame for her ill health. Freud concludes, 'I was not responsible for the persistence of Irma's pains,' and finishes triumphantly, '*When the work of interpretation has been completed, we perceive that a dream is the fulfillment of a wish.*'[4]

Freud introduced his own dreams into the book – thus creating its engagingly personal tone – because 'The only dreams open to me were my own'. It meant Freud had to 'reveal to the public gaze more of the intimacies of my mental life than I liked, or than is normally necessary for any writer who is a man of science and not a poet . . . [a] painful but unavoidable necessity'.[5] The book's emotional subtext was provided by Jacob's death. Indeed, the entire project was steeped in mourning, Freud confessing 'it was a portion of my self-analysis, my reaction to my father's death – that is to say, the most important event, the most poignant loss, of a man's life'.[6] His writing style matched the boldly imaginative material he presented. Though Freud complained to Fliess that he could not convey 'any idea of the intellectual beauty of this work', the finished product did exactly that.[7]

Racing to complete *The Interpretation of Dreams* during the summer of 1899, Freud was again on holiday, this time near Berchtesgaden in the Bavarian Alps. Set amid pine forests and hills of wildflowers, the rented house was not far from Salzburg, one of Freud's favourite shopping haunts. He deemed the place 'incomparably beautiful', and installed himself in a 'large, quiet, ground floor room with a view of the mountains'. He was not alone. 'My old and grubby gods,' he told Fliess, 'of whom you think so little, take part in the work as paperweights.'[8]

The organisation of Freud's desk, bristling with statues, as seen in Edmund Engelman's photographs, had been established. Having the works so close was an ideal way to study them. It was Charcot's advice: 'to look at the same things again and again until they themselves begin to speak'.[9] Freud told H.D. that the 'little statues and images helped stabilise the evanescent idea, or keep it from escaping altogether'.[10] Having the works so close also neatly symbolised the fecund role classical and preclassical art and myth began to play in Freud's thought, the direct manner in which such elements were incorporated in his writings and the intimate relationship he developed with his 'old and grubby gods'.

What did Freud's collection comprise in 1899? In Salzburg the summer before, he had bought 'a few good Egyptian antiquities' that put him 'in a good mood' because they suggested 'distant times and countries'.[11] That same summer at Innsbruck, he had purchased a Roman statuette, approving of Anna's description of it as 'an old child'.[12] Before leaving for Berchtesgaden, Freud had acquired 'a stone Janus who looks at me with his two faces in a very superior manner'.[13] He also had an Etruscan funerary urn, probably bought during a trip to Orvieto in 1897. Both the urn and the trip, which included a visit to an excavated Etruscan grave site, are mentioned in *The Interpretation of Dreams*. The book also provided Freud with the chance to comment on the business of collecting itself. He chides himself at one point for being too cautious and losing out on 'some nice acquisitions' and later remarks that a bachelor, by becoming an enthusiastic collector, displays a harmless case of displacement.[14]

Fliess, his closest friend and confidant, was dismissive of Freud's new hobby. Perhaps it is why, in his letters to Fliess, which form a diary of his thought and life in the late 1890s, Freud abjured from discussing his growing collection in any detail. Fliess was no philistine. Freud took seriously Fliess' injunction to study Italian art not for 'cultural-historical' reasons but for purely aesthetic ones: the 'absolute beauty in the harmony between ideas and the form in which they are presented'.[15]

Freud's taste was changing. No longer satisfied with plaster casts of Renaissance masters, he had begun to acquire original artworks, exquisite sculptures that offered a visceral experience. Freud enjoyed stroking their time-scored surfaces and gaining a palpable contact with antiquity. Hanns Sachs recalled that, while talking, Freud had the habit of taking one or another piece from its place and 'examining it by sight and touch'. Another visitor, given a tour of Freud's objets d'art, remembered 'he handled them lovingly'.[16] Like the theories Freud was developing, he was on a quest for origins, for the childhood memories of his patients and for the basis of dreams, a journey that led him to explore the childhood of civilisation through its artefacts. Freud believed that the latent content of dreams, like the roots of hysteria, were linked to 'the most ancient experiences . . . reaching back to earliest childhood'.[17] Freud had grown increasingly confident in the originality and daring of his vision and it encouraged him to rely on his own taste, to choose authentic objects, not copies, and to please himself, and not Fliess or anyone else.

The first originals Freud mentions acquiring are Egyptian. He must have also quickly realised, given the flood of Egyptian artefacts into Europe, how cheaply he could buy them, as long as he chose relatively small things. Not only did the scale mean he could cram his rooms at Berggasse 19, it was also a question of economy. Each day between three and four P.M., Freud saw patients without appointments, and he determined that his budget for antiquities would come from these consultancies. Later, any royalties from his publications were dedicated to the same purpose.[18] The smallness of the works gave the added benefit of easy transportation. Dreams – short visual episodes – are also compact in size. Working on *The Interpretation of Dreams* at Berchtesgaden indicated to Freud how important the gods' company was to his work process. It meant the private realm of Freud's study was duplicated when he worked elsewhere.

It seems that Freud took care of the packing himself. Servants who dropped fragile articles and 'so destroyed them' were motivated by obscure, aggressive impulses. 'Nothing is more foreign to uneducated people than an appreciation of art and works of art', was Freud's opinion. Servants were dominated by 'mute hostility' towards art, especially when the objects 'whose value they do not understand' meant work for them.[19] Paula Fichtl, who began working for the family in 1929, mellowed such reservations and Freud trusted her to dust and move the antiquities. When travelling to Italy, he comforted himself from their absence by buying more.

By 1900, Freud's downstairs study at Berggasse 19 was filling up. In *The Psychopathology of Everyday Life*, published in 1901, he describes the shortage of space in his study forcing him 'to handle a number of pottery and stone antiquities (of which I have a small collection) in the most uncomfortable positions'. It unnerved his visitors who 'expressed anxiety that I should knock something down and break it'. Proudly, Freud remarked, 'That however has never happened.' His desk was decorated, as it would be forever after, with 'a ring of bronze statuettes and terra cotta figures'.[20]

Aside from these comments, few specifics about the collection's growth are known. A catalogue he made during the First World War has been lost and, aside from a handful of comments to Fliess and cryptic jottings in a late diary, Freud provides scant clues to the dates or descriptions of his purchases.[21] What his late diary does reveal, however, is that he bought, on average, one item a week. As he seems to have begun collecting seriously around 1898, that would add up to just over two thousand objects for the period until his death in 1939. The remaining items in the collection number around 2500.

While writing *The Interpretation of Dreams*, Freud created his 'foundation' collection, and his choices – Egyptian, Etruscan and Roman – indicate its future scope. What happened to those initial purchases? It is impossible to guess the identity of the 'good Egyptian antiquities' or the Roman statuette that resembled an old child. The head of Janus is no longer in the collection. The funerary urn was given away. Freud was an exuberant gift-giver, offering choice examples from his collection to close friends such as Ernest Jones and to family members. As his taste was developing, Freud may have been dissatisfied with early acquisitions and dispensed with them or exchanged them for others. But he did find 'replace-ments' for both the head of Janus and the Etruscan urn.

Freud regretted the loss of the urn and it triggered a dream. One night, he fell asleep feeling thirsty and, rather than waking to get a glass of water, he dreamt Martha gave him a drink from the Etruscan urn. He reflected that 'the introduction of the cinerary urn was probably yet another wish-fulfillment. I was sorry that the vase was no longer in my possession.'²² The Etruscans, Italy's early inhabitants whose civilisation was around 700–1000 B.C., cremated their dead, then interred the ashes in sculpted stone or terracotta urns that were placed along the ledges of the family vaults. The deceased was usually portrayed on the urn's lid, semi-recumbent in the classical position of a banqueter. The rest of the urn was decorated with mythological scenes or scenes related to the afterworld, often with a distinctly festive atmosphere, and brightly painted. A great quantity of such urns was produced and Freud could have purchased his either at Orvieto or Perugia, Etruscan centres he visited in 1897. Like the

Egyptians, the Etruscans spared no expense in the construction or decoration of tombs and the wealthy, at least, decamped for the afterlife in great style, taking with them their hunting gear, favourite wine, jewels and pictures. Still mourning his father, Freud may have been attracted to the Etruscans' capacity to transform melancholy events into objects of beauty and joy.

Memories of death and Orvieto were linked and the trip to Orvieto inspired another, more disturbing dream. Freud and Alexander had visited the town's major attraction, the necropolis of Crocefisso del Tufo, dating from the sixth to eighth century B.C., its 'streets' of tombs laid out in regular grid patterns. Freud commemorated the visit by buying a photograph of it.[23] Following Riccardo Mancini's discovery of the necropolis in 1874, the tombs' remains, including pottery, bronzes and weapons, were put on view in the local museum where Freud could have seen them. In *The Interpretation of Dreams* he described a dream in which the lower part of his body was being dissected and at the point when he 'really became frightened' he saw two adult men lying on wooden benches along the walls of a hut. He believed the wooden hut represented 'a coffin, that is to say, the grave', and it made him recall that he had 'already been in a grave . . . an excavated Etruscan grave near Orvieto, a narrow chamber with two stone benches along its walls, on which the skeletons of two adult men were lying'. The interior of the wooden hut in the dream, Freud felt, looked exactly like the necropolis. His admiration for the Etruscans led him to read the dream's message to be: 'If you must rest in a grave, let it be the Etruscan one,' transforming 'the gloomiest of expectations into one that was highly desirable.'[24]

Freud's 'substitute' for the loss of his Etruscan urn was a Roman glass urn from around 50–150 A.D. (pl. 13) containing cremated bones. The Romans were mad about glass. After the discovery of glass-blowing during the first century B.C., probably in Syria, glass vessels became common throughout the empire: the rich ate from glass as well as drinking wine from it. Glass was used for storing food, perfumes and medicine, as well as crafting jewellery and vases. Elaborate Roman funerary rites also included glass vessels. After the cremation of a person of rank, the ashes were cooled with wine, water or milk, then dried with a linen cloth before being placed in a jar such as Freud's. Sometimes roses and aromatic plants were added. Later the urn was deposited in a niche in a family tomb.[25] Freud had several examples of Roman glass including a brilliantly iridescent bottle.[26]

This funerary urn, a strange and lovely object made of greenish-gold, free-blown glass, is sturdy and round-bodied with a wide, flattened lip. Originally a storage jar, it may once have had a cover, also of glass. Bones half-fill its interior (the ashes have long since disintegrated) and odours of death, dust and decay remain pungent. To look within is to observe life's shattered, fragile and very human remains, a touching memento mori from the ancient world.

Freud's choice might seem ghoulish but collecting such items provided the 'highly desirable' example chosen for Freud by his family after he died. Following his cremation at Golders Green cemetery in London in 1939, his ashes were placed in a sumptuous red-figured Greek urn from around the fourth century B.C. (pl. 43), a gift from Princess Marie Bonaparte, which was mounted on a black marble base, designed by Freud's son Ernst. Usually the urn stood in Freud's study. When Martha died, her ashes joined Freud's there. The scene on the vase shows Dionysus and a maenad. Dionysus was a complex Greek deity who was not only the god of wine, revelry and orgiastic excess but who also had the power to bring the dead back to life. Dionysus is perhaps best understood as the god of the irrepressible and regenerative life-force. On the vase, Freud's funeral urn, the seated Dionysus holds his symbols – the phallic *thyrsus*, a fennel stick surmounted with pine cones and wreathed with ivy, and a *cantharus* or drinking vessel – while the maenad, a priestess of the god, offers him a libation.

Freud's statue of Janus, 'who looks at me with his two faces in a very superior manner', bought in 1899, has also disappeared from the collection. Janus, the Roman god of doorways and protector of the home, looked two ways at once to guard the home's interior and exterior. He was also the deity of beginnings, the promoter of all initiatives, a great 'father' and solar god, who was placed at the head of all human enterprises. January, the first month of the year, is named after him. In the Roman Forum the gates of Janus' temple were open in times of war and closed in times of peace. Perhaps Freud regarded Janus as auspicious for his own enterprise: the pioneering work of *The Interpretation of Dreams*.

Freud had a two-headed Etruscan bronze vase (pl. 14) that he arranged on the edge of his desk, so one face looked towards him and the other towards the room where he saw his patients. The tiny *Balsamarium*, a container for perfumed oil or ointments from the third century B.C., is another tomb item and its design, using the faces of a maenad and a satyr, was a popular one.[27]

Maenads and satyrs were both members of Dionysus' retinue. The dark-skinned satyrs, part-man, part-goat with cloven hooves and horns, terrified shepherds as they chased nymphs across the landscape. Maenads, the priestesses of Dionysus, could be equally intimidating as they caroused in ecstatic abandon, loudly playing drums and flutes or tearing live animals to pieces and devouring their flesh. In *The Bacchae*, Euripides described 'the whirling Maenads' who leapt 'up the valley, along by the stream, over the rocks ... possessed with the very breath of the god'. They were not averse to rending limb from limb the occasional male, such as Orpheus, who strayed onto their path. Maenads intersect with myth and reality. Women who worshipped Dionysus in ancient Greece periodically quit home and family to participate in all-female rituals that honoured the god. These seem to have involved frenzied dancing, leading to trance and ecstasy (*ekstasis*: standing outside oneself), sometimes assisted by copious quantities of wine. As mythical beings, maenads were assigned supernatural powers, suckling wild animals and, bedecked in panther skins, fighting in Dionysus' army.[28] Such stories provide images of women who shed conventional roles and become holy, powerful and dangerous.

Freud's maenad faces him, while the grinning satyr looks in the opposite direction. Her expression is still, her gaze fixed and wide-eyed, her lips slightly parted. She appears to be in a trance; in contrast her companion is earthy, cheeky and ugly, the counterpoint to the maenad's lovely otherworldliness. Despite their antics, the maenads usually remained chaste, unlike the priapic satyrs. Freud, a dualistic thinker, charted the divisions between Eros and the death wish, the life and death drives basic to humanity. In *Three Essays on the Theory of Sexuality*, published in 1905, he also explored the controversial notions that young children have sexual feelings and that everyone is fundamentally bisexual. Freud wrote that 'in human beings pure masculinity or femininity is not to be found in either a psychological or a biological sense. Every individual on the contrary displays a mixture of the character-traits belonging to his own and to the opposite sex.'[29]

The *Balsamarium* depicts such a fusion with male and female literally roped together by the headdress worn by both maenad and satyr. While the female face is the better realised of the two, each is dependent on the other: the woman's ecstatic, spiritual gaze and the libidinous male's alert, mischievous look. Freud believed that libido is 'invariably and necessarily of a masculine nature, whether it occurs in men or in women and irrespectively of whether its object is a man or a woman'.[30] By turning the maenad towards him, Freud determined that the little bronze functioned like the head of Janus, protecting different areas: the satyr the 'external' zone where patients underwent analysis, and the maenad the inner sanctum where Freud wrote. Between them they create a deity of thresholds, a god of margins who symbolises Freud's proposition that there is a border where masculine and feminine meet and merge.

Discovering the antique, Freud found strong male personalities with whom to identify: the early archaeologists and art historians who expanded his knowledge and infused his search with the sense of personal destiny so necessary for his early endeavours. Heinrich Schliemann was just the sort of multi-faceted man Freud admired, a man who, like Freud's childhood heroes Hannibal and Napoleon, was imbued with an over-abundance of imagination, daring, energy and skill. Freud also admired the more refined talents of Johann Joachim Winckelmann and Jacob Burckhardt, especially as his collection expanded to include Greek and more Roman art.

If there were one person responsible for fostering the nineteenth-century western world's fascination with archaeology and transforming it into a popular science, it was Schliemann. An amateur archaeologist, as well as a braggart and a bluffer, Schliemann made several fortunes trading in cotton, gold, indigo and tea, as well as speculating on the Crimean War, before turning his talents to archaeology in 1868. As he told it in *Ilios*,

> the work of my later life has been the natural consequence of the impressions I received in my earliest childhood: and that, so to say, the pickaxe and spade for the excavation of Troy and the royal tombs of Mycenae were both forged and sharpened in the little German village in which I passed eight years of my earliest childhood . . . the great projects I formed when I was a poor little boy.[31]

Freud gave himself *Ilios* as a present and 'greatly enjoyed the account of [Schliemann's] childhood' as it dovetailed perfectly with Freud's theories. 'The man was happy when he found Priam's treasure, because happiness comes only with the fulfillment of a childhood wish.'[32] Little did Freud know that Schliemann's tale about his boyhood yearning to find Troy was an invention, a dramatic embellishment designed to make an heroic epic of his life. Schliemann was a relentless self-promoter, touchy, eccentric, ruthless and unwilling to allow worthy assistants, such as his wife Sophia, to share the spotlight with him, but he was truthful and correct about one thing: on the basis of Homer's *Iliad*, he discovered Troy.

In 1870, Schliemann began his first campaign at the hill of Hissarlik, in western Turkey not far from the Dardanelles. Scholarly opinion, if it even deemed the existence of Troy, put it beneath another nearby hill. But Schliemann was convinced and his approach was characteristically bold: he dug as hard, fast and deep as he could to reach the lower layers. Ironically, his great trenches resulted in the irretrievable loss of large portions of the higher levels, which scholars were later to identify as Troy. Schliemann's first dig was illegal but he was able to gain the necessary permits and returned to Hissarlik. In 1873 he literally struck gold. 'Priam's Treasure', so named after the Trojan king, included two magnificent headdresses, together with solid gold goblets and a mass of silver objects. Schliemann breathlessly described how he 'cut out the Treasure with a large knife', an action which required 'great risk' but 'the sight of so many objects, every one of which is an inestimable value to archaeology, made me reckless, and I never thought of any danger'.[33] As a result, Schliemann found himself an instant celebrity. 'All of a sudden Troy and its ingenious discoverer were a conversation topic in all the civilised centres of the world.'[34]

Schliemann may not have been the most painstaking archaeologist but he certainly was one of the luckiest. In 1876, on a break from Troy, he excavated the ancient, fabled site of Mycenae in Greece. According to Homer, the Myceneans, led by their king Agamemnon, had vanquished Troy. Once again, Schliemann had faith in the poet rather than the pundits. Within a short time, he had uncovered five graves filled with gold, including the gold funerary mask known as 'Schliemann's Agamemnon', now in the National Archaeological Museum, Athens.[35] He not only found more treasure, he had discovered a previously unknown civilisation. Freud read Schliemann's account of the dig and acquired an elegant, orange-glazed *Stirrup Jar*, laced with abstract patterns, similar to the kind Schliemann found at Mycenae.[36]

In 1900, Schliemann's endeavours prompted Arthur Evans to dig up Knossos in Crete, exposing another and even more mysterious civilisation, the Minoans. Freud asked Fliess: 'Have you read that the English excavated an old palace in Crete (Knossos), which they declare to be the real labyrinth of Minos? Zeus seems originally to have been a bull . . . This is cause for all sorts of thoughts too premature to write down.'[37] Freud did eventually comment on Evans and Crete in one of his final works, *Moses and Monotheism*. Evans believed an earthquake had destroyed Minoan civilisation, and Freud speculated that the decline of the Cretan mother-goddess and the rise in popularity of male deities such as Zeus was due to the goddess' inability to protect the people from catastrophe.[38] Freud longed to visit the island, telling his translator Joan Riviere in 1931, 'How I regret that it is impossible for me to take the short trip to Crete!'[39]

Freud grew up in an era of spectacular archaeological discoveries. In 1860 Giuseppe Fiorelli excavated Pompeii, in 1873 Alexander Conze was commissioned by the Austrian government to work on Samothrace and the eminent German archaeologist Ernst Curtius excavated Olympia in 1875. But none had quite the impact of Schliemann's Troy. Schliemann appealed to Freud because he cast himself in a crusading role as an isolated, embattled figure, derided by his colleagues, though he believed he had solved the greatest riddle in history.

The epigraph in *The Interpretation of Dreams* also has a connection with Troy. In 1896, Freud compiled a list of stirring quotations to grace his forthcoming books. He chose two from classical writers and two from Goethe. For the opening page of *The Aetiology of Hysteria*, published the same year, he thought of Aristotle's words, '*Introite et hic dii sunt*' ('Enter – for here too are gods'), and for a chapter of the same work, a quotation from Virgil's *Aeneid*,

'*Flectere si nequeo superos Acheronta movebo*': 'If I cannot bend the higher powers, I will move the infernal regions'.[40] As it turned out, he used only one – the latter for the opening page of *The Interpretation of Dreams*. The words are a curse by the Roman goddess Juno who, having bedevilled the hero Aeneas after he escaped from the siege of Troy, is furious to find him settling at Latium, at the mouth of the Tiber, the future settlement of Rome. Juno decides to make more trouble and, realising her own powers are not adequate to the task, swoops to the underworld where she summons one of the Furies, Allecto, 'the creatress of grief . . . the Daughter of the Dark', with a cluster of black snakes sprouting from her head, and sets her loose to wreak havoc.[41]

In 1899 Freud could not bend the higher powers – the forces of professional neglect and disdain that had so far greeted his endeavours in Vienna – but he could reach down into the unconscious, the realm of dreams, of prehistoric childhood thought and memory, where sexual energies swirled, and release them into the world. Juno's frustration finds a parallel with Freud's: he, too, was aware of the disruption and distaste his ideas would provoke. But, like Schliemann, he had every faith in his final triumph. Though Freud did not use the motto 'Enter – for here too are gods', it serves as a fine epigraph for the rooms in which his growing collection was housed.

Freud had another guide to classical art and archaeology, this time closer to home. Emmanuel Löwy was a schoolfriend who, in 1889, had become a professor of archaeology at the University of Rome, where he taught courses on Mycenea and archaic Greece. When Löwy made his annual visit to Vienna to see his family, he and Freud had stimulating discussions about ancient civilisations, and about Freud's collection, that could last until three in the morning. Freud found Löwy 'a scholar as solid as he is honest and a decent human being'.[42]

Löwy's powers of inspiration were considerable. Attending his lectures in Rome in 1896 convinced Gisela Maria Richter to study classical art. She became a distinguished scholar and curator in Greek and Roman art at New York's Metropolitan Museum. When Löwy returned to Vienna in 1915, he became a mentor to the influential art historian Ernst Gombrich, later the director of London's Warburg Institute. Ernst Kris, another student of Löwy's, was not only an authority on Renaissance gold work and engraved gems and a curator at the Kunsthistorisches Museum but he later trained as a psychoanalyst and was co-editor of the psychoanalytic monthly *Imago*. Kris, too, was an admirer of Freud's collection and assisted him with purchases. Was Löwy the dinner guest at Berggasse 19 remembered by Martin Freud, the man 'whose life was devoted to the study of the Ancients and their world', who began to recite *The Iliad* 'so magnificently', indeed 'endlessly ... becoming more inspired every minute, and shouting louder and louder until, carried away by the beauty of the ancient poem, he showed signs of deep emotion' and 'a tear trickled down his beard'?[43] At that moment, Martin, about to burst out laughing, was gently but effectively silenced by a look from his father.

Löwy's major work, *The Rendering of Nature in Early Greek Art*, published the same year as *The Interpretation of Dreams*, reveals the 'scientific' formalism that came to dominate the Vienna School of Art History. Löwy gave Freud a signed copy. It may have been Freud's influence that led Löwy to pursue a psychological approach, penetrating 'beyond the actual phenomena of art to the causes which give them rise'. Löwy describes the 'memory pictures' of the 'primitive imagination' as having a resistance to depth with the result that form in archaic Greek art could be 'nothing but flat'.[44] Gombrich hailed his former teacher as 'one of those nineteenth century optimists', a bold mind whose theories about archaic Greek art stressed the priority of conceptual methods.[45] But Löwy's approach is schematic and reductionist, a fault in Freud's thinking too. Freud went to Greece but it took him until 1904, and then the trip was only by chance. Until that time he had to be satisfied chatting with Löwy and 'reading Greek archaeology and revelling in journeys I shall never make and treasures I shall never possess'.[46]

The two remained firm friends. In a home movie from 1931, narrated by Anna Freud, Löwy and Freud, two dapper old men, are seen chatting in the garden of Freud's summer house at Poetzleinsdorf, near Vienna. Freud seems to be doing most of the talking and uses his hands expressively. Anna comments the scene was 'most natural' because the two did not know they were being filmed and that Löwy was an 'especially nice, lovable man'.[47]

Travelling and collecting were dual activities for Freud, the one stimulating the other. *The Interpretation of Dreams* is a map of Freud's travels, especially the recent journeys to Italy. Even the book's structure used travel as a metaphor, Freud explaining to Fliess that in the early sections 'The whole thing is planned on the model of an imaginary walk. At the beginning, the dark forest of authors (who do not see the trees), hopelessly lost on the wrong tracks. Then a concealed pass through which I lead the reader ... and then suddenly the high ground and the view and the question: which way do you wish to go now?'[48] Then Freud, the tour guide, announces, 'We find ourselves in the full daylight of a sudden discovery.'[49]

Verona, Siena, Perugia, Orvieto, Padua, Ravenna, Venice and the Adriatic are all fondly recalled, glowingly described and incorporated into the book as the potent landscapes and localities of Freud's dreams. Italy pervaded Freud's thoughts and on days when his patients exhausted him he 'longed to be away from all this grubbing about in human dirt and . . . visit the beauties of Italy . . . That lovely country.'[50]

Freud's dream 'A Castle by the Sea' is packed with references to Italy: a trip to Aquileia with Alexander at Easter 1898, a 'magically beautiful day' on the blue lagoon at Venice with Martha the year before and a visit to an Etruscan museum. In the dream, Freud is standing with his brother in a castle by the sea and fearfully watching the arrival of enemy warships. The governor of the castle suddenly dies, leaving in charge Freud, who feels responsible for the governor's death. Though Freud's dream contained 'the most cheerful recollections' of Italy, it actually concealed 'the gloomiest thoughts of an unknown and uncanny future': anxieties about his health, his death and the fate of his family.[51] The dream work, condensing several different but similar memories, was rather like the way Freud arranged objects of the same type together.

If Freud was intrigued by a particular object, he would buy plenty. For example, when Freud was in Aquileia, he visited the local museum with its 'inexhaustible wealth of Roman finds: tombstones, amphorae, medallions of gods from the local amphitheatre, statues, bronzes, and jewellery'. He was also struck by 'several priapic statues', including Priapus as an old man and 'a priapic stone ornament of the penis as a winged animal, which has a small penis in the natural place, while the wings themselves end in a penis'. Freud collected around twenty little phalluses, one winged, mostly Roman but also Egyptian, Etruscan and Japanese (pl. 15). Though similar items were on display in the Kunsthistorisches Museum, it seemed Freud's travels supplied him with a more direct incentive to collect. Though Freud believed 'Priapus stood for permanent erection, a wish fulfillment representing the opposite of psychological impotence', the god also signified good luck.[52] To the Romans, Priapus was a protective fertility god and they placed statues of him in their gardens, as well as in their fields as scarecrows. The original role of the little phalluses Freud collected were not so much erotic pleasure but portable talismans, offering magical protection from evil. As a symbol of good fortune and male power, the phallus had been worshipped since neolithic times. Freud was critical of conservative contemporary mores that designated the genitals as 'objects of shame . . . and even disgust', while in earlier civilisations 'they were the pride and hope of living beings; they were worshipped as gods'. It made him reflect that in 'the course of cultural development so much of the divine and sacred was ultimately extracted from sexuality that the exhausted remnant fell into contempt'.[53]

Freud also amassed quantities of Roman oil lamps and Etruscan mirrors. One reason was that 'clay lamps are very appropriate as gifts' and Freud enjoyed giving presents.[54] Robert Lustig visited Berggasse to bargain over a magnificent Egyptian mummy case (c.600 B.C.) made of gilded cartonnage that Freud wanted but felt he could not afford. He was taken by its 'nice Jewish face' and offered Lustig a sum of money plus the choice of some works from his collection.[55] When Freud opened a drawer filled with Etruscan mirrors, Lustig was so overwhelmed by their numbers he did not stop to examine them but just 'took the top layer' and left.[56] Because such items were cheap and plentiful, Freud may have collected them for their intrinsic charm and as bargaining chips for more expensive purchases.

Freud's *Engraved Mirror* (pl. 16), from the late fourth to early third century B.C., with its delicately incised and graceful figures, is typical of the many thousands produced for the toilettes of Etruscan women. In his 'Castle by the Sea' dream, Freud recounts how Etruscan toilettes (toilet sets) intrigued him when visiting Etruscan museums in towns such as Orvieto. He jokingly remarked it would be a good idea to take one home 'for the lady of the house', Martha.[57] There is no record that Freud gave Martha antiquities. In his dream, the black pottery toilet set becomes a reference to death. In life, the *Engraved Mirror* is another gift Freud gave, not to Martha, but to himself, another souvenir of his 'most cheerful' Italian travels. As Susan Stewart notes, 'souvenirs are magical objects' because they 'envelop the present with the past'.[58]

Though *The Interpretation of Dreams* radically redefined the tasks and the symbols of dreaming for the modern mind, in the book's final, poetic paragraph, Freud connects the past with the present in a way that is typically dynamic and deterministic.

Nevertheless the ancient belief that dreams foretell the future is not wholly devoid of truth. By picturing our wishes as fulfilled, dreams are after all leading us into the future. But this future, which the dreamer pictures as the present, has been moulded by his indestructible wish into a perfect likeness of the past.[59]

After pouring his hopes and energies into the book, Freud was shattered by its poor reviews and sales. By March 1900, Freud had noted 'not a leaf has stirred to reveal that *The Interpretation of Dreams* has had any impact on anyone'.[60] The reviews were largely unfavourable and few copies sold. The stir and outcry he expected, the unleashed powers of the underworld, did not eventuate. At least, not immediately. Freud confided to Fliess that he underwent 'a deep inner crisis', a 'catastrophic collapse' during which he felt 'deeply impoverished, I have had to demolish all my castles in the air, and I am just now mustering enough courage to start rebuilding them again'.[61] He distracted himself with 'chess, art history, and prehistory' and by May, when spring was in the air, came the plaint, 'If only I had money or a travel companion for Italy!'[62]

7

Roman Holiday

*Even to myself, I hardly dared admit where I was going and all the way I was
still afraid I might be dreaming; it was not until I had crossed through the Porta
del Popolo that I was certain it was true, that I really was in Rome.*

GOETHE, ITALIAN JOURNEY[1]

FREUD DREAMED OF ROME. In letters to Fliess, he canvassed his
desire to visit the city, admitting his longing was 'deeply neurotic',
connected as it was with 'my high school hero worship of the
Semitic Hannibal'.[2] In 1897, Freud got as far as Lake Trasimene,
the place where Hannibal had retreated from his attack on Rome,
and then returned to Vienna. Not only did Freud chronicle his
dreams about Rome in *The Interpretation of Dreams* but, suffering
from a block while writing the book, amused himself by studying
maps of the city.

In 1901, Freud finally conquered the cluster of reservations and anxieties that had prevented the journey and Rome became his favourite city, one that he visited seven times. He wanted to live there and, as late as 1938, when flight from Vienna was imminent, he was still considering such a move. Rome offered Freud the authentic grandeur Vienna could never provide: the remains of a great civilisation that appeared literally before his eyes. Rome affirmed his belief, and the driving metaphor of psychoanalysis, that the past could be unearthed. No matter how ancient or repressed, it could arise and change the present, and that old and new, past and present, could inform one another and co-exist. Rome was also a sensual place, offering pleasures for the aesthete and the collector, and Freud luxuriated in its charms.

September 1901 was an excellent time to visit Rome. After an intensive three-year programme, Giacomo Boni had judiciously excavated much of the Forum, as well as making startling discoveries in its precincts, including the Black Stone, a monument meant to mark the tomb of Romulus, Rome's mythical first king. Above the Forum, the Palatine Hill had also been restored and nearly all of it was open to the public. It became a special place for Freud where he liked to stroll in the evening 'in the heavenly weather . . . among the ruins'.[3]

The Forum, once the political and spiritual centre of ancient Rome and the empire, had been in a state of disrepair for centuries, provoking Byron's exclamation, 'Chaos of ruins!' Rodolfo Lanciani, who had also done excavations there, put it more bluntly: 'There is no edifice in Rome from the fifteenth century the erection of which did not simultaneously carry with it the destruction or the mutilation of some ancient structures.'[4] The Forum had become a cow paddock and the Palatine, where the Roman emperors had lived, was planted with cabbages. At the entrance to the Forum, the magnificent arch of Septimus Severus was half buried and sprouting weeds. Boni changed all that. He was also a man of taste and, as Michael Grant points out, it was his idea to plant the wisterias, roses, laurels and oleanders that make the Forum such an enchanted place today.[5]

Boni corresponded with John Ruskin and agreed with the latter's conservationist concerns. Opposed to the overzealous restoration of monuments, Boni's plan was to turn the Forum into a kind of archaeological park, thus preserving it as an historic district in the centre of the city. Freud could have watched Boni's remarkable digs taking place. Tourists were well catered for. In Henry James' *Portrait of a Lady*, Isabel Archer and her friends avail themselves of the services of 'one of the humble archaeologists who hover about' the Forum inviting them to see 'the process of digging on view'.[6] To keep abreast of developments, Freud read a glowing account of Boni's work as well as Lanciani's record of the destruction of Roman monuments and Umberto Leoni's equally impassioned concerns about the Palatine.[7] In Rome, archaeology was a living thing.

Freud bought an engraving of the Forum by prolific Viennese printmaker Luigi Kasimir which he hung in a well-lit corner of his consulting room. *Forum Romanum* (c.1923), created more than two decades after Freud's first visit, indicates how Rome's ruins continued to fascinate him.[8] Looking from the Capitoline Hill, the Colosseum is seen in the distance, nearer are the remains of the Temple of Castor and Pollux and, immediately to the left, the Temple of Saturn. The contemplation of ruins evokes nostalgia and melancholy. Kasimir's brooding, monochromatic study of the Forum's shattered remains also shows how much imagination and historical knowledge were needed by the visitor to mentally 'rebuild' the site and appreciate it.

In 1930, Freud was still rebuilding Rome. In *Civilization and its Discontents*, he asks the reader to take a flight of imagination and 'suppose that Rome is not a human habitation but a psychical entity with a similarly long and copious past'. Freud conjures a spatial history of Rome, where 'the palaces of the Caesars . . . would still be rising to their old height on the Palatine' and on the piazza of the Pantheon 'we should not only find the Pantheon of today, as bequeathed to us by Hadrian, but, on the same site, the original edifice erected by Agrippa'. In Freud's healing fantasy, all that is lost has been restored, and he draws the analogy 'that in mental life nothing which has once been formed can perish'.[9]

That first visit was 'a high point of my life', Freud told Fliess, providing the opportunity to be 'totally and undisturbedly absorbed in antiquity'. But it was also tinged with regret, Freud reflecting if 'one has waited too long . . . such fulfillments are . . . slightly diminished'. For Freud, the good pagan, it was also a profoundly emotional experience. 'I could have worshipped the abased and mutilated remnant of the Temple of Minerva,' he declared. But he was less enthusiastic about medieval, Christian Rome: 'the atmosphere troubled me'.[10]

Perhaps one reason was because Minerva's temple had been wrecked by Christian Rome. The little temple, built in 97 A.D. across from the Forum, was destroyed in the seventeenth century by Pope Paul V, who used its marble to build a fountain. Freud saw what remained of it: the statue of Minerva set high into a wall above a frieze of women — representing the arts and weaving, activities specially protected by the goddess, buttressed by two battered Corinthian columns. Minerva, the Roman equivalent of Athena, is a goddess of war, wisdom and the arts. She wears a helmet, like the statue of *Athena* Freud kept on his desk.

Freud's aversion to Christian Rome did not stop him visiting its splendours. On the first morning he set off at 7.30 for St Peter's and the Vatican museums where he admired the Sistine Chapel and Raphael's Stanze frescoes. Then he tossed a coin in the Trevi fountain and stuck his hand into the Bocca della Verità, the mouth of truth. According to popular legend, anyone throwing a coin in the fountain would return to Rome and those who put their right hand into the Bocca, an ancient drain, while telling a lie would have it bitten off. 'A superfluous gesture for a man of such integrity,' sniffed biographer Ernest Jones.[11] But Freud revelled in being a tourist. In the following days, he went to San Pietro in Vincoli where he discovered Michelangelo's *Moses*, as well as to the Pantheon, the Borghese Gardens (rather like the Prater, Freud observed) with its magnificent museum and the Museo Nazionale, one of the most important archaeological museums in the world. Then Freud returned to the Vatican museums where he was impressed by the Hellenistic sculpture *Laocoön* with its frenzied, writhing forms, and the *Apollo Belvedere*, a Roman copy of a Greek original, regarded at the time as sculpture's highest achievement.

Rome also offered Egyptian treasures. Outside Freud's hotel in Piazza Montecitorio stood an Egyptian obelisk over twenty metres high. Dating from the sixth century B.C., it was hauled to Rome by Augustus, who incorporated it within an ingenious giant sundial. The piazza itself was home to the Italian parliament, the enormous building designed by Bernini. Freud stayed at the Hotel Milano, a gracious former palace, in the part of Rome locals regarded as its centre. In the adjacent square, Piazza Colonna, Freud sometimes spent balmy evenings, sitting 'spellbound' watching lantern shows with the locals. At one end was a column erected in 180 A.D. to commemorate the victories of Marcus Aurelius in Armenia, Persia and Germany. Next to the column was a fountain Freud regarded as 'beautiful'. So were the Roman women, who 'strangely enough, are beautiful even when they are ugly, and not many of them are that'.[12] Thrilled by its antiquity, art and atmosphere, enraptured by the 'glorious light everywhere', Freud felt he was living 'like a god'. Standing in front of the Pantheon, he mused, 'So this is what I have been afraid of for years!'[13]

Dissecting his fears about Rome in *The Interpretation of Dreams*, Freud creates a narrative that combines dreams, travel, art, history and his Jewishness, and reaches its conclusion in childhood, where Freud presents himself at play among cherished objects. It is also a touching self-portrait of a vulnerable, questing man. Freud starts with an excuse: 'At the season of the year when it is possible for me to travel, residence in Rome must be avoided for reasons of health.' Then he describes how, in a patient's sitting room, he sees an engraving of Ponte Sant' Angelo, one of Rome's most beautiful bridges which is decked with statues of angels. He dreams he is looking out of a railway carriage at the same spot thinking, 'I had not so much as even set foot in the city.' Next he dreams he sees Rome clearly from afar, noting 'the theme of "the promised land"'. Then he dreams he visits Rome but is disappointed at the look of the place and, in the last dream, he is disconcerted to find German posters at a Roman street corner.

The dreams were troubling but it was travel that offered the insight. A journey to Italy that took Freud past Lake Trasimene made him realise 'that finally – after having seen the Tiber and sadly turned back when I was only fifty miles from Rome – I discovered the way in which my longing for the eternal city had been reinforced by the impressions of my youth . . . I had actually been following in Hannibal's footsteps.'[14]

As a child, Freud's hero had been the brilliant Carthaginian military leader who made war on Rome. Following an incident when his father had failed to retaliate against a belligerent Czech who humiliated him in the streets of Freiberg, Freud wished he *were* Hannibal. But Freud was recasting history. At Lake Trasimene in 217 B.C., Hannibal had vanquished the Roman army in an ambush and slaughtered about twenty thousand men. As most historians agree, rather than follow a foolhardy plan to attack Rome, Hannibal wisely replenished his exhausted troops by travelling away from the city. It was rather like Jacob's tactical retreat from his aggressor in Freiberg. But Freud decided that he – and Hannibal – had failed. Freud saw himself as a man of destiny, like Hannibal, and even his failures had to have grand parallels. Hannibal also symbolises Freud's Jewishness and their mutual powerlessness against the might of Rome: in Freud's case, the church of Rome dominated Vienna and it meant he was excluded from the city's higher echelons.

But thoughts of Hannibal led Freud to recall childhood pleasures when the activities of reading and collecting were united in play. One of the first history books that Freud read was Adolphe Thiers' *History of the Consulate and Empire of France under Napoleon*. Like most small boys, Freud collected soldiers and organised battles. After reading Thiers, he stuck labels on the backs of his wooden soldiers identifying them as Napoleon's marshals — his hero was André Masséna, who was believed to be Jewish. Labelling, identifying and assigning names were activities later practised by Freud as a collector. Interestingly, the size of his toy soldiers, easy to fit in the hand, to move and to re-arrange, determined the size of most of the objects in his collection. As Maurice Rheims suggests, 'the taste for collecting is like a game played with utter passion'.[15] Freud finishes his Roman dream analysis by observing, 'the deeper one carries the analysis of a dream, the more often one comes upon the track of experiences in childhood which have played a part among the sources of that dream's latent content'.[16] The same parallel can be drawn with Freud's drive to be a collector.

What seemed to frighten Freud about Rome was a fear of failure. He did not visit the city until he had finished *The Interpretation of Dreams*, the major work that vouchsafed his place in history's pantheon. In 1901, just before he went to Rome, *The Psychopathology of Everyday Life* was serialised in a journal.[17] Published as a book in 1904, it would prove to be Freud's most popular and accessible work. Freud wanted to be a success, not a failure as he perceived Hannibal to be. In Freud's eyes, Jacob had also failed, because he was unable to meet life's challenges. These flawed Jewish 'heroes', associated with his childhood, needed to be vanquished and placed at a remove, even if it meant recasting history. With the dream book under his belt, and two disappointing male authority figures dispatched, Freud gave himself permission to enter Rome. If Freiberg represented the paradise of childhood, the place Freud idealised but did not revisit, then Rome was a victory, won after much agonising and circumspection, a place of longing, but one validated by the tests of reality and maturity.

***

Collecting had been a Roman fashion for millennia, and the greatest sign of affection that Caesar or Agrippa could give the populace was to donate their palaces and treasures to the city. Romans thronged to art exhibitions and wealthy private collectors opened their homes to the public.[18] In 70 A.D. Roman crowds gawped in admiration at the seven-branched Menorah and other spoils captured from the sack of Jerusalem. Freud saw the spoils commemorated, the Menorah carried shoulder high, in a relief on the Arch of Titus in the Forum. Though Freud regarded Hannibal as the potent symbol for his Rome journey, a triumvirate of influential writers guided him.

Freud regarded Johann Joachim Winckelmann as 'the founder of classical archaeology'. Winckelmann was also a decisive taste-maker and art historian. His passionate appreciation of Greek art assisted the rise of neoclassicism in the eighteenth century and it was he who subjected ancient art, for the first time, to systematic categories of style. Freud wondered, 'Which of the two, it may be debated, walked up and down his study with the greater impatience after he had formed the plan of going to Rome – Winckelmann, the Vice-Principal, or Hannibal, the Commander-in-Chief?'[19]

Sculptures that Freud admired in the Vatican museums, such as *Laocoön* and the *Apollo Belvedere*, had been memorably described by Winckelmann, whose writing was influential because it was both scholarly and disarmingly effusive. In the presence of the *Apollo Belvedere*, 'this miracle of art', he wrote,

My breast seems to enlarge and swell with reverence, like the breasts of those who were filled with the spirit of prophecy, and I feel myself transported to Delos and into the Lycaean groves – places which Apollo honoured by his presence – for my image seems to receive life and motion, like the beautiful creation of Pygmalion.[20]

Winckelmann dismissed Roman art, believing 'the only way for us to become great, or if it be possible, inimitable, is to imitate the Greeks'.[21] As Winckelmann never visited Greece, it is ironic he developed his ideas from Roman copies of Greek originals, like the *Apollo Belvedere*: to love Rome, its art and monuments, means to also love copies. Winckelmann made careful studies of the excavations at Pompeii and Herculaneum. In 1902, Freud visited Pompeii and later published a study of Wilhelm Jensen's short story, *Gradiva*, set there.[22] He also collected fragments of Pompeiian frescoes which transported him 'to my longed-for Italy'.[23]

The *Apollo Belvedere* also swept Goethe 'off my feet'. Goethe arrived in Rome for a two-year stay in 1786, recorded in his diary *Italian Journey*. 'The most important monuments I take very slowly; I do nothing except look, go away, and come back and look again.'[24] But Freud had no time to follow Goethe's advice, and raced around Rome like a modern-day tourist, gorging himself. On a later visit, he viewed Gustav Eberlein's 1904 monument to Goethe, surrounded by characters from his writings, in the Borghese Gardens. Freud thought it 'quite clever but nothing wonderful. Goethe looks too youthful; after all he was over forty when he first came to Rome.' Though he considered Eberlein's rendering of Faust 'quite good', he was not impressed with the devilish Mephisto, who looked 'rather grotesque, a Jewish face with a cox's comb and horns'.[25] In 1930, Freud was honoured to win the Goethe Prize, awarded by the city of Frankfurt for creative work worthy of Goethe.[26]

Freud's most esteemed cultural historian was Jacob Burckhardt, whose *Cicerone* provided him with an excellent art guide for his Italian travels. Burckhardt also offered stimulating company while Freud wrote *The Interpretation of Dreams*: 'For relaxation, I am reading Burckhardt's *History of Greek Civilization* which is providing me with unexpected parallels'.[27] Burckhardt had not visited Greece either, but his studies led him to one clear conclusion: 'Myth is the underlying factor in Greek existence. Whenever actual history might have established itself it was thrust down and overcome by the proliferation of legend.'[28] For Freud, myth often provided the best and most potent illustrations of the individual's, and society's, deepest instinctual impulses. Like Winckelmann, Burckhardt was a vital and opinionated writer with an original mind, and he galvanised the discipline of art history. It is easy to see why Freud admired him, both for his fresh ideas about antiquity and history and for his literary style. Burckhardt's and Winckelmann's popularity was largely due to their combination of meticulous research with an accessible writing style, characteristics of Freud's enduring influence.

On his first trip to Rome, Freud could not at first quite decide what to buy. A complete collection of cheap clay vessels? No, too many transport difficulties. But gradually, as he told Martha in one of his many postcards, 'the money is disappearing and that has been accelerated by several purchases of antiquities'.[29]

The major Roman artwork in Freud's collection shows that the Romans regarded Greek culture rather as did Winckelmann and Burckhardt: as having a vocabulary of myth and storytelling superior to their own. *Fragment from the Lid of a Sarcophagus* (160–210 A.D.; pl. 17) shows a crucial event from the battle of Troy. Hector, the hero of the Trojan side, has been slain by Achilles and is being carried back to Troy by his distraught followers. After Hadrian, the emperor-architect who admired all things Greek and who revived an interest in Greek culture in the second century B.C., burial became another way to promote Greek taste and style. Freud's *Sarcophagus* is an example of the kind of elaborately decorated object wealthy Romans favoured in death. To them, commemorating a hero meant aligning the deceased with similarly noble qualities. If a Roman family could afford it, a funeral procession was virtually a parade, rather like the one shown on the *Sarcophagus*, which could include mourning women, musicians and dancers proceeding through the city streets to the Forum where a funeral oration would have been given.

The story of how Freud literally put the *Sarcophagus* back together is an example of the collector's luck and persistence. Recently, Alfred Bernhard-Walcher of the Kunsthistorisches Museum solved the puzzle.[30] The *Sarcophagus* was in two pieces, both of which surfaced on the Rome antiquities market and were brought to Vienna in the 1920s. The larger, right-hand fragment was obtained by Freud in 1930 from a woman, perhaps Princess Marie Bonaparte, who gave it to him as a gift. In the same year, Ludwig Pollak, a Viennese antiquities dealer, came across the left-hand piece, and offered it to Freud. Freud could then reassemble the frieze so that the hero's big supine form, the subject and focus, was made whole. In November 1930 Freud had the two marble fragments joined and set on a wooden base that he placed on top of bookshelves in the consulting room. However, he was unaware the scene depicted Hector's death. He thought it was an earlier episode from *The Iliad*, the murder of Patroclus, Achilles' adored friend, by the Trojans.[31]

Freud not only brought treasures back from Rome but, informed by the museums and monuments there, continued to acquire Roman antiquities when he was back in Vienna. Over time, he also got to know antiquities dealers in Rome, including Ettore Sandolo, whom he regularly visited. Oil lamps, marble bowls and busts, plus fine intaglio stones, are among the many Roman objects in his collection. On his desk Freud arranged three favourite bronzes, statuettes of *Hermes, Zeus* and *Aphrodite* (c.2nd century A.D.), near one another: the lively little figures seem to be dancing.

Not that shopping in Rome was always fun. As a veteran of several visits, Freud complained, 'The most difficult thing in Rome, where nothing is easy, is shopping.' It was also difficult to restrain his spending, though he noted that for a while at least he had been 'very modest'. Freud was pleased with the quality of several marble bowls, gifts for 'the Wednesday gentlemen', remarking, 'for once this marble is genuine and not painted', even though that made it 'somewhat more expensive'.[32]

The 'Wednesday gentlemen' were Freud's first circle of colleagues including Wilhelm Stekel, the Socialist and doctor Alfred Adler and Otto Rank, the group's secretary, a bright young intellectual interested in myth, art and literature who trained as a psychoanalyst. 'A number of young doctors gathered round me,' Freud recalled, 'with the express intention of learning, practising and spreading the knowledge of psychoanalysis.'[33] It was balm for Freud's lonely soul. The meetings, held each Wednesday evening at Freud's home from 1902, mark the end of his isolation and the nucleus of what would become the Vienna Psychoanalytic Society. The early meetings were high spirited and convivial.

In 1907, when Freud was buying the marble bowls, the group was undergoing change. Due to the growth in membership, the proliferation of papers read at the meetings and other business, Rank had been appointed as a paid secretary. From Rome, Freud wrote to the members giving them the opportunity to resign if they chose: if they wished to remain, then it was a three-year commitment. He was tactfully trying to get rid of the dead wood, members who did not attend or only irregularly, as well as those with whom differences were developing. The move makes clear Freud's pre-eminence as the group's leader, a role he would enforce with military precision in the years ahead. Perhaps it was why he was buying gifts: to soothe any ruffled feelings among the troops.

Each Wednesday, the men crammed into Freud's little waiting room, furnished for the occasion with an oblong table arrayed with coffee and cakes. Freud's children were curious about the meetings 'of great minds . . . We heard people arriving but we seldom saw them.' Martin observed that each chair at the table was equipped with an ashtray from Freud's collection, some of fine Chinese jade. Looking in later when the guests had departed, Martin realised why. 'The room was still thick with smoke and it seemed to me a wonder that human beings had been able to live in it for hours, let alone speak in it without choking.'[34] Freud had always been fond of jade and collected examples of differing quality. Hanns Sachs, a regular visitor to Berggasse 19, recalled 'the prize of beauty went to a toad in dark green jade; it became a sort of totem to all of us which had to be present on every solemn occasion'.[35] Freud wanted his collection to take both emblematic and practical roles in his working life.

Another set of gifts indicates the altered circumstances of Freud's relation to his inner circle and of the psychoanalytic movement itself. In 1913, Freud presented each of his closest colleagues with a Roman intaglio gem. The 'Committee', as it was known, was the brainchild of British psychoanalyst Ernest Jones and its members included Jones, Otto Rank, Hanns Sachs, Sándor Ferenczi, Karl Abraham and Max Eitingon (pl. 44). Bitter dissensions had arisen in the budding psychoanalytic movement. The first two breakaways were Wilhelm Stekel and Alfred Adler, followed by the young Swiss analyst Carl Jung, for whom Freud had evinced great hopes. Jones' idea was to form 'a sort of "Old Guard" around Freud', a protective group of loyal lieutenants who would rigorously uphold the central tenets of psychoanalyis, provide 'comfort' for Freud in the event of further quarrels and supply 'practical assistance', such as 'replying to criticisms' launched at him.[36] But dissension continued, leading Freud to comment that 'psychoanalysis brings out the worst in everyone'.[37] Jones, meeting Freud for the first time in 1908, recalled his 'lively and perhaps somewhat restless or even anxious manner, with quick darting eyes that gave a serious and penetrating effect'. He also 'dimly sensed some slightly feminine aspect' in Freud's 'manners and movements'. Perhaps this was why Jones developed 'a helping or even protective attitude' towards Freud rather than the filial devotion he aroused in other followers.[38]

Freud was thrilled by the idea of a 'secret council' and it took hold of his imagination 'immediately', though he recognised it had its 'boyish and perhaps romantic element'.[39] When he met the Committee in May 1913, the gifts he chose for them – engraved stones chosen from his collection – were both beautiful and binding. To Freud 'the affection of a group of courageous and understanding young men is the most precious gift that psychoanalysis has brought me'.[40] The group then had their gems mounted in gold rings.

Hanns Sachs recalled Freud himself wore a Roman ring 'since he loved to have some relic of ancient beauty about him'. Freud's ring showed a delicately carved bearded head of Jupiter, ruler of the Roman pantheon, and 'Freud never tired of examining every detail by look and touch'.[41] The Romans worshipped the god as Jupiter Optimus Maximus (all-good, all-powerful), a name that refers not only to his sovereignty over the universe but also to his function as the god of the state who distributes laws, controls the realm and makes his will known through oracles. Jupiter was also a warrior god and the archetype of the father: strong, authoritative, protective. Freud's choice was apposite: he was the father of psychoanalysis and the ruler of its destiny who did not hesitate to attack those who tried to usurp his authority.

To the Egyptians, the circle was a symbol of eternity and the exchange of rings at a marriage or to seal a betrothal came to symbolise unending commitment, a public declaration of union. By the time of Augustus, rings had an array of functions in Roman society. They were used as seals – the owner's personal signature and identification on any document – while the engraved image not only denoted the wearer's beliefs but had magical properties, conferring luck and protection. They were also an addition to the Romans' opulent sense of style. Freud wore his ring, with its green stone, on the fourth finger of his right hand, where he wore his wedding band – a Central and Eastern European Jewish custom. In a photograph of Freud and Sándor Ferenczi taken in 1917 when Ferenczi was serving in the Hungarian army, Freud's large, dark-stoned ring can be clearly seen, as can Ferenczi's ring on his left hand. Freud was still wearing his ring in London twenty years later (pl. 45).

Later Freud gave rings to other highly regarded colleagues and supporters including his daughter Anna, Princess Marie Bonaparte and Lou Andreas-Salomé. In 1928, offering a ring to psycho-analyst Ernst Simmel, Freud reflected

> Once upon a time these rings were a privilege and a mark distinguishing a group of men who were united in their devotion to psychoanalysis ... and to practice among them-selves a kind of analytical brotherhood. [Otto] Rank then broke the magic spell; his secession and [Karl] Abraham's death dissolved the Committee ... My daughter suggested I renew the old custom with you ... Forms may pass away, but their meaning can survive.[42]

For Ferenczi, Freud chose a carnelian engraved with a Dionysian scene of a dancing maenad flanked by a flute player and a big-bellied satyr.[43] Did Freud know Goethe's poem from his Persian-inspired *West Eastern Divan* that begins 'Carnelian is a talisman / It brings good luck to child and man'? The translucent reddish-brown stone (now in the Austrian National Library) was a favourite of Roman gem engravers. The Egyptians buried the carnelian alongside their dead – it was supposed to assist the soul's safe passage to the afterlife – while to the Greeks and Romans it offered luck, vitality and protection against the evil eye. Gisela Richter writes that an engraving on a Roman gem often had special relevance to its possessor.[44]

Was the image of Dionysian abandon Freud's hint to Ferenczi to be more light-hearted? Ferenczi was a charming and affec-tionate fellow, though highly strung. Freud found him very appealing, as did Freud's children, with whom he was a firm favourite. Of the Committee members, he was the closest to Freud, who occasionally called him 'my dear son'. But Freud could find

Ferenczi's emotional dependency taxing. After holidaying together in Sicily in 1910, Freud was aware Ferenczi had been

> disappointed because you probably expected to swim in constant intellectual stimulation, whereas I hate nothing more than striking up attitudes . . . As a result I was probably most of the time a quite ordinary elderly gentleman, and you in astonishment kept measuring the distance between me and your phantasy ideal . . . I often wished that you would pull yourself out of the infantile role and place yourself beside me as a companion on an equal footing, something you were unable to do.[45]

The rings were tokens of Freud's love and gratitude towards the young men who, like stalwart Roman sons, sought to protect him. His fidelity was enduring; he rarely removed his ring. In *The Psychopathology of Everyday Life*, reflecting on the ring, 'an object of such rich symbolic meaning', Freud quotes the story of a doctor and his follower. A young man attached himself to the doctor, sharing his intellectual endeavours and developing a pupil-teacher relationship, rather like the Committee did with Freud. To celebrate their friendship, the doctor presents the young man with a ring.[46] The rings also represent the principles of psychoanalysis and collecting in which dreams, memories and objects, no matter how small or fragmentary, are replete with meaning.

The Romans took their cues from Greek culture, philosophy and art, but there was one area they made their own: portraiture. Freud's marble *Head from Statue of a Man* (31 B.C.–14 A.D.) is a good example. It was probably made during the reign of Augustus who, as the first emperor, turned the Roman state into a vast, fully organised empire. Restraint and dignity mark the art of this era. Freud's *Head* shows the lined face of a mature man with thinning hair. Freud placed the *Head* on a pedestal next to his chair in the consulting room, so Freud and the Roman look towards the window and to Kasimir's print of the Forum. Intelligence and moderation distinguish the Roman's lean features. His firm jaw, set mouth and calm gaze denote the steady character of a good citizen. Probably commissioned by the man's family after his death, such private portraits were usually funerary items meant to keep alive family history. Even though the *Head* is an ancient artefact, the man's distinctive personality creates a sense of presence, providing the vital and intimate link Freud enjoyed with antiquity.

At the end of his first Roman holiday, Freud returned to Vienna a new man. 'When I came back from Rome, my enjoyment of life and work was somewhat heightened and that of my martyrdom somewhat diminished,' he announced to Fliess. It emboldened him to take steps to change his professional status. Interestingly, it was a work of art that did the trick.

For some years, Freud was after a promotion to the rank of professor. Aside from the distinction so necessary in Vienna's competitive and hierarchical society, it meant increased fees. Freud was certainly deserving but for a number of reasons, including both the confronting nature of his work and Vienna's hidebound anti-Semitism, promotion had been withheld. Nor had Freud been willing to engage in the necessary subterfuge and politicking. But, returning from Rome, he observed that his practice had 'almost melted away . . . And I did want to see Rome again, take care of my patients, and keep my children in good spirits.' He enlisted the aid of a patient, Baroness Marie von Ferstel, whose husband was a diplomat and who 'warmly took up the cause'.

At a party, Ferstel button-holed Wilhelm von Hartel, the minister for culture and education, responsible for such advancements, and offered him a bribe. Von Hartel, a supporter of Klimt and the Secession movement, was organising the Modern Gallery that opened in 1903 at the Lower Belvedere Palace. He suggested the baroness donate a work by Arnold Böcklin, the well-known Swiss symbolist painter, in the possession of her aunt. When the Böcklin was not forthcoming, Ferstel offered an alternative work by Emil Orlik. 'I believed that if a certain Böcklin had been in her possession instead of her aunt,' Freud commented, 'I would have been appointed three months earlier. As it is, His Excellency will have to be content with a modern painting.'[47]

Baroness Ferstel was not only helping Freud: she was also assisting an up and coming artist. Perhaps Freud did not know that Orlik, born in Prague and a member of the Secession, was Jewish. In the Secessionist magazine *Ver Sacrum*, Rainer Maria Rilke had praised Orlik, whose work included incisive portraits of artists and other cultural figures such as Gustav Mahler and Camille Pissarro. After a successful exhibition at Brno in 1900, Orlik was increasingly well known, especially when wealthy industrialist Max von Gomperz became his patron.[48] After a visit to Japan in 1900, Orlik's brand of modernism became charmingly decorative, though Freud, with his distaste for contemporary art, may not have approved.

Ferstel was delighted with the results of her stratagem. She burst into Freud's rooms with the cry, 'I've done it.'[49] Freud's response was more laconic. 'Public acclaim was immense,' he told Fliess. 'Congratulations and flowers are already pouring in as though the role of sexuality has suddenly been officially recognised by His

Majesty, the significance of the dream certified by the Council of Ministers, and the necessity of a psychoanalytic therapy of hysteria carried by a two thirds majority in Parliament.' But he was aware of the advantages and that he had been dilatory. 'Others are that clever without first having to go to Rome.'[50]

1901 was perhaps the only time Freud returned to Vienna light-hearted. Usually the end of his holidays was a cause for complaint. Vienna was a Roman town, as Freud knew. On evening walks, Lou Andreas-Salomé recalled that Freud

> frequently analysed Vienna, as it were: the streets under their wintry snow reminded him of the city's remotest past. One sensed how easily such a re-creation of the past came to him and one was reminded of the antique objects in his study and that the archaeologist had created the psychoanalyst in him.[51]

From the late 1870s, Vienna's chief archaeologist Friedrich von Kenner had busily published information about his Roman finds. Named Vindobona in 14 B.C. by the Romans, Vienna was the last outpost before the barbarian territories of the north. The Romans built a large fort in what is central Vienna and where today, in Michaelerplatz, excavated ruins show the walls of Roman houses. At its peak, Vindobona included around twenty thousand inhabitants and had all the luxuries Romans insisted on, even in the outposts of the empire: baths, brothels, formal gardens and running water. Marcus Aurelius arrived in 180 A.D. to battle the Teutons and died there from the plague, making Freud remark that in death the emperor 'became a Viennese'.[52] In 1913, to attend an exhibition of the latest Roman finds, Freud cancelled that night's session of the Vienna Psychoanalytic Society.[53]

Roman remains were being discovered, and plundered, throughout eastern Europe. Freud was part of the trade. In 1910 Ferenczi in Budapest alerted Freud that he had been contacted by a man from Duna Pentele offering Roman antiquities for sale. Duna Pentele, a town about sixty kilometres down the Danube from Budapest, was the site of the Roman fort of Intercisa, abandoned by the troops in the fourth century A.D. Ferenczi's informant turned out to be an unreliable and unscrupulous intermediary for local farmers, who were sacking the Roman cemetery and selling the finds for piddling amounts. Like many tomb robbers, they were poor and desperate for cash. Freud was eager to take advantage of the situation and entertained 'beautiful, fantastic hopes' about the results.[54]

In the early months of 1910, Ferenczi negotiated with his 'treasure hunter' for an array of objects, including strings of glass beads, bronze brooches and clay oil lamps and jugs.[55] Freud's *Globular Jug* (2nd–4th century A.D., Sigmund Freud Museum Vienna) is probably one of them. Ferenczi smuggled these goods to Freud in Vienna. Freud regarded the finds as 'certainly quite modest' but mused, 'it doesn't matter if it gives the old guy pleasure'. He also wondered whether Ferenczi was canny enough about the deal, telling him, 'You have to learn antiquities . . . from me.'[56]

The illegality of the situation seemed to give Freud no concern, making him typical of the collectors of his time. All over Europe, observes Maurice Rheims, 'in town and country, everything was for sale'.[57] Freud's attitude was also typical: the collector's make-up often included 'an enquiring mind; a penchant for secrecy' as well as 'a propensity for rationalisation'.[58] Freud explained to Ferenczi that he had to keep acquiring 'very beautiful things, essentially to keep me in a good mood'. When the situation in Duna Pentele proved 'vexing', Freud assuaged his frustrations by splurging on antiquities in Vienna. Some extra cash had come his way and it 'should be spent'.[59] The collector's need to acquire was relentless and like 'the mountaineer, the sportsman, and such people', he was always preoccupied with the next challenge, the next object, the next prize.[60] Freud well understood the urge. 'For I am actually not a man of science,' he told his friend Fliess, 'not an observer, not an experimenter, not a thinker. I am by temperament nothing but a conquistador – an adventurer, if you want it translated – with all the curiosity, daring, and tenacity characteristic of a man of this sort.'[61]

8

Conversations with the Sphinx

And now you are already prepared to hear that psychology too is unable to solve the riddle of femininity.

SIGMUND FREUD, NEW INTRODUCTORY LECTURES
ON PSYCHOANALYSIS[1]

Your enemy is yourself.

SOPHOCLES, KING OEDIPUS[2]

IF ROME WAS A QUEST, Athens was an accident. In 1904, Freud and Alexander were on their annual pilgrimage to Italy. After meeting in Trieste, the brothers were planning to spend a few days on the island of Corfu. But when a friend of Alexander's strongly advised against it, citing the heat, they set out for Athens instead.[3]

{ 198 }

Freud recalled the entire incident over thirty years later, giving it a dreamlike sense of destiny. The brothers were in 'remarkably depressed spirits' after receiving the advice and spent hours 'wandering about [Trieste] in a discontented and irresolute frame of mind'. But then, without discussing the problem or even consulting one another, they suddenly booked their passage for Athens. 'Such behaviour,' Freud noted, 'was most strange.' What happened on the Acropolis was stranger still. Though Freud rejoiced at being there, there was a discomfiting jolt from his unconscious: 'So all this really *does* exist, just as we learnt at school!'[4] Freud pondered this moment of 'derealization' for decades. Finally, it led him back to his father, just as the Oedipus complex did, 'the nucleus of all neuroses'. Life's governing force was 'man's relation to his father . . . the simultaneous existence of love and hate towards the same object'. In an extraordinary bid for the power of Greek myth, Freud believed 'the beginnings of religion, morals, society and art converge in the Oedipus complex', and it was he who had solved the riddle.[5]

Freud might have arrived in Athens by chance but he had been longing for it, probably encouraged by Emmanuel Löwy. In 1900, Freud was 'reading Greek archaeology and revelling in journeys I shall never make and treasures I shall never possess'.[6] In 1904 he made the most of his trip, visiting the Acropolis twice, spending the entire day there on his second visit. To celebrate the event he put on his best shirt. 'The Acropolis,' he told Martha, 'goes beyond everything we have seen and that we could have imagined.'[7]

The Parthenon, the temple to Athena the Virgin (*parthenos*), is the crowning glory of the Acropolis. As Walter Burkert reflects, 'it has come to epitomise all Greek art' and, though severely damaged, it is arguably 'the most nearly perfect building ever erected'.[8] Finished in 432 B.C., its main room housed a colossal gold and ivory statue of Athena, the city's protective deity and symbol. Despite the restrictions placed on women in classical Athens – they could not receive an education, vote, own property, conduct business or even leave their homes except under surveillance – in art and myth their place was powerful and assured.

In 1904, the city of Athens did not crowd the slopes as it does today: the Acropolis, meaning 'upper city', stood in solitary majesty on its rocky mount. What happened to Freud there? His moment of 'derealisation' bothered him for decades. Analysing it, Freud typically returned to his childhood, recalling 'the limitations and poverty' of that time and the 'passionate desire to travel and see the world' that was a result of 'dissatisfaction with home and family'. Travel expressed the wish to escape from such pressures, from the sense of restriction and responsibility that the family's straitened circumstances, and by implication his father's failure to adequately provide, aroused in Freud. Reaching the Acropolis meant experiencing as 'realities' places that 'for so long had been distant, unattainable things of desire – one feels oneself like a hero who has performed deeds of improbable greatness'.

Freud believed it was guilt that detracted from his pleasure on the Acropolis: 'it was something to do with a child's criticism of his father', with 'the son's superiority' that lurked behind the recognition that ' "We really *have* gone a long way!" '[9] Culture shock, which Freud experienced in Paris, Florence and again in Athens, was analysed by him, in the last instance, as the act of contesting and surpassing the father, all the while registering loss and dismay. Travel remained Freud's escape, not only from his own family but perhaps from all that 'family' represented, a time when he relaxed and indulged in his favourite pastimes: looking at art and buying antiquities, creating the special private realm mirrored in his study. But no matter how far from home he strayed, it seemed the father always awaited him.

On a more mundane level, Freud's journey also involved the usual tourist dilemmas: misunderstandings and missed opportunities. Though he had learned ancient Greek as a schoolboy, he could not make himself understood to the carriage drivers and was reduced to writing down the name of his hotel – the Athens, the city's best. During the boat trip over, Freud realised Wilhelm Dörpfeld, who had been Heinrich Schliemann's assistant at Troy, was a fellow passenger. After Schliemann died in 1890, Dörpfeld had continued the excavations. Freud was unable to get close enough to make his acquaintance.[10] Perhaps shyness held him back. There was a more satisfactory connection with Schliemann: in the National Archeological Musem in Athens, Freud could see the archaeologist's rich finds from the tomb at Mycenae, including the so-called mask of Agamemnon.

After three days in Athens, where Freud made 'a few small purchases, the continuation of my dealing with antiquity', the brothers continued on to Patras, to catch the boat back to Italy.[11] Stopping at Corinth, Freud could see the systematic excavations being conducted by a team from the American School of Classical Studies at Athens who were unearthing the agora of the ancient town as well as shrines, fountains, baths and other monuments, excavations that continue to this day.

What did Freud's journey inspire him to collect?

Corinth was famous for its vases. Around 700 B.C. vase painters in Corinth revitalised their wares by 'orientalising' them with wildly exuberant, curvilinear patterns. They also created a bold, black, silhouette technique. To decorate their works they borrowed from West Asia's bestiary of fabulous creatures: the Sphinx, the Siren, the Griffin and the Gorgon, as well as the fire-breathing, three-headed Chimaera, composed of a lion, a goat and a serpent's tail. In the fully developed Corinthian style that flourished until 550 B.C., the vases are crowded with figures set against backgrounds of elaborately patterned floral ornament.

Freud collected nearly a dozen Archaic period Corinthian vases. The largest and most impressive is *Corinthian Black-figured Alabastron* (c.600 B.C.; pl. 18), an oil or perfume flask, that shows a winged Mistress of Animals.[12] The Mistress of Animals was a West Asian goddess, often depicted in Minoan and Mycenean art, and assimilated into Greek art as Artemis, goddess of the hunt. A popular subject in Corinthian art, she displayed power over nature and was usually shown, as on Freud's vase, subduing wild creatures.[13] Seen in profile, the goddess holds a swan by the neck in either hand, their extended wings echoing her own. On her head, she wears a *polos*, the tall crown worn by goddesses in this period. At first, the dense, all-over patterning in red and black makes the figures difficult to decipher, like a visual puzzle, a characteristic of Corinthian vases.

Freud also had an energetic little statue of *Artemis* (2nd century B.C.; pl. 9) that comes from Myrina, the same site that delivered his *Eros* (c.150–100 B.C.).[14] *Artemis* has lost her arms and, presumably, her bow and arrows but it does not detract from her vigour and personality, emphasised by her stance and flowing robes. She is on the move and inspires others to do the same. A virgin goddess like Athena, the realm of Artemis was nature, the wilder the better, where she roamed and hunted with a band of women.[15]

West Asia was the source of another fabulous winged female who made her way into Greek art and into the heart of Freud's collection and his theories: the Sphinx. She remains a mystery. Even the origin of her name is open to conjecture.[16] The first representations of the Sphinx are male. In Egypt, the Sphinx was a wise and benevolent guardian, a valuable ally and the representative of the pharaoh. The Sphinx was kindred to the Assyrian lamassu, the winged protector of entrances, that Freud had seen in the Louvre. By the time the Sphinx arrived in archaic Greece, she was transformed into a winged female with an ecstatic smile who guarded funerary monuments. Freud could see some fine examples in Athens' National Archaeological Museum.[17] Like the Chimaera, the Sphinx was a popular subject on Corinthian vases but her role was purely decorative and she had no narrative context. In the fourth century B.C., Sophocles cast her in *Oedipus Rex* as the destructive trickster who besieged the city of Thebes. By solving her riddle, Oedipus defeated her and sealed their mutual doom.

Freud collected different images of the Sphinx, as if exploring the various meanings she offered. His free-standing, terracotta *Sphinx* (1st–2nd century A.D.) has the face and breasts of a woman, together with the lower quarters of a lion and beautifully curled wings. She wears the *polos*. *Athenian Red-figured Hydria* (c.380–360 B.C.) shows Oedipus in conversation with the Sphinx. The two face one another, he looking relaxed and making a conversational gesture, she erect and alert, seated on a rock. On another vase, *Athenian Black-figured Lekythos* (c.490–470 B.C.) the Sphinx, elegant as a cat, sits on a small column between Theban elders. In *Fragment of a Wall Painting* (1st century B.C.–1st century A.D.) the Sphinx has a decorative role, holding a spray of ivy. Freud's other Sphinxes include a tiny Egyptian amulet (716–332 B.C.), a good-luck charm like the winged phalluses, as well as Heinrich Ulbrich's engraving *Great Sphinx at Giza* (1905).

But it was the dramatic scene in which Oedipus ponders the Sphinx's riddle that was a favourite not only with Greek vase painters but of later artists such as Ingres. As well, Freud would have seen sphinxes on his daily walks through Vienna: they decorate the bases of the lanterns outside the Parliament on the Ringstrasse. Two more guard the Egyptian galleries at the Kunsthistorisches Museum and, of course, there are many more inside. In nineteenth-century decoration, the Sphinx had returned to her role as guardian of entrances.

Parentage proves nearly as troublesome for the Sphinx as it did for Oedipus. Some ancient writers regarded her as born of the monsters Echidna and Typhon, others of the dreaded Chimaera and the dog Orthrus.[18] In Sophocles' play, Oedipus describes her as 'the dog-faced witch', so the latter were probably her parents. The Sphinx alights at Thebes and positions herself either on the road into the city or on a nearby mountain and asks a riddle, prepared for her by the Muses. Each man who fails to correctly answer is promptly devoured. Why was the Sphinx terrorising Thebes? Again there are conflicting accounts. Was she sent by the gods to avenge a crime or was she merely a literary device, added for dramatic flair?[19] The scene in *Athenian Black-figured Lekythos*, in which the Sphinx sits amid Theban elders, shows the dilemma faced by the town. Before Oedipus arrived, the Thebans gathered daily in their assembly to ponder the riddle, since they could not rid themselves of the Sphinx until they had answered it.[20]

Meeting the Sphinx, Oedipus may have felt he had nothing to lose. Raised as the son of the king of Corinth, Oedipus had recently heard a prophecy that he would kill his father and marry his mother. He fled his home to escape his fate and, on the road to Thebes, had an altercation that resulted in the death of several men, including an older man in a carriage. Following the incident, Oedipus confronts the Sphinx. The Thebans were so eager to rid themselves of the creature that it was decreed that the man who could solve her puzzle would marry Jocasta, the widowed queen, and assume the throne. Sophocles does not bother repeating the riddle because his audience knew it well: 'Which is the animal that has four feet in the morning, two at midday and three at evening?' Oedipus, thinking laterally, gave the right answer, 'Man, who in infancy crawls on all fours, who walks upright on two feet in maturity, and in his old age supports himself with a stick.' Devastated at being out-tricked, the Sphinx commits suicide by throwing herself into the sea.

For Oedipus, the tragedy has just begun. Welcomed as a hero by the Thebans, he weds Jocasta, has four children and for many years enjoys a prosperous reign. But when an epidemic, droughts and famine ravage Thebes, the Delphic oracle is consulted. The answer comes back that the murder of Laius, Jocasta's first husband, has not been avenged. Oedipus is determined to discover the culprit. While interrogating the blind sage Teresias, Oedipus boasts how he vanquished the Sphinx and 'stopped the riddler's mouth, guessing the truth'. Unimpressed, Teresias remarks, 'Your enemy is yourself.'[21] In a series of terrible revelations, Oedipus discovers that the older man he killed on the road to Thebes was his father, Laius, and that Jocasta is his mother. It transpired that when his parents had heard the prophecy that their child would kill his father and marry his mother, they had abandoned him to the elements. But a shepherd, feeling pity for the infant, had taken him to the king of Corinth, who raised Oedipus as his son. Discovering the truth, Jocasta commits suicide and Oedipus blinds himself. Later, he is exiled with his daughter Antigone.

Though Oedipus suffers a hideous punishment, he acted in complete ignorance. H.D.F. Kitto suggests it makes nonsense of the play to interpret it as meaning that humans are playthings of fate. 'What Sophocles means is this, that in the most complex and apparently fortuitous combination of events there is a design, though what it means we may not know.'[22] Freud was captivated by the tale. While writing *The Interpretation of Dreams*, he told Wilhelm Fliess:

> A single idea of general value dawned on me. I have found, in my own case too [the phenomenon of] being in love with my mother and jealous of my father, and I now consider it a universal event in early childhood ... If this is so, we can understand the gripping power of *Oedipus Rex*, in spite of all the objections that reason raises against the presupposition of fate ... [T]he Greek legend seizes upon a compulsion which everyone recognises because he senses its existence within himself. Everyone in the audience was once a budding Oedipus in fantasy and each recoils in horror from the dream fulfillment here transplanted into reality.[23]

Freud had read *Oedipus Rex* in Greek as a schoolboy and was tested on translating sections of it for his final examinations. Passages from Sophocles were among the most difficult to translate and were reserved for the most gifted students.[24] Freud's results were the best in his class, meaning he had a long-standing and thorough knowledge of the play. 'Gripping power' is a good description of the play's driving rhythmic structure, adding to the pressure of moral force and sense of inevitability as Oedipus plays detective of his own fate. The horrifying and bloody conclusion makes *Oedipus Rex* one of the greatest dramatic works ever written. Freud had found a myth he made central to psychoanalysis and that he continued to develop, one that, to him, explained men, women, the family, sex and civilisation. The construction of the Oedipus complex shows Freud at his most imaginative and reductive, coupling his universalising tendency, which made him long for the grand idea, with a neat, epigrammatic solution.

In formulating the theory, Freud erased the Sphinx, the tricky, troublesome feminine, and re-interpreted the tale as a tragic, triangular equation: son loves mother and resents father or daughter loves father and resents mother. Either way, all were destined to enact the same scenario of desire, jealousy and repression. Like the dream, the Oedipus complex was not only the province of neurosis but everyone's shared territory. By 1920, Freud was declaring 'every new arrival on this planet is faced by the task of mastering the Oedipus complex; anyone who fails to do so falls a victim to neurosis'.[25] Though Freud first used the term 'Oedipus complex' in 1909, he originally canvassed it in *The Interpretation of Dreams* in which he likened the structure of Sophocles' play with its 'cunning delays and ever-mounting excitement . . . to the work of psychoanalysis'.[26] He believed the play's enduring popularity was due to its content. The destiny of Oedipus moves us 'only because it might have been ours – because the oracle laid the same curse upon us before our birth as upon him'.[27] The Oedipus complex helped to inspire *Totem and*

Taboo, Freud's 1913 anthropological study of tribal cultures which took the prohibition against incest as a central theme.

Though the Oedipus complex was controversial enough, it was the interpretation of femininity that Freud developed from it that led to the theory that remains today his most fervently debated: penis envy. Initially, he believed a boy and a girl experienced the Oedipal struggle more or less symmetrically: both desired the parent of the opposite sex and resented the other and both, usually as a matter of course, grew out of the attraction to form healthy and satisfying adult relationships. But after his research for *Totem and Taboo*, Freud was keen to explore the dark recesses of guilt and fear he believed were implicit in the Oedipus complex and that governed social systems. In tribal societies, it was by threat of castration that the older males controlled incestuous longings among the younger men, because only the severest prohibitions could 'deter this persistent infantile tendency from realization'.[28]

By 1925, Freud was arguing that girls and boys experienced the Oedipus complex, and the blossoming of their sexuality, quite differently. Little girls regarded the clitoris as the same as the little boy's penis, and masturbating gave them pleasure. But, noticing the penis of a brother or playmate, girls 'at once realise it as the superior counterpart of their own small and inconspicuous organ, and from that time forward fall a victim to envy for the penis'.[29] It provided a turning point in a girl's growth. Castrated because she is in possession of 'an inferior clitoris', the girl extends to her mother, and to all females (including herself), a sense of disappointment, of lack, even of shame. Masturbation is abandoned, 'passivity now has the upper hand', smoothing the ground for femininity.[30] Once the girl accepts the vagina as her prime erogenous zone, maturity is guaranteed. Penis envy also contributed to women's narcissism because 'in the physical vanity of women ... they are bound to value their charms more highly as a late compensation for their original sexual inferiority'.[31]

Freud admitted his conclusions were 'incomplete and fragmentary' and did not 'always sound friendly'. But how to decode 'the riddle of the nature of femininity'? He told his audience: 'Nor will *you* have escaped worrying over this problem – those of you who are men; to those who are women this will not apply – you are yourselves the problem.'[32] The Sphinx had returned and it seemed she was as enigmatic as ever. 'What does a woman want?' an ageing, baffled Freud asked Princess Marie Bonaparte.[33] When the princess remarked to Freud, 'Man is afraid of woman', he exclaimed, 'He's right.'[34]

Little is known about Freud's sexual life after his marriage. Emma, Jung's wife, was astonished when, in 1911, Freud announced that his marriage had long been 'amortised' and 'now there was nothing more to do except – die'.[35] Amortise, meaning to extinguish or deaden, was an interesting word to choose. It is a legal term whereby a debt is cancelled by gradual liquidation, but its roots are in 'amor', love, and 'mort', death – literally 'the death of love'.[36] A few years later, however, Freud was congratulating himself on a 'successful coitus', an all-too-rare event perhaps.[37] The theory of penis envy suggests Martha's pleasure was limited to the erogenous zone Freud demarcated – the vagina. Did Marie Bonaparte take penis envy too literally? From the late 1920s, Bonaparte was Freud's good friend, his analysand, as well as being an analyst herself and a champion of psychoanalysis in France. She gave him lovely things for his collection, including *Venus* (1st–2nd century A.D.), which she bought from Parisian antiquities dealer Manoly Segredakis. Bonaparte was obsessed with her fridigity. In 1927, she underwent the first of two operations, effectively clitorectomies, in which her clitoris was moved nearer to her vagina.[38]

Freud identified with Oedipus. He, too, was a man of destiny, a hero who defeats the obstacles in his path. Similar to Freud's other big idea about dreams and the unconscious, the Oedipus complex derives from his personal life. It seemed for Freud to develop new ideas they needed to be grounded in a vivid, specific, private world, a realm of autobiography and self-portraiture. The Oedipus complex comes from Freud's potent, cherished zone – early childhood – the same place from which his need to collect art also arose. In that sense, Freud's creativity was not detached or 'scientific' but intuitive, lateral and self-referential. Early childhood, the world of play, of myth, legend and fairy tale, of heroes, toy soldiers and imaginary battles, continued to inspire him.

On his fiftieth birthday, two years after the trip to Greece, Freud's followers gave him a bronze medallion designed by Karl Maria Schwerdtner (pl. 46). On one side was a portrait of Freud in profile, on the other Oedipus facing the Sphinx, together with Sophocles' words in ancient Greek, 'Who divined the famed riddle and was a man most mighty!' The presentation gave Freud a shock. Ernest Jones recounts the event. Reading the inscription, Freud became pale and agitated and in a strangled voice demanded to know who came up with the idea. After Paul Federn, a doctor and psychoanalyst, admitted it was he, Freud told the group that, as a young man at Vienna University, he had admired the busts of famous past professors. Not only had Freud longed to see his own image so honoured one day, he had imagined the bust inscribed with the very words on the medallion.[39] Freud's dream of glory had come true, manifest in a handsome artwork.

To Freud, the image on the medallion was ideal, and he described it to Jung as his 'best and most flattering' portrait.[40] Schwerdtner has diminished the size of his nose which Freud, ever sensitive to his appearance, approved. But Schwerdtner also reduced the alert intensity of Freud's gaze, transforming him into a calm sage. Oedipus, also in profile, is deep in thought. The Sphinx, as represented on Freud's Greek vases, is small, neat and demure: she does not seem capable of attacking anyone. On the medallion, she is large, aggressive and womanly – a real lioness. Bigger than Oedipus, her muscles are tensed, she is ready to strike. In contrast, Oedipus is passive and contemplative and his naked-ness makes him seem vulnerable. Unlike the ancient Greeks, Schwerdtner depicts the Sphinx as a threatening, frightening creature, an uncontrollable feminine force. It seems Schwerdtner was less influenced by classical art and more by the femmes fatales of the late nineteenth century with whom Klimt and the Secession artists adorned Vienna. In 1924, Max Pollak decorated Freud's certificate as an honorary citizen of Vienna with an illus-tration of an even larger sphinx. She ignores Oedipus, who is as tiny as an insect, and gazes furiously at the viewer. By then, it seemed that Oedipus + the Sphinx = Freud.

A small print of Ingres' *Oedipus and the Sphinx* (1808, Musée du Louvre) hung in Freud's consulting room near the couch, where he could contemplate it as he decoded his patients' conundrums. Painted the same year as his masterpiece of the nude, *The Bather of Valpinçon*, Ingres addresses his neoclassical vision of the body beau-tiful as a male. Freud may have seen both paintings in the Louvre, during his first visit to Paris, when he described the city as 'a vast overdressed Sphinx who gobbles up every foreigner unable to solve her riddles'.[41]

Ingres shines the spotlight on a handsome, curly-haired Oedipus, with athletic thighs and deliciously realised muscles. Naked, he leans towards the Sphinx, his outstretched finger close enough to stroke her firm little breasts with their erect nipples, while she reaches towards him with her paw. Snugly housed in her cave, the Sphinx seems no more than a strange, cute creature. If she attacked Oedipus, he could easily dispose of her with his javelins since she is so much smaller than he. Nor does she meet his gaze: her eye rolls back towards the shadows, the interior of her rookery. Though a grisly arrangement of bones and a foot in the lower left corner indicate the fate of previous riddlers, Ingres' scene offers no sense of threat. It is a foregone conclusion that Oedipus will triumph. But by defeating the Sphinx, Oedipus instigates a more terrible fate for himself. The Sphinx continues to act in the role of protector, as she did in Egyptian myth – she is trying to protect Thebes from Oedipus and Oedipus from himself. Camille Paglia suggests that 'the riddle by which she defeats all men but Oedipus is the ungraspable mystery of nature, which will defeat Oedipus anyway'.[42] Freud decoded the Sphinx's riddle as fundamentally sexual: it was 'the question of where babies come from'.[43]

Freud's free-standing *Sphinx*, his best representation, shows her alone, the troublesome Oedipus nowhere in sight. She is a noble creature wearing the crown of a goddess. Her association with Greek funerary monuments make her a daimon, meaning a 'divine power' or 'fate'. Good daimons were guardian spirits, who acted as helpful advisors between gods and humans. Freud referred to Wilhelm Fliess as his daimon. The Sphinx is also a trickster, described by Jung as 'a primitive cosmic "being" of *divine-animal* nature', an anima, the archetype who represents man's unconscious feminine aspect, 'who sums up everything that a man can never get the better of and never finishes coping with'.[44] Freud felt the same about the female sex whose 'soul', he complained, he had endlessly searched without finding an answer to their riddle.[45]

Freud's construction of femininity as both problematic and phallic indicates his questing and unsatisfactory relation to women. The anima brings man to awareness, to consciousness — the illuminating role Freud had attested that Martha performed during their courtship. Freud's women patients were also inspiring. They had helped him to discover and elaborate 'the talking cure', as well as some of his early theories. But Freud seemed incapable of imagining women's potential beyond the pale of convention. His attitude parallels that of ancient Greece: in myth and art, women were worshipped as goddesses but, in daily life, their roles were passive and restricted. Yet Freud, especially in his later years, was surrounded by smart, ambitious, attractive women such as Marie Bonaparte, Lou Andreas-Salomé, Joan Riviere and his daughter Anna, who became a pioneering child psychoanalyst. Freud referred to Anna as his Antigone, the loyal daughter who followed Oedipus into exile. Once again, Freud was adept at demarcating zones: theories of the feminine occupied one area while Freud's vital admiration and encouragement of such women occupied another.

Freud collected sculptures of another terrifying, winged female represented in his theories: Medusa the Gorgon. *Antefix in the form of a Gorgon Head* (2nd half of the 1st century B.C.–early 2nd A.D.; pl. 19) shows Medusa grinning widly. Medusa had two sisters and all had serpent-entwined hair, staring eyes, lolling tongues, fangs and beards – in short, they were so hideous that a glimpse of them would turn a man to stone. They were usually depicted running, winged and grinning. Poor Medusa. Once renowned for her loveliness, she was seduced by Poseidon in the shrine of Athena, who, as a punishment, transformed Medusa's hair into 'revolting snakes'.[46] Still not satisfied, Athena assisted Perseus in her murder. Sneaking up on Medusa as she slept, Perseus used the reflection in his shield to avoid her death stare and, guided by Athena, severed Medusa's head. Afterwards, Athena wore the head on her breastplate, as she does in Freud's little statue of the goddess: it was an *apotropaion*, a protective device worn to safeguard the wearer and to terrify the enemy during battle. Even in death, Medusa's gaze was awesome.

Freud began compiling dream dictionaries while writing *The Interpretation of Dreams*. In his mythology, a snake symbolised a penis, though he knew snakes had many alternate cultural meanings.[47] To the Egyptians, snake-handling was the attribute of a magician; in Minoan civilisation, the Great Goddess was represented as a mistress of animals, subduing nature by holding a serpent in each hand. Such interpretations make snake-haired Medusa less a victim of the gods' capricious will and more an enduring image of unconventional female power: a monster who was magical, strong and feared. Nanno Marinatos argues that Medusa was a protector, specifically of men, and that Perseus' defeat of the Gorgon symbolises a male initiation ritual conferring maturity, with Athena as the presiding deity.[48] Athena performs a similar though less dramatic role at the beginning of *The Odyssey* when her wise words to Telemachus, Odysseus' son, transform him from an irresolute youth into a determined man.[49]

In his essay 'The Medusa's Head', Freud rewrote the myth,

constructing an equation that combined snakes, genitals and castration. 'To decapitate = to castrate,' he states. When the boy catches sight of the mother's genitals surrounded by hair, the sight terrifies him because she lacks a penis, making the boy recognise the threat of castration is real. His stiffness, his erection, offers consolation; 'he is still in possession of a penis, and the stiffening reassures him of the fact'. Even the snakes are appropriated by the male gaze: 'they replace the penis, the absence of which is the cause for the horror'. Athena, the virgin goddess, by wearing the Gorgon's head, 'repels all sexual desire – since she displays the terrifying genitals of the Mother'.[50] In Greek mythology, Athena was Gorgopis, 'the gorgon-faced', literally 'the staring one'. By placing the Gorgon's head on her breastplate, Athena was incorporating Medusa's power for the good, to protect the state in times of threat.

Freud could see a marvellously gruesome example of a gorgon in the Kunsthistorisches Museum. Peter Paul Rubens' *Head of Medusa* (c.1618) shows the moment post-decapitation. Medusa stares balefully, blood gushes from her neck, and her skin takes on a deathly pallor as the tangled tresses of snakes writhe and squirm. Perhaps she looks so angry because, like the Sphinx, she has been outwitted.

Freud recognised the ancient power invested in the display of female genitals: it was also an 'apotropaic act'.[51] In his collection, he had a statue of the provocative goddess Baubo. It is likely Freud bought it after he came across a representation of Baubo that 'tallied exactly' with an obsessive image haunting one of his patients.[52] A tiny stone figure, *Baubo* (Egypt, Ptolemaic period, 323–30 B.C.) lies on her back, spreads her legs and exposes her genitals. In case the point is missed, she points to her vulva with her finger. In Greek myth, Baubo was a goddess of childbirth and fecundity, a ribald character symbolising humour and light-heartedness in the face of trouble, as well as sympathetic female bonds.[53] When Demeter, exhausted and dispirited from searching for her daughter Persephone, rests at Eleusis, she is entertained by Baubo with some lewd jokes and lascivious dancing. 'Thereupon,' Freud continues, 'Baubo made (Demeter) laugh by suddenly lifting up her dress and exposing her body.'[54] Demeter's laughter 'earths' and rejuvenates her.

The female with spread legs first appears on West Asian seals in the second millennium B.C. though the posture was already used in Neolithic times to suggest birth, a source of sexual potency, even the origins of life.[55] The 'eye' of Baubo's vagina, staring like the Gorgon, locates female energy. Like Medusa, Baubo is bizarre, not beautiful, a wild unrestrained being who represents aspects of the feminine that are both confronting and profound. Perhaps it explains why Freud's favourite work was *Athena*. The good daughter of Zeus was prepared to do battle but only in order to defend the stability of the state. Athena was the worldly wise diplomat and negotiator, respectful and dignified, not a bad girl like Medusa or a show-off like Baubo.

On a visit to New York in August 1909, Freud made a beeline for the Metropolitan Museum to see its excellent collection of Greek antiquities, particularly vases. He also went shopping at Tiffany & Company's palatial emporium on Fifth Avenue and came away with a jade bowl and a bronze Buddha bust. Freud had long been a jade fancier but the Buddha indicates an interest in oriental art. Tiffany's stocked original designs, so these works were not antiquities.[56]

Freud had been invited, together with Carl Jung, to give a series of lectures at Clark University, Massachusetts (pl. 48). It was during the lectures, in which Freud gave a condensed history of psychoanalysis, that he used the term 'Oedipus complex' for the first time.[57] Freud was touched by the invitation (and the honorary doctorate he received) believing it was 'the first recognition of our endeavours'.[58] But it did not endear America to him. He told Ernest Jones, 'America is a mistake; a gigantic mistake, it is true, but none the less a mistake.'[59] New York's hustle and bustle, as well as its sheer scale, put him out of sorts. 'I'm not going to allow myself to be impressed,' he declared and, as for 'the famous sky-scrapers, beautiful they are not'.[60] Freud was for once the bad traveller, suffering from a bevy of minor health problems and grumbling about the food, the toilets, the lack of a good barber as well as the laissez-faire manners of the New World. America became for him another Vienna: no matter what it offered, it could not get it right.

It was probably Emmanuel Löwy who told Freud that not only had the Metropolitan just established its department of classical art but that his former student Gisela Richter was cataloguing its collection. At twenty-four, Richter was attracting attention as a brilliant young scholar. Persuaded by Edward Robinson, assistant director of the Metropolitan and himself an archaeologist, Richter moved to New York and a temporary assignment over summer became an illustrious career. In 1910 she was made assistant curator and a full curator in 1925, the only woman at that time to hold such a post.[61] The Jacob S. Rogers Fund, a fabulously generous bequest, provided Richter with the resources to build a world-class collection. The accession figures speak for themselves. In 1907, she could afford to buy forty-five Greek vases. In 1917,

$45,000 was spent on acquisitions, $94,000 in 1923 and $185,000 in 1926.[62] Richter was a hands-on curator. In order to fully understand Greek pottery, she attended a modern pottery school in New York to gain practical experience.[63]

Richter made many fine purchases. *Drinking Cup* (c.575 B.C.) shows the Gorgon in all her glory: hirsute, grinning, fanged and flying, a creature both horrible and hilarious. Her image is on the bottom of the cup: as the liquid drained, the Gorgon became visible, giving the drinker a fright. Freud could have also seen a cup by the Makron painter displaying maenads cavorting with priapic satyrs (c.490–480 B.C.) as well as magnificent large vases.

There was another collection at the Metropolitan Freud was keen to see after he discovered that 'the largest collection of Cyprian antiquities had made its way to New York'.[64] It was the personal treasure of Luigi Palma di Cesnola whose 1877 book *Cyprus: Its Ancient Cities, Tombs, and Temples* Freud had read. Cesnola was the kind of buccaneering impresario who appealed to Freud. A general, a diplomat and an amateur archaeologist on a grand scale, Cesnola regarded himself as Schliemann's rival. Between 1865 and 1876, while American consul to Cyprus, Cesnola accumulated an array of local antiquities, including statuary, sarcophagi, pottery, glass and jewels, a hoard of over 35,000 objects that he shipped off the island. As far as the Cyprians were concerned Cesnola was 'the looter'.[65]

Soon Cesnola was bargaining for the best price with the Louvre, the Hermitage and the British Museum before selling the bulk of the objects to the fledgling Metropolitan Museum.[66] Though the collection offered a fresh view of Mediterranean culture, not everyone was impressed. 'There are too many of these Cyprian objects,' complained one visitor. 'They may illustrate quite exhaustively a certain early period but . . . [a]re they beautiful? Are the Cyprian statues, save with the rarest exceptions, either elegant or classic?'[67] Cesnola also created a scandal because he tampered with the antiquities. As Vassos Karageorghis puts it '[i]n his effort to present complete works, Cesnola did not hesitate to put heads and limbs on bodies to which they did not belong'.[68] But Cesnola persevered, winning the job as the museum's first director.

The history of Cyprus is one of successive invasions by Egyptians, Phoenicians, Persians, Greeks, Romans, Turks, English and Venetians – the cultures that, at least in ancient times, influenced its art. Alexander the Great liberated the island from the Persians and was pleased to take a Cypriot sword with him (Cyprus was famous for its bronze weaponry). So close to Turkey and the Levant, Cyprus formed a tantalising transition point between West and East. Aphrodite was 'born in wave-washed Cyprus', making her a major deity of the island; there are statues of her in the Cesnola collection.[69] Freud may have been struck, too, by the armed Jewish resistance that took place against the Romans during the reign of Trajan and that led, after much bloodshed, to the expulsion of all Jews from the island. Freud never visited Cyprus.

The strength of Cypriot art is shown in its pottery, especially from the early and middle Bronze Age. Much Cypriot sculpture, when compared to contemporary examples from Egypt, Greece or Rome, seems heavy and lifeless, as is Freud's *Statuette of a Man* (1st half of the 6th century B.C., Sigmund Freud Museum Vienna). After seeing the Cesnola collection, the Cypriot pottery objects Freud bought are mainly pottery and his choices are well represented in the Sigmund Freud Museum Vienna.[70] The halcyon days for Cypriot art were around 2700–1600 B.C., prior to the invaders' arrival, when the pottery was imaginative, delicate and playful. Freud's *Handmade Vessel* (c.1650–1475 B.C., Sigmund Freud Museum Vienna) indicates how the Cypriot potter's use of zoomorphic shapes, such as the bull's head that serves as a spout, could make a household utensil into a charming decorative object. Freud's Cypriot works indicate his expanding interest in antiquities and his desire to have representative examples from Mediterranean civilisations.

In New York there were other museums to visit, including the American Museum of Natural History where Freud saw 'lizards as big as elephants', as well as the more populist pleasures of Coney Island and a moving-picture show that left Freud distinctly underwhelmed.[71] Further afield was Niagara Falls, 'greater and more brutal' than Freud had expected.[72] Writing to his daughter Mathilde on the return journey, Freud summed up: 'East, West – Home best'.[73]

9

Tomb Raider

Around us are the old images or 'dolls' of pre-dynastic Egypt, and Moses was perhaps not yet born when that little Ra or Nut or Ka figure on the Professor's desk was first hammered by a forger-priest of Ptah on the banks of the Nile.

H.D.[1]

(T)he archaeologist had created the psychoanalyst in him.

LOU ANDREAS-SALOMÉ.[2]

IN 1908, WHEN A small apartment next to the Freuds became available, Freud moved his practice upstairs. His rooms, now connected to his home by an interior door, had the advantage of increased space to display the collection. Also in 1908, Freud visited London for the first time and immersed himself in the collection of

Egyptian antiquities at the British Museum, bigger and better than the one at the Kunsthistorisches Museum.

Egyptian art formed the heart and the majority of Freud's collection. What were its attractions? More than any other culture, Egypt revered elegance and grace, celebrating the body beautiful with sublime clarity and precision. 'The Egyptians were the first aesthetes,' writes Camille Paglia, and Freud was an aesthete par excellence: finicky, precise, carefully attired, always prepared to be seduced by beauty.[3] Furthermore, Egyptian art's greatest achievement is sculpture – Freud's favourite art form. The Egyptians were also master builders. What they constructed lasted – in particular the pyramids: an inspiring metaphor for Freud, master builder of psychoanalysis, and he enjoyed showing off his collection to his distinguished guests. Egypt was a prime topic of conversation when Thomas Mann came to visit in 1932.

Egypt's myth and history emerged in *Leonardo da Vinci and a Memory of his Childhood*, Freud's first attempt to interpret art and biography using psychoanalysis, 'The Moses of Michelangelo' and *Moses and Monotheism*, his final, major work. Freud also decoded Egyptian hieroglyphics and eagerly followed the latest archaeological finds. The twentieth century's most spectacular discovery, Tutankhamun's tomb in 1922, sent the world Egypt-mad. Freud wanted to travel to Egypt, but missed his chance. In 1913 Sándor Ferenczi, Freud's regular travelling companion after Alexander married, encouraged him to make plans for the following September. But Freud cavilled about the heat at that time of the year, though he agreed 'it would, of course, be *very* nice, and we should keep it in mind'.[4] Freud, so keen on what was authentic and fundamental in his theories and his collection, had to make do with others' interpretations of Egypt. When H.D. arrived for analysis, she described Ramesses II's magnificent temple at Abu Simbel, a print of which hung above the couch. 'I had visited that particular temple,' she remarks, 'he had not.'⁵

Much Egyptian art, especially the small objects Freud collected, was destined for the tomb, accompanying the deceased on their journeys to the afterlife. It was an art of mourning that Freud began to collect while mourning his father and it expanded until his rooms, crowded with magical artefacts, began to resemble the tombs from which they were taken. Tombs, after all, not only house the dead but pay homage to them and what is mourning but an act of homage?

Egypt had been on Freud's mind for a long time. The Philippson Bible, which had first attracted him as a boy of seven, was filled with illustrations of Egyptian gods, monuments and landscapes. Jacob had made an emotional gift of the book to his son on his thirty-fifth birthday. Freud's earliest recalled dream, triggered by the illustrations, concerned the death of his mother, Amalia, who was 'carried . . . by people with birds' beaks and laid upon the bed'.⁶

When writing *The Interpretation of Dreams* Freud joked with Wilhelm Fliess about his 'Egyptian dream book', a reference to popular, nineteenth-century dream dictionaries based on ancient Egyptian texts.⁷ For millennia, books have been written proposing the interpretation of dream images and Egypt produced the most numerous, imaginative and memorable. By the Late Period, around 700–330 B.C., not only were dream dictionaries readily available but there had arisen a class of professional interpreters of dreams, usually members of the temple priesthoods.⁸ Many gods had dream temples and people wishing to have their dreams decoded stayed at the temple for a period known as 'dream incubation' when they underwent rituals of fasting, cleansing or abstinence.

As Freud knew from his Bible, a Jew had proved to be Egypt's best known dream expert. When Joseph correctly translated the pharaoh's dream of the seven fat cows and the seven lean ones, it led not only to the prevention of famine but Joseph's promotion to grand vizier.[9] Freud identified with Joseph, commenting that 'it will be noticed that the name Josef plays a great part in my dreams . . . My own ego finds it very easy to hide behind people of that name, since Joseph was the name of a man famous in the Bible as an interpreter of dreams.'[10]

A lovely dream story surrounds the Great Sphinx of Giza, a print of which hung in Freud's rooms. When Tuthmosis IV, out on a hunting trip, fell asleep in the shadow of the Sphinx he dreamt that Harmakhis, the sun god embodied in the Sphinx, told him that if he cleared away the accumulated sand and established a temple, he would become pharaoh. Tuthmosis followed the advice with the predictable result. The 'Dream Stele' that records the tale was erected by Tuthmosis during his reign in 1419–1386 B.C. and remains today between the Sphinx's paws. Prophecy and divine revelation were the dream's time-honoured functions.

In the first chapters of *The Interpretation of Dreams*, Freud was keen to separate his new dream analysis from the older symbology, realising that, for many, dream analysis meant nothing more than quackery and superstition. Freud was aware that 'it seemed quite inconceivable that anyone who had done serious scientific work could make his appearance as an "interpreter of dreams"'.[11] Even the title of his book aroused suspicion, because it was similar to that of the disreputable dream books sold in cheap book-shops. But Freud's belief that dreams had meaning put him on the side of popular opinion that, 'led by some obscure feeling', assumed 'in spite of everything, every dream has a meaning'. Freud, ardent promoter of past cultures, also believed that the respect paid to dreams in antiquity was based on 'correct psychological insight' because it emphasised 'the uncontrolled and indestructible forces in the human mind' and 'the "daemonic" power which produces the dream-wish'.[12] Instead of dismissing dream divination, Freud commented that 'psychoanalysis arrived at a different conclusion'.[13]

Freud had been acquainted with Egyptian artefacts since boyhood. The collection in Vienna, begun by the Habsburgs, was an excellent introduction. Over the years, it was swelled by additional donations from private benefactors. Freud first saw the collection when it was housed in the Lower Belvedere Palace where major items such as the *Sarcophagus of Nes-schu-tefnut* (c.300 B.C.) were crowded together with myriad Greek statues and Roman busts, rather as Freud arranged his own collection.

When the Kunsthistorisches Museum opened in 1891, the Egyptian collection was given its own exquisitely decorated galleries. Gustav Klimt painted a mural in the museum's entrance showing a svelte, naked Egyptian woman surrounded by a collage of Egyptian objects. The Egyptian galleries create an impressive ambience by combining original objects with stylish ornamentation. Ernst Weidenbach's charming, detailed scenes from Egyptian life decorate the walls and Carl von Hausenauer's sumptuous design of red and black vultures covers the ceiling. Both artists took their ideas from original tomb paintings. Three columns from the Eighteenth Dynasty, collected by Emperor Franz Josef while attending the opening of the Suez Canal in 1869, provide both grandeur and architectural support. On display is a good sample of Egyptian art from all periods.[14] Freud bought similar works, making his collection an echo of the Kunsthistorisches Museum's. Was it was part of Freud's antagonism towards Vienna that meant he never acknowedged the museum's pivotal role? Freud developed friendly relations with museum staff, who authenticated works for him, and the curator Hans von Demel's deliberately low estimate of Freud's collection in 1938 meant he was able to whisk it out of the country.

Max Pollak's 1914 etching shows Freud at his desk with important Egyptian works including *Head of Osiris* (1075–716 B.C.; pl. 21), *Baboon of Thoth* (30 B.C.–395 A.D.; pl. 20) and *Neith* (c.600 B.C. [Late Period]). A quarter of a century later, when Edmund Engelman photographed Freud, the statues were in virtually the same position. Stability and continuity, prized by Egyptian civilisation and determinants of its artistic style, were bequeathed by Freud to his favourite antiquities, giving his rooms the sense of timelessness noted by visitors. It also indicates the affectionate bonds he developed with key works: once close, they remained so – easy to touch, observe and admire over the years.

Osiris was Egypt's most popular deity, beloved because he combined the roles of god, man and saviour. Osiris prefigured the Christian myth of Jesus' death and resurrection, an important link explored by British anthropologist James Frazer in *The Golden Bough* and by the Egyptologist E.A. Wallis Budge. Both authors were influential for Freud. Killed by his brother Seth, Osiris was returned to life by the rituals of Isis. In the resurrection of Osiris, writes Frazer, 'the Egyptians saw the pledge of life everlasting for themselves beyond the grave'.[15] Osiris was the lord of the underworld who guided the dead on their journeys to the afterlife and who presided at their trial, which was known as the Weighing of the Heart, a poetic version of Judgement Day.

The Egyptians fervently believed that if their families did for them what Isis did for Osiris they, too, would enjoy life eternal. The facts of the matter were rather more prosaic. Few could afford the costly and elaborate rituals of mummification and burial in a designated tomb, surrounded with magical objects: the number of tombs that have been discovered is minuscule when compared with Egypt's population over the millennia. Peasants and slaves, who made up the bulk of the population, were buried in shallow graves on the edge of the desert where, in the hot dry climate, a natural process of mummification took place. The narrow strip of Egypt's fertile land was too valuable to house their mortal remains. The realm of the afterlife all hoped to enter was Tuat, a duplicate of Egypt.[16] The poor were admitted but, because they could not afford the correct burial, they were consigned to Tuat's first, lesser, realm. The wealthy, however, travelled first class all the way to the afterlife.

On Freud's vividly coloured *Frontal Covering of a Mummy* (c.332–330 B.C; pl. 22), Osiris is depicted twice in his traditional representation as a dead king, swathed in the wrappings of a mummy and wearing 'a kingly crown and grasping in one of his hands, which were left free from the bandages, a kingly sceptre'.[17] He is accompanied by his female protectors: Isis, on the left, and his other sister, Nepthys, on the right. Above are the four sons of Horus, minor deities, whose role was the elimination of the deceased's hunger and thirst. Wood of any size and quality has always been scarce in Egypt and a popular alternative was carton-nage, alternating layers of linen (or papyrus) and glue, moulded around a form and gessoed to take the painted design.

Freud's *Covering of a Mummy*, made of cartonnage, was prepared for a woman and would have been placed over her legs. 'May Anubis who is in his bandages, lord of the Sacred Land, come to you; may he give you a goodly burial' reads the inscription.[18] Anubis, jackal-headed god of the dead, was the presiding deity of mummification. Freud's knowledge of hieroglyphics was adequate to decipher the inscription though he had problems with Egyptian script, complaining it was 'left to the arbitrary decision of the scribe' whether the pictographs were arranged from left to right or in vertical columns, and the most disturbing feature was 'that it makes no separation between the words'.[19]

To master hieroglyphs Freud consulted E. A. Wallis Budge, prolific author and curator of the British Museum's Egyptian collection from 1894 to 1924. Budge's command of his subject and his fluent writing style made him an excellent populariser of Egyptology. After his visit to the British Museum, Freud continued to stock up on Budge's volumes, including *An Egyptian Reading Book for Beginners, Osiris and the Egyptian Resurrection* and his famous translation of *The Book of the Dead*.[20]

The Book of the Dead is a collection of spells written in an exultant, lyrical style, with accompanying illustrations, which were chanted by priests over the deceased. Such protective invocations were meant to help the departed negotiate their journey through the underworld. One of Freud's *Mummy Bandages with Vignettes from the Book of the Dead* (c.100 B.C.–200 A.D; pl. 23) shows Osiris on his throne with a hieroglyph that explains he is 'lord of eternity, ruler of forever'.[21] *The Book of the Dead* is Osiris' biography. Aside from Plutarch, it is where much of the information about the god is recorded.[22] Purchased in 1933, Freud's mummy bandages must have been an especially thrilling acquisition. Stained by the aromatic embalming ointments used to preserve the bodies of the dead, the bandages are delicate, ghoulish, tactile and informative. Messages from the tomb, they carry the imprint of death and are as close to the visceral reality of ancient Egypt as Freud ever got.

After studying hieroglyphs, Freud observed the connection with psychoanalysis. 'If we reflect that the means of representation in dreams are principally visual images not words, we shall see that it is even more appropriate to compare dreams with a system of writing than with a language. In fact the interpretation of dreams is completely analogous to the decipherment of an ancient pictographic script such as Egyptian hieroglyphs.'[23] Part of Freud's attraction to Egyptian culture was its intensely visual emphasis. Words were images. Concepts, such as the existence of balance in the underworld, were represented pictorially. *The Book of the Dead*, filled with prayers and litanies, was also filled with images, not merely 'illustrations' that were secondary to the spells but their visual equivalents.

Freud's bronze *Head of Osiris* enjoyed a privileged position on his desk. By 1938, Freud had moved Osiris further to the right, placing him near his family members: *Isis Suckling the Infant Horus* and *Harpocrates* (c.600 B.C. [late Ptolemaic Period]), the name for the child Horus. *Osiris'* expression is calm and dignified, yet he seems youthful, perhaps fitting for a god who dies only to live again, a boy-god who defeats old age and death. Frazer points out that Osiris was a vegetation god, a corn god whose annual cycle included death and rebirth.

Curiously, when Freud investigated the taboo of incest in *Totem and Taboo*, he did not include the complex family arrangements of ancient Egypt, with its sanctification of both divine and royal incest, did not use what was in front of him: Osiris and Isis, siblings, lovers and parents. Instead he focused on indigenous Australian tribes, whom he described as 'the most backward and miserable of savages'.[24] Later, he commented that though incest was the practice of the pharaohs it was 'merely brother-and-sister incest, which even at the present time is not judged so harshly'.[25] Ernest Jones was mystified why Freud did not investigate mythologies in which he was well versed instead of 'the quite unfamiliar field of Australian Aborigines'.[26] Freud was always interested in what had been forgotten or repressed but in the case of tribal cultures he chose merely to skim the surface. He had a point to make about 'the primal horde', and miserable savages were his example. As Edward Said writes, 'Freud's was a Eurocentric view of culture – and why should that not be? . . . [T]he peoples of Ancient Greece, Rome and Israel . . . were his real predecessors in terms of psychoanalytic images and concepts.'[27] Freud collected tribal artefacts, including neolithic tools. *Stone Club* (c.8000–5500 B.C., Sigmund Freud Museum Vienna) is a redoubtable-looking weapon carved from bone with a stone blade.

Freud's *Osiris* wears a crown decorated with a uraeus, the sacred cobra of Egypt. Poor *Osiris* has lost much of his magnificence over time. His eyes, now empty sockets, would once have been inlaid with precious stones. The Egyptians were particularly fond of lapis lazuli and carnelian. He is also missing his beard and the plumes and disc of his crown. Nose, mouth and cheeks are scored, probably by the hands that robbed him of his adornments. Once *Osiris*' head would have sat atop an impressive bronze torso, a cult figure presented to the god by a wealthy worshipper. Freud honoured what remained of him.

Osiris' most important role was to supervise the Weighing of the Heart. To the Egyptians, the heart represented the soul and the intelligence as well as the emotions. It was the source of 'all life and thought'.[28] Each individual had to undergo the ceremony before being allowed to enter the afterlife and several major gods were involved. Osiris, on his throne, observed Anubis weighing the heart on the scales. On one side was Maat, the goddess of balance, the personification of truth and justice who was usually represented by a feather; on the other was the human heart. The results were recorded by Thoth, the ibis-headed god of writing. If a person had led a good life and was deemed worthy to enter paradise, the heart balanced with the feather. Otherwise the deceased was thrown to a monster known as The Devourer, part-hippopotamus, part-crocodile and part-lioness.

The deceased also had to make a confession of innocence, a tricky business because the heart might suddenly testify against its owner. Freud's *Heart Scarab* (1540–1190 B.C. [18th–19th Dynasties; pl. 24) is a magical amulet designed to prevent that happening. Tiny, around five centimetres long, and made of grey-green steatite, it would have been folded into the mummy bandages, close to the heart it was meant to protect. The Egyptians loved amulets: they placed them under their houses and tombs, set them up in their temples, wore them while living and buried them with their dead. They also worshipped the humble scarab, making Freud's choice of amulet extremely popular. The scarab beetle laid its eggs in balls of dung well hidden in the sand so the newly hatched beetles seemed to appear from nowhere. The Egyptians wore scarab amulets, symbolising rebirth, to imbibe the strength of Ra, the sun god of creation. In death, the amulet assisted resurrection. Amulet means 'protector', 'the thing which keeps safe' or 'the strengthener'.²⁹ The hieroglyph on Freud's *Heart Scarab* was taken from *The Book of the Dead* and asks 'O my heart . . . Do not stand up / against me as a witness / before the guardian of balance!'³⁰

Why would the heart condemn its owner? The symbolic triangular structure combining soul, mind and emotions, which the Egyptians ascribed to the heart, is similar to Freud's structuring of ego, super-ego and id, as well as to the triangular character of the Oedipus complex. 'The super-ego retains the character of the father,' Freud wrote in *The Ego and the Id*. It dominates the ego either in the form of a conscience or an unconscious sense of guilt. It not only represents the 'higher nature of man' but 'moral censorship', thereby containing 'the germ from which all religions have evolved'. The super-ego decrees 'Thou shalt.' It can act independently of the ego and its destructive component can succeed in 'driving the ego into death', just as a bad report from the heart sent the deceased to the maw of The Devourer.³¹ The super-ego (and the heart that speaks out) are dreaded by the ego (and the deceased) because they represent the reproaches of conscience. Did Freud contemplate these connections as he gazed at his Egyptian idols?

Thoth, recording angel of the Weighing of the Heart, was one of Egyptian mythology's most complex and interesting deities. He was regarded as the inventor and god of all the arts and sciences and the special patron of medicine, writing and magic. *The Book of the Dead* was assumed to have been composed by Thoth and certain chapters written 'with his own fingers.'³² Freud's marble *Baboon of Thoth* shows the god in his manifestation as a dog-headed ape, symbolising wisdom and equilibrium. On his head, he wears the lunar crescent and disc, associating him with the moon and the measurement of time. Seated with his paws on his knees, *Thoth's* expression is sagacious and reflective. Thoth sometimes appeared twice in depictions of the Weighing of the Heart: as the ibis-headed scribe and as a tiny baboon seated atop the scales, their equalising force. In his role as royal scribe, Thoth was represented as a bird; as a household god, he was depicted as a baboon and meant to confer good fortune. Exactly why Thoth had two animal identities remains a mystery.[33] The Egyptians were fond of apes, regarding them as lusty and canny, and often kept them as pets. *Thoth's* genitals are displayed and realistically rendered, unusual in Egyptian art, which prized dignity and the asexual schematisation of form. Thoth's attributes as the patron of writing, knowledge and healing, as well as being a protective household deity, made him an ideal muse for Freud's writerly journeys. Once again Freud must have known, from the collections with which he was familiar, that he had obtained a first-class work.

The Greeks and Romans found the Egyptians' obsession with death and burial peculiar. As Freud remarked, 'No other people of antiquity did so much [as the Egyptians] to deny death or took such pains to make existence in the next world possible.'[34] Freud was doubtless intrigued by their rituals for rebirth. The items with which he surrounded himself – amulets, fragments of mummy cases, masks and bandages as well as images of Osiris, Isis and Thoth, the chief deities of death and resurrection – symbolically chart a preoccupation with mourning. Creating the collection is an act that represents birth: from the pain of loss comes new life in the form of a body of objects, a collection of awakening interests and aesthetic pleasures. Freud described mourning as work. Equally, it is a journey from the darkness of grief to the light of recovery and renewal, the same journey that Egyptians believed literally took place in the afterlife.

Mourning as work is represented by an Egyptian tomb object known as the *shabti*. Meaning 'I am here', *shabtis* or 'answerers' came to be regarded as 'the deputies of the deceased whose job was to carry out on his behalf in the next world any menial agricultural tasks that he might be called on to perform'.[35] The Egyptians were obviously concerned about the amount of work they might have to do. If a family could afford it, hundreds of *shabtis* were interred with the deceased. Freud owned several types of *shabtis* and he arranged them together on a cabinet in the consulting room, just as they would have been arranged in a tomb. *Shabti of Imhotep Born of Bastetirdis* (380–342 B.C. [30th Dynasty]; pl. 25) is made of subtle, pale green Egyptian faience. He has a pick in his left hand and in his right he holds a hoe and a rope that is attached to a basket suspended down his back. From his expression, he looks ready to perform his duties cheerfully. The hieroglyph inscribed on *Shabti* reveals the deceased was a priest who was probably interred at a necropolis at Saqqara. In October 1936, Freud took *Shabti* to Hans von Demel at the Kunsthistorisches for authentication, a practice he pursued with relatively few pieces.[36]

The cool, formal beauty of Egyptian art eventually underwent change, but it took the combined onslaught of Greece and Rome. In 30 B.C., Egypt became a Roman province under the rule of Augustus and one of the world's most beautiful civilisations came to an end. But all was not lost. The Romans favoured the Egyptian gods, particularly Isis, and she became a revered deity across the empire. *Mummy Portrait I* (c.250–300 A.D; pl. 26) shows how the individualistic style of late classicism combined with the Egyptian tradition of funerary art. The portrait of a middle-aged man, painted in tempera on wood, is vibrantly rendered, no longer a 'type' but a personality, the artist emphasising his large eyes, thick brows and well-formed features. Equally distinctive is *Plaster Coffin Mask of a Female Egyptian* (2nd century A.D.) due to the woman's expressive face and confronting, kohl-rimmed eyes. These portraits of the dead are vitally alive. But Freud also found character in the older-style Egyptian funerary art. The magnificent *Mummy Covering* (c.600 B.C.) he acquired from Robert Lustig in 1934, in exchange for a selection of Etruscan mirrors, has a gilded cartonnage cover decorated with a figure of Maat, the goddess of truth and balance. Freud told Lustig he liked the deceased's 'nice Jewish face.'[37]

Freud bought *Mummy Portrait* I from the collection of Theodore Graf for 600 florins. The Austrian collector, associated with nineteenth-century archaeological discoveries in Egypt, was an impressive tomb robber. In 1887, Graf took possession of more than three hundred portrait panels that had been whipped out of a cemetery in the ancient city of Philadelphia, in the Fayum region. Graf exhibited 'The Fayum Portraits', as they became known, to great acclaim throughout Europe and at the 1893 Chicago World Fair, as well as publishing an extensive catalogue. When parts of the Graf collection came up for sale, Freud eagerly bought this and *Mummy Portrait* II (c.250-300 A.D.).[38]

Occasionally, the Egyptians did permit a little ugliness to enter the pantheon. Freud's statue of *Bes* (c.600 B.C.), which also stood on his desk in 1914, was Egypt's only coarse god. Freud described Bes as one of few caricatures in Egyptian religion.[39] An angry-looking dwarf with one raised arm, Bes was beloved of women as the patron of childbirth. Other Egyptian deities on Freud's desk include the striding warrior goddess *Neith* as well as small bronzes depicting the feline goddesses *Sekhmet* (c.600 B.C. [Late Period]) with her fierce leonine head and her bloodthirsty reputation for war and vengeance, and *Bast* (c.600 B.C. [Late Period]) the popular cat-faced goddess identified with pleasure whose festivals were celebrated with rude gaiety. Cats were sacred to Bast and, as incarnations of the goddess, they were worshipped in her temples. When they died they were carefully mummified and buried in their own cat-shaped coffins in extensive cat cemeteries. The Greeks and Romans found it laughable that the Egyptians worshipped animals, but to the humble Egyptians animals represented important concepts such as continuity and a tangible connection with the natural world. Animals had always been worshipped in Egypt and, once established, Egyptians rarely relinquished their beliefs. Cats – elegant, sleek and dignified – are the animal equivalents of Egyptian style.

Freud had no love of cats. Until his later years, when he had a succession of chows, pets did not seem to interest him. When Lou Andreas-Salomé asked whether he had any pets, Freud replied he had not acquired 'either a dog or a cat; I have enough women in the house as it is'.[40] But there was a feline visitor who was made welcome in his downstairs study at Berggasse 19. Climbing in the open window, a neighbourhood cat made itself comfortable on the couch before inspecting some of the antiquities that were placed, perhaps due to a lack of space, on the floor. Freud watched, anxious lest the cat knock something over. But when the cat acquitted itself with grace and balance, and purred with satisfaction, Freud rewarded it with a bowl of milk. Despite his affection, the cat remained distant and 'coldly turned its green eyes with their slanting pupils toward him as toward any other object'. Freud tried to woo the cat by playing with it, all to no avail. 'After this unequal relationship had lasted a long time without change', one day Freud found the cat feverish and gasping on the couch and, despite painstaking remedies, it succumbed to pneumonia and died. Freud dubbed it 'the narcissistic cat'.[41]

Freud was not endowed with the same grace and balance. Though in 1901 he could congratulate himself he had not broken 'any object in my house', a few years later the list of damaged antiquities was growing.[42] Freud freighted such occurrences with symbolic meaning. By 1907, he had smashed several works. A 'beautiful little marble Venus' met its fate when Freud hurled one of his slippers at it. Mathilde, Freud's oldest daughter, was gravely ill and, in secret despair, Freud had resigned himself to her death. But the morning when news of a great improvement came, Freud jettisoned his anxieties with a sudden, impulsive shot. He mused, 'My attack of destructive fury served therefore to express a feeling of gratitude to fate and allowed me to perform *"a sacrificial act"*.'[43] Freud was quite astonished that, with so many objects close by, Venus was the only thing he hit.

A 'handsome glazed Egyptian figure' suffered a similar fate. The figure was standing directly in front of him, the spot for his latest acquisition, where he could gaze at it while writing. Like the Venus, this work remains unidentified. Freud, always quick to suspect disloyalty, had criticised a friend, ascribing hostile, unconscious motives to him. Wounded, the man advised Freud not to psychoanalyse his friends. Writing back to acknowledge that his friend was right, Freud's pen-holder slipped from his hand, breaking the figurine. The action had 'the significance of a sacrifice' but now it took the form of 'a propitiatory sacrifice to avert evil', Freud commenting that he could luckily 'cement both of them together — the friendship as well as the figure — so that the break would not be noticed'.[44] Perhaps Freud could have avoided the accident had he kept the statues at a distance. But he crowded his desk with them, so there was little room to move.

Rather like the Egyptians, Freud was preoccupied with thoughts of his own death. He was superstitious, too, especially about numbers. This may partly account for his enthusiastic support for the bizarre theories of periodicity propounded by his friend Wilhelm Fliess. The Berlin ear, nose and throat specialist believed that a range of physical and psychological illnesses could be predicted and diagnosed according to a monthly cycle of twenty-eight days for women and twenty-three days for men. Fliess believed twenty-eight was a 'feminine' number and twenty-three, a masculine one. He also decided that the nose was connected with sex. Not only did it swell with genital arousal, it governed neuralgic pains and was an instigator of the neuroses. It seems hard to credit that Freud was bewitched by Fliess' 'biological numerology'.[45] In order to help prove these theories, Freud offered to Fliess minutely detailed accounts of his own array of illnesses, as well as Martha's menstrual cycle, and the times of the month they occurred. In 1895, he allowed Fliess to operate on his nose. Commenting on a photograph taken of the two men shortly afterwards, Freud writes, 'Beautiful we are not (or no longer), but my pleasure having you close by my side after the operation clearly shows.'[46] Freud's nose looks none the worse for wear.

Numerology is an ancient occult system. The Egyptians believed the universe was founded on magical mathematical principles: numbers were either male or female and, according to their animist tradition, very much alive. Major works like pyramids and temples were constructed on the harmonic proportions of sacred geometry, which incorporated seasonal and astrological calculations. Numerology was further developed and used by the Greeks and Romans, remaining popular in Freud's time, just like dream interpretation. Freud knew the Kabbala, the Jewish mystical tradition, ascribed all Hebrew letters with a numerical value. In 1909, when he was sixty-three, Freud wrote to Jung about his conviction that he would die when he was around sixty.

Visiting Athens, Freud remarked that 'it was really uncanny how often the number 61 or 60 in connection with 1 or 2 kept cropping up in all sorts of numbered objects, especially those connected with transportation'. It made him feel depressed, even more so when he reached the hotel to find he was given room thirty-one, 'which with fatalistic licence could be regarded as half of 61 or 62'. Freud described it as 'another confirmation of the specifically Jewish nature of my mysticism' as well as 'the hidden influence of W. Fliess at work'.[47] In his library, Freud had books on the Kabbala as well as a French translation of the *Zohar*, the Jewish mystical tradition's most important text.[48]

Ernest Jones was not sure if Freud ever entirely freed himself from Fliess' theories. Fliess had predicted the date of Freud's death. Long after the friendship with Fliess had ended and the date passed uneventfully, Freud came up with another time to die: February 1918. Jones recalled how he 'kept looking forward to that date, usually with resignation' and, during the First World War, 'with a sense of welcome'.[49] Colleagues sometimes felt that Freud was credulous, yet his willingness to plunge into realms of creative speculation allowed full rein to what he described as 'my phantastic self'.[50] It is worth remembering that Fliess encouraged Freud during the loneliest and most inventive phase of his intellectual life and was the chief witness at the birth of psychoanalysis. He was also responsible for proposing, before Freud, the idea of a nascent, universal bisexuality. Fliess was the sort of wild theoriser who Freud relished. Similar characteristics attracted Freud to Jung with the same finale: disagreement, disappointment, disaffection and disunity.

Freud's shift to the larger rooms at Berggasse 19 was made possible when Rosa, his favourite sister, left. In March 1908, Freud quit the little flat he had occupied for seventeen years and moved upstairs[51]. Prior to Rosa, the flat had belonged to Victor Adler, a fellow university student who became leader of the Social Democratic Party. As a young doctor, Freud had visited Adler there, with schoolfriend Heinrich Braun, later a German Socialist politician. Freud's study had a history. It had been the nursery of Adler's son, Friedrich, who, in 1916, imbued with revolutionary fervour, assassinated the prime minister Count Karl von Sturgkh. Sturgkh, an arch conservative who imposed strict censorship rules, was not sorely missed. After the Armistice, Friedrich's sentence was commuted and he was set free. Freud remembered lunching at the Adlers' and catching a glimpse of young Friedrich.[52]

Now Freud had nearly double the amount of space in which to arrange his antiquities, books, furniture and Persian rugs. It was brighter, too, as all three rooms looked on to the courtyard and its chestnut tree.[53] There were a few structural changes: Freud had an extra door set into the consulting-room wall, so patients could leave discreetly without being seen by those in the waiting room, and another door that joined the flats together. In the general clearance he took the opportunity, for the second time in his life, to destroy a mass of documents and letters.[54]

Soon after, he wrote '"Civilized" Sexual Morality and Modern Nervous Illness', where he quoted the distinguished German neurologist Wilhelm Erb to bolster his argument that in contemporary life, 'All is hurry and agitation. The exhausted nerves seek recuperation in increased stimulation and in highly-spiced pleasures, only to become more exhausted than before.' Enclosed in his study and surrounded by ancient artefacts, Freud agreed with Erb that modern art was 'repellent, ugly and suggestive', confronting the viewer with 'the most horrible sights that reality has to offer'.[55] By repressing the sexual drives, modern life's 'civilising' effects had turned its citizens into nervous wrecks. The collection provided Freud with an oasis from such pressures. Freud admitted he liked to 'turn away from the present ... Strange secret longings rise up in me, perhaps from the legacy of my forebears, for the Orient and the Mediterranean, and for a life of a completely different kind.'[56] In 1914, Freud's eldest son Martin volunteered for the army and was training as a gunner. Anxious about Martin's fate and marooned in Vienna that summer, Freud distracted himself by minutely examining and cataloguing the antiquities. Unfortunately, the catalogue has been lost.

A visit to London in September 1908 gave Freud the opportunity to immerse himself in the British Museum's Egyptian collection. There was plenty to see: three galleries on the ground floor and four upstairs. On his first visit he stayed for two hours – 'Longer I couldn't stand it' – only to return at 3 P.M. He was staying at Ford's Hotel in Manchester Street, Westminster, 'exactly half an hour' from the museum and, though he enjoyed the walk, he wanted to be closer. London impressed Freud with its 'glory, nobility, purity and elegance . . . The English are really agreeable people and, by the way, the cigars are excellent.'

The first part of Freud's cherished summer holidays had been spent with his family near Berchtesgaden. At Manchester and Blackpool he visited his half-brothers Emmanuel, now seventy-four, and Philipp, seventy-two, of whom he was very fond. Then he had a week alone in London. He didn't bother going out much at night. 'I'd rather prepare myself to visit the [British] Museum.'[57] That meant studying guides to the Egyptian galleries, as well as the writings of Wallis Budge.[58] Freud could also view the Elgin Marbles, the magnificent sculptural friezes Lord Elgin had prised from the Parthenon.

The British Museum had done well from Napoleon's invasion of Egypt. After the defeat of the French in 1801, the English confiscated Napoleon's spoils and deposited them in the museum, where new galleries were built to house them. The Rosetta Stone (Ptolemaic Period, 196 B.C.) was arguably the famous single object: its inscriptions had helped Jean-François Champollion to crack the code of the hieroglyph. More works arrived courtesy of Giovanni-Battista Belzoni and Henry Salt. In 1816 Belzoni, a former circus strongman, was hired by Salt, the British consul to Egypt, to gather treasure for the museum. Many of the outstanding large sculptures were found by them, including the bust of Ramesses II known as *Young Memnon* (c.1250 B.C. [19th Dynasty]). Getting the colossal bust back to London was the first task Salt set the intrepid Belzoni. In his book, Belzoni described digging the bust from the sands of Luxor before hauling it onto a massive sledge, and dragging it to the Nile. There he waited for the river to rise so he could send it by water to England.[59] Belzoni was another successful archaeological buccaneer combining physical stamina with personal charisma, insatiable curiosity and the happy knack of finding just the right spot to dig, plus a fine disregard for the legal and ethical niceties of his task.

Wallis Budge, who made many visits to Egypt and purchased large quantities of antiquities for the museum, eloquently made the case for looting the country. 'Every unprejudiced person must admit that, once a mummy has passed into the care of the Trustees and is lodged in the British Museum, it has a far better chance of being preserved than it could possibly have in any tomb, royal or otherwise, in Egypt.'[60] But the museum, as Salt and Belzoni found, did not want to pay handsomely for the privilege. As a result, in 1824 Salt sold the huge sarcophagus of Sethi I (c.1370 B.C.) to Sir John Soane when negotiations with the British Museum broke down. Freud could have seen the sarcophagus because Soane's London home, crammed full of artworks and curiosities, was open to the public. In Manchester Square, close to Freud's hotel, was another magnificent private treasure trove: the Wallace Collection. Hertford House, the former residence of the Hertford-Wallace family, exhibited a wealth of paintings, furniture, sculpture and a fine collection of Sèvres.

Freud referred to Egyptian culture in two problematic works: 'Leonardo da Vinci and a Memory of his Childhood' and *Moses and Monotheism*.

Leonardo was a hero of Freud's, 'among the greatest of the human race', a renaissance man with whom he identified.[61] The essay, published in 1910, was a bold gambit designed to subject art and biography to psychoanalysis and to place the new science firmly in the realm of cultural discourse. 'We must also take hold of biography,'

Freud told Jung. 'The riddle of Leonardo da Vinci's character has suddenly become clear to me.' Freud relished the task of writing about Leonardo who, he told Jung, 'has been posing for me'.[62] Freud linked Leonardo's aversion to completing projects with the artist's cool repudiation of sexuality. Leonardo 'converted his passion into a thirst for knowledge . . . He has investigated instead of loving.' Naturally, Freud was keen to link his thesis with Leonardo's childhood. He noted an early memory of Leonardo's: as he lay in his cradle, a vulture flew down 'and opened my mouth with its tail, and struck me many times with its tail against my lips'.

Freud pointed out that in Egyptian myth the great mother goddess Mut is represented by a vulture. 'Can the similarity to the sound of our word *Mutter* ['mother'] be merely a coincidence?' Freud wondered.[63] Thus Leonardo was recollecting the pleasures of maternal breastfeeding as well as creating a homosexual fantasy of fellatio. Freud also observed that Mut, often represented with a phallus, was an androgynous being, a mother-father figure, like Caterina, Leonardo's mother, who was sole parent of her illegitimate son in his early years. It followed that Leonardo's dependent, erotic relationship with his mother had predisposed him to homosexuality.

Though Freud would have been familiar with the images of Mut as a vulture that decorate the ceiling of the Egyptian rooms at the Kunsthistorisches Museum, in his exquisitely rendered limestone *Donation Stele* (301 B.C. [Ptolemaic Period]), Mut is seen in her human representation. She stands with her consort, the sky god Amon, their son, Khonsu, and Horus as they accept an offering from the pharaoh Ptolemy. Freud had acquired the *Stele* by 1909 but may not have known the identity of the deities.

Freud erred in translation. The word Leonardo used for the bird was *nibbio*, meaning kite, a member of the hawk family. The German translations Freud had consulted erroneously used the word *Geier*, meaning vulture. Though no one commented on the blunder during Freud's life, the criticism aroused by his brave but flawed excursion into biography was sufficient to make him reflect that it was as though he had 'merely written a psychoanalytic novel'.[64]

The red kite, a large and graceful bird of prey, was common throughout western Europe in Leonardo's time. During the nineteenth century, however, its numbers had begun to dwindle due to hunting and the spread of human habitation. It was a bird with which Freud, nature lover and intrepid hiker, would have been familiar. It is a pity Freud did not correctly translate *nibbio*. After all, Horus, the son of Isis and Osiris, was depicted with a falcon's or a hawk's head, as Freud's *Falcon-headed Figure* and *Donation Stele* show. If Freud had connected the bird with Horus, the divine and original pharaoh, perhaps he could have still constructed a fellatio fantasy for Leonardo and a longing for glory to boot.

Moses and Monotheism, published in 1939, was Freud's last major work. A larger project than *Leonardo*, its central tenet was even more fraught with difficulties. Freud's opinion, that Moses was an Egyptian and not a Jew, brought him, as he predicted, opprobrium from fellow Jews. 'To deprive a people of the man whom they take pride in as the greatest of their sons is not a thing to be gladly or carelessly undertaken, least of all by someone who is himself one of them,' Freud observed.[65] But it gave him the chance to deepen his knowledge of Egyptian myth and history by examining the most divisive and fascinating of pharaohs, Amenophis IV (also known as Akhenaten). *Moses and Monotheism* is distinguished by Freud's best and worst traits: big, provocative ideas; reductive, dualistic thinking; a selective use of historical sources; and brilliantly honed prose. Writing it during 1934, Freud was troubled by this 'historical novel', as he called it, and wondered whether his arguments were 'mounted on a foundation of clay'. They were dark times. Assailed by cancer, Freud also faced the spectacle of Europe in the midst of the Depression, encroaching fascism and the threat of war. To Arnold Zweig, he confided that his 'final attempt to create something has run aground', but Moses 'and what I wanted to make of him, pursues me incessantly'.[66]

When Moses led the Jewish people out of slavery in Egypt, he also introduced them to a new religion, 'a rigid monotheism on the grand scale'. The Egyptians' prolific pantheon manifested itself in an 'insatiable appetite . . . for embodying their gods in clay, stone or metal (to which our museums owe so much today)'. And his own collection, Freud could have added. Freud theorised that Moses had been converted to the ideas of Amenophis IV. The young pharaoh, who came to the throne in 1375 B.C. during the 'glorious Eighteenth Dynasty', banished the gods in favour of Aten, the sun god, naming himself Akhenaten ('pleasing to Aten').[67] He shifted the capital from Thebes to Tell el-Amarna where, for the next seventeen years, in increasing isolation, Akhenaten, his principal wife, Nefertiti, and the court followed the new religion.

Freud's view of Akhenaten was formed by American archaeologist James Breasted, the pharaoh's fervent apologist. Freud quoted Breasted's ringing description of Akhenaten as 'the first individual in human history'. According to him, Akhenaten was not a monomaniacal tyrant who disrupted his country, but 'the beneficent father of all men' whose 'discerning eye' had caught 'a universal truth'.[68] It was a popular but largely erroneous nineteenth-century view of the pharaoh.[69] Freud explained that while polytheism is 'very close to primitive phases [of development]', monotheism 'has risen to the heights of sublime abstraction'.[70] It was the same spurious version of Darwinism that informed James Frazer's *Golden Bough*, as well as *Totem and Taboo*: pagans were savages.

The Egyptians, who disliked change and loved their gods, resisted Akhenaten's system and when his reign ended, the cult of Aten was banished and Tell el-Amarna was reclaimed by the desert. Ironically, Akhenaten the iconoclast was condemned to the same fate — many of his images were defaced, consigning him to eternal damnation. Akhenaten was heretical and disruptive and, as described by Breasted, a high-minded social revolutionary, all good reasons for Freud to identify with him. But Freud wanted it both ways. Akhenaten was ultimately a loser. His new religion foundered and his story was buried beneath the Sahara for centuries. It was not the fate Freud wanted for himself or the new faith of psychoanalysis. Enter Moses. Freud regarded Moses as Akhenaten's son and heir, not 'the dreamer' who had 'alienated his people and let his empire fall to pieces' but a man of 'energetic nature . . . more at home with the plan of founding a new kingdom'.[71] Moses would lead the children of Israel to the promised land and transform Akhenaten's idea into a reality. The comparison between the dreamy, hopeless 'father' and the determined, confident son recalls Freud's relationship with his father, his need to strive against Jacob and to best him. But it is not Freud's familiar positioning of the contest between father and son that makes *Moses and Monotheism* notable.

The 'glorious Eighteenth Dynasty' included a period of rampant iconoclasm during which the very items that Freud treasured were earmarked for destruction. If polytheism was 'primitive' and monotheism represented a 'sublime abstraction', how did Freud accommodate his predilection for Egypt's magical and sacred objects?

If Akhenaten had had his way, none would remain. In 'The Moses of Michelangelo', Freud had pondered the prophet's fierce expression, triggered by the sight of the Israelites gaily worshipping the Golden Calf.[72] Freud cherished his antiquities. In the 1930s, he gained several key works including *Isis Suckling the Infant Horus*, *Mummy Covering*, the *Mummy Portraits* from the Graf collection and the two *Mummy Bandages*. Why dismiss their worth?

Freud drew divisions. Moses could not be both Egyptian *and* Jew, as other scholars had suggested. He had to be one or the other. Nor could Freud allow his collection to extend beyond his rooms. It must be contained – though by 1938, when finishing *Moses and Monotheism*, the rooms were so crowded that Freud could barely move. His collection was his consolation, his private realm, his retreat, crammed with the emblems of past cultures that inspired him. Images of Isis, Osiris and Horus were not empty idols but redolent metaphors for sexuality and family relationships, areas that proved fruitful for Freud. The collection represents an act of reverence for pagan cultures, the painstaking recovery and organisation of objects symbolising restitution for the vicissitudes they suffered.

But Freud was prepared to sacrifice private homage in the arena of public debate. To prove that Moses 'civilised' the Jews by converting them to a superior form of worship, one that reviled images, Freud repressed his collection's importance to him. Why does the ego repress what is deep and instinctual? '[E]ither because it is paralysed by the magnitude of the demand or because it recognises it as a danger.' God the Father was deemed of greater historical and cultural value than Freud's old and grubby gods. He was still querulously arguing the case just before he died, though *Moses and Monotheism* had been condemned for its uncritical use of sources, among other things. Freud did not furnish his rooms with 'sublime abstraction' but its opposite, *horror vacui*. By the 1930s, he was so obsessed with the antiquities that, when he departed for his summer holidays on the outskirts of Vienna, much of the collection accompanied him. As Freud argued the case for the significance of monotheism, he continued to surround himself with the artefacts of polytheism, just as the repressed drive, despite the ego's attempts to block it, returns as strongly as ever because it has 'either retained its forces, or collects them again, or it is reawakened by some new precipitating cause'.[73]

Tutankhamun was almost certainly Akhenaten's son-in-law. Not as lucky in life as Akhenaten — he died from an infection in his leg when he was sixteen — in death he became an international celebrity thanks to Howard Carter, who discovered his tomb in November 1922. Thus far it is the greatest archaeological discovery, and the triumphant finale to the long and exciting series of excavations that Freud had been tracking since boyhood.

Egypt's Valley of the Kings had been visited by the most illustrious tomb raiders. Belzoni arrived for a few spectacular days in 1817. After clearing the entrances to the tombs of Ramesses I and Sethi I, he found himself, with characteristic good fortune, standing in one of the greatest royal sepulchres of any age. The rock-cut tomb of Sethi I became known as 'Belzoni's tomb'. In 1829, Jean-François Champollion arrived with a team of artists and architects to record inscriptions and tomb designs.

In 1898, just after Freud began his collection, a fresh round of sensational finds began when Victor Loret discovered the tombs of Tuthmosis III and Amenophis II. From 1902, Theodore M. Davis, a wealthy American lawyer and art collector, held the excavation rights in the Valley of the Kings. He had the enviable reputation of uncovering a new tomb every season, and his finds now fill a gallery in the Cairo Museum. In 1914, believing the opportunities were exhausted, Davis transferred his concession to Lord Carnarvon. After years of failures and expense, Carnarvon was ready to quit the Valley when Howard Carter, who had also worked for Davis, offered to finance a new campaign from his own pocket. Impressed, Carnarvon agreed to push on.

Carter knew Tutankhamun's tomb was there but he had no idea of its wealth. It had been left relatively unharmed by local tomb robbers, who usually began their work soon after a burial was completed, because another tomb lay directly above it. It meant that when the upper tomb was pillaged, the entrance to the one below was buried under tonnes of rubble and saved from any further attempts at disturbance.[74] Opening the tomb, Carter was stunned. In his notebook he recorded that 'Lord Carnarvon said to me, "Can you see anything?". I replied to him, "Yes, it is wonderful" . . . Our sensations and astonishment are difficult to describe . . . The first impressions suggested the property-room of an opera of a vanished civilization.'[75] Freud knew Carter's words well: he had the three-volume set of Carter's account of the discovery. Carter was able to bring to the surface nearly five thousand objects of breathtaking and unparalleled beauty, including the golden mask of the young king. James Breasted, Akhenaten's apologist, arrived to assist him. Freud was fortunate to receive a statuette 'directly from the tomb of Tutankhamun'.[76]

The discovery made world news and a fresh wave of Egyptomania, the strongest since Napoleon's invasion of Egypt, flooded western culture influencing film, art, design and fashion and providing the subject for popular literature and song as well as scholarship. Egyptianising motifs formed the essential ingredi-ents of Art Deco. There was even the sensational 'curse of the pharaohs', a legend that arose from Lord Carnarvon's sudden death and believed to haunt those involved with the tomb's opening. In commercial terms, the Egypt-frenzy signalled the increase in value, as well as the rarity, of ancient Egyptian artefacts.

If he had been interested in selling it, Freud's collection had become an investment offering handsome returns. But, aside from the 1938 valuation given by Hans von Demel that Freud needed to take the collection out of Austria, it seems he never bothered with pecuniary assessments. He continued methodically buying and selling, adding to his store of quality Egyptiana whenever he could. And he continued to follow discoveries eagerly. In 1935, when a report about Tell-el Amarna was published, 'a certain Prince Thothmes' was mentioned. Freud told Arnold Zweig that 'if I were a millionaire in pounds, I would finance the continued excavations. This Thothmes could be my Moses and I would be able to boast I had guessed right.'[77]

With the onset of old age and illness, Freud was mostly confined to Berggasse 19. When Karl Abraham sent him newspaper clip-pings about the discovery of Tutankhamun's tomb, he replied, 'My chief feeling is of annoyance at not being able to be there, and above all the prospect of descending to the Styx without having sailed on the Nile.' Abraham tried to encourage him, suggesting 'if you cut your summer holidays by a month, you could surely be absent for a few months at the beginning of the next year and enjoy Egypt'.[78] Freud replied in the negative. Gradually his rooms, aside from summer breaks spent near Vienna, became his sole domain, the empire of the old king crowded with gods who whispered of dream journeys that would never take place.

10

Idols

I formally adopted you as eldest son and anointed you . . . as my successor and crown prince.

FREUD TO JUNG, 16 APRIL 1909[1]

The stirring up of conflict is a Luciferian virtue in the true sense of the word. Conflict engenders fire, the fire of affects and emotions, and like every other fire it has two aspects, that of combustion and that of creating light.

C.G. JUNG, 'PSYCHOLOGICAL ASPECTS OF THE MOTHER
ARCHETYPE'[2]

FREUD'S CLOSE FRIENDSHIPS with men struck deep and transfor-
mative chords in him and were marked by a passionate enagage-
ment similar to his early relationship with Martha. Only two men

were so privileged: firstly Wilhelm Fliess and later Carl Jung. Freud's other male intimates, such as Ernest Jones and Sándor Ferenczi, were not welcomed into his heart quite as openly. It is also true to say that, after the break with Fliess, no man, not even Jung, was so close to Freud again. The Fliess and Jung friendships were characterised by intense comradely discussions, shared ideas and ambitions, longed-for meetings and bitter public finales.

Freud was an anxious friend. He often replied to Jung's letters as soon as he received them, then chafed when an immediate reply was not forthcoming. For example, Jung wrote to Freud from Zurich on 3 March 1908. Freud wrote the same day, then followed with a long letter on the 5th and a shorter one on the 9th. A few days later Jung wrote, 'I am sorry I can't get around to answering letters as promptly and fully as you do. I have a mass of other things to attend to.'[3] When Jung did not contact Freud for a month, explaining that he had been ill and was recuperating in northern Italy, Freud replied unfeelingly, 'With your youthful stamina you ought to make short shrift of any illness.' Jung responded, 'Your last letter upset me.'[4]

The rhythms of hope, need and disappointment symbolised by such exchanges presage the larger problems the two encountered. Although Freud's characterisation of Jung and himself as 'the Teuton and the Mediterranean man' is not wholly accurate, it reveals the differences Freud perceived between them, about reserve and effusiveness, coolness and warmth.[5] But they inspired one another. During the friendship, Freud began writing art and literary criticism, and acknowledged Jung's work as a guiding light for *Totem and Taboo*, while Jung plunged into the study of myth. There was a shared taste for archaeology and Egyptian art, and both disliked modern art. Both had phobias about visiting Rome, though Freud, unlike Jung, conquered his. They aroused turbulent feelings in one another: Freud fainted twice in Jung's presence. The first time followed a discussion about archaeology and the second, about Akhenaten. Myth was the catalyst that drove them apart.

In 1907, Freud was eager to send *Delusions and Dreams in Jensen's 'Gradiva'* to his new friend. It was Freud's first excursion into arts criticism and it was followed, in the next few years, by *Leonardo da Vinci and a Memory of his Childhood*, 'Creative Writers and Daydreaming' and 'The Moses of Michelangelo'. Freud was delighted that Jung regarded his analysis of *Gradiva* as 'magnificent. I gulped it at one go.'[6]

Jung admitted it had taken him some time to fully absorb *The Interpretation of Dreams*. When he did, he became Freud's able lieutenant, ready to go into battle to defend the cause of psychoanalysis and Freud himself. To Freud, Jung must have seemed like a dream come true. Vividly intelligent with a commanding presence, Jung had the added advantages of the academic recognition denied to Freud, and being Aryan. Freud confided to Karl Abraham that Jung guaranteed psychoanalysis would not become 'a Jewish national affair'.[7]

After graduating in medicine from the University of Basel, Jung had specialised in psychiatry, working at Zurich's famed Burghölzli sanatorium under Eugen Bleuler. Jung's childhood was wretched. His father, though descended from a noted Basel family, was an impoverished country pastor while his mother had 'routine nighttime visitations by spirits and poltergeists' and had the habit of making uncanny predictions, all the more bizarre for often coming true.[8] Jung grew up with an abiding interest in spiritualism and folklore. Both parents were moody, unstable and constantly bickering and, as a youth, Jung led an isolated, often friendless existence that made him driven and self-reliant. He had to fight unhelpful relatives in order to attend university and he raised the money to maintain himself, as well as his widowed mother and sister, by trading in antiques. At the Burghölzli, where he was an assistant physician, his workload was gruelling and he was accustomed to eighteen-hour days. Jung was not exaggerating when he told Freud he had 'a mass of other things to attend to'. It was a plea that Freud largely ignored during the course of their friendship. Life eased somewhat in 1903 when Jung married Emma Rauschenbach, a sensitive and intelligent young woman who was also the heir to a fortune.

In 1906, Jung had sent Freud *Diagnostic Association Studies*, which contained essays by Jung and Eugen Bleuler that cited Freud's work and demonstrated that psychoanalysis had found acceptance at the Burghölzli sanatorium. In the foreword to Jung's *The Psychology of Dementia Praecox*, published in 1906, he wrote that he was 'indebted to the brilliant discoveries of Freud'.[9] As a lively correspondence began between the two men, Jung was making an international name for himself as an academic and a clinician. His most prominent achievement was the development of word association. Unlike Freud, Jung was dealing with the incarcerated insane, the kind of extreme cases Freud had observed years earlier at Charcot's Salpêtrière clinic. Warning bells were sounded early in the relationship. When Freud wrote in *Gradiva* that 'many who are sensible in other respects find it possible to combine spiritualism with reason', he defined Jung's attitude.[10] Another sticking point was that Jung could never quite accept – and Freud could not accept that Jung could never quite accept – sex as the foundation of the neuroses, the driving force of personality and the basis of civilisation.

Freud told Jung that *Gradiva* was written 'on sunny days' in the open air, while staying in South Tyrol at Lavarone. 'I myself derived great pleasure from [writing the book]. True, it says nothing that is new to us, but I believe that it enables us to enjoy our riches.'[11] Freud had first travelled through south Tyrol in 1900 with Minna. Impressed by the high plateau with its 'magnficent forest of conifers and undreamed of solitude', he took the family back in 1906.[12] Seven-year-old Martin kept a diary of that enchanted summer, recording daily swims in the 'small green mountain lake' – Freud loved the water – and 'long walks with father through the beautiful forest'.[13] Freud's enjoyment of the place, and his holiday spirits, seem to have seeped into *Gradiva*, with its engaging storytelling and sparkling wit.

Wilhelm Jensen's 1903 novel *Gradiva*, set in Pompeii, was bound to please an armchair archaeologist such as Freud. As Peter Gay writes, Norbert Hanold, the central character, is 'the withdrawn, unworldly product of cool northern climes who will find clarity and a very Freudian cure through love in the sun-baked south'.[14]

With relish, Freud retells the tale. Hanold, an archaeologist, is so captivated by an antique relief of an attractive young woman he sees in a Rome museum that he buys a plaster copy to hang in his study 'and gaze at with interest'. Hanold is particularly taken by the gait of the girl with the fluttering drapery. He begins to make up a story about her, giving her a name – Gradiva, 'the girl who steps along' – a distinguished family and a life in ancient Pompeii. Soon afterwards, he has a terrifying dream of the eruption of Vesuvius and the destruction of Pompeii; he sees Gradiva lying on the steps of the Temple of Apollo 'with a peaceful expression, like someone asleep, till the rain of ashes buried her form'. After the dream, Hanold is restless and decides to travel to Italy, and to Pompeii. Wandering alone in the ruined town 'at the hot and holy mid-day hour, which the ancients regarded as the hour of ghosts', Hanold is startled to see Gradiva stepping lightly over the cobblestones, just as she does in the relief. He follows her to the House of Meleager, where he confronts her, first in ancient Greek, then Latin. With a smile, she replies, 'If you want to speak to me you must do it in German.'[15]

Gradiva, it transpires, is none other than Hanold's childhood sweetheart Zoe Bertgang, whose memory he has 'buried'. (Zoe means 'life' and Bertgang, 'someone who steps along brilliantly'.) Science has ossified Hanold's libido, leaving him interested 'only in women of marble and bronze'.[16] It was the same theme that Freud explored in *Leonardo* in which the single-minded pursuit of knowledge leads to sexual repression. Ridding Hanold of his delusion by explaining who she really is, Zoe plays a charming and clever game of psychoanalysis, telling Hanold it is strange that someone has 'to die so as to come alive; but no doubt that must be so for archaeologists'. Freud approved of her tactic, commenting in the book's margin, '*schön*' – beautiful. Freud believed there was

no better analogy for repression, by which something in the mind is at once made inaccessible and preserved, than the burial of the sort to which Pompeii fell a victim and from which it could emerge once more through the work of spades.[17]

Pompeii also featured in Freud's treatment. In the case of the Rat Man, a patient who had a dream he was being gnawed by rats, Freud alluded to the destroyed city. Describing to his patient the difference between the conscious and the unconscious, between what was subject to change and what was relatively unchanging, Freud indicated his antiquities. They were 'only objects found in a tomb', he explained, 'and their burial had been their preservation: the destruction of Pompeii was only beginning now it had been dug up'.[18]

Just after his birthday in May 1901, Freud acquired 'a fragment of a Pompeiian wall with a centaur and a faun' that 'transports me to my longed-for Italy'.[19] Freud delighted in giving gifts to himself as well as others, and his birthday was probably the occasion for buying the work. The following year with his brother Alexander, he visited Pompeii as well as Naples' National Archaeological Museum, which holds treasures from the site. The museum impressed Freud but Naples did not. It was 'inhumanly hot' and the ugly inhabitants belonged in a monkey cage, but Vesuvius was smoking and there was a glimpse of fire.[20]

Pompeii had been excavated, and ransacked, for centuries. When Winckelmann arrived in 1762, he was shocked at the chaos, writing that the engineer supervising the excavations 'knew as much of antiquities as the moon does of lobsters'.[21] Prior to that, Pompeii was in the hands of the Habsburgs, who plundered it to obtain statues to display in their Viennese residences. Finally, in 1860, under the direction of Giuseppe Fiorelli, proper scientific and methodical procedures were instigated. Fiorelli also invented a method of plaster casting that preserved the positions the Pompeians adopted at the moment of death, creating haunting images of mortality. When Freud visited, recent discoveries included the House of the Vettii, one of the most splendid houses in Pompeii, and the remains of a temple dedicated to Venus, the city's principal goddess.

Freud spent only a day there but, as he had with Rome, he had studied maps of its streets and had been dreaming about Pompeii for years. In 1897, he dreamt he received a telegram concerning the whereabouts of Fliess, then on holiday, that included the words 'Via' and 'Villa'. Freud was 'stirred up ... at not knowing where you are staying and at having no news of you', so the dream was 'the fulfillment of a wish if you would telegraph your address to me'. Freud believed 'Via' meant 'the streets in Pompeii, which I am studying'.[22] From his handsome copy of Johannes Overbeck's *Pompeii*, with its large, fold-out map, Freud knew the Via Mercurio where the House of Meleager stands, the place where Hanold follows Zoe and where she disabuses him of his fantasy. With its generous rooms, tall columns and deep pond set in the garden, the villa is an example of the wealthy Pompeians' elegant lifestyle.

Near the entrance is a faded fresco of the hero Meleager and the 'girl warrior' Atalanta, that gives the house its name.[23] Nineteenth-century archaeologist August Mau, who classified Pompeian wall painting for the first time, pointed out that while the House of Meleager had numerous frescoes, many had been transferred to the museum at Naples, and those left on the walls had suffered from exposure to the weather.[24] The tale of Meleager and Atalanta was famous in Greek myth. When a wild boar ravaged the countryside, Meleager, smitten by Atalanta, insisted she join the hunt. Atalanta acquitted herself well, being the first to wound the animal, and Meleager sought to please her by offering her the slain boar's head and pelt. When his uncles objected to bequeathing such an honour on a woman, Meleager killed them. His mother was furious and, through magic, caused his death. Perhaps Jensen admired the sure aim of the huntress Atalanta, incorporating her as a symbol for Zoe.

Aside from Leonardo's work, Freud was not a great admirer of painting. It was literature and sculpture, and 'less often . . . painting', that exercised 'a powerful effect' on him.[25] The paintings in his collection are either fragments of sarcophagi – three-dimensional objects that, over time, had been transformed into two-dimensional ones like *Portrait of a Mummy* – or frescoes, such as *Fragment of a Wall Painting*, items that had been part of a house, a larger, three-dimensional whole. A painting lacks the visceral appeal of sculpture: it does not invite the touch, nor is it readily transportable. Not only did Freud like to hold and stroke his antiquities, he wanted to surround himself with them and to replicate their arrangement wherever he was staying. When he moved to London in 1938, the objects on his desk were placed in the same positions as they were in Vienna.

Freud's 1901 purchases, *Archer with Centaur* (c.1st century B.C.– 1st century A.D.) and *Archer with Faun* (c.1st century B.C.–1st century A.D.), are framed separately, though they probably once belonged to the same wall design. At Berggasse 19, Freud arranged them at the corners of the consulting-room walls, creating a dynamic movement so it appears the archers are shooting at one another. In his London study, where they were hung by Freud's son Ernst, they face the other way.

The Pompeians decorated their villas with expertly rendered frescoes, choosing from a wide variety of mythological themes.

From the city's busy workshops, artists were selected to depict an image of Venus or the story of Meleager, home owners often choosing deities or heroes whose protection and goodwill they sought. The technique of mixing pigments with limewater before applying the final layer to wet plaster walls, perfected in Pompeii, has endured for centuries. After being prised from the walls, Pompeian frescoes were either transported to the museum at Naples or found their way to the international market. As is often the case, Freud does not mention where he bought the *Archers* frescoes, or their price. It is unknown whether the frescoes are Pompeian or Roman.[26]

Centaurs, half-man and half-horse, were members of the reckless retinue of Dionysus, like the satyr, the half-man, half-goat whom Freud described as 'a faun'. Though the centaur Chiron, gifted in the arts of learning and healing, was responsible for the education of Achilles, most centaurs were a wild bunch, boisterous, wine-loving and sensual. Both satyrs and centaurs were hybrids, composites of human and animal species. The Greeks were fond of such creatures, populating myths, legends and works of art with them. They represent uncivilised, natural forces, the instinctual, sexual drives that Freud championed and whose suppression, he believed, led to 'modern nervous illness'.[27] Freud's fresco fragments, however, do not illustrate a myth but, like many wall paintings, were purely decorative, employing a common language of symbolism to exquisite effect. The satyr and the centaur cheerfully wave branches and the archers spring from the stems of flowers. The satyr stands on a yellow frame, or door-way, within which a child is set against a shadowy, dark blue ground. Both works have become worn over time, especially *Archer with Centaur*.

There were plenty of reasons why Freud liked Jensen's *Gradiva*. At one point, Jensen describes how Hanold, disturbed by his encounter with Zoe/Gradiva, wanders the nearby countryside until he finds himself at an inn. The landlord, doubtless like many locals, was dealing in plundered artefacts and takes the opportunity to show Hanold 'his excavated treasures'. He tells Hanold he was present when the bodies of a young couple, locked in an embrace, were dug up. Eager to make a sale, the landlord produces a metal clasp 'covered with a green patina, which was said to have been retrieved from the ashes from beside the girl's remains'. Hanold banishes his 'critical doubts' and snaps it up.[28] It was the sort of situation, and the sort of cock-and-bull story, Freud must have grown familiar with hunting for antiquities.

Jensen's *Gradiva* also led Freud to his *Gradiva*. After its publication, Freud contacted Jensen who, he told Jung, 'has been really charming'. Jensen agreed that 'in all essential points my analysis corresponded to the intention of his story'.[29] Jensen also told Freud that the ancient relief actually existed and he had bought a copy from an art dealer in Munich, though he had never seen the original.[30] Freud wanted one, too, and soon a plaster cast of *Gradiva* was hanging in the consulting room (pl. 48), starting a fashion for the casts among psychoanalysts.

Freud also contacted Emmanuel Löwy in Rome, who sent him a postcard showing a reconstruction of the relief by German archaeologist Friedrich Hauser.[31] In a neat job of detective work, Hauser had reassembled the relief from three fragments: 'Gradiva', the most complete section, is in the Vatican's Chiaramonti Museum and the other two are in museums in Florence and Munich. Hauser suggested that the three beautiful maidens depicted were the Horae, 'goddesses of vegetation, and the deities of the fertilising dew' and that the relief was a Roman copy of a Greek original dating from the second half of the fourth century B.C.[32] A few months later, Freud visited the Vatican where he saw the original, 'the dear familiar face' of Gradiva, 'high up on a wall' among a host of other Greek and Roman antiquities.[33]

When *Gradiva* was republished in 1912, Freud added a post-script, describing the relief as belonging to 'the zenith of Greek art'.[34] The ancient Greeks divided the year into three seasons corresponding to the planting, harvesting and fallow cycles: spring, summer and winter. The Horae (the seasons or the hours) were goddesses of time, of fruitfulness and growth. Swift, graceful movement was their trademark. They were particularly honoured by farmers who sought their protection for the crops. Hesiod described them as 'the Watchers, Lawfulness, Justice, and flourishing Peace, who watch over the works of mortal men'.[35] *Gradiva* may represent winter. Dressed more warmly than her companion goddesses, one of whom bares a breast while the other pauses to water the earth, she walks briskly, her gaze resolute. She represents time, inexorably moving on.

Freud offered his *Gradiva* relief a suitable tribute. During travels in Sicily, he picked a papyrus plant that he placed in the frame above her head, so the flowing strands resemble hair, streaming behind her.[36]

By the time Freud and Jung departed for America in 1909, their friendship was firmly established. Jung, though full of admiration for Freud, was not a sycophant. '[L]et me enjoy your friendship not as one between equals but as that of father and son,' Jung wrote. 'The distance appears to me fitting and natural.' Jung predicted, rather too confidently as it turned out, that it would 'prevent misunderstandings and enable two hard-headed people to exist alongside one another in an easy and unstrained relationship'. Freud did not want to be idolised: 'I shall do my best to show you that I am unfit to be an object of worship,' he told Jung.[37]

At their first meeting, at Berggasse 19, the two men had talked without a break for thirteen hours. Before sailing to New York in August 1909, they met at Bremen where Freud was joined by Sándor Ferenczi, who was accompanying them. Jung, who knew the city, led a tour that included the famous lead cellar and crypt of Bremen Cathedral, quite a chamber of horrors, where corpses buried there had become mummified and were on display. Freud explained in his travel journal that four hundred years earlier, a workman who had accidentally fallen from the roof was buried in the cellar and, years later, was discovered to have been preserved like a mummy. Even corpses of birds hung there. Keen on the effect, wealthy citizens of Bremen arranged to be entombed in the cellar. Freud, however, thought it was a case for cremation.

Later, the three lunched at one of Bremen's top restaurants where, after a few glasses of wine, the conversation turned to the mummified corpses. Jung confused the Bremen mummies with the prehistoric 'peat-bog corpses' found occasionally in northern Germany and Sweden. The bog water preserved the dead bodies perfectly so 'a process of natural mummification' took place. It was the sort of topic that would usually intrigue Freud but, in Jung's version of the event, Freud took umbrage. 'Why are you so concerned with these corpses?' he asked Jung several times. Then he fainted. He later told Jung that 'all this chatter about corpses' meant Jung harboured 'death wishes towards him'.[38] In his travel journal, Freud merely notes that he was light-headed from the wine and a bad night's sleep, resulting in 'a sweat and weakness . . . [that] naturally was soon over'.[39]

Jung knew fainting could be a protective device. After being bullied at school, he had used fainting fits to stay at home, only relenting when he overheard his father despairing about his son's future prospects. Through an effort of will, Jung overcame the debility and never fainted again, reflecting, '[t]hat was when I learned what a neurosis is'.[40]

For the next seven weeks, Freud and Jung were 'together every day, and analysed each other's dreams'.[41] They visited museums, an event all too rare for Jung, whose workload at the sanatorium did not permit the luxuriously long holidays that Freud took. Jung's interest in Egyptian art had been fired when he visited the Louvre in 1902, so he particularly enjoyed the collection at New York's Metropolitan Museum. Having trained himself to sell antiques to fund his university education, Jung had developed a sharp eye for beautiful things. After a shopping spree with Freud, he complained that Freud's contagious example had let him in for 'some diabolical expenses', including a painting and three 'marvellous drawings'. Jung admitted 'where objets d'art are concerned I easily go *non compos mentis*'.[42]

On his return from America, Jung was brimming with confidence and ideas: indeed, the direction of his life's work had coalesced. In order to follow his own star and to give himself more time, Jung resigned from the Burghölzli sanatorium, a move resembling Freud's professional daring after his journey to Paris when he went into private practice. 'Archaeology or rather mythology has got me in its grip,' Jung told Freud, 'it's a mine of marvellous material. Won't you cast a beam of light in that direction?' Freud was glad that Jung shared his belief that 'we must conquer the whole field of mythology'. Freud, too, felt inspired, telling Jung that 'the riddle of Leonardo's character has suddenly become clear to me'.[43]

Soon Jung was so immersed in the study of mythology that he neglected to reply to Freud's letters, and earned a rebuke. 'Pater, peccavi,' Jung wrote: 'Father, forgive me'. Though gently poking fun at Freud's possessiveness, Jung was worried. He believed his explorations were rich and meaningful but would Freud dismiss them as mere 'spookery'?[44] Late one night, the two were ensconced in Freud's study, discussing the occult. As Jung remembered it, Freud 'rejected this entire complex of questions as nonsensical' and Jung 'had difficulty in checking the sharp retort on the tip of my tongue', giving him 'a curious sensation . . . as if my diaphragm were made of iron and were becoming red-hot – a glowing vault'.[45] Suddenly there was a crash from the bookcase. Jung announced that another would soon follow – which it did. Jung believed he had detected a poltergeist.

Freud offers another interpretation. It seems that Jung had been trying to conjure occult phenomena, perhaps to convince Freud of their existence. Freud had an open mind on the matter, admitting to Jung that the experiment left a 'deep impression' on him. After Jung left, Freud kept trying to summon the poltergeist, without result. He deduced that the creaking floorboards in the consulting room were due, not to spirits, but to the weight of the Egyptian stelae on top of the bookshelves. It was 'the magic of your personal presence' that led to his 'willingness to believe', and, alone in his study, Freud wrote to Jung that he confronted 'the despiritualised furniture as the poet confronted undeified Nature after the gods of Greece had passed away'.[46] Freud reflected that his own life 'had been particularly poor in an occult sense'.[47]

But, as Freud reminded Jung, he was not averse to exploring the paranormal. The story about his fatalism regarding numbers was told to underline the point. He had 'grown humble since the great lesson Ferenczi's experiences gave me. I promise to believe anything that can be made to look reasonable.'[48] After their return from America, Freud had stayed briefly in Berlin with Ferenczi, who visited a medium named Frau Seidler. Ferenczi conveyed his excitement about Frau Seidler's mind-reading abilities to Freud who, though impressed, surmised 'it is only a matter of thought transference . . . certainly a novelty of the first rank'.[49] In 1913, a seance was conducted at Berggasse 19 by the so-called 'Professor' Alexander Roth and a female medium. In attendance were Otto Rank and Hanns Sachs, as well as Anna and several other members of Freud's family. 'It went very miserably,' Freud told Ferenczi,'hardly any indication of success.'[50] But he remained intrigued. In 1921 Freud told British author Hereward Carrington, who founded the American Psychical Institute and Laboratory, that 'if I were at the beginning rather than at the end of a scientific career, as I am today, I might choose this field of research, in spite of all the difficulties'.[51] Three years later, Freud conducted 'thought-transference' experiments with Anna and Ferenczi that were 'remarkably good, particularly those in which I played the medium and then analyzed my associations'.[52] In the 1930s, when discussing telepathy and clairvoyance with a patient, Freud remarked, 'There is something in it . . . Now, telepathy is a possibility and is worth study.'[53]

Deeply involved in myth, Jung's spiritual sense was heightened and he was having 'the most marvellous visions, glimpses of far-ranging interconnections'. Freud was intrigued and delighted, though he reminded Jung that 'the ultimate basis for religion is *infantile helplessness.*' He wanted to hear more of Jung's investigations, especially, since the return from America, 'something has diverted me from working in those fields'.[54] Was Jung occupying the ground that previously belonged to Freud? Jung was undergoing an intense inner journey, similar to the one experienced by Freud after his father's death which led to his self-analysis and *The Interpretation of Dreams*. But Jung did not want to fully share his researches with Freud. He was too fearful of his mentor's reaction. Meanwhile, he was working at a furious rate: Freud had cajoled him into becoming president of the International Psychoanalytic Association as well as editing a yearbook devoted to psychoanalysis.[55] In the latter, Jung published the fruits of his labours, *Wandlungen und Symbole der Libido* (Symbols of transformation), in two parts in 1911 and 1912.[56] Jung based the study on the dreams, visions and writings of Frank Miller, a young American woman, who was not his patient but whose case had attracted his attention.

Symbols opens with a homage to Freud, and what better device to use than archaeology? Jung likens the effect of reading about the Oedipus legend in *The Interpretation of Dreams* to 'that wholly peculiar feeling which arises in us if, amid the noise and tumult of a modern street, we should come across an ancient relic'. Freud directed attention towards 'things of another order; a glimpse away from the incoherent multiplicity of the present to a higher coherence of history', the same impression gained by 'the first acquaintance with the monuments of antiquity'.[57]

Shortly after the first part of *Symbols* was published, Freud announced that 'my work in these last weeks has dealt with the same theme as yours, to wit, the origin of religion'. He had started writing *Totem and Taboo*.[58] Aware how anxious this development would make Jung, Freud assured him that 'probably my tunnels will be far more subterranean than your shafts and we shall pass each other by'. But Jung was not so easily placated, telling Freud, 'the outlook for me is very gloomy if you too get into the psychology of religion. You are a dangerous rival — if one has to speak of rivalry.'[59]

Freud based *Totem and Taboo* on Darwin's notion of 'the primal horde', developing the theory that a possessive, polygamous father who asserted exclusive rights over the women of the tribe was challenged, then killed and eaten, by his sons. Though anthropologists have debunked Freud's theory, he regarded *Totem and Taboo* as the historical explanation of the incest prohibition and the Oedipus complex. Jung was engaged in a complementary but opposite area: 'This time I have ventured to tackle the mother.' From that angle, Jung examined incest, surmising the cornerstone of Freudian theory was 'a fantasy problem'. He believed that the 'tremendous role of the mother in mythology has a significance far outweighing the biological incest problem'.[60]

Though Freud acknowledged the existence of influential female social and religious forces, such as the great goddess worshipped by the Minoans, mother goddesses were usurped by male gods and so 'matriarchy was succeeded by patriarchal order'.[61] It worried Jung that Freud made few comments about *Symbols*, aside from telling him that matriarchy did not mean women escaped being members of the tribal chief's harem, their 'polygamous abasement'. With disagreement looming about the role that mothers and fathers took in the formation of society and the psyche, Jung became even more close-lipped about the second part of *Symbols* and, quoting Goethe's *Faust*, told Freud he was 'hidden' in the underworld in 'the realm of the Mothers'.[62]

In Vienna's Natural History Museum, Freud could see one of
the most famous mother goddesses of all time. In 1908, a small
limestone statue of a woman was discovered near the Austrian
town of Willendorf on the Danube. Named the *Venus of
Willendorf*, she was first thought to date from around 15,000 B.C.,
the same period as the Lascaux cave paintings, but subsequently
she has been dated to around 25,000 B.C., making her an artefact
of the Ice Age and one of the world's oldest and most mysterious
icons.[63] Only eleven centimetres high, *Venus* is a powerful and
compact image of a faceless woman with exaggerated breasts, belly
and labia. Braids around her head could be hair or a cap. Hers is
a surprisingly erotic presence. Debate continues about her identity
and function. Was she a fertility goddess or an example of palaeolithic pornography? A plaything or a sacred object designed for
worship and travel with the hunter-gatherer tribe who produced
her? In Freud's time, she was regarded as the symbol of an earth
goddess cult.

Freud had a similarly mysterious female in his collection.
Found in the Orontes Valley in Syria, *Female Figure* (c.2000–1750
B.C.; pl. 27) is a fraction bigger than the *Venus*, less sensual and more
elegant. Made from terracotta, she has a flat schematised body and
a birdlike face with enormous eyes. Once she was adorned: her
pierced ears held earrings and there were decorations in the socket
in her forehead and her doughnut-shaped navel. Incisions on her
thighs indicate her pudenda.[64] Without exaggerated sexual characteristics, can she be classed as a fertility goddess? Among recent
excavations at the ancient Syrian city of Ebla (Tell Mardikh),
figurines like Freud's were found in a *favissa* (pit used for the
disposal of objects used in a temple) in the acropolis, an area sacred
to Ishtar.[65] *Female Figure* may have been an offering to Ishtar –

afterwards, like other offerings, she was disposed of. Due to the vast numbers of figures offered to the gods as gifts by devout pilgrims, temple repositories had to be cleared out periodically and the old offerings buried in the vicinity of the god's shrine. Such caches, frequently stumbled upon by diggers, are the source of most divine figures encountered today in private and public collections.[66]

Ishtar was the region's super-goddess, in charge of love, storms, fertility and war. Sacred prostitution was part of her worship. When her lover Tammuz died, Ishtar descended to the underworld to find him, as Isis had searched for Osiris and revived him. Jung explored the Isis/Osiris myth in *Symbols*. To Jung, Isis was the kind of mother goddess whose 'tremendous role' remained significant; Freud positioned rivalries between males as the prime cultural determinant. Both agreed that the revival of classical civilisation was essential to understand modern society and the neuroses. But Freud's view was bleak: there was no spiritual consolation, no transcendence. Jung's universe was kinder and more optimistic, balanced between male and female, and galvanised by the spirit rather than by sex. Myth, Jung wrote, 'gives man assurance and strength', it is *'psychologically true,* because it was and is the bridge to all the greatest achievements of humanity'.[67] As the gulf widened between Freud and Jung, they bickered about fathers and mothers by letter.

At their next meeting at a conference in Munich in November 1912, Freud and Jung set off on a two-hour walk to thrash out their problems. There were professional and personal misunderstandings to clear up, a cluster of suspicions, disappointments and hurt feelings. Jung was apologetic, begging Freud to '[p]lease forgive and forget the mistakes which I will not try to excuse or extenuate'.[68] The rift apparently healed, they joined the other conference members for lunch. Freud was in high spirits, elated at winning over Jung again. But the atmosphere remained tense.

Freud sniped at the Swiss delegates because their recent publications had omitted his work and even his name. Then followed a discussion about Karl Abraham's paper on Akhenaten in which he suggested the pharaoh's negative attitude towards his father, Amenophis III, had led him not only to destroy the latter's images but that a father complex lurked behind Akhenaten's monotheism. Jung rushed to Akhenaten's defence. In *Symbols*, Jung had described the pharaoh's reforms as 'psychologically important'.[69] He was 'a profoundly religious person whose acts could not be explained by personal resistance to his father'. Just as he had done at Bremen, Freud swooned. Jung swept Freud up in his arms and carried him into another room. As Freud came to, Jung would 'never forget the look he cast at me. In his weakness he looked at me as if I were his father.'[70]

Amenophis III revelled in opulence and luxury and, like his son, showed little interest in governing the country. He initiated a costly building programme that included a vast new temple at Luxor, where he was depicted on a wall relief being blessed by the god Amon. When it was his turn to reign, Akhenaten systematically destroyed the images of Amon. Jung argued it was not his father's image Akhenaten sought to eradicate but evidence of polytheism. In *Moses and Monotheism*, Freud, too, praised Akhenaten, noting he expunged the name Amon 'from every inscription – even when it occurred in the name of his father, Amenophis III'.[71] Though in 1912 Freud seemed overwhelmed by the heady mix of controlling his heir apparent and then hearing an argument about a son's brutal treatment of his father's legacy, in *Moses and*

Monotheism, written two decades later, he sided with the son. Even though Akhenaten's experiment failed, both Freud and Jung agreed that it was a bold attempt to achieve a higher stage of cultural development.

Freud's bronze statue of *Amon-Re* (c.716–332 B.C; pl. 28) shows the god who survived Akhenaten's programme of destruction. One of the oldest Egyptian deities, Amon means 'the hidden one', indicating his pervasive yet abstract nature. Over time, Amon attained an almost unrivalled position and was known as 'the king of the gods' and 'the lord of heaven'. To his name was added that of the sun god Ra, forming a great being who combined solar energy with invisible creative power.[72] *Amon-Re* is a quietly energetic figure, who strides forward wearing his symbolic crown of double plumes with a solar disk. He provides an apposite emblem of Freud's collection: despite his varied fortunes over time, *Amon-Re* has endured, his patina a little corroded but none the worse for wear.

Despite the reconciliation at the Munich meeting, relations between Jung and Freud continued to decline. Freud behaved with admirable sangfroid, clinging to the idea that their professional relationship at least could be saved. But Jung made it impossible and his final letters to Freud are studies in invective. He accused Freud of 'treating your pupils like patients' which 'is a *blunder*' and meant 'you either produce slavish sons or impudent puppies'. Jung, however, was 'objective enough to see through your little trick . . . You go around sniffing out all the symptomatic actions in your vicinity, thus reducing everyone to the level of sons and daughters who blushingly admit the existence of their faults. Meanwhile you remain on top as the father, sitting pretty.'[73]

Jung was experiencing a kind of nervous breakdown, brought on by a constellation of pressures, including the need to distance himself from Freud and to develop his own theories. There was also the factor of sheer exhaustion – Jung had been working at a frantic pace since he was at school, driving himself to achieve. Even Emma's fortune offered little respite as Jung strove to demonstrate that he was not dependent on her. Between 1912 and 1914, Jung divested himself of many of his professional responsibilities, resigning as editor of the journal, president of the International Psychoanalytic Association and lecturer at the University of Zurich. Though he did not cease work, he spent hours each day playing in silence with self-made toys on the shores of the lake near his home. It was not until 1921 that he published his next major work, *Psychological Types*, and began to develop such influential ideas as the anima and the animus, the archetype and the collective unconscious. If Jung had stayed faithful to Freud, he would have become another 'Freudian', like Jones or Ferenczi. As it was, he founded his own school – analytical psychology.

Freud seemed relatively unruffled by the breach. In 1913, after a final, nasty interlude with Jung, he travelled to Rome with Minna Bernays, staying at the swank Hotel Eden near the Spanish Steps. He assured Karl Abraham, 'I have quickly recovered my spirits and zest for work in the incomparably beautiful Rome.' There were 'visits to museums, churches, and the Campagna' plus time to write the introduction to *Totem and Taboo*.[74] No doubt plenty of shopping therapy was involved. Then he hurried into print with 'History of the Psychoanalytical Movement', which firmly put Jung in his place. Freud had selected Jung as his successor due to his 'exceptional talents', but Jung had to relinquish 'certain racial prejudices' – that is, anti-Semitism – before friendly relations could be established. Soon Freud recognised his choice was 'a most unfortunate one' because Jung was a person not only 'incapable of tolerating the authority of another' but who was 'relentlessly devoted to the furtherance of his own interests'.[75]

Jung had demonised others in Freud's cause, attacking the opponents of psychoanalysis and gleefully reporting to Freud on his stoushes, so he knew exactly what to expect. Jung was vulnerable because he lacked the supporters that surrounded Freud, which included the Committee, the band of young stalwarts instigated by Ernest Jones. After parting with Freud, Jung admitted he was in 'a state of disorientation. I felt totally suspended in mid-air.'[76]

Was Freud immune from grief? As Louis Rose notes, 'After 1914, Freud never returned to the interpretation of visual art, as if he had lost that feeling for images whose emotional power over him had once been so remarkable.'[77] Had Jung helped to illuminate a path in the forest of images that was extinguished on his departure, a fire that had created both clarity and combustion? Perhaps Jung represented an animus for Freud, a bright, inspiring masculine force that heralded change and encouraged the exploration of new horizons. A member of his circle recalled that Jung 'had such radiance he was overwhelming. The man had so much charisma . . . He could not help it, it was just his personality. But I also believe it was why women fused with him and why men had to quarrel and leave.'[78] Masculine and feminine, fathers and mothers – these roles represented divergences between Freud and Jung.

Jung wished to give the 'mother complex' a positive emphasis because in psychoanalysis it was 'always associated with injury or illness'. Freud minimised the power of the mother in accounts of his own life and in the development of civilisation. Jung's mother, with her uncanny predictions and seances, was the portal to the realm of the spirits. Freud's mother was an erotic object, the desired bounty in the war between father and son. Describing a man with a mother complex, 'a finely differentiated Eros', Jung creates an interesting portrait of Freud. Such a man may have

> a great capacity for friendship, which creates ties of astonish-ing tenderness between men . . . He may have good taste and an aesthetic sense which are fostered by the presence of a feminine streak. Then he may be supremely gifted as a teacher because of his almost feminine insight and tact. He is likely to have a feeling for history, and to be conservative in the best sense and cherish the values of the past.

His other characteristics may include an 'ambitious striving after the highest goals . . . perseverance, inflexibility and toughness of will; a curiosity that does not shrink even from the riddles of the universe; and finally, a revolutionary spirit which strives to put a new face upon the world'. [79] Jung's portrait could only be uncon-scious. For the rest of his life, his feelings about Freud remained tangled. But Freud managed to salvage something from the rela-tionship. Typically, it was from the world of objects. When he left Vienna, he had to select which books to take with him to London – included were all of Jung's.

II

Family, Friends and Dealers

On June 29 there was the annual social evening . . . in the Prater, and I remember an ex-patient presenting Freud with an Egyptian figure which he kept in front of his plate as a totem.

ERNEST JONES, SIGMUND FREUD[1]

AFTER FREUD'S PREDILECTION FOR antiquities became known, he was often given presents. Some came from the furthest reaches of Freud's new empire, such as Japan and India; others were from close friends, like Princess Marie Bonaparte, who knew Freud's taste and offered him choice examples. But most objects joined the collection the time-honoured way: from the antiquities dealers of Vienna. With Anna, his youngest child, Freud shared not just the enterprise of psychoanalysis but a taste for beautiful things.

The only time his antiquities took their place elsewhere in the apartment was when Anna borrowed several to place on her desk.

During the First World War, Freud's three prime pleasures – antique hunting, travelling and smoking the best cigars – were seriously curtailed. Confined to Vienna during August 1914, Freud was anxious about the fate of his son Martin, who was in training before joining his artillery regiment. Freud was forced to 'sit at home and economise, which is a disgustingly unaccustomed activity'. His colleague Otto Rank, 'in order to overcome boredom', decided to catalogue Freud's library, 'and I have thought up a similar game; I take my antiquities and study and describe every piece'.[2] Cigars were in short supply owing to wartime restrictions and, with the borders closed, the antiquities market had slowed. Freud was reduced to bartering Minna's embroideries with a local tobacconist for cigars. Nor did he have ready cash. His practice, which had been growing nicely by 1914, had dissipated by the war's end. Soaring inflation destroyed Freud's savings and it was only the arrival of British and American clients, paying in the stable currencies of pounds and dollars, that redeemed him financially. Ernest Jones evokes the gloom of post-war Vienna:

> Everything had come to a standstill in Vienna and life there was scarcely bearable. The monotonous diet of thin vegetable soup was far from being adequately nourishing and the pangs of hunger were continuous. The winters of 1918–19 and 1919–20 were the worst of all, with completely unheated rooms and feeble illumination. It needed a tough spirit to

endure sitting still and treating patients for hour after hour in that deadly cold, even if equipped with an overcoat and gloves.[3]

Anna, then nineteen years old, returned from holidaying in England at the outbreak of war. She was the last child left at home, a girl longing for her father's attention, after having had to compete with older siblings including Sophie, the favoured child of both parents. Anna admitted to Freud there was an 'unending quarrel' between herself and Sophie. 'It was no matter for her,' Anna reflected bitterly, 'because she did not care for me, but I liked her very much and admired her a bit.'[4] When Sophie died in 1920, pregnant with her third child, Anna was there to comfort her parents. When Freud was diagnosed with cancer of the palate in 1923, the result of his addiction to cigars, Anna became his nurse and ministering angel. Freud dubbed her Antigone, the dutiful daughter of Oedipus.

The Freuds were not keen for their three daughters to enter higher education, so the girls were educated at the Lyceum, not the Gymnasium with its classical curriculum that provided the doorway to university. The girls' destiny was to be good wives and mothers, like Martha, not independent professional women. Freud forbade his sons to study medicine. One doctor in the house was obviously enough. Nor did Freud, with his concerns about Oedipal struggles, want to raise a rival. Martin studied law and the younger sons seem have inherited their father's topographical imagination: Ernst became an architect and Oliver a mechanical engineer.

Anna, bright, imaginative and headstrong, had been attending meetings of the Vienna Psychoanalytic Society since she was

fourteen and avidly read her father's work. In 1914, she enrolled
in a teaching training course, finally graduating as a primary
school teacher, and earned Freud's esteem. 'She is, incidentally,
developing charmingly,' he told Ferenczi, 'more gratifying than
any of the other children.'[5] Freud began interpreting her dreams,
often adventures with Anna as the hero. 'I dreamed you were a
king and I was a princess,' she wrote to him. 'Someone wanted to
separate us by political intrigues. It was not at all nice and quite
thrilling.'[6] Her sojourn in England had caused Freud anxiety, and
not only because war broke out and she had to make her way
home under the wing of the Austrian ambassador. In London,
Ernest Jones, ladies' man and Freud's lieutenant, might try to
seduce the princess and secure a dynastic marriage. Freud need
not have worried. Anna had decided she would never leave
Daddy, and certainly not for a man.

Their relationship is captured in a photograph from 1913
(pl. 49). That August, Freud, accompanied by Martha, Minna
and Anna, travelled to San Martino di Castrozza, high up in the
Dolomites, in the heart of the Primiero valley. Freud told Ferenczi,
who joined them later, 'my closest companion will be my little
daughter'.[7] It was prior to the psychoanalytic conference in Munich
where Freud and Jung had their final unhappy encounter. Freud
was dreading the conference and Anna recalled it was the only time
she saw her father depressed.[8] In between hikes with Anna, Freud
planned tactics with Ferenczi and Karl Abraham.

In the photograph Freud and Anna are dressed in elaborate
holiday outfits. When the Viennese went out to play, dress codes
still applied. Freud wears a hunter's kit – knickerbocker suit, stout
walking boots and a green fedora with a cockade – and carries a
knapsack, a walking stick and a pipe, it being too difficult to puff

Plate 31: Jacob Freud. 1890. (Courtesy Mary Evans Picture Library/ Sigmund Freud Copyrights.)

Plate 32: Max Pollak. *Sigmund Freud at his desk.* 1914. Etching. (Courtesy Freud Museum London.)

Plate 33: Amalia and Sigmund, 1872. (Courtesy Freud Museum London.)

Plate 34: Amalia (seated centre), Sigmund (standing behind her) and Jacob (seated far right) with family members, 1876. (Courtesy Freud Museum London.)

Plate 35: Freud and his fiancée, Martha Bernays, in Wandsbek in 1885. Freud was on his way to Paris to study under Charcot. (Courtesy Mary Evans Picture Library/ Sigmund Freud Copyrights.)

Plate 36: Andre Brouillet, *Une Leçon Clinique à la Salpêtrière*. Lithograph by Eugene-Louis Pirodon. (Courtesy Freud Museum London.)

Plate 37: The Freud family, c.1898. Rear: Martin and his father. Middle, from left: Oliver, Martha Freud and Minna Bernays. Front, from left: Sophie, Anna and Ernst. (Courtesy Freud Museum London.)

Plate 38: Berggasse 19. 1938. (Edmund Engelman, courtesy Thomas Engelman.)

Plate 39: Freud and Wilhelm Fliess in the 1890s. (Courtesy Mary Evans Picture Library / Sigmund Freud Copyrights.)

Plate 40: The family at Jacob's grave, 1897. Freud (second from left), Amalia (far right). (Alexander Freud, courtesy Freud Museum London.)

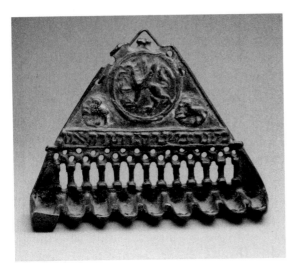

Plate 41: *Hanukkah Lamp*. Northern France or Germany. 13th century. Copper alloy, cast in the lost wax method. 12.7 × 17 × 5 cm. Cat. no. 4515. (Courtesy Freud Museum London.)

Plate 42: Freud with plaster cast of Michelangelo's *Dying Slave*, c.1905. (Martin Freud, courtesy Freud Museum London.)

Plate 43: Freud's ashes, Golders Green Cemetery, London. The red-figured Greek urn from around the 4th century B.C. was given to Freud by Princess Marie Bonaparte. The black marble plinth was designed by Ernst Freud. Martha's ashes are also interred in the urn.
(Courtesy Mary Evans Picture Library / Sigmund Freud Copyrights.)

Plate 44: The Committee, 1922. Standing, from left: Otto Rank, Karl Abraham, Max Eitingon and Ernest Jones. Seated, from left: Freud, Sándor Ferenczi and Hanns Sachs. Sachs and Ferenczi are wearing their intaglio rings. (Courtesy Freud Museum London.)

Plate 45: 39 Elsworthy Road, London, 1938. Freud is wearing his intaglio ring and holding the inevitable cigar. (Courtesy Mary Evans Picture Library/Sigmund Freud Copyrights.)

Plate 46: Karl Maria Schwerdtner, *Oedipus and the Sphinx* (reverse of bronze medal).
1906. Freud Museum Vienna. Freud was given the medal on his 50th birthday.
(Courtesy Mary Evans Picture Library/ Sigmund Freud Copyrights.)

Plate 47: In America, 1909. Standing, from left: Abraham A. Brill, Ernest Jones, Sándor Ferenczi. Seated, from left: Freud, G. Stanley Hall, Carl Jung. Hall, Professor of Psychology and President of Clark University, Worcester, Massachusetts, had invited Freud and Jung to give a series of lectures there. (Courtesy Freud Museum London.)

Plate 48: Freud's consulting room. *Centaur with Archer* (far left). Above couch, print of *The Great Temple of Ramesses at Abu Simbel* (Egyptian Nineteenth Dynasty, c.1260 B.C.). *Gradiva* (Far right). (Edmund Engelman, courtesy Thomas Engelman.)

Plate 49: Freud and Anna in the Dolomites, 1913. (Courtesy Freud Museum London.)

Plate 50: *White Vishnu*. Indian. 1931. Ivory. 0 × 10 × 5 cm.
Cat. no. 3004. (Courtesy Freud Museum London.)

Plate 51: H.D. (Hilda Doolittle). 1922. (Man Ray, courtesy Beinecke Rare Book and Manuscript Library, Yale University.)

Plate 52: *Freud's consulting room*. Photograph shows (above) *Centaur with Archer* and *Centaur with Satyr*; (centre) *Head from Statue of a Man*; (left) *Frontal Covering of a Mummy*. (Edmund Engelman, courtesy Thomas Engelman.)

Plate 53: *Freud's desk*. 1938. (Edmund Engelman, courtesy Thomas Engelman.)

Plate 54: *Freud at his desk*. 1938. (Edmund Engelman, courtesy Thomas Engelman.)

Plate 55: Salvador Dalí. *Portrait of Sigmund Freud*. 1938. Pen on paper. 34.8 × 28 cm. Cat. no. 6388. (Courtesy Freud Museum London.)

a cigar on a hike. Anna wears Austrian national dress, a dirndl with an apron and a loose sleeved blouse. It was a style, with modifications, she assumed for the rest of her life. Father and daughter make a handsome couple. Freud is a fit, alert fifty-seven. Anna, the slender, sweet-faced teenager, squints in the sunshine, her expression quizzical, a little shy, her outfit emphasising her innocence. As Freud strides forward, she grips his arm tightly. Her feet are together, she does not move. In the posed and frozen moment, Anna anchors her father, the companion who, with quiet determination, has attached herself to him.

Anna adored travelling with Freud. When he went to America in 1909, she ached to accompany him. It was a role that, like the others she desired in her father's life, she achieved slowly, subtly and decisively. In the Dolomites, Martha and Minna went strolling together; anything more vigorous tired them. It gave Anna the chance to set off alone with her father. Holidays were precious to the Freud children because they provided them with their annual allotment of their father's time. Freud was a delightful and informative guide on such excursions, taking them on mushroom hunts and rambles through 'wild forests and woods' where he would describe butterflies, flowers and anything else that caught his fancy.[9] Earlier in 1913, Freud had taken Anna to Venice for a week, which she loved, developing a liking for Italy similar to his own. Nature was a necesary pleasure for her, too. In 1930, she bought a weekender at Hochrotherd, not far from Vienna. Each week she visited the property, bringing fresh milk, eggs and other produce back to Berggasse 19. By then, Anna's wage was an important part of the family economy.

Anna liked dressing up, the shy girl creating an individual look and a persona that both masked and revealed her identity.

She developed a taste for necklaces and Freud gave her some fine examples as birthday presents, including pearls and jade. Like Freud, she enjoyed both giving and receiving, and often made gifts of necklaces to her friends. Anna's Austrian costume, common to the entire alpine region, was, in the post-war period, fashionably uncluttered. Loose and comfortable outfits for women, with straight skirts and dropped waists, were the rage in the 1920s when a boyish figure without the hint of a curve became the ideal. Her frocks with their wide, simple necks were also ideally suited to display her necklaces. Anna represented the 'new independent young woman with her career, her pay packet, her improved job prospects and her freedom to live her own life'.[10]

Equally, Anna's style was her own. She incorporated features sentimentally important to her: the dress identified the places she had holidayed as a child, reminiscent of both the natural world she cherished and precious times spent with her father. Her interest in handcrafts, especially knitting and weaving, meant her clothes often incorporated fine embroidery. If, as Jean Baudrillard has written, modernity is a code and fashion is its emblem, Anna's commitment to modernity was expressed, like Freud's, with ambivalence.[11] The father of the twentieth-century mind surrounded himself with the mementos of ancient cultures. His daughter, a pioneer in the psychoanalysis of children, arrayed herself in nostalgic peasant garb.

In post-war Europe, traditional costumes were rarely worn among countryfolk, except on special occasions. The places where such traditional dress, known as *Tracht*, remained important were in parts of Bavaria and Austria, the Black Forest, Lower Saxony and the Harz mountains.[12] From the nineteenth century, adopting regional costume became a popular statement by young city dwellers to symbolise community, ethnicity and the importance of rural handcrafts – aspects of culture eroded by mass production and urbanisation. In the streets of Vienna, Anna looked as though she belonged in the country; in the country, the sophisticated, middle-class woman tried to look like a peasant. In either place, she looked 'other'.

Traditional dress was a way of identifying with *Heimat*, homeland. But where was the homeland of the Jewish-Austrian intellectual? Anna, it seemed, wanted to fashion an answer. She wanted the best of both worlds. The country symbolised health, holidays and freedom, as well as stability and continuity. The city offered other freedoms and challenges, the exciting pace of change, as well as such unpleasant features as overcrowding, noise and pollution. As Joanne Finkelstein writes, fashion can become a masquerade. 'Instead of positioning individuals in a fixed social universe, it promises to fulfill their desires to perform multiple social identities.'[13] Anna constructed her femininity, her identity as a woman, dualistically: she appeared as ultra-feminine in her long skirts and blouses but not sexy or seductive, not 'womanly'. She belonged to the city, to modernity, but her clothes associated her with unchanging values, epitomised by the conventions of rural dress. She was Jewish and without a homeland, yet her *Tracht* costumes defined her as a patriotic Austrian. Freud, who liked slim girlish youthfulness and not the 1920s flapper craze for short skirts or shingled hair, probably approved. '[A]rty but neat', is how H.D. summarised Anna's appearance.[14]

Synthesising what she treasured from her past and desired from the present led Anna to specialise in the treatment of children. It was an area she could explore without becoming engaged in border disputes of the kind that had bedevilled Jung's and Freud's researches into the psychology of religion. Though her father had published a case study on 'Little Hans', the boy had not been his patient and children were not his speciality.[15] Childhood, the foundation zone of psychoanalysis, became Anna's realm. She was a gifted teacher of children – warm, kind, firm and methodical – and was remembered fondly by her young charges.[16]

In 1918, she won her father's permission to train as a psycho-analyst and began a four-year analysis with him (extremely long by standards then), a secret kept from all but their closest colleagues. Though it seems bizarre that a daughter could undergo analysis with her father, at the time it was difficult to find another analyst in Vienna whom Anna did not know and in whom she could fully put her trust. The history of psychoanalysis was one of bruising dissensions and defections, so there was the worrying possibility that intimate details, even among staunch friends, might eventually leak out. For Anna, it offered the chance of a closer bond with her father, as well as an incomparable education in her chosen profession. As Paul Roazen notes, Anna's work with children had a distinctive cast from the outset. She was interested in 'adapting classical psychoanalytic technique to the special capacities and strengths of young children who will not lie on a couch and free associate'. Her view was that children needed to establish 'an educative relationship' with the therapist before accepting interpretations.[17]

In 1922, when Anna set up her practice at Berggasse 19, her rooms were, in their own way, as distinctive as Freud's. But her taste was not uncompromising. Governed by a characteristic attraction to synthesis, Anna included a combination of modernist and folk furniture, plus some of her father's antiquities. In her consulting room, the couch, with its casually arranged cushions, gave the place a relaxed air, somewhat diminished by Ferdinand

Schmutzer's stern portrait of Papa glowering on the wall.[18] She asked architect and interior designer Felix Augenfeld to design a bookcase. Augenfeld, a friend of her brother Ernst, made a sleekly handsome, dark wood object with the clean lines and simplified style of modernism, inset with an abstracted landscape painting. (Augenfeld received another commission from the Freud family: he made Freud's unusually shaped desk chair.) Nearby, Anna placed a distinctive folk art cabinet, contextualising her contemporary instincts with an example of rural handcraft. She also included chairs by major modernist designers Mies van der Rohe and Alvar Aalto.

At Anna's desk, where she interviewed prospective patients as well as attending to business matters, she invoked her father's authority by arranging several of his antiquities. In the centre was *Neith* (c.600 B.C. [Late Period]), the Egyptian warrior goddess. Freud had several statues of Neith: one stood on his desk with two more on the bookcase in the consulting room. Anna's *Neith*, on her desk around 1920, was returned to Freud's rooms where Edmund Engelman photographed it in 1938. In Egyptian mythology, Neith commanded several powerful roles. In predynastic times, she was an androgynous creator god, later assuming female characteristics and becoming the mother of Ra, the sun god. Like Athena, she was a level-headed mediator chosen by the other gods to solve their disputes. Neith was interchangeable with Isis, a goddess of magic and mysteries. She was also a warrior and a huntress, often depicted with bow and arrows, and a protector of Egypt's royal house. Neith was a weaver of the universe, of time and space leading, as E.A. Wallis Budge points out, to her becoming patroness of weaving, Anna's favourite craft.[19]

Athena, another masculine warrior goddess, was at the centre of Freud's desk. Her birth was spectacular. She sprang fully formed from the head of her father, Zeus, 'with a triumphant cry of victory, armed and brandishing a sharp javelin'.[20] Responsible and fair-minded, as well as a fierce fighter for those to whom she was committed, Athena was the embodiment of intellect and reason. Freud knew that Athena was 'the veiled Isis or Neith'.[21] Nor can he have missed the point of the myth as it applied to Anna, the daughter who became her father's representative and a warrior for the cause of psycho-analysis. Both Athena and Anna were skilled tacticians.

Combining masculine and feminine roles, as Neith and Athena did, was Anna's ideal, and her strategies were surprisingly success-ful. Needing her father's respect and attention made her a dutiful daughter, but ambitions to participate in the psychoanalytic movement, and become her father's 'right-hand man', meant assuming power in a competitive and intellectually rigorous arena. She also yearned for her own fulfilling love and family life but she did not want to leave home to get it. Though Anna enjoyed close friendships with older women in Freud's circle such as Lou Andreas-Salomé, she was not a lesbian, nor, as far as it is known, were there affairs with men.

In 1925, Dorothy Burlingham arrived in Vienna with her four children, having fled a cluster of family problems in America. She, too, was the youngest child of an illustrious father. For more than two decades, Louis Comfort Tiffany was regarded as America's leading designer, helping to shape both the Arts and Crafts and Art Nouveau movements. He was also the proprietor of the 'palatial and . . . thoroughly modern emporium' on Fifth Avenue where Freud bought a jade bowl and a bronze Buddha bust on his visit to New York.[22] After the death of Louise, his second wife and Dorothy's mother, Tiffany retreated into depression and drink. He was not an easy man, obsessed with excellence, and feared by his staff. Dorothy recalled that she and her siblings regarded him as 'eccentric'.[23] Her marriage to Robert Burlingham, a surgeon, was strained by her husband's episodes of manic depression, making her fearful for the safety of her children and herself. In 1938, Robert's problems finally led to his suicide. Dorothy had come to Vienna seeking psychoanalysis for her son, and soon the family was in analysis, with Dorothy being treated by Freud and two of the children by Anna.

A friendship between Anna and Dorothy blossomed, and soon the Burlingham family became part of the Freud family, moving in upstairs at Berggasse 19. It seems that Anna took the lead in all things in the happy, lifelong and platonic relationship she shared with Dorothy. Like Anna's rooms, in Dorothy's apartment modernism was mixed with antiquities. When H.D. visited, she noted the 'art-craft simple' room, designed by Ernst Freud, where Dorothy, 'like the Professor', had 'a few Greek treasures'. Dorothy was 'quiet, slim and pretty' though her 'reserved, shy manner' rather disconcerted H.D.[24] Dorothy not only followed Anna into the profession of child psychoanalysis, she also imitated Anna's dress. When the two set off for Hochrotherd in Dorothy's automobile, they both wore *Tracht* costumes. Anna had found a sister-self, complete with children to mother. In their letters, Dorothy and Anna agreed they were each other's twins, or twins for each other in their 'ideal friendship'.[25] Photographs of Anna from the late 1920s show her as calm, radiant and strikingly attractive, her own woman, loved and satisfied. By then, Freud had rewarded Anna with an intaglio ring and welcomed her to the inner circle of the Committee.

Anna's destiny as her father's chosen helper was explored by Freud with eerie prescience in 'The Theme of the Three Caskets'. In the summer of 1912, Sophie announced she was getting married. As Mathilde, Freud's eldest daughter, was also wed, it meant only Anna remained, leading Freud to ponder relations between fathers and daughters. He thought of *King Lear*, in which the old king makes a tragic mistake in assessing the integrity of his three daughters. After the essay was published, Freud, writing to Ferenczi, mentioned how well Anna was developing, and added 'you will long ago have guessed the subjective condition for the choice of "The Three Caskets" '.[26]

Lear told his daughters that their inheritance of his kingdom would be determined by how convincingly they expressed their love for him. Goneril and Regan wax lyrical but Cordelia, the youngest, remains silent except for a few curt words. 'He should have recognised the unassuming, speechless love of his third daughter and rewarded it,' writes Freud. Instead, Lear disinherits Cordelia and divides the kingdom between the other two, 'to his own and the general ruin'. *Gradiva* was still on Freud's mind and, further exploring the 'sacred' symbolism of the number three, he returned to the Horae. Originally goddesses of the waters of the sky, the Horae 'became divine representatives of the Seasons ... guardians of natural law and of the divine Order'.[27] Freud then relates these mistresses of time to the Morae (the Fates), the inexorable spinners of human destiny, who cut the thread of life on a whim. To Freud, such ancient triple goddesses represent

the three inevitable relations that a man has with a woman — the woman who bears him, the woman who is his mate and the woman who destroys him; or ... they are the three forms taken by the figure of the mother in the course of a man's life – the mother herself, the beloved one who is chosen after her pattern, and lastly the Mother Earth who receives him once more. But it is in vain that an old man yearns for the love of a woman as he had it first from his mother; the third of the Fates alone, the silent Goddess of Death, will take him into her arms.[28]

Gradiva, the relief that hung in his room, was winter, the third Horae and the angel of death, who, in Freud's reading, also stood for the youngest daughter, Cordelia / Anna. It was a rare occasion in his writings when Freud focused on the feminine and made it the subject of the work.

In 1923, when Freud was diagnosed with cancer, his life changed dramatically. Afterwards, he rarely travelled abroad or spoke in public due to his self-consciousness about his distorted speech. He did not even like to eat in public. Freud had contracted the disease from smoking – it was known then that nicotine caused cancer – and he had been chain-smoking twenty cigars a day since he was a young man. Jacob, his father, also smoked heavily until his death, though he did not have cancer. In letters to Fliess while writing *The Interpretation of Dreams*, Freud recounted the anguish of withdrawal as he tried to quit: 'the misery of abstinence has been far greater than I ever imagined'. With it came 'a feeling of depression which took the form of visions of death and departure in place of the usual frenzy of activity'.[29] But Freud never regretted smoking and never gave it up. When his nephew Harry refused the offer of a cigarette, Freud told him, 'My boy, smoking is one of the greatest and cheapest pleasures in life, and if you decide in advance not to smoke, I can only feel sorry for you.'[30] Freud underwent major, brutal, initial surgery that removed most of his palate and upper jaw on the right side, and probably saved his life. Undeterred, he took a clothes-peg and used it to prise open his mouth so he could jam in a cigar.[31] It was the beginning of more than thirty surgical procedures he would endure in the next fifteen years. He also lost hearing in his right ear, and the consulting room was re-arranged so he sat on the left of his patients.

It became Anna's job to speak for Freud at conferences, to travel with him, act as his secretary, shield him from unwanted attention and minister to him. When Freud won the Goethe Prize in 1930, Anna travelled to Frankfurt to read his acceptance speech. She performed the same service the following year when Freiberg honoured Freud. Each morning, in a little room near his study set aside for the purpose, she carefully examined his mouth to check the status of the disease. Even there, art was included: a small bust of a boy stood among the medical paraphernalia. It was a difficult intimacy that Anna managed with admirable dispassion. She also helped him to adjust the prosthesis – he had a series, each larger than the last, that irritated his mouth and never quite seemed to fit. In 1923, not long before he learnt the diagnosis, he took Anna to Rome, Freud's last visit to his beloved city. They luxuriated in its charms, Freud commenting, 'Anna was splendid. She understood and enjoyed everything, and I was very proud of her.'[32]

Freud described collecting antiquities as 'second only in intensity to his nicotine addiction'.[33] In *Civilization and its Discontents*, Freud described art itself as a 'mild narcosis' that brought about 'a transient withdrawal from the pressures of vital needs'.[34]

Similar to his passion for collecting, Freud chose not to analyse his dependence on nicotine. Keeping it in the realm of the unconscious meant he did not have to deal with the challenge of relinquishing it.

Though Freud believed all addictions were substitutes for 'the primary addiction', masturbation, it seems possible that oral gratification – the warm, wet pleasures of sucking, savouring and swallowing – could originate in suckling the mother's breast. Were the compulsions of collecting and smoking substitutes for the mother, for nurture and contentment? Can Freud's favourite objects – antiquities and cigars – be interpreted as symbols of desire, as embodiments of the mother's love and care? Freud's theories repress the feminine but perhaps it returned in the pleasures he could not live without. He described smoking as a form of sustenance but did not develop a theory about addiction, perhaps too bedevilled by his own. Recent research speculates that nicotine's deep and enduring psychological grip may mask depression, especially when the drug takes on 'totemistic meaning' for its adherents, as it did for Freud, who described smoking as his 'protection and weapon in the combat with life'. To the cigar he ascribed 'the greatest share of my self-control and tenacity in work'.[35] Like many writers, his habit was linked to the rhythms of creative work and he repeatedly told his doctor Max Schur that 'he could do no creative work without smoking'.[36] Even so, his massive literary output decreased once he contracted the disease. 'Since I can no longer smoke freely, I no longer want to write,' he complained to Arnold Zweig, adding 'or perhaps I am just using this pretext to veil the unproductiveness of old age.'[37]

Cigars added to Freud's mystique. Raymond de Saussure, analysed by Freud during the 1920s, recalled that 'contact was established by means of his voice and the odour of the cigars he ceaselessly smoked' and in that 'rather dark room ... [l]ight came not from the windows but from the brilliance of that lucid, discerning mind'.[38] In fact, Freud's rooms reeked, the pungent aroma of cigars lingering in the Persian rugs and the air, emanating from his clothes and the pores in his skin. Once Freud nearly gassed himself because, 'swathed in cigar smoke', he did not detect a leaking gas pipe in his study, though he felt its effects, 'strange headaches . . . and . . . annoying lapses of memory'.[39]

In *Beyond the Pleasure Principle*, Freud explored 'the profound and regressive attraction of death'.[40] When the instincts of self-preservation replace the pleasure principle with the reality principle, the latter 'demands and carries into effect the postponement of satisfaction . . . and the temporary toleration of unpleasure . . . on the long indirect road to pleasure'. But good sense does not prevail and the pleasure principle overcomes the reality principle 'to the detriment of the organism as a whole'. Freud concludes 'the pleasure principle seems actually to serve the death instincts', neatly summarising the tragic results of his indulgence in tobacco.[41] Even Freud's prostheses found their way into his work. 'Man,' he wrote, has become, 'a kind of prosthetic God. When he puts on all his auxiliary organs he is truly magnificent; but those organs have not grown on to him and they still give him much trouble at times.'[42]

Death pervaded those years: Sophie's was followed by that of her younger son Heinele, a delicate child of whom Freud was very fond. As well there was the war's awful resonance. It seemed the world had been robbed of its beauties, Freud reflected, but mourning was necessary so that the individual is free 'to replace the lost objects by fresh ones equally or still more precious'.[43] By the mid 1920s, Freud's most precious object was undoubtedly Anna.

***

As Freud's life grew increasingly circumscribed, the collection was, more than ever, a refuge and a delight. Gifts arrived with almost the same regularity as purchases. Some were fine examples of South-East Asian art. Freud's Buddha, bought from Tiffany & Company, is the first indication of interest in that area. Though fewer in number than Egyptian, Greek or Roman artefacts, Freud acquired some excellent examples of oriental art, mostly Chinese. He did not visit the region – the furthest east he got was Athens – and he referred only in passing to eastern civilisations in his writings.

Freud arranged his most exquisite Chinese work in pride of place on his desk, directly behind *Athena. Table Screen* (Qing Dynasty, 19th century; pl. 29) is inset with the figure of a scholar, carved in white jade, and surrounded by delicate, curving, wooden leaves and branches. A meditative object for the scholar's desk, the natural forms were meant to encourage thoughts to roam in an ideal landscape. Freud was familiar with such imaginary journeys and his similarity to the Chinese scholar does not end there. Scholars were collectors of high-quality art objects, some functional, some inspirational, most small enough to decorate their desks or complement their studies. The scholar's studio was a place of study and contemplation where he surrounded himself with specially created 'treasures' – brushes, ink stones, water droppers, netsukes and figurines that embodied the shared wisdom, traditions and values of the Chinese literati. Objects of beauty as well as status symbols, the treasures projected 'allusive and symbolic meanings' that 'encouraged and inspired [the scholar] in his work'.⁴⁴

Freud had been collecting jade, mainly bowls, for many years. It was his introduction to Chinese art. Called the 'stone of heaven', jade was the sacred gem of China, symbolising a range of virtues, including justice, wisdom and courage, and meant to confer good luck and protection. As Jane Portal writes, the Chinese have treasured jade even more than westerners have valued gold.[45] Jade is an extremely hard stone, so carving it is a slow and difficult process, another reason it is regarded as precious. During the Qing Dynasty, which lasted from 1644 to 1911, jade carving improved substantially due to the ruling Manchu emperors establishing workshops where carvers refined their techniques. *Table Screen* is an elegant example of their craft. The Qing Dynasty was 'an antiquarian age when, as never before, men looked back into the past, burrowing into the Classics, dabbling in archaeology, forming huge collections of books … porcelain and archaic bronzes'.[46] Freud collected other decorative items designed for the scholar's desk, including a jade *Buddhist Lion Paperweight* (Qing Dynasty, 18th–19th centuries) and, brilliantly carved in ivory, a tiny Japanese *Netsuke in the Form of a Shishi* (Edo Period, 18th–19th centuries).

Jade Screen (Qing Dynasty, 19th century), placed in front of *Athena*, was one of Freud's most highly regarded items. Leaving Vienna in 1938, and fearing he would lose the whole collection, Freud selected two objects to be smuggled out by Princess Marie Bonaparte: *Athena* and *Jade Screen*. It is another scholar's treasure. As Mae Anna Pang points out, 'the strong design in the centre is the stylised Chinese character of "shou" meaning longevity' and on each side of the character bunches of flowers shoot from the mouths of dragons. Pang regards the elegant and unusual work as a credit to Freud's taste.[47]

Flowers refer to life, happiness and fertility. In Chinese astrology, dragons symbolise visionary and outspoken qualities and those born under their sign are supposed to have similar attributes. In pre-revolutionary China, the dragon was a symbol of the power of the emperor and so those born in the year of the dragon have the characteristics considered desirable in an emperor – such as zeal, enthusiasm and leadership abilities. Freud's birthdate of 6 May 1856 means he was born into a year of the dragon, under the elemental influence of fire. As Chinese astrologer Shelly Wu writes, 'the Fire Dragon is a natural leader and born to be in the public eye. Unpredictable and strong-willed . . . egotistical and supremely self-confident, those born into Fire Dragon years are articulate and have a tremendous desire to succeed.'[48] *Shou* also means birthday, so perhaps the screen was either a birthday present from an admirer or, as was Freud's habit, a birthday gift to himself. With his interest in arcane symbols, it is probable Freud knew the dragon's relevance to his birthdate.

Marie Bonaparte, who began her analysis with Freud in 1925, was generous, offering him excellent Greek vases, a Roman statue of *Venus* (Roman, from France or the Rhineland, 1st or 2nd century A.D.) as well as Tang statues. In February 1932, Freud bought a terracotta *Woman Polo Player* (Tang Dynasty, 618–906 A.D.), a lively rendering of an unusual subject in Chinese art: a woman playing sport. The early period of the Tang Dynasty was dominated by women, particularly Empress Wu Zeitan and Empress Wei, and women were accorded new freedoms that allowed them to ride, hunt and play polo with the men, as well as mix in society with fewer restrictions.[49] Polo, which probably originated in Persia, spread to China where the ruling classes were mad about the game. Fluid, dynamic movement is created by the rider, who leans forwards after striking the ball as her horse leaps, all four legs outstretched in mid-air. A few months later, in June, Freud bought two Tang horses, unfortunately both fakes.

The following year, for his birthday, Marie Bonaparte gave him a Tang camel, the first of two that entered the collection.[50] Like the horses, *Camel* (early Tang style, 20th-century forgery) is also a fake, albeit a charming one. During the late seventh to early eighth century, great numbers of unglazed terracotta figures were placed in tombs. Like the objects in Egyptian tombs, they indicated the wealth and status of the deceased and were meant to accompany them in the afterlife. Subjects included horses and Bactrian camels as well as figures of officials, servants, dancing girls and musicians. Camels and horses were considered 'auspicious signs of material comfort', representing a connection with the Silk Road and its luxuries and exotic goods.[51] Tang tomb figures, dug up during the 1920s and 1930s, became so popular in the West that the market for original works was soon exhausted and their manufacture began. Freud's two-humped Bactrian *Camel* is impressive but, new to the study of Chinese art, Freud could not read the tell-tale signs of fake Tang: paint that flakes off easily and a poor imitation of its hallmark unfired colours.

During the Han Dynasty in the first century A.D., Buddhism became popular in China and Freud collected different representations of the Buddha and his devotees. On a table in his study, he arranged several large busts including *Head of a Bodhisattva* and *Head of a Guardian Figure* (both 15th–17th centuries [Ming Dynasty]) as well as a large marble *Kannon* (Sung style, 20th-century forgery). A Bodhisattva is a saintly follower of the Buddha who refrains from attaining nirvana out of compassion for others. The expressive *Guardian Figure* protects Buddhist temples. A Kannon, known as Avalokitesvara, is a popular Buddhist deity who, like the Bodhisattva, postpones nirvana until others achieve enlightenment. Did the serene faces of Buddhism appeal

to Freud during his afflictions? He also collected two rare eighteenth-century ivory Buddhas, both from the Burma-Thailand
border.

On his desk, Freud had an ivory figure of Vishnu, a belated
birthday present from the Indian Psychoanalytical Society, and
the only Indian work in the collection. Freud admitted his knowledge of India was slight. When, in 1930, Romain Rolland, the
Nobel Prize winner for literature, sent Freud his recent books on
the Indian spiritual leaders Ramakrishna and Vivekananda, Freud
replied, 'I shall now try with your guidance to penetrate into the
Indian jungle which until now an uncertain blending of Hellenic
love of proportion, Jewish sobriety, and philistine timidity have
kept me away.'[52]

Though Freud's birthday was in May, the statue did not arrive
until December 1931. Girindrashekhar Bose, founder of the
Indian Psychoanalytical Society, explained the delay was because
the work was made especially for Freud. It was modelled on a
statue from an eighteenth-century temple dedicated to Vishnu
at Thiruvananthapuram, 'the city of the snake god' and capital of
Kerala in southern India. Vishnu, the preserver and restorer, is
one of Hinduism's major deities. Freud's *White Vishnu* (pl. 50)
shows the god holding his attributes – a lotus flower, his club, a
discus and a conch – while behind him rears a five-headed
serpent, representing the universe, on whose coils he sits. H.D.
noted the 'beautiful quality and design of the ivory'.[53] Vishnu
represents a powerful healing force, perhaps signalling the august
role that Freud's Indian followers ascribed to him.

Freud wrote to Bose that 'the Statuette is charming. I gave it
a place of honour on my desk. As long as I can enjoy life it will
recall to my mind the progress of Psychoanalysis[,] the proud

conquests it has made in foreign countries and the kind feelings it has aroused in some of my contemporaries at least.' But when the statue developed cracks, Freud wondered, 'Can the god, being used to Calcutta, not stand the climate in Vienna?'[54]

As Michael Molnar notes, Freud's diary, the record of the last decade of his life, contains more references to Japanese translations of his works than to those in any other language.[55] In 1931, the Japanese psychoanalytical group had been provisionally accepted into the International Psychoanalytic Association. The following year Japanese psychologist Heisaku Kosawa, who became Freud's patient, gave him a print of Kiyoshi Yoshida's justly famous view of *Mount Fuji*. Freud thanked Kosawa for the 'beautiful picture which presents to my eyes what I have read so much about and a sight which I myself have not been granted'.[56] Freud hung the print in the waiting room that he now shared with Anna, at Berggasse 19.

Though Freud rarely mentioned his transactions with antiquities dealers, he was well known to many, both in Vienna and abroad. Over the years, he proved an excellent customer and local dealers often visited him at home, bringing their wares. In Rome, he saw Ettore Sandolo and Alfredo Barsanti. Visiting Berlin in 1930 meant several visits to Dr Philipp Lederer's shop. Afterwards, Freud congratulated himself, 'It would be nice if everything this year went as well as my purchases from Lederer . . . They are all standing here together on the table.'[57] Freud converted most of the money from the Goethe Prize into antiquities courtesy of Lederer.[58]

In Vienna, between 1927 and 1938, Freud bought around two hundred items from Robert Lustig.[59] Freud's other Viennese dealers included Frölich and Glückselig. Lustig means 'merry', Frölich 'happy' and Glückselig 'blissful'. Freud means 'joy'. From the eighteenth century, Jews living in the Habsburg empire were required to have German surnames, as well as to speak German. Some paid a fee and selected names with an optimistic ring.

Lustig's gallery, Antike Kunst (Antique Art), was on Wipplingerstrasse in the Inner Stadt, the lovely, medieval heart of Vienna, its narrow streets crowded with small speciality shops. Each day, when Freud took his constitutional after lunch, he walked briskly along the Ringstrasse, then made his way back through the old city, visiting his publishers, stocking up on cigars and surveying antiquities. That was how he and Lustig met.

In 1927 Lustig was twenty-two, personable, charming and jovial. His father, Ludwig, was a watchmaker and Robert had learned his father's craft and worked in his shop. But the young man loved antiquities and spent his lunch-hour studying the collections at the Kunsthistorisches Museum. At auction, Robert bought some small urns which he placed in the shop window. One day, 'an old gentleman with a beard and a cane' stopped by. Freud asked the price of the urns and invited Lustig to bring them to Berggasse 19. Visiting Freud's rooms, Lustig's 'eyes nearly popped out of his head. He had never seen so many antiquities in a private home.'[60]

Freud bought major works from Lustig including *Isis Suckling the Infant Horus* and the large, gilded *Mummy Case*. The story of how Lustig acquired *Isis* offers a good example of how under-valued antiquities were in Freud's lifetime. Lustig spotted the statue in a junk shop near Vienna. When he asked the price, the shop owner put the statue on the scale to weigh it, and Lustig bought it for the price of the metal. When he first met Lustig,

Freud explained, 'I am not a rich man. We can trade.'[61] Lustig
recalled that, of the several hundred antique dealers in Vienna in
the 1920s and 30s, only about five specialised in antiquities. The
others dealt primarily in Renaissance, Baroque and Biedermeier
works.[62] Lustig specialised in original Roman, Greek, Egyptian
and prehistoric works as well as antique silver and jewellry. In
those days, Greek vases could be purchased for the equivalent of
a few hundred dollars.

In April 1936, Freud made his last recorded purchases of an-
tiquities. Two were from Lustig: an Egyptian funerary barge and
a ploughing scene, both ritual tomb items. But it seems they may
be forgeries.[63] Fakes were cunningly produced and fooled not only
Freud and Lustig but curators at the Kunsthistorisches Museum.
In the 1930s, the curator, Hans von Demel, regularly provided
Freud with authentication certificates and Freud often asked
Lustig to have works appraised by von Demel before buying them.
When Lustig showed von Demel an Egyptian stone head that
Freud fancied, the curator told him, 'It's a fake: don't sell it.' But
several wooden sculptures belonging to Freud and authenticated
by von Demel have proved to be forgeries, including *Falcon-headed
Figure*. Lustig recalled that if Freud found he had a fake, he usually
got rid of it.[64]

In 1936, Freud turned eighty. His health had continued to
deteriorate and he rarely left home. Unless Lustig and other
dealers visited him, he could no longer make the journey to the
Inner Stadt. It may be why Freud's rate of purchasing slowed for
the first time in forty years. Holidays, often a time to splurge, were
spent close to Vienna in furnished villas at Hohe Warte or
Grinzing. Freud would move to a villa in early spring and, taking
advantage of the good weather, stay until the end of summer. At

Grinzing, he rejoiced in 'the most beautiful garden and the most charming house in which we have ever spent our summer holidays'.[65] He was accompanied by the antiquities, Martha observing, 'all his pictures and also the majority of his antiquities were in their places!' Freud took some of his library and Persian rugs, too. He continued to see patients while on holiday and recreated his rooms just as they were at Berggasse. Anna, who supervised the operations, commented that 'moving with us is always a lengthy and a strenuous business'.[66]

Anna had the assistance of Paula Fichtl, a lively young woman who had worked for Dorothy Burlingham before becoming the Freuds' maid in 1926. It proved to be a lifelong association. When the Freuds left Vienna to settle in London, Paula accompanied them. It was her task to wrap the precious artworks before packing them in a succession of wooden boxes – if Freud took the majority of his collection, that would mean nearly two thousand objects. But Freud had not retired as a collector. Waiting to leave Vienna in 1938 and wondering about the fate of his antiquities, he wrote to his son Ernst, 'If I were to arrive [in London] a rich man, I would start a new collection.'[67]

12

Analysis Among the Ruins

He was very beautiful,
the old man,
and I knew wisdom,
I found measureless truth
in his words,
his command
was final

H.D., 'The Master'[1]

What [Freud] said — and I thought a little sadly — was, 'You are the only
person who has ever come into this room and looked at the things in the room
before looking at me.'

H.D., Tribute to Freud[2]

FREUD ADVISED HIS PATIENTS not to record their analysis with him, neither to make notes nor to discuss the matter with their nearest and dearest. Thankfully, Hilda Doolittle (pl. 51) ignored him, commenting, 'the Professor is not always right'.[3] It makes her memoir, *Tribute to Freud*, together with letters to her friend Bryher, the only detailed account of an analysis with Freud, even though over the years he treated hundreds of people. According to H.D., Freud's attitude towards conducting an analysis was open and flexible and he was quite prepared to change his own guidelines. For example, he not only befriended H.D., forming a lasting and tender bond, but insisted she accept the gift of a dog, though he recognised that gifts between analyst and patient could provoke 'difficulties'. H.D. was not the first patient to comment on Freud's 'soft and easy manner' but it seems she was its particular recipient.[4]

Tribute to Freud also provides the most informed and sensitive account of the collection by any contemporary of Freud's. Others responded to the antiquities but without H.D.'s erudition and poetic élan.

Sergei Pankejeff's parting present, in the summer of 1914, was the large *Neith* that stands on Freud's desk. When, years later, Pankejeff saw a photograph of Freud's desk, 'his' Egyptian statue immediately caught his eye. The work 'symbolized my analysis with Freud who himself called me "a piece of psychoanalysis"'.[5] Freud gave Richard Knight, who was visiting Berggasse 19, a tour of the collection, and he watched as Freud handled the objects 'lovingly and spoke about certain specimens in detail'. Though 'entirely ignorant regarding such matters', Knight nevertheless expressed interest. Freud, unconvinced, remarked, 'You do not have much appreciation for such things, do you?'[6]

No wonder Freud was pleased to have H.D. as a patient. She was a distinguished modernist poet, steeped in classical Greek literature and myth that she used as the inspiration for her work. Eileen Gregory comments that 'no modern writer takes "the gods" more seriously than H.D.'.[7] As well as writing prose, H.D. also completed translations of classical texts that were hailed by T. S. Eliot for their vitality and innovation. A nature-worshipper as well as an unabashed pagan, H.D. revelled in visits to the Mediterranean, just as Freud did. She also was fortunate enough to be travelling in Egypt when Tutankhamun's tomb was opened, and saw relics being brought up from the excavation.

Freud was acquainted with H.D.'s work. A friend had given him her novel *Palimpsest*, which he read, together with her poetry, before the analysis began. H.D. described *Palimpsest*, published in 1926, as 'a rather loosely written long-short-story volume' in a series of historical and classical tales that included *Pilate's Wife* and *Hedylus*.[8] The title would have appealed to Freud: a palimpsest is a parchment on which the writing has been partially or completely erased to make room for another text, an image similar to the one he explored in 'A Note Upon The "Mystic Writing Pad"'.[9]

H.D.'s mainstay, lifelong friend and sometime lover was the daughter of millionaire English industrialist Sir John Ellerman, Annie Winifred Ellerman, who had changed her name to Bryher, after one of the Scilly Isles that she loved. Poet, writer and ardent supporter of psychoanalysis, Bryher had been in analysis with Hanns Sachs, Freud's Berlin colleague, and wished to practise as an analyst. Both Bryher and Sachs recommended that H.D. see Freud. Bryher had built a Bauhaus-style home above Lake Geneva where she lived in a marriage of convenience with Kenneth

Macpherson, who had initially been H.D.'s lover. It was H.D.'s home, too. In 1919, she had given birth to a daughter, Perdita, whom Bryher adopted. All lived together in a complex ménage – H.D., Perdita, Bryher and Macpherson.

H.D. was born in Bethlehem, Pennsylvania, in 1886, the daughter of astronomer and mathematician Charles Doolittle, her revered but distant father, and Helen Wolle Doolittle, an art and music teacher. Growing up in the intense, communal atmosphere of the Moravian church, founded by German migrants to America, shaped H.D.'s predilection for an ecstatic spirituality. (Freud had been born in Moravia.) While at school, she met Ezra Pound, an early friend and mentor who encouraged her poetic endeavours. It was he who dubbed her H.D.[10] The First World War was a disturbing time for H.D. She was living in England, with her husband, the poet Richard Aldington, as part of the avant-garde. In 1918, her older brother was killed on the western front and six months later her father died. When she became pregnant with Perdita (a previous pregnancy had resulted in a stillbirth), not to her husband, but to the composer Cecil Gray, she left Aldington to live briefly with Gray. This caused a rupture in her close, platonic friendship with D. H. Lawrence. She contracted influenza during her pregnancy and, without Bryher's intervention and assistance, would probably have died. The years since then had been spent writing, publishing and translating, as well as travelling – 'drifting', as H.D. would describe it to Freud – between America and Europe.

There were two reasons that brought H.D. to Freud. While trying to come to grips with her wartime experiences and commit them to the page, a hiatus had occurred in her writing. Secondly, the rise of fascism in the 1930s brought with it the expectation of another war. In the strained atmosphere, H.D.'s anxieties bloomed. In her 1931 collection *Red Roses for Bronze*, she writes, 'Dark / days are past / and darker days draw near.'[11] Previous psychoanalytic sessions with Mary Chadwick in London and Hanns Sachs in Berlin had proved unsatisfactory. 'There was something beating in my brain . . . I wanted it to be let out.'[12]

H.D. was thrilled to undergo analysis with Freud, regarding it as a feather in her cap. She told sexual psychologist Havelock Ellis, 'Sigmund Freud is sold on artists.'[13] In March 1933, she arrived in Vienna and moved into the luxurious Hotel Regina, near Berggasse, a favourite haunt of visiting psychoanalysts. For H.D. did not see herself as merely a patient: she was a pupil and hoped to practise as an analyst herself.[14] Though H.D. was comfortably off, Bryher covered all her costs, including payment to Freud. Her sessions, at 5 P.M. six days a week, lasted for the next three months, and were conducted in English. The analysis began at Berggasse, and when the Freuds moved outside Vienna for the summer, H.D. travelled out by tram.

There are four versions of H.D.'s analysis with Freud: 'Writing on the Wall' and 'Advent' are published as *Tribute to Freud*. The latter is based on notes she kept during the first analysis in 1933 and the former, written in 1944, was based on recollections without relying on her notes. Then there are her irreverent and chatty letters, written daily to Bryher. Finally there is her poem 'The Master', which she refused to publish during her lifetime. Though all explore different facets of the analysis, they attest to one fact: H.D.'s appreciation of the collection and Freud's delighted response. The antiquities proved an intersecting point of interest and a fruitful metaphor in the analysis. A friendship developed, and Freud and H.D. became something of a mutal admiration society. H.D. was another of Freud's collection of 'Athenas', the group of smart, glamorous, questing women who gathered around him in his later years.

The first session began with an argument. H.D. was nervous when Freud, 'a little white ghost who appeared at my elbow', led her into his rooms. Showing patients the collection was obviously a method of encouraging them to relax and H.D. admired 'some authentic coffin paintings' – the *Mummy Portraits* from the Graf collection – and 'a bit of Egyptian cloth' – probably *Mummy Bandages with Vignettes from the Book of the Dead*.[15] Later, she admitted she felt overwhelmed. 'I had not expected to find him . . . in a museum, a temple.'[16] But Freud assessed H.D.'s enthusiasm as resistance, remarking 'rather whimsically and ironically', that she had looked at the artworks, 'preferring the mere dead shreds of antiquity to his living presence'. But H.D insisted that 'you are priest, you are magician', to which Freud responded, 'It is you who are poet and magician.' In other words, the analysand is responsible for directing the analysis. H.D. burst into tears, telling Freud that 'in looking at antiquity, I was looking at him'. Freud agreed that he and H.D. had arrived at the same place: 'we met, he in the childhood of humanity – antiquity – I in my own childhood'.[17] H.D. referred to a rather alarming feature of Freud's, noted by others – to make a point, he hammered on the pillow of the couch, 'like a child hammering a porridge-spoon on the table'.[18]

But she was enchanted by him, gracing him with epithets: 'the old Hermit', 'the Old Man of the Sea', 'Oedipus Rex' and 'O lovely, lovely little old Papa'.[19] The collection played its part, H.D. telling Havelock Ellis that she was 'surprised and touched' by Freud's 'little de lux museum of objects d'art [sic] . . . I knew his mind was exquisite, I had no idea of such a practical demonstration.'[20]

Freud, pleased to have such a learned analysand, went 'in and out of his rooms' to find her 'some little god or other', demonstrating the visceral approach he took to the work of analysis and the role the antiquities played. Objects Freud drew H.D.'s attention to included *Athena* and *White Vishnu*, as well as 'the most lovely old Tanagras and archaic Greek and Egyptian statuettes'.[21] In 'On Beginning the Treatment', Freud notes that a 'helpful factor' is the patient's 'intellectual interest and understanding'.[22] There were excited discussions about Arthur Evans' excavations on Crete. H.D. longed to give Freud a Minoan snake goddess statue, though realising its rarity, Freud said, 'I doubt if even *you* could do that.'[23] To Ezra Pound, who was disdainful of psychoanalysis, H.D. declared, 'I adore Freud who is a great artist.'[24] But she wondered about Freud's motives.

> I did not know if the Professor's excursions with me into the other room were by way of distraction, actual social occasions or part of his plan. Did he want to find out how I would react to certain ideas embodied in those little statues, or how deeply I felt the dynamic *idea* still implicit in spite of the fact that ages or aeons of time had flown over many of them? Or did he mean simply to imply that he wanted to share his treasure with me, those tangible shapes before us that yet suggested the intangible and vastly more fascinating treasures of his own mind?[25]

Why did Freud chose *Athena* and *White Vishnu*? Freud believed that because H.D.'s father was cold and remote she had not made the transition to the Oedipal phase, so instead of desiring her father, she still longed for union with the pre-Oedipal mother. He deduced this from her dreams and a 'vision' she had while staying on Corfu, as well, of course, from her bisexuality. It was an unusual analytic procedure for Freud, who regarded the bond with the father as fundamental. It meant that H.D.'s 'transference' was to Freud as mother, which made him rather uncomfortable. He confided, 'I do *not* like to be the mother in transference – it always surprises me and shocks me a little. I feel so very masculine.' For H.D. 'the Professor's surroundings and interests [that is, the collection] seem to derive from my mother rather than from my father'.[26] Was it an element H.D. found attractive and sympathetic – Freud the art collector rather than Freud the austere physician? Was it why the first impression of his rooms had made her feel 'overwhelmed and upset'? Instead of finding a cool scientist (like her father), she had discovered a passionate art lover (like her mother).

Freud picked up *Athena*, telling H.D., '*This* is my favourite,' and placed it in her hands. 'She is perfect, *only she has lost her spear*.' Having lost her spear, that is, symbolically lacking a penis, *Athena* images the castrated woman. H.D. was 'rather annoyed with the Professor' because she had read in one of his volumes that 'women did not creatively amount to anything or amount to much, unless they had a male counterpart or male companion from whom they drew inspiration'.[27] In 'The Master', H.D. is incensed by 'the old man / with his talk of the man-strength /.../ I argued till day-break.' Later in the poem she writes, '*woman is perfect*'.[28] Yet Freud treasured *Athena*, the masculine, intellectual virgin goddess who belonged to no man, who gave birth to herself. H.D. was aware Freud meant that 'this little piece of metal you hold in your hand (look at it) is priceless really, it is *perfect*, a prize, a find of the best period of Greek art'. H.D. appreciated that he was 'speaking as an ardent lover of art and an art-collector'. Freud also reminded H.D. that Athena 'is the veiled Isis, or Neith the warrior-goddess'.[29]

Veiled Isis, interchangeable with Neith, locates the goddess in her role as magician and guardian of mysteries. An inscription on the temple to Isis at Sais reads, 'I am that which is, hath been, and which shall be; and no man has ever lifted the veil that hides my Divinity from mortal eyes.' It was at Sais that Neith also had her temple. In *Moralia*, Plutarch wondered if Isis was the daughter of Hermes, in his form as the magician and alchemist known as Hermes Trismegistus. Worship of Isis continued, not only through Greek and Roman times but, as Freud's *Isis Suckling the Infant Horus* indicates, during the rise of Christianity when she was reconfigured as the Madonna. Occult societies such as the Freemasons, the Rosicrucians and the Theosophists continued to explore the significance of Isis as the guardian of hermetic knowledge. The first book published in 1893 by Helena Petrovna Blavatsky, founder of the Theosophical Society, was *Isis Unveiled: A Master Key to the Mysteries of Ancient Science and Theology.*

The connections Freud drew between Athena, Isis and Neith were, as he no doubt realised, fecund and alluring to H.D., who was as immersed in the occult as she was in Greek myth and art. In the late 1920s, she had begun to study astrology, numerology and the tarot. Two months into her analysis, she wrote to Bryher

> I am not, as you know a sloppy theosophist or horoscope-ist, but you know I do believe in these things and think there is a whole other-science of them. And that is where, in a way, S.F. and I part company.[30]

During her analysis, H.D. was reading books by the well-known American astrologer Evangeline Adams and flagged her interest with Freud. Born in May, Freud was Taurus, the bull, a type whose 'original tendency is to be obstinate but, if once convinced of the necessity of a revolutionary course, they will pursue it to the bitter end'.[31] H.D. told Bryher that 'he pretends he knows nothing of the [astrological] tradition and bust himself when I said Venus was the ruler of his "house"'.[32] But Freud resisted H.D.'s efforts to lead the analysis in that direction. In 'Dreams and Occultism', he wrote that interest in the occult was motivated by religious belief and the occult movement was trying to assist religion, 'threatened as it is by the advance of scientific thought'.[33] Thwarted, H.D. observed, 'we must not talk astrology. In that, at least, my father and Sigmund Freud agree.' Though 'in spite of them, or to spite them' she found 'enchanting parallels' exploring Freud's, and her father's, astrological signs.[34]

As Barbara Guest observes, H.D.'s analysis is a curious mixture of Freud's scientific technique and her own belief in magic. In theory, she believed in psychoanalysis; actually she wanted to go to the original magician, the Merlin or Theseus, as she would later call him in her epic poem *Helen in Egypt*. Superstition and intuition were the controls under which she worked, which Freud must have recognised immediately.[35] 'I am sure he IS the absolute inheritor of all that eastern mystery and majic [sic],' H.D. told Bryher, 'just IS, in spite of his monumental work and all that, he is the real, the final healer.'[36]

Athena represented an artistic standard, a balance between masculine and feminine, a commanding being who could reveal secrets, draw aside the veil and inspire others. The myth of Perseus' defeat of the Gorgon can be decoded as an initiation ritual conferring maturity, with Athena as the presiding deity. To Freud, though not to H.D., the goddess was lacking. *Athena* was also Freud's most treasured object. He offered *Athena* to H.D. as a rich and lovely symbol of herself as both poet and woman. By giving her the statue to hold, he was also emphasising the power was in her hands. What did *White Vishnu* symbolise?

When H.D. visited Freud's rooms, the Indian statue stood at the centre of his desk. H.D. felt 'a little uneasy' before its 'extreme beauty . . . which compelled me, yet repelled me at the same time'. During her second session, Freud 'took the ivory Vishnu with the upright serpents and canopy of snake heads, and put it into my hands'. It looked like 'a half flower cut lengthwise', 'a half-lily', leading her to remember that, as a child, an old gardener had given her a lily. Rushing home, she showed it to her mother (or grandmother) who said, 'that will look beautiful on your grandfather's new grave'. The ivory Vishnu was like 'the piston of a calla-lily' or 'a jack-in-the-pulpit', an image that identified the plant with H.D.'s grandfather, a clergyman, 'a jack-in-the-pulpit'.[37]

Disturbed by the *Vishnu*, H.D. reflected that 'the subject did not especially appeal to me'. But it continued to work on her unconscious, as Freud perhaps meant it to, leading her to reminisce about her religious life in the Moravian church. At the Christmas Eve service conducted by grandfather, all the children were given candles to hold, prompting Freud to say, 'There is no more significant symbol than a lighted candle . . . That is the true heart of all religion.'[38] To Freud, the old gardener stood for God. So too, perhaps, did H.D.'s grandfather. To H.D., the lily was the 'Annunciation-lily', the flower offered to the Virgin Mary by the angel Gabriel when he tells her she is pregnant with Jesus, and therefore it is a symbol of both virginity and fertility.

What made H.D. ambivalent about *White Vishnu*? She described it as 'this Oriental, passionate yet cold abstraction' and, though it sat in the centre of Freud's desk, she was relieved to realise 'it was not his favourite'.[39] According to Hindu mythology, the world rests on a multi-headed serpent that represents desire and, by sitting on the coiled snake, Vishnu masters desire. The king cobra, one of the largest and most venomous snakes, is found in southern India where it is worshipped. The cobra heads frame Vishnu like a throne, the rearing, hooded posture indicating the serpent is about to strike. In Indian myth, the snake has dual qualities, both protective and destructive, and to charm or control a snake is a magical act. To Freud, the meaning was obvious: in dreams, snakes were phallic symbols. The statue had made H.D. think of lilies – calla lilies with their white flutes and golden stamens, and dark Jack-in-the-pulpit lilies. Did she know that Jack-in-the-pulpit was also called the cobra lily? In 1930, Georgia O'Keeffe did a series of paintings titled 'Jack-in-the-Pulpit', rendering the flower in an increasingly abstract manner and focusing on the fluid, eroticised stamen, the undisguisedly phallic Jack. By interpreting the statue as a flower with Vishnu as the erect stamen and the cobras as the petals, H.D. reads it as a double male image of immense but threatening power.

H.D. worshipped great men and, equally, she rebelled against them. No wonder she called her poem about Freud 'The Master'. She had been seeking, and losing, masters all her life. As Adalaide Morris writes, H.D.'s masters were brilliant, magnetic men. Pre-eminent among them were Pound, Lawrence and Freud, and with each the pattern was similar: intense contact leading to a period of submission, a long period of incorporating and reworking their teachings, and a final tribute releasing her from their power.[40] The first man she worshipped was her brilliant but remote father. H.D. had a 'habitual awe for scholarly paternal authorities, for their intelligence, their breadth of learning, their impersonality'.[41] Being in Freud's study made H.D. recall her father's study, where on his table he, 'like the Professor, had old, old sacred objects'.[42] She also remembered the silence imposed upon her there. The mother was associated with images of art and beauty, and in H.D.'s analysis Freud stood for the mother, and so did his rooms, replete with art. In Freud's rooms, H.D. was commanded to speak.

The features that attracted her to *White Vishnu* – its elegance and perfection – were the ones that repelled her. H.D. was drawn to fathers, and to cool, 'masculine', scientific scholarship, yet she yearned to subvert them. Her project was not truth but poetry, not facts but visions, not accuracy but magical acts of transformation. In triumphant lines from 'The Master', she recognised it was Freud's project for her, too.

> And it was he himself who set me free
> to prophesy,
>
> he did not say
> 'stay
> my disciple,'
> he did not say,
> 'write,
> each word I say is sacred,'
> he did not say 'teach',
> he did not say,
> 'heal
> or seal
> documents in my name,'
> no,
> he was rather casual,

'we won't argue about that'
(he said)
'you are a poet.'[43]

Poetry and psychoanalysis were liberating, connected enterprises
for H.D., as both made space for the excavation and expression of
unconscious processes. In May 1933, H.D. wrote to Bryher that
she felt 'different all over, as if I had changed an electric current
in myself . . . Everything now will work forward with new
meaning.'[44] But there was an abrupt halt to the analysis. In June,
a bomb scare on the tracks of a tram on which H.D. was travelling panicked her, and she fled Vienna. In August 1934, at her
home near Lake Geneva, she suffered a breakdown. It encouraged
her to return to Vienna at the end of October 1934 and resume
the analysis.

But Vienna was a different and more frightening place.
Swastikas were drawn on the sidewalks. H.D. followed them
down Berggasse 'as if they had been chalked on the pavement
especially for my benefit. They led to the Professor's door.'[45] The
city was in turmoil. In 1932, Engelbert Dollfuss became Austrian
chancellor, heading a right-wing coalition government. But
Dollfuss' policies, designed to combat the effects of the Depression,
were unpopular and he struggled to maintain power. Both left-
wing and right-wing parties opposed him, the Social Democrats
as well as the National Socialists. Early in 1933, civil war erupted
in the streets of Vienna, which Dollfuss brutally suppressed. Then
he suspended parliament, banned both the Socialists and the Nazi
party, and governed by decree. Dollfuss wanted to form an alliance
with the Italian fascist leader, Benito Mussolini. But Adolf Hitler,
who had been made German chancellor in 1933, ordered the

assassination of Dollfuss. In July 1934, a group of Austrian Nazis entered the Chancellery and shot him.

One day, on her regular visit to Berggasse, H.D. noticed the streets were strangely quiet. Freud was astonished to see her. 'But why did you come out?' he asked. 'No one has come here today, no one. What is it like outside? Why did you come out?' It was another occasion of civil unrest. Freud, worried about current events, believed the local newspapers did not supply accurate information and asked H.D. to have Bryher send him cuttings from the English papers she received in Switzerland. In May 1933, Hitler organised a book burning at Berlin University – Freud's books were among those thrown to the flames. Conjuring the atmosphere of those times gives *Tribute to Freud* its measured, elegiac tone. 'We are here today in a city of ruin,' reflected H.D., 'a world ruined, it might seem, almost past redemption.'[46] But, despite the tensions, H.D. persisted and the second analysis ended in December 1934 by mutual agreement. Even after such a brief analysis, Freud gave H.D. permission to offer informal psychoanalytic sessions, which she occasionally did for friends between 1935 and 1936.

Freud told H.D. that, due to the loss of her parents, 'a sort of perfect bi-sexual attitude arises . . . I have tried to be man, or woman, but I have to be both.' But 'it will work out, papa says'.[47] In 1915, Freud had written that sexual preference was not decided until after puberty and that 'all human beings are capable of making a homosexual object-choice'. He continued, 'Psychoanalytic research is most decidedly opposed to any attempt at separating off homosexuals from the rest of mankind as a group of a special character.'[48] Freud also suggested that H.D. write factually about the wartime experiences that haunted her. She tried.

In 1918, she had begun her roman-à-clef *Bid Me to Live* (*A Madrigal*) which she rewrote in the 1930s and finished in 1948. It was not published until 1960, shortly before her death. *Bid Me to Live* charts H.D.'s claustrophobically intense relationships with the London literary avant-garde including D. H. and Frieda Lawrence, Ezra Pound and Richard Aldington. H.D. cast herself as the protagonist, Julia Ashton. They were 'the late-war intellectuals' who 'gabbled of Oedipus across tea-cups or Soho café tables'.[49]

Did Freud help H.D.? Her mental health remained fragile. Another breakdown, a series of psychiatrists and long periods of rehabilitation formed painful continuing rhythms in her life. But, as a poet, analysis liberated her. *Ion*, a translation of Euripides' play, begun during the war and put aside, was taken up once more after the first analysis. Published in 1937, H.D. sent a copy to Freud who was '[d]eeply moved by the play (which I had not known before)'.[50] Her great achievement in poetry, *Trilogy*, was completed between 1944 and 1946, and, in her later years, she was acknowledged with honours and awards.

Meeting in their love of antiquity, Freud and H.D. were able to offer one another particular gifts. The analysis, underscored by the stimulating atmosphere of the collection, gave Freud a special kind of authority with H.D. and the result was a renewed confidence in her creativity. She returned the favour, presenting him with *Ion*, a classical text in her own words, the direct result of Freud's inspired manner of healing. At the play's end, Pallas Athene tells Ion, 'for you / I came / to reveal / mystery'. It is Athena in her role as veiled Isis, 'the most beautiful abstraction of antiquity and of all time', who pleads 'for the great force of the under-mind or the unconscious'. Athena 'makes all things possible for us', so 'nothing is misplaced' and all is 'illuminated by the inner

fire of abstract understanding; hate, love, degradation, humiliation, all, all may be examined, given due proportion and dismissed
finally, in the light of the mind's vision'.[51] H.D. casts Athena as
both symbol and ringing endorsement for psychoanalysis. For
Freud, H.D.'s presence was another gift – she proved the perfect
visitor to his private museum.

13

Under the Protection of Athena

Everything is still unreal, as in a dream.
FREUD TO MAX EITINGON, 6 JUNE 1938[1]

IN MARCH 1938 THE GERMAN army occupied Austria. Not that the majority of Viennese minded: they welcomed Hitler with open arms, crowding into Heldenplatz in their thousands to cheer their führer. A quarter of a million people, over a third of the population of Vienna, participated in the spontaneous, unorchestrated public jubilation.[2] It surprised even Hitler, who had expected a bloody denouement to his long-cherished goal to merge Austria with Germany.

Hitler identified with Germany and despised Austria, the land of his birth, regarding it as a second-rate version of the Fatherland, a view Freud shared. Living in Vienna before the First World War, Hitler aimed to study art, only to be rejected by the Academy of Fine Arts, which gave him another reason to resent the city and wish to humble it. He had been desperately poor and in *Mein Kampf* referred to his time in Vienna as 'the saddest period of my life'.[3] But he admired the architecture of the Ringstrasse and later witnesses confirmed his knowledge of it. According to Albert Speer, Hitler could draw the Ring Boulevard and the adjoining districts with the large buildings true to scale and from memory.[4]

On 12 March, when Freud read his favourite newspaper, the formerly liberal *Neue Freie Presse* trumpeted the glorious unification of Austria with Germany, and he threw it away in disgust. That day he wrote tersely in his diary, 'Finis Austriae'. It was also the end of a glittering epoch that began around the turn of the century and had made Vienna one of Europe's most notable cities. Freud had helped to put it on the map, too, whether the Viennese liked it or not. He was part of a wave of gifted and determined Jewish men and women who had helped transform the city, not only through the arts, sciences and business but as patrons, as the audience for the cultural display for which Vienna was renowned. That Vienna was destroyed overnight.

The most immediate evidence of Nazi rule was shameless attacks on Jewish people, their homes and businesses. Jews were not safe to walk the streets because they no longer had the protection of law. Nazi gangs roamed Vienna, beating up Jewish citizens, smashing their shops, looting their homes and forcing them to perform demeaning public acts, such as scrubbing pavements or writing 'Jud' (Jew) on the walls or windows of their businesses, watched by jeering crowds. German Nazis were impressed by the

Viennese, and took their style of terror campaign back home. Not that it shocked Edmund Engelman: 'The hatred of Jews in Vienna was nothing new to me. We had always lived with it, without a thought of leaving the city. It was part of Vienna, just like the Prater and the cafes – it seemed almost taken for granted, the price we paid for our pleasures. But now it was different.'[5] With lightning speed, Jewish businesses were forcibly liquidated, dwellings seized and religious and cultural institutions confiscated or destroyed.

Panic gripped Vienna's Jewish population and plans to emigrate dominated the conversation. Jews stood in queues at embassies, consulates, shipping companies and government offices, desperate for papers: exit visas, transit visas, receipts for tax payments, clearance forms, boat and train tickets.[6] Though Freud had always reviled Vienna, he could not accept that he had to leave. He prevaricated, like many who did not believe that Germany would allow itself to be ruled by barbarians, telling a friend, 'A nation that has produced Goethe could not possibly go to the bad.'[7]

In mid-March, Ernest Jones flew from London and Marie Bonaparte arrived from Paris to persuade Freud to go. Both were already actively engaged in securing his safe passage to London. But the event that changed Freud's mind occurred on 22 March, when the Gestapo raided Berggasse 19 and arrested Anna, taking her to the infamous Hotel Metropole, the Gestapo headquarters. It was not the first time the Freuds had been raided. A week earlier, a ragtag band of thugs, a kind of Nazi home guard, had pushed their way in. The Freuds behaved with admirable calm, Martha inviting them not only to take cash and valuables but to avail themselves of seats in the living room, while Freud came in from his study and quietly joined his wife. As that was happening, the rest of the gang were a few doors down at Freud's publishing house where they bailed up Martin Freud, who managed the press, and held him captive for several hours.

Freud was terrified for Anna, knowing she could be summarily dispatched to a concentration camp or shot. He spent the day in his study with Max Schur, his doctor. 'The hours were endless,' Schur recalled. 'It was the only time I saw Freud deeply worried. He paced the floor, smoking incessantly.'[8] Anna, however, successfully conducted her interview with the Gestapo, convincing them that the International Psychoanalytic Association was scientific and non-political, and not a terrorist organisation. When she arrived home at seven that evening, plans to leave Vienna were immediately put in place.

Though neither Anna nor Martin told their father, they had asked Schur to supply them with lethal doses of veronal in case of arrest and torture. Freud's attitude was more robust. 'Wouldn't it be better if we all killed ourselves?' Anna had suggested. 'Why?' retorted Freud. 'Because they would like us to?'[9] In the months following the Nazi occupation, there were more than thirteen hundred suicides, and many of those were Jewish.[10] Others fled by whatever means they could, and to whichever country would take them – and few would. A joke circulated in the Jewish community: 'What language are you learning?' Answer: 'The wrong one.'[11] Signs went up at the British and French consulates in Vienna, stating no more visas would be issued. As Paul Hofmann recalls, 'No one who was a witness can evade the memory of the overwhelming majority of the Viennese denying help to, or active compassion for, their Jewish fellow citizens.'[12] Even shopping became a humiliating experience as many non-

Jewish shopkeepers refused to serve their Jewish customers, even if they had known them for years.

But Freud had some powerful angels. Firstly, Bonaparte and Jones had considerable international contacts. When Anna was arrested, Bonaparte, a protective presence at Berggasse 19, had gamely asked to be arrested too, but the Gestapo refused: the diplomatic consequences of having a princess of Greece in custody was too much of a headache. The Americans also became involved in Freud's case. William Bullitt, the U.S. ambassador to France, was a friend of President Franklin D. Roosevelt. An energetic man with wide interests and a former analysand of Freud, Bullitt had persuaded him to co-author a psychoanalytic study of Woodrow Wilson, and the two had remained in touch.[13] John Wiley, the chargé d'affaires at the American Embassy in Vienna, visited Freud to discuss his situation. Wiley and Bullitt took the matter directly to Roosevelt, who instructed Cordell Hull, the Secretary of State, to personally supervise Freud's passage to England.

Such high-level diplomatic negotiations assured Freud of preferential treatment. He asked for, and got, British visas for fourteen people besides himself: included were Martha and Minna, his children and their families still in Vienna, Max Schur and his family, as well as Paula Fichtl. Freud's brother Alexander had fled to Canada, and his son Ernst had already settled in London. Of his five elderly sisters, only Anna was safely living overseas in New York; the remaining four — Mitzi, Dolfi, Rosa and Paula — were in Vienna. Anna Freud sought to help her aunts, as did Marie Bonaparte who tried to organise visas so they could travel to France where she would be able to shelter them, but all attempts failed. Freud's sisters were trapped in Vienna, forced to live in cramped, miserable conditions in a collective apartment until, between 1942 and 1943, they were transported to different concentration camps, including Theresienstadt, where they perished.

Even when Jews had obtained visas, the Nazis placed bureaucratic hurdles in their way. First was the *Reichsfluchtsteuer* (refugee tax), an assessment of taxable assets that stripped them of their money and property, so they left Austria as paupers. Next was the *Unbendenklichkeitserklärung* (declaration of no impediment), a document that meant all taxes and debts had been paid and without which no one could leave. For Freud, there was an added complication: he wanted to take his furniture, library and, of course, the collection, making the tax a special worry. Fortunately, the person selected to value the collection was the Kunsthistorisches curator Hans von Demel. Freud waited anxiously to hear von Demel's assessment, 'suffering from the lack of occupation' and 'putting the library and collection in order'.[14] He made choices about his library that he refused to make for the collection: he gleaned what he felt was unnecessary, and passed around five hundred books to a Viennese dealer, Paul Sonnenfeld, who sold most of them to an antiquarian bookseller.[15] Freud kept all his archaeological books and the bulk of the library is today in the Freud Museum London.

On 23 May, Freud announced to Minna, who had left for England under the care of Dorothy Burlingham two weeks earlier,

The one good piece of news is that my collection has been released. Not a single seizure, only a small payment of 400 Reichsmarks. Director Demel of the Museum was very merciful, he assessed it all at only 30,000 RM but that leaves us far below the tax limit for refugees. The removers can begin packing without delay.[16]

To his credit, von Demel deliberately undervalued the collection, saving it from being confiscated and looted by the Nazis, and on 25 May Freud received the required certificate. But still he waited on the declaration of no impediment.

In the tense days of late May, a young photographer arrived at Berggasse 19. Edmund Engelman had turned a childhood enthu- siasm for photography into a profitable career. Born in 1907, he had grown up in the Leopoldstadt and attended the same high school as Freud. Trained as an engineer, he had been unable to find work because of the Depression and anti-Semitism. In 1932, he opened Photo City (Photo Stadt), an innovative shop and studio centrally located in Kärntnerstrasse, which became well known for the latest photographic equipment, ideas and tech- niques. Engelman expressed his talents in photojournalism and, in film-enthralled Vienna, cinematography.[17] Vienna had a strong photographic tradition, especially in portraiture, which included the dominating figure of Heinrich Kühn as well as the famous studio of Dora Kallmus, known as Studio d'Ora. There was also a radical weekly, *Kuckuck*, illustrated by local photojournalists.[18]

It was a dangerous time to be a photographer, especially a left- wing Jewish one, as Engelman was. In 1934, during an uprising by workers, Engelman photographed the *Goethehof* housing develop- ment, where the insurgents had taken refuge, after government troops had shelled it. There were many casualties: 109 civilians had been killed and 233 were wounded. The Social Democratic Party, of which Engelman was a member, was dissolved during the fighting and its leaders arrested. Before he left Vienna in 1938, Engelman destroyed all the *Goethehof* negatives. 'If the Nazis had found them,' he reflected, 'they would have been "evidence", indeed fatally incriminating evidence, against me.'

On the day Freud's tax certificate was issued, August Aichhorn, a friend and colleague of Freud's, asked Engelman to meet him at a café. Aichhorn, who was not Jewish and belonged to a well-to-do Austrian family, was a socially concerned teacher who employed psychoanalytic techniques in the treatment of troubled adolescents. Aichhorn's controversial theories meant he was unpopular with the authorities. That day, Engelman remembered Aichhorn 'was very upset and looked around nervously to see if we were being watched or overheard'.[19] Aichhorn told Engelman that Freud was leaving for London within days, and it was of the utmost importance that the apartment and the collection be recorded. Engelman, an admirer of Freud's, was thrilled at the prospect. But Aichhorn alerted him to the problems. Having issued the tax certificate, the Gestapo then warned the Freuds not to bring into the apartment other valuables to be smuggled out with Freud's possessions. To make sure, and probably to keep the Freuds on tenterhooks, the Gestapo were conducting a surveillance of the apartment. Undue attention must not be drawn to Engelman's project, therefore no flash or floodlights could be used. It created a technical problem for Engelman: film then was not as light sensitive as it is today. Aichhorn also advised Engelman that Freud, now very frail, would not be present. Though disappointed not to meet his hero and recognising that he was placing himself in danger, Engelman agreed.

Aichhorn had chosen the right photographer for the job. Engelman's precise, sensitive and luminous studies of Berggasse 19 not only provide a record of its contents but are works of art in themselves, a homage to the collection akin to H.D.'s writings. As Susan Sontag observes, even functional photographs 'become studies in the possibilities of photography'.[20] They are the best example of Engelman's photographs that remain, and the only complete record of Freud's living quarters and of his collection.[21]

That cool, rainy morning, Engelman was nervous as he approached Berggasse 19. In a small valise, he had packed two excellent cameras, a Leica and a Rolleiflex, together with a tripod and as much film as he could fit. He began by documenting the street, the building and the staircase 'on which Freud had walked thousands of times, following the route taken by everyone who had ever visited there'. His plan was to 'take as many pictures as I could from positions where Freud usually stood or sat. I wanted to see things the way Freud saw them, with his own eyes, during the long hours of his treatment sessions and as he sat writing.' When Engelman entered Freud's sanctum, he was 'overwhelmed by the masses of figurines which overflowed every surface'.[22] Though he knew Freud had a collection – his best friend was the son of one of Freud's antiquities dealers – he had no idea of its extent. He had to tear himself away from examining each work in detail and address himself to his task. There was little available light, especially as the weather was gloomy, so Engelman turned on all the electric lights, hoping he wouldn't attract the attention of the Gestapo.

Engelman's photographs show that, by 1938, Freud could barely move in his study because of the number of antiquities. Rising from his desk, he had to swing his chair at a ninety-degree angle to slide out between the desk and table, both loaded with statues and other items. Nor was the collection static. Over Engelman's three-day visit, he observed how objects were moved, both by Freud and Paula Fichtl when she dusted them, so from one day to the next, they would be in slightly different positions. The most telling absence is *Athena*, missing from its customary place in the centre of the array on Freud's desk (pl. 53). He had given it and *Jade Screen* to Marie Bonaparte to smuggle out of Vienna. Bonaparte took them out separately. Freud tried to be sanguine, telling his son Ernst in London, '[h]ow much of my own collection I can send on is quite uncertain'. He might 'have to be content with the two little pieces the Princess rescued'.[23]

No area in the apartment (Engelman did not photograph the bedrooms) bears evidence of preparation for flight. Perhaps Freud was waiting for the *Unbendenklichkeitserklärung* before the massive task of packing commenced: clearing out the home where the Freuds had spent forty-seven years, with its accumulation of furniture, crockery, linen, clothes and mementos. Also involved were the delicate logistics of packing the collection, a duty put in the trusted hands of Fichtl. The atmosphere in the apartment is calm, comfortable and orderly (pl. 52). Pot plants thrive in window boxes, a lamp shines on a group of family photographs, a cushion is slumped casually on a couch. Even Minna's sitting room seems ready for her to enter, sit at her desk, pick up a pen and write a letter, though she had already left for London. The camera creates an illusion. What seemed stable and solid was melting into air. Engelman staged a recreation not only of Berggasse 19 but of a world that was being destroyed. Freud's home and Engelman's own were disappearing, and so was a cherished way of life. For many Jewish people, life was not only changing, it was ending.

Though Engelman's task did not include taking photographs of the family, a chance meeting with Freud changed that. While the photographer was working in the study, Freud arrived unexpectedly. The two 'stared at each other with equal astonishment'.[24] Then Aichhorn stepped in, and defused the situation by explaining Engelman's assignment to Freud. Until then, Engelman's presence was kept secret from him. Perhaps Aichhorn thought Freud would find it too bothersome to have a photographer about the place. Engelman, who had prepared an album of the pictures he had already taken, immediately offered it to Freud as a souvenir. Freud was gracious with his thanks and Engelman, seizing the opportunity, asked if he could take Freud's photograph. The images show Freud's uncompromising gaze as well as the ravages of cancer on his right cheek. In one photograph (pl. 54), Freud sits at his desk, gazing at his antiquities, a touching farewell to his personal museum. Engelman also photographed Martha and Anna, and these shots were used for the new passports the family required.

Engelman's photograph of Anna captures the mood of the times. She had just returned from standing in a queue at the Jewish emigration office set up by Adolf Eichmann in the palace of Baron Louis von Rothschild.[25] She was 'somewhat agitated by the sad experience,' recalled Engelman, 'having stood in line outside of the mansion with hundreds of frightened and depressed human beings who were subjected to indignities by Nazi officials.' The Rothschilds, an immensely wealthy Jewish banking family, had branches in Paris, London and Vienna. When they annexed Austria, the Nazis placed Louis von Rothschild in detention, where he remained for a year, arranging his exit from the country by sacrificing part of his vast fortune, including his art collection.[26] By situating the emigration office in the Rothschild palace, the Nazis were sending the Jewish population a clear message: no Jew was safe, no matter how rich or powerful. Engelman took Anna's portrait, capturing 'the fine beauty of her sad and sensitive face during those hard days'.[27] It was Anna who had to be 'untiringly active' securing the necessary papers.[28]

On 2 June, Freud finally received the declaration of no impediment. Since Freud's bank account had been frozen, Marie
Bonaparte loaned him the necessary cash to pay for it. Freud was
not entirely broke. Wisely, he had exchanged much of his cash
for gold ingots and Bonaparte had had them smuggled out in
diplomatic pouches belonging to the Greek Embassy. On 4 June,
Freud and his entourage left Vienna on the Orient Express
and, with great relief, crossed into France. 'Now we are free,'
commented Freud.[29] He managed the journey well, though he
suffered some painful heart irregularities.

Marie Bonaparte, William Bullitt and Freud's son Ernst,
together with journalists and photographers, eagerly awaited the
arrival at the Gare de l'Est in Paris. Bonaparte whisked the Freuds
off to her mansion at St. Cloud, on the outskirts of the city.
Thoughtful and generous as ever, Bonaparte had some special
treats for Freud. Not only did she reunite him with *Athena* and
Jade Screen, she had also bought him a dozen or so small Greek terracotta statues and vases on a recent trip to Athens. Knowing how
important antiquities were to his creative work and well-being,
Bonaparte's gifts meant Freud could decorate his desk with them
while waiting for his collection to arrive. Freud was overwhelmed.
On reaching London, he wrote to Bonaparte, 'The one day in your
house in Paris restored our good mood and sense of dignity; after
being surrounded by love for twelve hours we left proud and rich
under the protection of Athene.'[30] At St Cloud, Freud also repaid
Bonaparte the money she had loaned him.

Soon the Freuds were settled in 'the beautiful city of London',
in a furnished house at 39 Elsworthy Road while a search began
for a permanent residence. Freud liked the place, 'at the foot of
Primrose Hill', because from his window he saw 'nothing but

greenery'. The enchantment of his new surroundings, Freud told Max Eitingon, made him want to shout 'Heil Hitler!' But he admitted the feelings aroused by leaving Vienna were 'hard to grasp, almost indescribable. The feeling of triumph on being liberated is too strongly mixed with sorrow, for in spite of everything I still greatly loved the prison from which I have been released.'[31] Finally, Freud revealed his true sentiments for the city he had affected to disdain.

Freud was a celebrity in London, deluged with flowers, gifts and letters of welcome, making him declare England was 'a blessed, a happy country inhabited by well meaning, hospitable people'. Soon he was receiving letters addressed to 'Dr Freud, London' or 'Overlooking Regent's Park'. The mail included letters from friends as well as 'a surprising number from complete strangers who simply wanted to express their delight at our having escaped to safety and who expect nothing in return ... In short, for the first time and late in life I have experienced what it is to be famous.'[32]

There were visitors, too. On 19 July, Salvador Dalí arrived. It is Freud's only known contact with a leading avant-garde painter. Dalí had visited Vienna three times in the hope of meeting Freud, but each time had missed him. 'On each of these voyages,' Dalí recalled, 'I did exactly the same thing: in the morning I went to see the Vermeer in the Czernin Collection and in the afternoon I did *not* go to see Freud because I invariably learned he was out of town for reasons of health.' Dalí amused himself by eating *Sachertorte*, Vienna's famous chocolate cake, visiting antiquities dealers and having 'long and exhaustive imaginary conversations with Freud'.[33]

Freud was critical of modernists in general and Surrealists in particular. He regarded the latter 'who apparently have adopted me as their patron saint, as complete fools (let us say 95% as with alcohol)'.[34] In 1921, André Breton had visited Freud in Vienna, finding himself 'in the presence of a not very attractive little old man, who receives one in the somewhat shabby offices of a general practitioner'.[35] Breton later apologised for this derogatory account, describing it as 'a regrettable sacrifice to the Dada spirit', and he was grateful that Freud 'had the good grace not to hold it against me and to keep up our correspondence'. Though Breton maintained his 'enthusiastic admiration' for Freud, it seems that the feeling was not mutual.[36] Freud's failure to welcome Breton into the study and show him the collection indicates reserve.

The Surrealists were not interested in psychoanalysis as treatment but in a poetic and anarchic pillaging of its treasures: the dream, the unconscious and the libido. Freud was a revolutionary force and the Surrealists owed him a great deal, as Breton was keen to point out in the first Surrealist manifesto. Automatic writing, which privileges the power of the unconscious, is founded upon Freud's technique of free association. Just after the First World War, Breton, a doctor, practised lay analysis with the patients he was treating for war injuries. In 1937, he opened Galerie Gradiva in Paris, named after Freud's essay. In *Gradiva*, the Surrealists found an explicit justification for their own attempt to determine the relationship between artistic expression and the unconscious. However, they were not interested in 'cures' but in trances and hallucinations, the fantastic and the marvellous, the wild pleasures of the unfettered imagination. In *Les vases communicants*, Breton took Freud to task for failing to reveal the true, personal sources of his dreams. After Breton sent Freud the book, in which Freud is referred to as 'a petit bourgeois from Vienna who aspired for a long time to become a professor', the two engaged in a few hair-splitting exchanges, then Freud curtailed the correspondence by explaining that, although he had received 'many testimonies of the interest that you and your friends show for my research, I am not able to clarify for myself what Surrealism is and what it wants. Perhaps I am not destined to understand it, I who am so distant from art.'[37]

Between 1936 and 1938, major exhibitions in London, Paris and New York displayed the talents of the French Surrealist circle – Dalí, Max Ernst, Yves Tanguy, Joan Miró and André Masson – as well as representatives from many other countries. Like psychoanalysis, Surrealism's enterprise was determinedly international. In London in 1936, Dalí stole the limelight when he gave a lecture inside a diver's suit and nearly suffocated in the process.

Dalí regarded Freud as one of his two father figures (the other was Picasso). While an art student in Madrid, Dalí had read *The Interpretation of Dreams*, regarding it as 'one of the capital discoveries of my life', which seized him with 'a real vice of self-interpretation, not only of my dreams but of everything that happened to me'.[38] Seeing a photograph of Freud arriving in London, Dalí decided to try to see him again. He contacted Stefan Zweig, who was living in England, and asked for an introduction. Zweig was an admirer of Dalí's, describing him to Freud as 'the only painter of genius of our epoch ... and the most faithful and grateful disciple of your ideas among the artists'. Freud agreed, it seems rather reluctantly, and Zweig arrived 'in a little caravan' with Dalí, his wife Gala and his wealthy patron Edward James. With him, James brought Dalí's *The Metamorphosis of Narcissus* (1937, Tate Gallery), then in his possession.[39] Zweig, never shy of hyperbole, told Freud the work, which 'may have been painted under your influence', had 'a perfection with which all paintings of our time seem to pale' and colours that 'since the old masters nobody has ever found'.[40]

Dalí wrote that '[m]y whole ambition in the pictorial domain is to materialize the images of concrete irrationality with the utmost imperialist fury of precision'.[41] From 1926, his impeccable illusionistic style delivered an array of startling new imagery including the limp watches and other melting forms. Dalí refined his technique by studying the old masters and, like Freud, especially admired Leonardo.

In *The Metamorphosis of Narcissus*, he uses the warm tones of Umbrian art to create a disquieting landscape. In Greek myth, Narcissus was the beautiful boy so transfixed by his reflection in a pool that he wasted away and died. As Ovid tells it, when the wood nymphs prepared the funeral pyre for the departed youth, his body was nowhere to be found. 'Instead of his corpse, they discovered a flower with a circle of white petals round a yellow centre.'[42] A trademark of Dalí's 1930s paintings is the 'doubling' of images, which he uses to both literal and symbolic effect in *Narcissus*. The boy and his reflection in the pool create a mirror image, and a large hand positioned on the pool's edge, holding an egg from which the narcissus flower bursts, duplicates Narcissus' pose. As David Lomas observes, Narcissus, who 'unconsciously yearns to re-create the blissful solitude of life in utero', crouches in a fetal position.[43]

During the 1920s, Dalí read Freud's collected works in Spanish, including 'On Narcissism', in which the neuroses of self-love are discussed. Homosexuals, Freud argued, sought 'their own selves' as their love object because their libidinal development had suffered a disturbance.[44] In *Leonardo*, he wrote that homosexuals had repressed the love for their mother by 'running away from other women'.[45] What did the self-mythologising Dalí, married but drawn to homoerotic male friendships, make of that? Perhaps unsurprisingly, his depiction of the myth redeems Narcissus and subverts Freud's theory. From Narcissus' introspection and self-absorption, fresh life and energy is generated in the form of a pure, white flower, a triumphant image of the creative process.

That day at Elsworthy Road, Dalí dressed up for his father figure, 'trying to appear as a kind of dandy of "universal intellectualism"'. In Dalí's memory, the meeting ended badly. Trying to draw Freud's attention to an article he had written on paranoia, Dalí raised his voice, becoming 'involuntarily sharper and more insistent' while Freud continued to stare at him with 'imperturbable indifference'. Then Freud exclaimed to Stefan Zweig, 'I have never seen a more complete example of a Spaniard. What a fanatic!'[46] Could Freud have been guilty of such a gaffe? It is unlikely a Viennese gentleman would utter such an uncouth remark in the presence of a guest. In fact, as Freud told Zweig by letter the next day, he was impressed by 'that young Spaniard, with his candid fanatical eyes and his undeniable technical mastery', making him change his opinion of the Surrealists. Perhaps, when Zweig relayed Freud's comments to the anxious, sensitive artist, he misunderstood them and believed he had been criticised. He was also intrigued by *The Metamorphosis of Narcissus*. 'It would indeed be very interesting to investigate analytically how [Dalí] came to create that picture.'[47] He told Dalí that 'in classic paintings, I look for the sub-conscious – in a Surrealist painting, for the conscious'.[48] In other words, the Surrealists were presenting too literally the concepts of psychoanalysis. The comment deflated Dalí, who believed Freud's words sounded the movement's death knell.

Zweig had advised Freud that Dalí wished to sketch him. Dalí's *Portrait of Sigmund Freud* (1938, Freud Museum London; pl. 55), executed in Indian ink on blotting paper, was a preparatory work completed prior to the meeting.[49] Fascinated by synchronicity, Dalí had made a connection with Freud's face – and snails. When he saw the photograph of Freud arriving in London, Dalí was eating a meal of snails: 'I uttered a loud cry. I had just that instant discovered the morphological secret of Freud! Freud's cranium is a snail! His brain is in the form of a spiral ... This discovery strongly influenced the portrait drawing I later made from life, a year before his death.'[50] In Dalí's brilliantly succinct drawing, stippled pen strokes whirl in opposing arcs to create the shape of Freud's head. The morphology of snails seems less an inspiration than his admiration for Freud's genius, as Dalí positions his subject's dogged, little clenched fist of a face beneath a towering skull, swirling with energy and crowned with radiance. *Portrait of Sigmund Freud* (1938, Fundació Gala-Salvador Dalí, Figueres), produced during the visit, is clumsy and unconvincing. Perhaps Dalí's nerves got the better of him. Zweig was horrified by the sketch and 'dared not show it to Freud because clairvoyantly Dalí had already depicted death in the picture'.[51]

There was good news about the antiquities. Freud's diary entry for 7–8 August is understated: 'Things arrived.'[52] But his relief was immense. Even though the Nazis agreed to release the collection, Freud had remained unsure of its status, telling Max Eitingon, 'The gangsters are unpredictable.'[53] Shortly after, Freud's first visit to his new home at 20 Maresfield Gardens in Hampstead took place. 'Our own house!' Freud wrote in delight to a colleague. 'You can imagine the demands its purchase made on our shrunken savings. And far too beautiful for us.' Meanwhile Ernst, an architect, was renovating the house, restoring it 'anew in a more suitable state for us . . . sheer sorcery translated into architectural terms'.[54] A major task for Ernst was to accommodate Freud's study by making one large room from two downstairs connecting rooms.

Number 20 Maresfield Gardens (pl. 30) is a big, comfortable, sunny home in a good bourgeois neighbourhood. Though in Hampstead, the Freud house is closer to the bustle of Finchley Road than to the greenery of Hampstead Heath. Built in the 1920s in Queen Anne style, Ernst described it as 'neo-Georgian'.[55] With its spacious, light-filled rooms and large back garden, it is reminiscent of the houses the Freuds rented during their summer holidays in Vienna's suburbs, the kind of house they could never afford to buy. On 27 September, the family moved in, Freud telling Eitingon, 'We have it incomparably better than at Berggasse.'[56]

Soon the task of unpacking the antiquities was underway. Even after the boxes were deposited at Maresfield Gardens, Freud was uncertain that everything had arrived safely. In November, when H.D. came to visit, she heard the family's doubts 'as to whether or not the entire treasure-trove, or even any of it, would be found intact'. Afterwards — anonymously — she sent Freud some gardenias with a note, 'To greet the return of the Gods.' Freud replied,

> Dear H.D.,
> I got today some flowers. By chance or intention they are my favourite flowers, those I most admire. Some words 'to greet the return of the Gods' (other people read: Goods). No name. I suspect you to be responsible for the gift. If I have guessed right don't answer but accept my hearty thanks for so charming a gesture. In any case,
>
> affectionately yours,
> Sigm. Freud

When H.D. next visited – the last time she saw Freud – she observed that '[t]he Gods or Goods were suitably arranged on ordered shelves'.[57]

Remarkably, nothing had been broken, lost or stolen. The gods had undergone another perilous journey across time and space, and survived. The collection was arranged in its spacious new premises by the team of Ernst Freud, Ernst Kris and Paula Fichtl. Kris, a psychoanalyst and former curator at the Kunsthistorisches, was an authority on Renaissance gold work and engraved gems. A colleague of Freud's, he was familiar with the collection and had assisted with the display of works at Berggasse 19 as well as authenticating various items. He had also fled Vienna and was waiting to leave for New York. Paula Fichtl, the collection's loyal curator, had memorised the arrangement of the key works on Freud's desk in Vienna and reproduced it at Maresfield Gardens.

Freud was too unwell to engage in such a laborious and finicky operation. He had recently undergone another terrible operation on his mouth from which he never fully recovered, becoming more and more frail. His appearance had been a great shock to H.D., who wrote to Bryher, 'I simply feel he died this is his resurrected Pharaoh or Ka, all rather alarming to the UNK (unconscious)'.[58] But, ever the aesthete, Freud's condition did not stop him from appreciating his new surroundings. He particularly revelled in the large garden, its beds and borders well stocked with flowers and shrubs, and the rows of high trees that secluded it from neighbouring houses. As Ernest Jones recalled,

Freud spent as much time as possible in this garden, and he was provided with a comfortable swing lounge couch shaded by a canopy. His consulting room, filled with his loved possessions, opened through French doors directly into the garden.[59]

The natural world, always a place of regeneration and inspiration for Freud, was now closely linked to his collection. Previously, Freud had moved the bulk of the antiquities to his summer homes. Now at Maresfield Gardens, the two environments were comple-mentary, art and nature flowing into one another. Nature, the title of the essay that had enticed Freud to study medicine, is the source of all myth, but he also recognised the dark side of Mother Earth, the inescapable 'silent Goddess of Death' who 'will take him into her arms'.[60] That goddess now drew near. Freud continued to see patients and was delighted with the publication of *Moses and Monotheism*, his final, inflammatory text.

On 3 September 1939, after Hitler had invaded Poland, Churchill declared war against Germany. Freud was extremely ill. That day, when an air siren sounded in Hampstead, he was lying on his couch in the garden, watching as Paula and his family took steps to safeguard the antiquities. Though the siren turned out to be a false alarm, Freud's bed was moved to the 'safe' zone of the house – his study – from where he could still see the garden and where he was surrounded by his antiquities. Freud retained his interest in current affairs and, when Max Schur wondered if this could be the last war, commented dryly, 'My last war.'[61]

Freud was suffering. It was difficult to feed him, his nights were miserable and he could hardly leave his bed. The skin over his right cheekbone became gangrenous and had to be removed. The odour was foul, making Lün, his devoted dog, keep away from him, something that distressed Freud greatly. On 21 September, when Schur was sitting at his bedside, Freud took his hand and said, 'My dear Schur, you certainly remember our first talk. You promised me then not to forsake me when my time comes. Now it's nothing but torture and makes no sense anymore.' Reluctantly, Schur agreed. Freud paused. 'Tell Anna about this.'[62] Schur then asked Anna to agree to her father's decision which, sorrowfully, she did. Then Schur administered two centigrams of morphine, and Freud fell into a peaceful sleep. Schur repeated the dose twelve hours later, and Freud slipped into a coma from which he did not wake, dying at 3 A.M. on 23 September. He died surrounded by the objects that were precious to him and that symbolised the journey to the afterlife.

The funeral took place three days later at Golders Green Crematorium, where his ashes were placed in the impressive red-figured Greek urn that had been given to him by Marie Bonaparte. Ernst designed the marble plinth on which it sits. When Martha died in 1951, her ashes joined her husband's.

Freud left his antiquities and his library to Anna. She proved a most reliable conservator, keeping the entire collection intact, aside from donating some works to the Sigmund Freud Museum Vienna when it opened in 1971. Occasionally Anna held meetings and ceremonies relating to psychoanalysis in Freud's study, and guests were often given a quick tour, but by and large the room was kept closed. As Elisabeth Young-Breuhl notes, Anna 'wanted to keep her father's part of the house just as it was, a memorial to him'.[63] In 1947, Anna founded the Hampstead Clinic (now the Anna Freud Clinic) at 21 Maresfield Gardens. Dorothy Burlingham also worked with her and lived in a nearby flat. When Minna died in 1947, making space available both for living quarters and private consulting rooms, Dorothy moved in with

Anna. They were together until Dorothy's death in 1979. Anna died in 1982.

When in July 1986 Maresfield Gardens opened to the public as the Freud Museum, everything was just as Freud had left it. The antiquities stand on his desk with *Athena* and *Jade Screen* in central position. Nearby are *Isis Suckling the Infant Horus*, the *Head of Osiris* and *Baboon of Thoth*. In a glass-fronted cabinet, *Eros* takes his place with other winged deities. The exquisite rug woven by the women of the Qashqai tribe is on the couch. The visitor's first impression is of a marvellous museum, quiet as a tomb. But gradually the objects, in their abundance and diversity, their beauty and vitality, clamour for attention, making it not a silent place but one animated by the pagan splendour that Freud adored.

Acknowledgements

I AM INDEBTED TO ERICA DAVIES, former director, Freud Museum London, for her encouragement when I first discussed this book with her. At the Freud Museum London, I am also grateful to Michael Molnar, acting director, and to Keith Davies for answering a multitude of queries so swiftly, as well as to all the staff for making my visits so pleasurable. I would also like to thank the staff at Sigmund Freud Museum Vienna, especially Christian Huber. I am particularly grateful to Christfried Tögel, Sigmund-Freud-Zentrum, for his scholarship and his unstinting help.

I would also like to thank Lynn Gamwell, State University of New York at Binghamton, whose pioneering 1989 exhibition and catalogue provided the foundation of my research and who showed such encouragement when I began this book.

I am also grateful to Pim Allison, Australian National University; Walpurga Antl, Naturhistorisches Museum; Melanie Aspey, The Rothschild Archive; Donald Bailey; Alfred Bernhard-Walcher, Kunsthistorisches Museum; Catherine Bridonneau, Musée du Louvre; Dominique Collon, British Museum; Thomas Engelman; Heather Jackson, University of Melbourne; Rabbi John Levi; Ernest Lustig; Marcella Marongiu, Casa Buonarroti; Mae Anna Pang, National Gallery of Victoria; Klaus Pokorny, Österreichische Galerie Belvedere; Christa Prokisch, Jewish Museum Vienna; Nicholas Reeves; Professor Frank Sear, University of Melbourne; Michael Schweller, Liechtenstein Museum; Emeritus Professor Bernard Smith; Professor Jack J. Spector, Rutgers University; Peter Struthers; Judith Swaddling, British Museum; Arnold Werner, Michigan State University; David Whitehouse, Corning Museum of Glass; Helen White-house, Ashmolean Museum; Ming Wilson, Victoria and Albert Museum; Shelly Wu.

I am very grateful to the psychoanalysts – David Periera, María-Inés Rotmiler de Zentner and Oscar Zentner – and to Professor Isaac Schweitzer, University of Melbourne, who generously read the manuscript and who offered such excellent advice. Norbert Loeffler was a most able translator. My guide in Příbor was Jiří Jurečka whose kind assistance made possible a rather daunting journey. At Random House Australia, I would like to thank my publisher Jane Palfreyman whose enthusiasm for this book, right from the start, was as keen as my own. Thanks also to Nerrilee Weir. At Walker Books, I would like to thank Michele Lee Amundsen for her warm encouragement. I would also like to thank my agents, Joe Veltre and Diane Bartoli, Artists Literary Group.

Last but not least I would like to thank my colleagues at Monash University for their interest in this project: Geraldine Barlow, Max Delany, Maryanne Dever, Professor Merran Evans, Jane Montgomery Griffiths, Rose Lucas, Associate Professor Pauline Nestor, Nina Philadelphoff-Puren and Kate Rigby. Staff at the Monash University Library, especially Averil Dent, did a sterling job of assistance.

Endnotes

INTRODUCTION NOTES

The abbreviation S.E. refers to *The Standard Edition of the Complete Psychological Works of Sigmund Freud*, ed. and trans. by James Strachey in collaboration with Anna Freud, 24 vols (Hogarth Press, London, 1953–1974), Vintage, London, 2001.

The abbreviation Jones I, II or III refers to Ernest Jones, *The Life and Work of Sigmund Freud*, 3 vols, Basic Books, New York, 1953–1957.

1. 'The Moses of Michelangelo' (1914), S.E., vol. XIII, p. 211.

2. Maurice Rheims, *Art on the Market: Thirty-five Centuries of Collecting from Midas to Paul Getty*, trans. David Pryce-Jones, Weidenfeld and Nicolson, London, 1959, p. 33.

3. William McGuire (ed.), *The Freud–Jung Letters: The Correspondence Between Sigmund Freud and C. J. Jung*, trans. Ralph Manheim and R. F. C. Hull, Princeton University Press, Princeton, 1974, p. 292.

4. Jeffrey Moussaieff Masson (ed.), *The Complete Letters of Sigmund Freud to Wilhelm Fliess, 1887–1904*, Harvard University Press, Cambridge, Mass. & London, 1985, p. 202.

5. Sergei Pankejeff, 'My Recollections of Sigmund Freud', in Muriel Gardiner (ed.), *The Wolf-Man and Sigmund Freud*, Hogarth Press and the Institute of Psycho-analysis, London, 1972, p. 139.

6. H.D. (Hilda Doolittle), *Tribute to Freud*, Carcenet, Manchester, 1974, pp. 96–97.

7. Pankejeff, 'My Recollections', p. 139.

8. Ernst L. Freud (ed.), *Letters of Sigmund Freud*, trans. Tania and James Stern, introduction by Steven Marcus, Basic Books, New York, 1975, p. 403. The essay on Freud appeared in Zweig's *Die Heilung durch den Geist: Franz Anton Mesmer, Mary Baker Eddy, Sigmund Freud*, Inselverlag, Leipzig, 1931. (Published as *Mental Healers*, Viking, New York & Cassell, London, 1933.)

9. Jones, II, p. 393.

10. Masson (ed.), *Complete Letters of Freud to Fliess*, p. 363.

11. Freud (ed.), *Letters of Sigmund Freud*, p. 334.

12. Freud (ed.), *Letters of Sigmund Freud*, pp. 330–331; Oscar Pfister, 'Der psychologische und biologische Untergrund expressionitischer Bilder', Berne, 1920; *Expressions in Art, Its Psychological and Biological Basis*, London, 1922.

13. Jones, III, p. 235. Dalí's *Portrait of Freud* was later presented to the Freud Museum London, in memory of writer Helene Eliat van de Velde (1894–1949).

14. Hanns Sachs, *Freud, Master and Friend*, Harvard University Press, Cambridge, 1945, p. 20.

15. Rheims, *Art on the Market*, p. 138.

16. Masson (ed.), *Complete Letters of Freud to Fliess*, p. 398.

17. Jean Baudrillard, 'The System of Collecting', in John Elsner and Roger Cardinal (eds), *The Cultures of Collecting*, Reaktion, London, 1994, p. 7.

18. Ernst Freud, Lucie Freud and Ilse Grubrich-Simitis (eds), *Sigmund Freud: His Life in Words and Pictures*, biographical sketch K. R. Eissler, trans. Christine Trollope, Norton, New York & London, 1998, p. 313.

19. In 1980, the Sigmund Freud archives, a registered English charity, purchased the land and buildings at 20 Maresfield Gardens with funds from the New-Land Foundation Inc. Muriel Gardiner, founder of the New-Land Foundation, a friend of Anna Freud's as well as a psychoanalyst, was instrumental in founding the museum. On Anna's death in 1982, the contents of the house were bequeathed to the English charity to establish the Freud Museum London that opened in July 1986. Sigmund Freud Archives Inc. and Freud Museum London Trustee Ltd are trustees. The

museum is operated through a joint committee of Sigmund Freud Archives and the New-Land Foundation, and managed with the assistance of the London Advisory Committee.

20. Lynn Gamwell, 'The Origins of Freud's Antiquities Collection', Lynn Gamwell and Richard Wells (eds), *Sigmund Freud and Art: His Personal Collection of Antiquities*, State University of New York, Binghamton, and Freud Museum London, 1989, p. 29.

CHAPTER 1: NATURE BOY

1. John Paul Riquelme (ed.), *Bram Stoker, Dracula: Complete, Authoritative Text with Biographical, Historical and Cultural Contexts, Critical Essays from Contemporary Critical Perspectives*, Palgrave, New York, c.2002, p. 28.

2. Freud (ed.), *Letters of Sigmund Freud*, p. 5.

3. 'Screen Memories', S.E., vol. III, p. 312.

4. Letter to the Burgomaster of Príbor, S.E., vol. XXI, p. 259.

5. Walter Boelich (ed.), *The Letters of Sigmund Freud to Eduard Silberstein, 1871–1881*, trans. Arnold Pomerans, Harvard University Press, Cambridge, 1990, p. 16.

6. Suzanne Cassirer Bernfield, 'Freud and Archaeology', *American Imago*, vol. 8, 1951, p. 115.

7. 'Screen Memories', S.E., vol. III, p. 311; 'A Childhood Recollection from *Dichtung und Wahrheit*' (1917), S.E., vol. XVII, p. 149.

8. Masson (ed.), *Complete Letters of Freud to Fliess*, p. 50.

9. *The Psychopathology of Everyday Life*, S.E., vol. VI, p. 110.

10. Masson (ed.), *Complete Letters of Freud to Fliess*, p. 322.

11. Freud (ed.), *Letters of Sigmund Freud*, p. 78.

12. Freud (ed.), *Letters of Sigmund Freud*, p. 140.

13. Boelich (ed.), *Letters of Freud to Silberstein*, p. 33–36.

14. H.D. (Hilda Doolittle), *Tribute to Freud*, p. 11.

15. Masson (ed.), *Complete Letters of Freud to Fliess*, p. 440.

16. Masson (ed.), *Complete Letters of Freud to Fliess*, p. 326; p. 336.

17. 'The Theme of the Three Caskets', S.E., vol. XII, p. 301.

18. J. G. Kohl, *Austria, Vienna, Prague, Hungary, Bohemia and Moravia*, Chapman and Hall, London, 1843, p. 527.

19. Quoted in Derek Sayer, *The Coasts of Bohemia: A Czech History*, Princeton University Press, Princeton 1998, p. 113.

20. Lion Phillimore, *In the Carpathians*, Constable and Company, London, 1912, p. 131.

21. Petr Bogatyrev, *Vampires in the Carpathians: Magical Acts, Rites, and Beliefs in Subcarpathian Rus'*, trans. Stephen Reynolds and Patricia A. Krafcik, East European Monographs & Columbia University Press, New York, 1998, p. 127.

22. Wilma Abeles Iggers (ed.), *The Jews of Bohemia and Moravia, A Historical Reader*, trans. Wilma Abeles Iggers, Káca Poláčková-Henley and Katharine Talbot, Wayne State University Press, Detroit, 1992, p. 197.

23. Boelich (ed.), *Letters of Freud to Silberstein*, p. 17.

24. *Civilization and its Discontents*, S.E., vol. XXI, p. 91.

25. Freud (ed.), *Letters of Sigmund Freud*, p. 22; p. 86.

26. *The Interpretation of Dreams*, S.E., vol. IV, p. 197.

27. Eva Brabant, Ernst Falzeder and Patrizia Giampieri-Deutsch (eds), *Correspondence of Sigmund Freud and Sándor Ferenczi*, trans. Peter T. Hoffer, Belknap Press of Harvard University Press, Cambridge, Mass. & London, 1993–1996, vol. I, p. 72.

28. 'A Childhood Recollection from *Dichtung and Wahrheit*', S.E., vol. XVII, p. 156.

29. Jones, I, p. 3.

30. Martin Freud, *Glory Reflected: Sigmund Freud — Man and Father*, Angus and Robertson, London, 1957, pp. 11–12.

31. Judith Bernays Heller, 'Freud's Mother and Father', Hendrik M. Ruitenbeek (ed.), *Freud As We Knew Him*, Wayne State University Press, Detroit, 1973, p. 338.

32. Ludwig Philippson's *Die israelitische Bibel* (1858); *The Interpretation of Dreams*, S.E., vol. V, p. 583.

33. Freud (ed.), *Letters of Sigmund Freud*, p. 140.

34. Freud (ed.), *Letters of Sigmund Freud*, p. 327.

35. Freud (ed.), *Letters of Sigmund Freud*, p. 327.

36. Bruno Bettelheim, *Freud and Man's Soul*, Pimlico, London, 2001, p. 26.

37. *The Interpretation of Dreams*, S.E., vol. IV, p. 192.

38. Kohl, *Austria*, p. 149.

39. Sachs, *Freud, Master and Friend*, p. 62.

40. 'A Disturbance of Memory on the Acropolis' (1936), S.E., vol XXII, p. 246.

41. Arthur Schnitzler, *My Youth in Vienna*, Weidenfeld and Nicolson, London, 1971, p. 14.

42. Edward Crankshaw, *Vienna, The Image of a Culture in Decline*, Macmillan, London, 1976, p. 39.

43. Freud (ed.), *Letters of Sigmund Freud*, p. 79.

44. Paul Hofmann, *The Viennese: Splendour, Twilight and Exile*, Doubleday, New York, 1988, p. 127.

45. 'Some Reflections on Schoolboy Psychology', S.E., vol. XIII, p. 241. I have used Suzanne Cassirer Bernfeld's translation of this passage from 'Freud and Archaelogy', *American Imago*, vol. 8, 1951, p. 107.

46. T. H. Huxley (trans.), 'Nature: Aphorisms by Goethe', *Nature*, vol. I, 1869, pp. 9–10.

47. Ernst L. Freud, 'Some Early Unpublished Letters of Freud', *International Journal of Psychoanalysis*, vol. L. 1969, p. 424.

48. *Totem and Taboo* (1913), S.E., vol. XIII, pp. 76–77. Italics Freud's.

49. *Totem and Taboo* (1913), S.E., vol. XIII, p. 90.

50. 'Address in the Goethe House', S.E., vol. XXI, p. 208.

51. *The Interpretation of Dreams*, S.E., vol. V, p. 440. Harry Trosman points out that '*unvergleichlich schön*' should be translated as 'incomparably beautiful', rather than 'striking', as it is in Strachey's translation in S.E., vol. V, p. 440. See Trosman, *Freud and the Imaginative World*, The Analytic Press, Hillsdale, 1985, p. 9.

52. *The Interpretation of Dreams*, S.E., vol. IV, p. 196.

53. Schnitzler, *My Youth in Vienna*, p. 63.

54. Freud (ed.), *Letters of Sigmund Freud*, p. 212.

55. Sachs, *Freud, Master and Friend*, p. 26.

56. Schnitzler, *My Youth in Vienna*, p. 13.

57. Boelich (ed.), *Letters of Freud to Silberstein*, p. 63.

58. Preface to the Hebrew Translation, *Totem and Taboo*, S.E., vol. XIII, p. xv.

59. See Yosef Hayim Yerushalmi, 'The Purloined Kiddush Cups: Reopening the Case in Freud's Jewish Identity', in *Sigmund Freud's Jewish Heritage*, State University of New York, Binghamton, 1991, n.p. Published as a supplement to Gamwell and Wells (eds), *Sigmund Freud and Art*, State University of New York, Binghamton & Freud Museum, London, 1989.

CHAPTER 2: LOVE OBJECT

1. 'Some Character Types Met With in Psychoanalytic Work' (1916), S.E., vol. XIV, p. 312.

2. Anna Freud Bernays, 'My Brother, Sigmund Freud', Hendrik M. Ruitenbeek (ed.), *Freud As We Knew Him*, Wayne State University Press, Detroit, 1973, p. 141. None of the homes the Freud family occupied in those years now exist.

3. Boelich (ed.), *Letters of Freud to Silberstein*, p. 126.

4. 'Creative Writers and Daydreaming' (1908), S.E., vol. IX, p. 152.

5. Harry Freud, 'My Uncle Sigmund', in Reuitenbeek (ed.), *Freud*, p. 312.

6. 'Creative Writers and Daydreaming' (1908), S.E., vol. IX, p. 152.

7. Jones, I, p. 25.

8. Freud (ed.), *Letters of Sigmund Freud*, p. 6.

9.   Boelich (ed.), *Letters of Freud to Silberstein*, p. 78.

10. Jacob's inscription to Freud is reproduced in Freud, Freud and Grubrich-Simitis (eds), *Sigmund Freud: His Life in Words and Pictures*, p.134. This translation in Peter Gay, *Freud: A Life for Our Time*, W. W. Norton & Company, New York, 1998, p. 12. Jacob bought a copy of the first edition of the Bible in 1848 and had it rebound to give to Freud on his thirty-fifth birthday. See Emanuel Rice, *Freud and Moses: The Long Journey Home*, State University of New York Press, Albany, 1990, p. 31.

11. Boelich (ed.), *Letters of Freud to Silberstein*, p. 24; pp. 60–61; p. 70; p. 78; p. 54.

12. *The Interpretation of Dreams*, S.E., vol. V, p. 450.

13. *An Autobiographical Study* (1925 [1924]), S.E., vol. XX, p. 10.

14. Laible, '"Through Privation to Knowledge", Unknown Documents from Freud's University Years', *International Journal of Psychoanalysis*, vol. 74, 1993, p. 788.

15. *An Autobiographical Study* (1925 [1924]), S.E., vol. XX, p. 10.

16. Boelich (ed.), *Letters of Freud to Silberstein*, p. 41.

17. Schnitzler, *My Youth in Vienna*, p. 67.

18. 'The Uncanny' (1919), S.E., vol. XVII, p. 237.

19. Paul Ferris, *Dr Freud*, Counterpoint, Washington, 1997, p. 36. Freud made a second trip to Trieste in 1878.

20. Boelich (ed.), *Letters of Freud to Silberstein*, p. 142; p. 153; p. 144.

21. Boelich (ed.), *Letters of Freud to Silberstein*, pp. 92–93.

22. Boelich (ed.), *Letters of Freud to Silberstein*, p. 155.

23. Boelich (ed.), *Letters of Freud to Silberstein*, p. 153.

24. Freud (ed.), *Letters of Sigmund Freud*, p. 89.

25. Quoted in Theodor Reik, *Listening with the Third Ear: The Inner Experience of the Psychoanalyst*, Farrar, Straus, New York, 1948, p. 72.

26. Quoted in Jones, I, p. 132.

27. Freud (ed.), *Letters of Sigmund Freud*, p. 30; p. 23

28. Freud (ed.), *Letters of Sigmund Freud*, p. 158.

29. Quoted in John Follain, 'Freud's Dream Girl', *Sunday Times*, August 2003, p. 26. From Katja Behling-Fischer, *Martha Freud: Die Frau des Genies* (Martha Freud: Wife of the Genius), Aufbau Taschenbuch Verlag, 2003.

30. Gay, *Freud: A Life for Our Time*, p. 39.

31. 'Group Psychology and the Analysis of the Ego', S.E., vol. XVIII, p. 91.

32. H. D. F. Kitto, *The Greeks*, Penguin, Harmondsworth, (1957), 1985, p. 251.

33. Lucilla Burn suggests *Eros* may have been holding a lyre or other musical instrument, a common attribute of figures of this type. See Lynn Gamwell and Richard Wells (eds), *Sigmund Freud and Art*, State University of New York, Binghamton, and Freud Museum London, 1989, p. 103.

34. Hesiod's *Theogony*, probably written in the last third of the eighth century B.C, provides the earliest reference to Eros. He is described as 'the most handsome among the immortal gods, dissolver of flesh, who overcomes the reason and purpose in the breasts of all gods and men'.

Hesiod, *Theogony* and *Works and Days*, trans. with an introduction and notes by M. L. West, Oxford University Press, Oxford & New York, 1988, p. 6.

35. Plato, *The Symposium*, trans. with an introduction and notes by Christopher Gill, Penguin, London, 1999, p. 35.

36. *Beyond the Pleasure Principle*, S.E., vol. XVIII, p. 52.

37. Plato, *The Symposium*, p. 35.

38. Freud (ed.), *Letters of Sigmund Freud*, p. 8.

39. Freud (ed.), *Letters of Sigmund Freud*, pp. 202–203.

40. Freud (ed.), *Letters of Sigmund Freud*, p. 27.

41. Freud (ed.), *Letters of Sigmund Freud*, pp. 58–59; p. 28; p. 46.

42. Freud (ed.), *Letters of Sigmund Freud*, p. 202.

43. A popular representation of the goddess, a similar work, *Isis Enthroned*, also from the Late Period, is in the Kunsthistorisches Museum, Vienna. For dating Egyptian works in Freud's collection, I am grateful to acknowledge the research of Nicholas Reeves in Gamwell and Wells (eds) *Sigmund Freud and Art*, p. 53.

44. E. A. Wallis Budge, *The Gods of the Egyptians, or Studies in Egyptian Mythology*, vol. 2, Dover Publications, New York, (1904), 1969, p. 204.

45. *Moses and Monotheism*, (1939), S.E., vol. XXIII, p. 83.

46. Freud (ed.), *Letters of Sigmund Freud*, p. 81.

47. Freud (ed.), *Letters of Sigmund Freud*, pp. 81-82.

48. Freud (ed.), *Letters of Sigmund Freud*, p. 132.

49. Freud, *Glory Reflected*, p. 25.

50. *The Psychopathology of Everyday Life*, S.E., vol. VI, p. 194.

51. Freud (ed.), *Letters of Sigmund Freud*, p. 43; Walter Benjamin, 'Louis Philippe or the Interior', *Charles Baudelaire: A Lyric Poet in the Era of High Capitalism*, trans. Harry Zohn, Verso, London, 1973, pp. 167–168; Freud (ed.), *Letters of Sigmund Freud*, p. 76.

52. 'The Theme of the Three Caskets', S.E., vol. XII, p. 301.

53. Follain, 'Freud's Dream Girl', p. 26.

54. Freud (ed.), *Letters of Sigmund Freud*, p. 117; p. 48; p. 18.

55. Freud (ed.), *Letters of Sigmund Freud*, p. 89.

56. Follain, 'Freud's Dream Girl', p. 26.

57. Theodor Reik, *The Search Within: The Inner Experiences of the Psychoanalyst*, Funk and Wagnalls, New York, 1968, p. 9.

58. Boelich (ed.), *Letters of Freud to Silberstein*, p. 17.

59. Freud (ed.), *Letters of Sigmund Freud*, p. 160.

60. Freud (ed.), *Letters of Sigmund Freud*, p. 57; p. 141.

CHAPTER 3: PARIS

1. Freud (ed.), *Letters of Sigmund Freud*, p. 187.

2. Georges Didi-Huberman, *Invention of Hysteria: Charcot and the Photographic Iconography of the Salpêtrière*, trans. Alisa Hartz. MIT Press, Cambridge, Mass., 2003, p. xi.

3. Freud (ed.), *Letters of Sigmund Freud*, p. 188. In *The Interpretation of Dreams*, written fifteen years later, Freud wears rose-coloured glasses to represent his initial feelings about Paris, describing the 'blissful feelings with which I first set foot on its pavement seemed to me a guarantee that others of my wishes would be fulfilled as well'. (S.E., vol. IV, p. 195.)

4. Honoré de Balzac, *Lost Illusions*, trans. Herbert Hunt, Penguin, London, 1971, p. 160.
5. Quoted in Hortense Koller Becker, 'Carl Koller and Cocaine', *Psychoanalytic Quarterly*, vol. XXXII, 1963, p. 357.
6. Freud (ed.), *Letters of Sigmund Freud*, p. 188.
7. Quoted in Sachs, *Freud, Master and Friend*, p. 48.
8. Walter Benjamin, 'Paris, Capital of the Nineteenth Century', *The Arcades Project*, trans. Howard Eiland and Kevin McLaughlin, Belknap Press of Harvard University Press, Cambridge, Mass., & London, 1999, p. 5.
9. Freud (ed.), *Letters of Sigmund Freud*, p. 206.
10. Freud (ed.), *Letters of Sigmund Freud*, p. 173.
11. Freud (ed.), *Letters of Sigmund Freud*, p. 173.
12. Kenneth Clark, *The Nude: A Study of Ideal Art*, Penguin, Harmondsworth, 1970, p. 83. For detailed discussion of Venus's discovery and arrival in Paris see Gregory Curtis, *Disarmed: The Story of the Venus de Milo*, Knopf, New York, 2003.
13. Freud (ed.), *Letters of Sigmund Freud*, p. 173.
14. Freud (ed.), *Letters of Sigmund Freud*, p. 173.
15. Donald Malcolm Reid, *Whose Pharaohs?: Archaeology, Museums and Egyptian National Identity from Napoleon to World War I*, University of California Press, Berkeley, 2002, p. 33.
16. In 1881, Auguste Mariette founded the Egyptian Antiquities Service and was instrumental in setting up the old Cairo Museum, as well as discovering fresh

monuments, clearing others and working at thirty-five different sites. With C. du Locle he wrote the libretto of Verdi's *Aida*, which premiered in Cairo in 1871. But his methods could be unorthodox and autocratic. See Peter A. Clayton, *The Rediscovery of Ancient Egypt: Artists and Travellers in the Nineteenth Century,* Thames and Hudson, London, 1982, p. 26 and Charles Keith Maisels, *Early Civilizations of the Old World: The Formative Histories of Egypt, the Levant, Mesopotamia, India and China,* Routledge, London, 1999, p. 22.

17. Freud (ed.), *Letters of Sigmund Freud,* p. 173.

18. *Cylinder Seal,* Mesopotamian, Sumerian (Early Dynastic III), c.2500 B.C., cat. no. 4242, Freud Museum London. The white plaster tablet showing the seal's images was probably made for Freud. *Cylinder Seal,* Old Babylonian, c. 19th–18th century B.C., cat. no. 4234, Freud Museum London. The creamy-coloured tablet was made for the exhibition 'Sigmund Freud and Art: His Personal Collection of Antiquities' (1989). I am grateful to Dominique Collon, Department of Western Asiatic Antiquities, British Museum, for information about the seals. In Freud's library are Franz Philipp Kaulen's *Assyrien und Babylonien nach den neuesten Entdeckungen* (Assyrian and Babylonian according to the latest discoveries), 5th ed., illus. Herder, Freiburg, 1899 and Leonard William King's *Assyrian Language: Easy Lessons in the Cuneiform Inscriptions,* Kegan Paul, Trench, Trubner and Company, London, 1901. In the latter book are some marginal markings, signed 'Dr Freud, January 22, 1902'.

See Wendy Botting and J. Keith Davies, 'Freud's Library and An Appendix of Texts Related to Antiquities', in Gamwell and Wells (eds), *Sigmund Freud and Art*, p. 184ff.

19. Edward W. Said, *Culture and Imperialism*, Vintage, London, 1994, p. 142.

20. *The Interpretation of Dreams*, S.E., vol. V, p. 469.

21. Freud (ed.), *Letters of Sigmund Freud*, p. 183; p. 185; p. 188.

22. Freud (ed.), *Letters of Sigmund Freud*, p.183; Victor Hugo, *Notre-Dame of Paris*, Penguin Books, London, 1978, p. 123.

23. Hugo, *Notre-Dame of Paris*, pp. 128–129.

24. Hugo, *Notre-Dame of Paris*, p. 164.

25. Freud (ed.), *Letters of Sigmund Freud*, p. 203.

26. Hugo, *Notre-Dame of Paris*, p. 200; p. 165.

27. Georges Guillain, *Jean-Martin Charcot, 1825–1893: His Life – His Work*, ed. and trans. Pearce Bailey, Paul Hoeber Inc., New York, 1959, p. 24.

28. Quoted in Didi-Huberman, *Invention of Hysteria*, p. 17; p. 15.

29. Michel Foucault, *Madness and Civilization: A History of Insanity in the Age of Reason*, trans. Richard Howard, Vintage, New York, 1973, p. 64.

30. Freud (ed.), *Letters of Sigmund Freud*, pp. 175–176.

31. *An Autobiographical Study*, S.E., vol. XX, p. 11.

32. Freud (ed.), *Letters of Sigmund Freud*, p. 185.

33. Freud (ed.), *Letters of Sigmund Freud*, p. 185.

34. 'Charcot', S.E., vol. III, p. 17.

35. Freud (ed.), *Letters of Sigmund Freud*, p. 185.

36. Mark Micale, *Approaching Hysteria: Disease and its*

Interpretations, Princeton University Press, Princeton, c.1995, p. 95.

37. 'Paris Report', S.E., vol. I, p. 13.

38. 'Charcot', S.E., vol. III, p. 18.

39. Didi-Huberman, *Invention of Hysteria*, p. 29.

40. 'Charcot', S.E., vol. III, p. 12.

41. 'Charcot', S.E., vol. III, p. 13. Jean-Martin Charcot and Paul Richer, *Demonaiques dans l'art* (1887), BM Israël, Amsterdam, 1972, and Jean-Martin Charcot and Paul Richer, *Difformes and les malades dans l'art* (1889), BM Israël, Amsterdam, 1972. Though Freud refers to the books in the essay, they are no longer in his library.

42. Quoted in Guillain, *Charcot*, p. 24.

43. Quoted in Jones, I, pp. 208-209.

44. Freud (ed.), *Letters of Sigmund Freud*, p. 195; Quoted in Jones, I, p. 84.

45. Freud (ed.), *Letters of Sigmund Freud*, p. 194.

46. Frederick Brown, *Zola: A Life*, Farrar, Straus, Giroux, New York, 1995, p. 563.

47. Freud (ed.), *Letters of Sigmund Freud*, pp. 196-197.

48. Quoted in Guillain, *Charcot*, p. 33.

49. Freud (ed.), *Letters of Sigmund Freud*, pp. 207–8.

50. *An Autobiographical Study*, S.E., vol. XX, p. 12.

51. Jean Baudrillard, 'The Systems of Collecting', Elsner and Cardinal (eds), *The Cultures of Collecting*, p. 12.

52. Quoted in Guillain, *Charcot*, p. 33.

53. Freud (ed.), *Letters of Sigmund Freud*, p. 211.

54. Freud (ed.), *Letters of Sigmund Freud*, pp. 211–215.

CHAPTER 4: AT HOME

1. Adolf Hitler, *Mein Kampf* (My Struggle), trans. and annotated by James Murphy, Hurst and Blackett, London, 1939, p. 30.

2. André Breton, 'Interview with Professor Freud' in Ruitenbeek (ed.) *Freud As We Knew Him*, p. 63.

3. Donald J. Olsen, *The City as a Work of Art: London, Paris, Vienna*, Yale University Press, New Haven & London, 1986, p. 154.

4. Jones, I, p. 143.

5. Koller Becker, 'Carl Koller and Cocaine', *Psychoanalytic Quarterly*, vol. XXXII, 1963, p. 357.

6. Freud (ed.), *Letters of Sigmund Freud*, p. 100.

7. Martin Freud, *Glory Reflected*, p. 24.

8. Freud (ed.), *Letters of Sigmund Freud*, p 217.

9. Quoted in *Diary of Sigmund Freud, 1929–1939: A Record of the Final Decade*, trans. and annotated with an introduction by Michael Molnar, Freud Museum Publications, London, & Scribner, New York, 1992, p. 237.

10. H.D. (Hilda Doolittle), *Tribute to Freud*, pp. 68–69.

11. 'The Moses of Michelangelo' (1914), S.E., vol. XIII, p. 211.

12. Freud, *Glory Reflected*, p. 34.

13. Masson (ed.), *Complete Letters of Freud to Fliess*, p. 336.

14. Carl E. Schorske, *Fin-de-siècle Vienna: Politics and Culture*, Weidenfeld and Nicolson, London, 1980, p. 43.

15. Edward Crankshaw, *Vienna: The Image of a Culture in Decline*, Macmillan, London, 1976, p. 18.

16. A. J. P. Taylor, *The Habsburg Monarchy: A History of the*

Austrian Empire, 1809–1918, Hamish Hamilton, London, 1972, p. 10.

17. Stefan Zweig, *The World of Yesterday*, Cassell, Sydney, 1945, p. 12.

18. Hitler, *Mein Kampf*, p. 57.

19. Schorske, *Fin-de-siècle Vienna*, p. 60.

20. Freud (ed.), *Letters of Sigmund Freud*, p. 217.

21. Schorske, *Fin-de-siècle Vienna*, p. 62.

22. Zweig, *The World of Yesterday*, p. 27.

23. Letter to Minna Bernays, 25 August 1886, in Ernst Freud, Lucie Freud and Ilse Grubrich-Simitis (eds), *Sigmund Freud: His Life in Words and Pictures*, p. 131.

24. Jones, I, p. 146.

25. Freud (ed.), *Letters of Sigmund Freud*, p. 27.

26. Freud (ed.), *Letters of Sigmund Freud*, p. 43.

27. Freud (ed.), *Letters of Sigmund Freud*, p. 189.

28. Quoted in Jones, I, p. 146.

29. Freud (ed.), *Letters of Sigmund Freud*, p. 71.

30. Freud, *Glory Reflected*, p. 34.

31. Koller Becker, 'Carl Koller and Cocaine', p. 356.

32. Edmund Engelman, *Sigmund Freud: Berggasse 19, Vienna*, trans. Lonnie R. Johnson, with an introduction by Inge Scholz-Strasser, Verlag Christian Brandstätter, Vienna, 1998, p. 100.

33. Sachs, *Freud, Master and Friend*, p. 51.

34. Masson (ed.), *Complete Letters of Freud to Fliess*, p. 78; p. 94.

35. Masson (ed.), *Complete Letters of Freud to Fliess*, p. 54.

36. Freud (ed.), *Letters of Sigmund Freud*, p. 224.

37. Casting doubt on Anna's memory, Ernest Jones remarks 'unfortunately no one else in the family ever knew of [the vase's] existence'. (Jones, I, p. 149.) There are no examples of nineteenth-century china in Freud's extant collection.

38. Martin Grotjahn, 'A Letter by Sigmund Freud with Recollections of his Adolescence' in Ruitenbeek (ed.) *Freud As We Knew Him*, p. 320.

39. Bruno Bettelheim, *Freud's Vienna and Other Essays*, Knopf, New York, 1990, p. 20.

40. Marsha L. Rozenblit, *The Jews of Vienna, 1867–1914: Assimilation and Identity*, State University of New York Press, Albany, 1983, p. 88.

41. Freud (ed.), *Letters of Sigmund Freud*, p. 202.

42. Freud, *Glory Reflected*, p. 28.

43. Koller Becker, 'Carl Koller and Cocaine', p. 359.

44. *An Autobiographical Study*, S.E., vol. XX, p. 18.

45. 'Report on My Studies in Paris and Berlin', S.E., vol. I, p. 13.

46. Freud (ed.), *Letters of Sigmund Freud*, p. 228–229.

CHAPTER 5: RENAISSANCE MAN

1. Masson (ed.), *Complete Letters of Freud to Fliess*, p.110.

2. Baudrillard, 'The System of Collecting', John Elsner and Roger Cardinal (eds), *The Cultures of Collecting*, p. 9.

3. Brabant, Falzeder and Giampieri-Deutsch (eds), *Correspondence of Sigmund Freud and Sándor Ferenczi*, p. 498.

4. Masson (ed.), *Complete Letters of Freud to Fliess*, p. 214.

5. Freud, *Glory Reflected*, p. 45.

6. Freud, *Glory Reflected*, p. 82.

7. Masson (ed.), *Complete Letters of Freud to Fliess*, p. 135.

8. Freud, *Glory Reflected*, p. 137.

9. For discussion of the Leipzig period, see Christfried Tögel and Michael Schröter, 'Jacob Freud mit Familie in Leipzig (1859). Erzählung und Dokumente' ('Jacob Freud with his family in Leipzig (1859). Anecdotes and Documents.') *Luzifer-Amor*, 33, 2004, pp. 8–32.

10. Masson (ed.), *Complete Letters of Freud to Fliess*, p. 285.

11. Freud, *Glory Reflected*, p. 126.

12. Freud, *Glory Reflected*, p. 51. For a complete list of Freud's travels see Sigmund Freud, *Unser Herz zeigt nach dem Süden: Reisebriefe 1895–1923* (Our Heart Points to the South: Travel Letters. 1895–1923), Christfried Tögel (ed.) in collaboration with Michael Molnar, Aufbau-Verlag, Berlin, 2002. For details of Freud's 1896 journey, see p. 51.

13. Freud, *Glory Reflected*, p. 47.

14. Karl Baedeker, *Italy, Handbook for Travellers, Central Italy and Rome*, 10th edition, Karl Baedeker, Leipzig, 1890, p. xvii.

15. E. M. Forster, *A Room with a View*, Penguin, Harmondsworth, 1988, p. 41.

16. Freud, *Unser Herz*, p. 64.

17. Freud, *Unser Herz*, p. 62; p. 64.

18. *The Interpretation of Dreams*, S.E., vol. V, p. 432.

19. Freud, *Unser Herz*, p. 64.

20. Freud, *Glory Reflected*, p. 39; p. 44.

21. Freud, *Unser Herz*, p. 64.

22. Francis King, *Florence: Literary Companion*, John Murray, London, 1991, p. 118.

23. Freud, *Unser Herz*, p. 67.
24. King, *Florence: Literary Companion*, pp. 220–221.
25. Freud, *Unser Herz*, p. 71.
26. Freud (ed.), *Letters of Sigmund Freud*, p. 187.
27. 'A Disturbance of Memory on the Acropolis' (1936), S.E., vol. XXII, pp. 246–247.
28. Freud, *Unser Herz*, p. 69.
29. The drawing, attributed to Jacopino del Conte, is in the collection of the Casa Buonarroti, Florence. *Portrait of Michelangelo*, c. 1535, 98.5 × 68 cm.
30. Freud, *Unser Herz*, p. 69.
31. Masson (ed.), *Complete Letters of Freud to Fliess*, p. 193; p. 195; p. 201.
32. Masson (ed.), *Complete Letters of Freud to Fliess*, p. 202.
33. Masson (ed.), *Complete Letters of Freud to Fliess*, p. 202.
34. *The Interpretation of Dreams*, S.E., vol. IV, p. 318.
35. Heller, 'Freud's Mother and Father', in Ruitenbeek (ed.) *Freud As We Knew Him*, p. 336. Judith Bernays Heller was the daughter of Anna, Freud's younger sister. In 1892–93, she stayed with Jacob and Amalia while her parents were settling in America.
36. *Totem and Taboo*, S.E., vol. XIII, p. xv.
37. Rabbi Tom Louchheim, *Jewish Customs of Mourning*, 1997, http://scheinermann.net/judaism/life-cycle.html. I would also like to thank Rabbi John Levi for his advice on Jewish funerary customs.
38. Shavuot, marking the end of the barley harvest and the beginning of the wheat harvest, is the only festival for

which no specific date is given in the Bible. This holiday takes place seven weeks after the second day of Passover and occurs in May or June.

39. Ana-María Rizzuto, *Why Did Freud Reject God?: A Psychodynamic Interpretation*, Yale University Press, London & New Haven, 1998, p. 252.

40. *Leonardo da Vinci and a Memory of his Childhood*, S.E., vol. XI, p. 123.

41. *Civilization and its Discontents* (1927), S.E., vol. XXI, p. 10.

42. I am grateful to acknowledge Susan L. Braunstein's research on the *Hanukkah Lamp* (Northern France or Germany, 13th century, copper alloy, cast in lost wax method, 12.7 × 17 × 5 cm, cat. no. 4515 Freud Museum London) in *Sigmund Freud's Jewish Heritage*, State University of New York at Binghamton, New York, 1991, n.p. Published as a supplement to Gamwell and Wells (eds), *Sigmund Freud and Art*, State University of New York, Binghamton & Freud Museum, London, 1989.

43. Freud (ed.), *Letters of Sigmund Freud*, p. 261.

44. *The Psychopathology of Everyday Life*, S.E, vol. VI, p. 7.

45. *An Autobiographical Study*, S.E, vol. XX, p. 30.

46. Susan L. Braunstein in *Sigmund Freud's Jewish Heritage*, n.p.

47. Freud (ed.), *Letters of Sigmund Freud*, pp. 411–412.

48. Masson (ed.), *Complete Letters of Freud to Fliess*, p. 254.

49. Masson (ed.), *Complete Letters of Freud to Fliess*, p. 202.

50. Freud (ed.), *Letters of Sigmund Freud*, p. 202.

51. Didier Anzieu, *Freud's Self Analysis*, trans. Peter Graham,

Hogarth Press and Institute of Psychoanalysis, London,
1986, p. 121.

52. *Studies on Hysteria*, S.E., vol. II, p. 139.
53. *Studies on Hysteria*, S.E., vol. II, p. 157.
54. *Studies on Hysteria*, S.E., vol. II, p. 160.
55. *An Autobiographical Study*, S.E., vol. XX, p. 28.
56. P. R. J. Ford, *Oriental Carpet Design: A Guide to Traditional Motifs, Patterns and Symbols*, Thames and Hudson, London, 1981, p. 122.
57. In 1886, Freud's sister Marie (Mitzi) married a distant Romanian cousin, Moritz Freud, who was a carpet dealer. It is unlikely, however, that Freud bought the carpet from his brother-in-law as the couple moved to Berlin after the wedding. Nor did Freud have much affection for them, telling Fliess, 'None of [the family] has a relationship with [Mitzi]; she has always been isolated and rather peculiar. In her mature years this has manifested itself in pathological parsimony, while the rest of us are spendthrifts.' As for Moritz, 'he is half-Asian, suffers from pseudologica fantastica, though he is otherwise good to his family. All of us (with the exception of my mother, of course) were much relieved when the family moved to Berlin.' (Masson (ed.), *Complete Letters of Freud to Fliess*, p. 311.)
58. P. R. J. Ford, *Oriental Carpet Design*, p. 110.
59. Jane Brown, *Gardens of a Golden Afternoon: A Social History of Gardens and Gardening*, Penguin, Harmondsworth, 1985, p. 34.

60. *An Autobiographical Study*, S.E., vol. XX, p. 41.

61. *An Autobiographical Study*, S.E., vol. XX, pp. 27–28.

62. 'On Beginning the Treatment' (1913), S.E., vol. XII, p. 134.

63. E. Gans-Ruedin, *Iranian Carpets: Art, Craft and History*, Thames and Hudson, London, 1978, p. 11.

64. *An Autobiographical Study*, S.E., vol. XX, p. 17.

65. Masson (ed.), *Complete Letters of Freud to Fliess*, p. 110.

66. *The Aetiology of Hysteria*, S.E., vol. III, p. 202.

67. *The Aetiology of Hysteria*, S.E., vol. III, p. 192.

68. Masson (ed.), *Complete Letters of Freud to Fliess*, p. 184.

69. *Civilization and its Discontents*, S.E., vol. XXI, p. 81.

70. Masson (ed.), *Complete Letters of Freud to Fliess*, p. 363.

71. Christian Huber, Sigmund Freud Museum Vienna, advises that Martin Freud's photograph was taken on the veranda of the consulting rooms Freud occupied between 1891 and 1908. (Email to the author, 26 August 2004.) Freud also had a study upstairs during the same period but it is unlikely the photograph was taken there as Freud did not include objects from his collection in his domestic environment. There has been some discussion about the date of this photograph. In Freud, Freud and Grubrich-Simitis (eds), *Sigmund Freud, His Life in Words and Pictures*, the photograph is dated 'around 1912' (p. 200). However, I am inclined to agree with the dating of around 1905 suggested by Lynn Gamwell in 'The Origins of Freud's Antiquities Collection' in Gamwell and Wells (eds), *Sigmund Freud and Art*, p. 31, fn 5.

72. Freud (ed.), *Letters of Sigmund Freud*, p. 293.

73. 'The Moses of Michelangelo' [1914], S.E., vol. XIII, p. 213.

74. Giorgio Vasari, *Lives of the Artists*, trans. George Bull, Penguin Books, London, 1988, vol. I. p. 342.

75. For discussion of the iconography of the tomb and *Dying Slave* see Vasari, *Lives of the Artists*, pp. 343–345, and Howard Hibbard, *Michelangelo: Painter, Sculptor, Architect*, Octopus, London, 1974, pp. 97–101.

76. The extant *Slaves* are: *Dying Slave* (1513–15) and *Rebellious Slave* (c. 1513–15) Musée du Louvre, Paris. The other *Slaves* are *Awakening Giant* (1520–23), *Bearded Slave* (1520–23), *Prisoner (Atlas?)* (1520–23) and *Young Slave* (1520–23), Accademia Gallery, Florence.

77. 'The Moses of Michelangelo' [1914], S.E., vol. XIII, p. 233.

78. Robert J. Clements (ed.) *Michelangelo: A Self-portrait*, Prentice-Hall, Englewood Cliffs, 1963, p. 55.

79. Erwin Panofsky, *Studies in Iconology; Humanistic Themes in the Art of the Renaissance*, Harper & Row, New York, 1962, p. 197.

80. Camille Paglia, *Sexual Personae: Art and Decadence from Nerfertiti to Emily Dickinson*, Penguin, London, 1992, p. 165.

81. Panofsky, *Studies in Iconology*, p. 177.

82. *Three Essays on the Theory of Sexuality* (1905), S.E., vol. VII, p. 156, fn 2, added 1915.

83. Jacob Burckhardt, *The Cicerone: Or, Art Guide to Painting in Italy*, trans. A. H. Clough, T. Werner Lawrie, London, 1917, p. 57. Freud's two-volume edition, which remains

in his library, is Jakob Burckhardt, *Die Cicerone: eine Anleitung zum Genuss der Kunstwerke Italiens* (The Cicerone: A Guide to the Enjoyment of Italian Artworks), E. A. Seeman, Leipzig, 1893.

84. Jacob Burckhardt, *The Civilization of the Period of the Renaissance in Italy*, trans. S. G. C. Middlemore, C. Kegan Paul, London, 1898, vol. 1, p. 182.

85. *Civilization and its Discontents*, S.E., vol XXI, p. 72.

86. Patrick Mauries, *Cabinets of Curiosities*, Thames and Hudson, London, 2002, p. 171.

87. Masson (ed.), *Complete Letters of Freud to Fliess*, p. 110.

88. 'Mourning and Melancholia' (1917 [1915]), S.E., vol. XIV, p. 244.

89. *The Psychopathology of Everyday Life*, S.E., vol. VI, p. 236.

90. In 1938, the Liechtenstein family fled, with their collections, to Vaduz in the Principality of Liechtenstein. The palace housed the Leopold Museum (the private collections of Rupert and Elisabeth Leopold) until 2001 when the Leopold Museum gained its own site in the Museum Quarter, behind the Kunsthistorisches Museum. In March 2004, the palace reopened, with its original collections, as the Liechtenstein Museum.

91. Masson (ed.), *Complete Letters of Freud to Fliess*, p. 274; p. 281; p. 272.

92. The Belvedere Palace was built in the eighteenth century for Prince Eugene of Savoy by Johann Lukas von Hildebrandt. The *Unteres* (Lower) Belvedere was built first (1714–16) with an orangery attached, and was the prince's

summer residence. Connected to it by a long, landscaped garden is the *Oberes* (Upper) Belevedere (1721–23), the venue for banquets and other festivities. In 1736, after the prince's death, Empress Maria Theresa bought the palace. The Habsburg art collections were housed there and opened to the public, before being transferred to the Kunsthistorisches Museum in 1891.

93. Thomas Dacosta Kaufmann, 'The Collections of the Austrian Habsburgs', in Elsner and Cardinal (eds), *The Cultures of Collecting*, p. 151.

94. *Picture Gallery of the Art History Museum Vienna*, introduction by Friderike Klauner, Paul Hamlyn, London, 1971, p. 12.

95. I am grateful to Christa Prokisch, Jewish Museum Vienna, for her assistance. See also Christa Prokisch, 'Chronologie einer Ansammlung Jüdisches Museum Wien (1893–1996)', in 'Papier ist doch weiss?', Eine Spurensuche im Archiv des Jüdisches Museum Wien, 30 January–22 March 1998, pp. 14–25.

96. 'Address to the B'nai B'rith', S.E., vol. XX, p. 274.

97. Masson (ed.), *Complete Letters of Freud to Fliess*, p. 309.

98. Brigitte Hamann, *Hitler's Vienna: A Dictator's Apprenticeship*, trans. Thomas Thornton, Oxford University Press, Oxford & New York, 2000, p. 290.

99. James Shedel, *Art and Society: The New Movement in Vienna, 1897–1914*, Society for the Promotion of Science and Scholarship, Palo Alto, 1981, p. 82.

100. Masson (ed.), *Complete Letters of Freud to Fliess*, p. 227.

101. Masson (ed.), *Complete Letters of Freud to Fliess*,
    pp. 231-232.

102. *An Autobiographical Study*, S.E., vol. XX, p. 34.

103. Masson (ed.), *Complete Letters of Freud to Fliess*, p. 228.

CHAPTER 6: DREAM COLLECTOR

1. Heinrich Schliemann, *Ilios: The City and Country of the Trojans*, John Murray, London, 1880, p. 18.

2. Masson (ed.), *Complete Letters of Freud to Fliess*, p. 240.

3. Gay, *Freud, A Life for Our Time*, p. 82.

4. *The Interpretation of Dreams*, S.E., vol. IV, p. 118; p. 121. Italics Freud's.

5. *The Interpretation of Dreams*, S.E., vol. IV, pp. xxiii–xxiv. Freud adds 'and those of my patients'.

6. *The Interpretation of Dreams*, S.E., vol. IV, p. xxvi.

7. Masson (ed.), *Complete Letters of Freud to Fliess*, p. 269.

8. Masson (ed.), *Complete Letters of Freud to Fliess*, p. 363.

9. 'On the History of the Psychoanalytic Movement', S.E., vol. XIV, p. 22.

10. H.D. (Hilda Doolittle), *Tribute to Freud*, p. 175.

11. Masson (ed.), *Complete Letters of Freud to Fliess*, p. 366.

12. Masson (ed.), *Complete Letters of Freud to Fliess*, p. 322.

13. Masson (ed.), *Complete Letters of Freud to Fliess*, p. 361.

14. *The Interpretation of Dreams*, S.E., vol. IV, p. 207; p. 177.

15. Masson (ed.), *Complete Letters of Freud to Fliess*, p. 262.

16. Sachs, *Freud, Master and Friend*, p. 101; Robert P. Knight, 'A Visit with Freud', in Ruitenbeek (ed.) *Freud As We Knew Him*, p. 115.

17.   *The Interpretation of Dreams*, S.E., vol. IV, p. 218.

18.   Jones, II, pp. 389–90.

19.   *The Psychopathology of Everyday Life*. S.E., vol. VI, p. 173.

20.   *The Psychopathology of Everyday Life* was published in 1901. S.E., vol. VI, p. 167. Hanns Sachs observes that the collection was 'in its initial stages' when Freud moved into his upstairs study in 1909 but that seems unlikely given Freud's description. (Sachs, *Freud, Master and Friend*, p. 52.)

21.   See *Diary of Sigmund Freud, 1929–1939: A Record of the Final Decade*.

22.   *The Interpretation of Dreams*, S.E., vol. IV, p. 124.

23.   Freud's first visit to Orvieto was in September 1897. He visited twice more in August 1902 and September 1907. Luca Signorelli's fresco of the Last Judgement in Orvieto Cathedral made an impression on Freud. He discusses forgetting Signorelli's name in 'The Mechanism of Forgetfulness', S.E., vol. III, pp. 290–295, and again in *The Psychopathology of Everyday Life*. S.E., vol. VI, pp. 2–6.

24.   *The Interpretation of Dreams*, S.E., vol. V, pp. 453–455.

25.   Geoffrey Edwards, *Art of Glass: Glass in the Collection of the National Gallery of Victoria*, National Gallery of Victoria, Melbourne, 1998, p. 46. *Covered jar / Funerary urn*, late first century–second century A.D. (Western Mediterranean or Gaul). Blown glass, 21.8 × 24.4 × 23.4 cm. Collection National Gallery of Victoria. This work, similar to Freud's, has a lid but it is not the original. As Lucilla Burn notes, jars of this shape are generally found in the western

provinces of the Roman empire. They may have been used as storage jars in the house but most of those found have contained cremations. (Gamwell and Wells (eds), *Sigmund Freud and Art*, p. 118.)

26. See Lucilla Burn, in Gamwell and Wells (eds), *Sigmund Freud and Art*, pp. 116–121.

27. *Balsamarium*, Etruscan, third century B.C. Bronze, 9.4 cm high, cat. no. 3029 See Lucilla Burn, Gamwell and Wells (eds), *Sigmund Freud and Art*, p. 108.

28. M. Isidora Forrest, 'Notes on the Maenads and Ecstatic Dance', http://www.hermeticfellowship.org/Dionysion/Maenads.html.

29. *Three Essays on Sexuality*, S.E., vol. VII, p. 220. This sentence was added in 1915.

30. *Three Essays on Sexuality*, S.E., vol. VII, p. 219.

31. Schliemann, *Ilios*, p. 1.

32. Masson (ed.), *Complete Letters of Freud to Fliess*, p. 353. Freud also bought Schliemann's other major works *Mykenae: bericht uber meine Forschungen und Entdeckungen in Mykenae und Tiryns* (Mycenae: A Narrative of Researches and Discoveries at Mycenae and Tiryns), FA Brockhaus, Leipzig, 1878, and *Tiryns: der praehistorische Palast der Koenige von Tiryns, Ergebnisse der neusten Ausgrabungen* (Tiryns: The Prehistoric Palace of the Kings of Tiryns, the Results of the Latest Excavations), FA Brockhaus, Leipzig, 1886.

33. Schliemann, *Ilios*, p. 41.

34. Leo Deuel, *Memoirs of Heinrich Schliemann: A documentary portrait drawn from his autobiographical writings, letters and*

excavation reports, Hutchinson, London, 1978, p. 7.

35. The mask, from the second half of the 16th century B.C., predates the Trojan War by four centuries. It is thought to be of a Mycenean chieftain or king.

36. *Stirrup Jar*, Mycenean, Late Helladic IIIB, c. 1300–1200 B.C. Terracotta, 15 cm high. cat. no. 3757. See Gamwell and Wells (eds), *Sigmund Freud and Art*, p. 80.

37. Masson (ed.), *Complete Letters of Freud to Fliess*, p. 445.

38. *Moses and Monotheism*, S.E., vol. XXIII, p. 46 fn. In his library, Freud had Sir Arthur Evans' *The Palace of Minos: A Comparative Account of the Successive Stages of the Early Cretan Civilization as Illustrated by the Discoveries at Knossos*, Macmillan, London, 1921–1936.

39. Quoted in Anna Lucia D'Agata, 'Sigmund Freud and Aegean Archaeology: Mycenaean and Cypriote Material from his collection of Antiquities', *Studi Miceni ed Egeo-Anatolici*, Gruppo Editoriale Internazionale, Rome, 1994, p. 17.

40. Masson (ed.), *Complete Letters of Freud to Fliess*, pp. 205–206.

41. Virgil, *The Aeneid*, trans. W. F. Jackson Knight, Penguin, London, 1958, p. 185.

42. Masson (ed.), *Complete Letters of Freud to Fliess*, pp. 205–206.

43. Freud, *Glory Reflected*, p. 37.

44. Emmanuel Löwy, *The Rendering of Nature in Early Greek Art*, trans. John Fothergill, Duckworth, London, 1907, p. 2; p. 68. Freud also had copies of Löwy's other books, now in the library at the Freud Museum London.

45. E. H. Gombrich, *Art and Illusion: A Study in the Psychology of Pictorial Representation*, Phaidon, London, 1972, p. 18.

46. Masson (ed.), *Complete Letters of Freud to Fliess*, p. 427.

47. A video, compiled from several different Freud family home movies and with Anna Freud's voiceover, is screened continuously at the Freud Museum London and Sigmund Freud Museum Vienna.

48. Masson (ed.), *Complete Letters of Freud to Fliess*, p. 365.

49. *The Interpretation of Dreams*, S.E., vol. IV, p. 122.

50. *The Interpretation of Dreams*, S.E., vol. V, p. 470; S.E., vol. IV, p. 232.

51. *The Interpretation of Dreams*, S.E., vol. V, p. 465–466.

52. Masson (ed.), *Complete Letters of Freud to Fliess*, p. 308.

53. 'Leonardo da Vinci and a Memory of His Childhood', S.E., vol. XI, pp. 96–97.

54. Brabant, Falzeder and Giampieri-Deutsch (eds), *Correspondence of Sigmund Freud and Sándor Ferenczi*, vol. I, p. 138.

55. *Mummy Case* (c.600 BC) is made of gilded cartonnage and displays amulets of Maat, goddess of divine order. See *Diary of Sigmund Freud, 1929–1939: A Record of the Final Decade*, p. 168.

56. Edmund Engelman, *Berggasse 19: Sigmund Freud's Home and Offices, Vienna, 1938: The Photographs of Edmund Engelman*, introduction by Peter Gay, captions by Rita Ransohoff, Basic Books, New York, 1976, p. 66.

57. *The Interpretation of Dreams*, S.E., vol. V, p. 466.

58. Susan Stewart, *On Longing: Narratives on the Miniature, the*

Gigantic, the Souvenir, the Collection, Duke University Press, Durham, 1993, p. 151.

59. *The Interpretation of Dreams*, S.E., vol. V, p. 621.
60. Masson (ed.), *Complete Letters of Freud to Fliess*, p. 402.
61. Masson (ed.), *Complete Letters of Freud to Fliess*, p. 405.
62. Masson (ed.), *Complete Letters of Freud to Fliess*, p. 415

CHAPTER 7: ROMAN HOLIDAY

1. J. W. Goethe, *Italian Journey, 1786–1788*, trans. W. H. Auden and E. Mayer, Collins, London, 1962, p. 115.
2. Masson (ed.), *Complete Letters of Freud to Fliess*, p. 285.
3. Freud (ed.), *Letters of Sigmund Freud*, p. 293.
4. Rodolfo Lanciani, *The Destruction of Ancient Rome: A Sketch of the History of the Monuments*, Macmillan, London, 1901, p. 206.
5. Michael Grant, *The Roman Forum*, Weidenfeld and Nicolson, London, 1970, p. 205.
6. Henry James, *The Portrait of a Lady*, Oxford University Press, London, 1968, p. 311.
7. Luigi Borsari, *The Roman Forum in the Light of Recent Discoveries*, 2nd edition, Officina poligrafica romana, Rome, 1901; Lanciani, *The Destruction of Ancient Rome*; and Umberto Leoni, *The Palatine, Monuments of Rome*, no. 8, Frank, Rome, n.d.
8. Luigi Kasimir (1881–1962) specialised in topographical studies and landscapes. He did a series of engravings of the Forum including *Arch of Septimus Severus* (1923) and *Rome – Arch of Titus* (1924).

9. *Civilization and Its Discontents*, S.E., vol. XXI, p. 70; p. 69.

10. Masson (ed.), *Complete Letters of Freud to Fliess*, p. 449.

11. Jones, II, p. 20.

12. Freud (ed.), *Letters of Sigmund Freud*, p. 263.

13. Sigmund Freud, *Unser Herz*, p. 136.

14. *The Interpretation of Dreams*, S.E., vol. IV, pp. 194–196.

15. Rheims, *Art on the Market*, p. 33.

16. *The Interpretation of Dreams*, S.E., vol. IV, p. 198.

17. *The Psychopathology of Everyday Life* was first published in two parts in the journal *Monatsschrift für Psychiatrie und Neurologie*, in July and August 1901 and in book form in 1904.

18. Rheims, *Art on the Market*, p. 9.

19. *The Interpretation of Dreams*, S.E., vol. IV, p. 196. In a footnote added in 1925, Freud writes that the author he is quoting is probably novelist Jean Paul Richter.

20. Johann Joachim Winckelmann, *Writings on Art*, selected and ed. David Irwin, Phaidon, London, 1972, p. 140.

21. Johann Joachim Winckelmann, *Reflections on the Imitation of Greek Works in Painting and Sculpture*, trans. Elfriede Heyer and Roger C. Norton, Open Court, La Salle, Illinois, c.1987, p. 5.

22. 'Delusions and Dreams in Jensen's *Gradiva*' (1906 [1907]), S.E., vol. IX, pp. 2–95.

23. Masson (ed.), *Complete Letters of Freud to Fliess*, p. 440.

24. Goethe, *Italian Journey*, p. 123; p. 120.

25. Freud (ed.), *Letters of Sigmund Freud*, p. 260.

26. 'The Goethe Prize' (1930), S.E., vol. XXI, pp. 207-212.

27. Masson (ed.), *Complete Letters of Freud to Fliess*, p. 342.

28. Jacob Burckhardt, *The Greeks and Greek Civilization*, trans. Sheila Stern, ed. and with an introduction by Oswyn Murray, St Martin's Press, New York, 1998, p. 25. Freud had six of Burckhardt's books in his library, including *Geschichte der Renaissance in Italien* (The History of the Renaissance in Italy) (1891), *Griechische Kulturgeschichte* (The History of Greek Civilization) (1898–1902), *Die Zeit Constantins des Grossen*, (The Times of Constantine the Great) (1880), *Der Cicerone* (The Cicerone) (1855), *Die Cultur der Renaissance in Italien*, (The Culture of Renaissance Italy) (1896) and *Vorträge* (Lectures) 1844–1887 (1918).

29. Freud, *Unser Herz*, p. 141.

30. Gamwell and Wells (eds) *Sigmund Freud and Art*, p. 115.

31. *Diary of Sigmund Freud, 1929–1939: A Record of the Final Decade.* See pp. 86 and 279 for further discussion of the *Sarchophagus*.

32. Freud (ed.), *Letters of Sigmund Freud*, p. 260.

33. 'On the History of the Psychoanalytic Movement' (1914), S.E., vol. XIV, p. 25.

34. Freud, *Glory Reflected*, p. 110.

35. Sachs, *Freud, Master and Friend*, p. 102.

36. Jones, II, pp. 152–153.

37. 'On the History of the Psychoanalytic Movement', S.E., vol. XIV, p. 39.

38. Jones, II, p. 43.

39. Jones, II, p. 153.

40. Freud to Max Eitingon, quoted in Jones, II, p. 419.

41. Sachs, *Freud, Master and Friend*, p. 153.

42. Freud (ed.), *Letters of Sigmund Freud*, pp. 382–383.

43. *Committee Ring Sándor Ferenczi*. Roman Gem. Carnelian in modern setting. c.100 B.C.–100 A.D. (?), 1 cm × 1 cm diameter. Österreichische Nationalbibliothek. Some doubt remains about the stone's authenticity. See Lydia Marinelli (ed.), '*Meine ... alten und dreckigen Götter*': *Aus Sigmund Freuds Sammlung* ('My Old and Grubby Gods': From Sigmund Freud's Collection), Strömfeld Verlag, Vienna, 1998, p. 145.

44. G. M. A. Richter, *The Engraved Gems of the Greeks, Etruscans and the Romans*, Phaidon, London, 1971, vol. 2, p. 2.

45. Freud (ed.) *Letters of Sigmund Freud*, p. 283.

46. *The Psychopathology of Everyday Life* (1901), S.E., vol. VI, pp. 205–206. Freud added this story in 1919.

47. Masson (ed.), *Complete Letters of Freud to Fliess*, pp. 456–457.

48. The painting by Orlik is no longer in the collection of the Modern Gallery (now the Österreichische Galerie Belvedere). The von Gomperz family built up a large collection of Orlik's work that was exhibited at the Jewish Museum Vienna in 1997. Orlik formed a lifelong friendship with Max von Gomperz's daughter, Marie. The von Gomperz family, from Brno in Moravia, is not to be confused with Elise Gomperz (née Sichrovsky), a patient of Freud's, who also tried to help secure the promotion for Freud and who was a friend of Baroness Marie von Ferstel. For Elise Gomperz see Lisa Appignanesi and John Forrester, *Freud's Women: Family, Patients, Followers*, Basic Books, New York, 1992, pp. 172–174.

49. Jones, II, p. 340.

50. Masson (ed.), *Complete Letters of Freud to Fliess*, p. 457.

51. Quoted in Ernest Pfeiffer (ed.), *Sigmund Freud and Lou Andreas-Salomé: Letters*, Hogarth Press and the Institute of Psychoanalysis, London, 1972, p. 230.

52. Freud, *Unser Herz*, p. 216.

53. *The Freud Journal of Lou Andreas-Salomé*, trans. and with an Introduction by Stanley A. Leavy, Basic Books, New York, 1964, p. 101.

54. Brabant, Falzeder and Giampieri-Deutsch (eds), *Correspondence of Sigmund Freud and Sándor Ferenczi*, vol. 1, p. 135.

55. Peter Ucko, 'Unprovenanced Material Culture and Freud's Collection of Antiquities', *Journal of Material Culture*, November 2001, vol. 6 (3), pp. 269–322 for discussion of objects in Freud's collection held in Freud Museum London and most likely to have derived from Duna Pentele.

56. Brabant, Falzeder and Giampieri-Deutsch (eds), *Correspondence of Sigmund Freud and Sándor Ferenczi*, vol. 1, p. 137; p. 147; p. 152.

57. Rheims, *Art on the Market*, p. 182.

58. Mauries, *Cabinets of Curiosities*, p. 182.

59. Brabant, Falzeder and Giampieri-Deutsch (eds), *Correspondence of Sigmund Freud and Sándor Ferenczi*, vol. 1, p. 152; p. 169.

60. Masson (ed.), *Complete Letters of Freud to Fliess*, p. 110.

61. Masson (ed.), *Complete Letters of Freud to Fliess*, p. 398.

Chapter Eight: Conversations with the Sphinx

1. *New Introductory Lectures on Psycho-analysis* (1933 [1932]), S.E., vol. XXII, p. 116.
2. Sophocles, *King Oedipus*, in *The Theban Plays*, trans. E. F. Watling, Penguin, Harmondsworth, (1947), 1968, p. 36.
3. Freud and Alexander did manage a short visit to Corfu on their way to Athens. They found a guide and walked the streets, realising the signs in Greek would take some time to interpret. Freud found the town 'clean and friendly'. Despite the extremely hot weather, they climbed to the town's fortress – Freud noting that Alexander would not allow him to stop at an antiquities shop along the way. Freud regarded the view of the sea and surrounding hills as indescribably beautiful. (Freud, *Unser Herz*, p. 188.)
4. 'A Disturbance of Memory on the Acropolis' (1936), S.E., vol. XXII, pp. 240-241.
5. *Totem and Taboo* (1913), S.E., vol. XIII, p. 157; p. 156.
6. Masson (ed.), *Complete Letters of Freud to Fliess*, p. 427. The book Freud was probably referring to is Maxime Collignon's *A Manual of Greek Archaeology*, published in English in 1886. Freud's edition was *Handbuch der griechen Archaeologie*, P. Friesenhahn, Leipzig, n.d.
7. Freud, *Unser Herz*, p. 190. In his print collection, Freud had a nineteenth-century etching of the Acropolis by Albert Linke after George Nestel.
8. Walter Burkert, *Greek Religion, Archaic and Classical*, trans. John Raffan, Basil Blackwell, Oxford, 1985, p. 139; John

Fleming, Hugh Honour and Nikolaus Pevsner, *Penguin
Dictionary of Architecture*, Penguin, Harmondsworth, 1972,
p. 124.

9. 'A Disturbance of Memory on the Acropolis' (1936),
    S.E., vol. XXII, pp. 246–247.

10. Freud, *Unser Herz*, p. 185.

11. Freud, *Unser Herz*, p. 193.

12. *Corinthian Black-figured Alabastron*, Greek, Archaic Period,
    c.600 B.C., terracotta, 28.2 cm high. cat. no. 3699. See
    Lucilla Burn in Gamwell and Wells (eds), *Sigmund Freud
    and Art*, p. 83. Michael Molnar writes that early in 1931,
    Freud bought a Corinthian vase from a Viennese dealer
    named Frölich – but which one Freud does not specify.
    (*Diary of Sigmund Freud, 1929–1939: A Record of the Final
    Decade*, p. 94.)

13. Nanno Marinatos, *The Goddess and the Warrior: The Naked
    Goddess and Mistress of Animals in Early Greek Religion*,
    Routledge, London, New York, 2000, p. 97.

14. *Artemis*, Greek, Hellenistic Period, from Myrina, 2nd
    century B.C., terracotta, 25 cm high, cat. no. 3273. Lucilla
    Burn in Gamwell and Wells (eds), *Freud and Art*, p. 105.

15. Freud was amused by the vicissitudes a pagan deity like
    Artemis could undergo via Christianity. In his essay
    'Great is Diana of the Ephesians', he describes how, after
    the destruction of the temple to Artemis (Diana) at
    Ephesus in Turkey, a basilica to the Virgin Mary was built,
    'the new mother-goddess of the Christians . . . Now once
    again the city had its great goddess and, apart from her

name, there was very little change.' (S.E. (1911), vol. XII, p. 343.)

16. Nicholas Reeves writes 'it has been suggested that the term "sphinx" originated from an Egyptian expression, *shesep ankh*, which means "living image".' Reeves also points out that Egyptian sphinxes were usually but not always male. (In Gamwell and Wells (eds), *Freud and Art*, p. 50.) Andrew Wilson points out 'the derivation of the name "sphinx" is unknown (it is not Greek or Indo-European at all, although it first appears in Greek in the 5th century B.C.) and we don't know what the Egyptians called him. But a widely accepted theory is that he was called *shesepankh* . . . The Greek word would then be derived from an attempt at pronouncing this! The sphinx would be the living image of the (eternal) god and the (mortal) king simultaneously.' (*Oedipus and the Sphinx*, The Classics Pages, www.users.globalnet.co.uk/~loxias/ sphinx.htm). Robert Graves, on the other hand, suggests "Sphinx" means "throttler" and observes that in Etruscan ceramic art 'she is usually portrayed as seizing men, or standing on their prostrate figures, because she was fully revealed only at the close of the king's reign when she choked his breath.' (*The White Goddess: A Historical Grammar of Poetic Myth*, Faber, London, 1961, p. 417.) Camille Paglia writes the Greek Sphinx was 'born of the incest of the half-serpent Echidna with her dog-son Orthus . . . Her name means "the Throttler" (from the Greek *spiggo*, "strangle").' (Camille Paglia, *Sexual Personae*, p. 50.)

17. Works Freud could have seen in 1904 are *Statue of a Sphinx*, c.570–550 B.C., pentelic marble, found at Sparta, 0.69 m, cat. no. 56; *Statue of a Sphinx*, c.540 B.C., parian marble, found Piraeus 1880, 0.79 m, cat. no. 57 and *Statue of a Sphinx*, c.645 B.C., parian marble, found on Aegina, 0.70 m, cat. no. 58. See Nikolaos Kaltsas, *Sculptures in the National Archaeological Museum Athens*, J. Paul Getty Museum, Los Angeles, 2002, p. 54 and p. 63.

18. Hesiod described Orthrus (Orthos) as the son of the half-woman, half-serpent Echidna and Typhon, a 'terrible lawless brute'. (Hesiod, *Theogony* and *Works and Days*, p. 12.) See also Lowell Edmunds, *Oedipus: The Ancient Legend and its Later Analogues*, Johns Hopkins University Press, Baltimore & London, 1985, pp. 8–12; pp. 52–55.

19. Laius, Thebes' king, had raped a young man named Chrysippus and the goddess Hera demanded punishment. See Lowell Edmunds, 'The Sphinx in the Oedipus Legend', in Lowell Edmunds and Alan Dundas (eds), *Oedipus: A Folklore Legend*, Garland, New York, 1983, especially pp. 155–159.

20. Timothy Ganz, *Early Greek Myth: A Guide to Literary and Artistic Sources*, Viking Arkana, London, 1996, pp. 495–6. As Ganz points out, 'this type of scene with numerous men gathered around the column and no single figure identified as Oedipus repeats itself often in the late sixth and early fifth century'. The Kunsthistorisches Museum Vienna has a black-figured *Oedipus and the Sphinx*, Pelike (wine carrier), 39 cm 470–460 B.C., a work Freud

may have seen. Ganz identifies the pelike as representing a scene of the Sphinx with the Theban elders.

21. Sophocles, *King Oedipus*, p. 36.

22. H. D. F. Kitto, *The Greeks*, Penguin, Harmondsworth (1957), 1985, p. 177.

23. Masson (ed.), *Complete Letters of Freud to Fliess*, p. 272.

24. Peter L. Rudnytsky, *Freud and Oedipus*, Columbia University Press, New York, 1987, p. 12.

25. *Three Essays on Sexuality* (1905), S.E., vol. VII, p. 226, fn 1 (added 1920).

26. *The Interpretation of Dreams*, S.E., vol. IV, p. 262.

27. *The Interpretation of Dreams*, S.E., vol. IV, p. 262.

28. Introductory Lectures on Psychoanalysis, 1917, S.E., vol. XVI, p. 335.

29. 'Some Psychical Consequences of the Anatomical Distinctions between the Sexes' (1925), S.E., vol. XIX, p. 252.

30. *New Introductory Lectures on Psychoanalysis*, S.E., vol. XXII, p. 128.

31. *New Introductory Lectures on Psychoanalysis*, S.E., vol. XXII, p. 132.

32. *New Introductory Lectures on Psychoanalysis*, S.E., vol. XXII, p. 113.

33. Quoted in Jones, II, p. 421.

34. Appignanesi and Forrester, *Freud's Women*, p. 342.

35. Emma Jung to Sigmund Freud, 6 November 1911. Emma wondered that Freud's children, after he discussed his concerns about them, might need psychoanalysis. (McGuire (ed.), *The Freud–Jung Letters: The Correspondence Between Sigmund*

Freud and C. G. Jung, p. 456.) Freud's reply (now lost) made Emma Jung realise, 'You were really annoyed with my letter, weren't you?' Afraid of having offended Freud, Emma offered a grovelling apology and asked, 'Please write nothing of this to Carl.' (*Freud–Jung Letters*, p. 462.) Later, Emma told Freud that Jung was 'astonished to see one of your letters addressed to me; but I only revealed a little of their content.' (*Freud–Jung Letters*, p. 467.)

36. 'amort/ise. 1. to liquidate or extinguish (an indebtedness or charge) usually by periodic payments (or entries) made to a sinking fund, to a creditor, or to an account. 2. *Old Eng Law*. to convey to a corporation; alienate in mortmain.' (*The Macquarie Dictionary*, The Macquarie Library, Sydney, 1992, p. 55–56.)

37. Quoted by Peter Gay in *Freud, A Life for Our Time*, p. 163. See Gay, p. 673 for explanation of source.

38. Appignanesi and Forrester, *Freud's Women*, p. 343.

39. Jones, II, p. 14.

40. *Freud–Jung Letters*, p. 88. In the same letter to Jung, Freud writes, 'Two years ago I was obliged (by the regulations) to have my picture taken for the Hygiene Exhibition but I so detest the picture that I won't lift a finger to let you have it. At about the same time my boys took a picture of me; it is much better, not at all artificial.' Schwerdnter based his image of Freud on that photograph, probably taken by Martin Freud. The photograph is reproduced in Freud, Freud and Grubrich-Simitis (eds), *Sigmund Freud: His Life in Words and Pictures*, p. 186.

41. Freud (ed.) *Letters of Sigmund Freud*, p. 187.

42. Paglia, *Sexual Personae*, p. 50.

43. *An Autobiographical Study* (1925), S.E., vol. XX, p. 37.

44. Carl Jung, *Four Archetypes: Mother, Rebirth, Spirit, Trickster*, Arc, London, 1988, pp. 144–151.

45. Jones, II, p. 421.

46. Ovid, *Metamorphoses*, trans. and introduction by May M. Innes, Penguin, Harmondsworth, 1955, p. 115.

47. *The Interpretation of Dreams*, S.E., vol. V, p. 357.

48. Marinatos, *The Goddess and the Warrior*, p. 54.

49. Homer, *The Odyssey*, trans. Walter Shewring, Oxford University Press, Oxford, 1980, pp. 5–9.

50. 'Medusa's Head' (1940 [1922]), S.E., vol. XVIII, p. 273.

51. 'Medusa's Head' (1940 [1922]), S.E., vol. XVIII, p. 274.

52. 'A Mythological Parallel to a Visual Obsession' (1916), S.E., vol. XIV, p. 338.

53. In the *Homeric Hymn to Demeter*, Baubo is known as Iambe, like the iambic metre in which satirical poems were written. As Karolyi Kerenyi writes, 'Her role was to make Demeter laugh by jests and mockery, to turn her grief to tenderness. This she succeeded in doing by means of obscene gestures which the Homeric poet's style forbids him to describe.' But in another version of the myth, Iambe becomes Baubo (belly) whose home Demeter visits. 'She did not hesitate to perform an obscene dance before the goddess and to throw herself on her back. In this way she made Demeter laugh'. (Karolyi Kerenyi, *Eleusis: Archetypal Image of Mother and Daughter*, trans. Ralph

Manheim, Routledge and Kegan Paul, London, 1967,
pp. 39–40.) Donald Bailey, former curator, British
Museum, writes this figure is 'a beneficent fertility demon,
made to go into a household shrine for the well-being and
fecundity of a family and its animals. Made in Egypt, such
figures seem to be of the Ptolemaic period, not closely
dated with the third to the first century B.C. Such figures
are also found in the Cyrenaica, which was under
Ptolemaic control for much of the same period. The
modern identification of them with the Baubo met with
by Demeter during her search for Kore is very probably
wrong.' (Email to the author, 29 April 2005.)

54. 'A Mythological Parallel to a Visual Obsession' (1916),
S.E., vol. XIV, p. 338. Freud notes that, by exposing
herself, Baubo was enacting a forgotten magical ritual and
refers to Salomon Reinach's *Cultes, Mythes et Religions*
(1912). Eleusis became the site for the sacred mysteries of
Demeter and Persephone.

55. Marinatos, *The Goddess and the Warrior*, p. 57.

56. By 1900, Louis Comfort Tiffany was a world leader in the
Art Nouveau and Arts and Crafts movements and
America's leading designer. John Loring writes that
Tiffany & Company's store on Fifth Avenue, which
opened in 1905, was 'the new American temple of
decorative arts and industry . . . the temple of true
American style'. While inspired by a range of cultures,
including ancient Egypt, all goods sold at Tiffany's were
contemporary, original designs. John Loring, *Tiffany's 20th*

Century: *A Portrait of American Style*, Harry N. Abrams, New York, 1997, p. 26.

57. *Five Lectures on Psychoanalysis* (1910 [1909]), S.E., vol. XI, p. 47.

58. Quoted in Jones, II, p. 57.

59. Quoted in Jones, II, p. 60.

60. Sigmund Freud, *Unser Herz*, p. 299.

61. See entry for Gisela M. A. Richter at www.lib.duke.edu/lilly/artlibry/dah/richterg.

62. Calvin Tomkins, *Merchants and Masterpieces: The Story of the Metropolitan Museum of Art*, Longmans, London & Harlow, 1970, p. 124.

63. Gisela M. A. Richter, *The Craft of Athenian Pottery*, Yale University Press, New Haven, 1923, p. xii.

64. Brabant, Falzeder, and Giampieri-Deutsch (eds), *Correspondence of Sigmund Freud and Sándor Ferenczi*, vol. 1, p. 73. Freud could have also seen Cypriot objects bought from Cesnola in the Kunsthistorisches Museum Vienna.

65. Elizabeth McFadden, *The Glitter and the Gold: A Spirited Account of the Metropolitan Museum of Art's First Director, the Audacious and High-handed Luigi Palma di Cesnola*, Dial Press, New York, 1971, p. 163.

66. As McFadden points out, the collection was not intact. Cesnola was already involved in private sales, gifts and formal auctions that amounted to around 4000 pieces. See McFadden, *The Glitter and the Gold*, p. 127.

67. Quoted from the New York *Tribune*, 1880, in McFadden, *The Glitter and the Gold*, p. 186.

68. Vassos Karageorghis, *Ancient Art from Cyprus: The Cesnola Collection in the Metropolitan Museum of Art*, The Metropolitan Museum of Art, New York, 2000, p. 4. The Metropolitan did not keep its entire collection. In 1928 a large portion was auctioned by the museum and now 6000 pieces remain. Today Cesnola's collection is divided between numerous museums including the British Museum, Musée du Louvre, Paris, Museum of Fine Arts Boston, Kunsthistorisches Museum Vienna, Cantor Center for the Visual Arts at Stanford University and the Ringling Museum Florida.

69. Hesiod, *Theogony* and *Works and Days*, p. 9. For Aphrodite in the Cesnola collection see Karageorghis, *Ancient Art from Cyprus*, p. 212.

70. In 1971, together with other antiquities from Freud's collection, Anna Freud gave thirteen Cypriot works to the Sigmund Freud Museum Vienna. For catalogue details see Marinelli (ed.), '*Meine . . . alten und dreckigen Götter*': *Aus Sigmund Freuds Sammlung*, ('My . . . Old and Grubby Gods': From Sigmund Freud's Collection), pp. 125–129.

71. Freud, *Unser Herz*, p. 305.

72. Freud, *Unser Herz*, p. 307.

73. Freud, *Unser Herz*, p. 314. Written in English.

CHAPTER NINE: TOMB RAIDER

1. H.D. (Hilda Doolittle), *Tribute to Freud*, p. 42.

2. Quoted in Pfeiffer (ed.), *Sigmund Freud and Lou Andreas-Salomé: Letters*, p. 230.

3. Paglia, *Sexual Personae*, p. 60.

4. Brabant, Falzeder and Giampieri-Deutsch (eds), *Correspondence of Sigmund Freud and Sándor Ferenczi*, vol. 1, p. 513.

5. H.D. (Hilda Doolittle), *Tribute to Freud*, p. 9. Though H.D. refers to it as 'the Temple at Karnak', the print shows the Great Temple of Ramesses II at Abu Simbel, Nineteenth Dynasty, c.1260 B.C. In 1964–1968, the temple was dismantled and moved to a hill behind the original temple site in order to save it from the rising waters of Lake Nasser following the construction of the Aswan High Dam.

6. *The Interpretation of Dreams*, S.E., vol. V, p. 583.

7. Masson (ed.), *Complete Letters of Freud to Fliess*, p. 366.

8. E. A. Wallis Budge, *Amulets and Superstitions*, Oxford University Press, London, 1930, p. xxv.

9. As Kasia Szpakowska points out, the story of Joseph was written with an Israelite audience in mind. 'The point of the episode is that Joseph is the successful dream interpreter and not the Egyptian *hartummim* (dream interpreters) who appear unfamiliar with the practice of dream interpretation and indeed are singularly inept in helping their pharaoh.' (Kasia Szpakowska, *Behind Closed Eyes: Dreams and Nightmares in Ancient Egypt*, Classical Press of Wales, Swansea, 2003, pp. 63–64.)

10. *The Interpretation of Dreams*, S.E., vol. V, p. 484 fn2.

11. 'An Autobiographical Study', S.E., vol. XX, p. 43.

12. *The Interpretation of Dreams*, S.E., vol. IV, p. 96; vol. V, p. 614.

13. 'An Autobiographical Study', S.E., vol. XX, p. 43.

14. See Helmut Satzinger, *Das Kunsthistoriches Museum in Wien, Die Aegyptisch-Orientalische Sammlung*, (The Art History Museum in Vienna, The Egyptian-Oriental Collection) Kunsthistoriches Museum Wien und Verlag Philipp von Zabern, Mainz, 1994.

15. Sir James Frazer, *The Golden Bough: A Study in Magic and Religion*, Wordsworth Reference, Ware, 1993, (1922 abridged version), p. 367.

16. Egyptians believed there were several places to which spirits departed after death – they lived in the bodies of animals and birds, they entered the stars, they lived in the Boat of the Sun or they entered Tuat. (E. A. Wallis Budge, *Osiris and the Egyptian Resurrection*, Medici Society, London, 1911, vol. 2, p. 156.)

17. Frazer, *The Golden Bough*, p. 367.

18. Nicholas Reeves in Gamwell and Wells (eds), *Sigmund Freud and Art*, p. 75.

19. *Introductory Lectures on Psychoanalysis* (1915–1916), S.E., vol. XV, p. 230.

20. For a complete list of E. A. Wallis Budge's books in Freud's collection see Wendy Botting and J. Keith Davies, 'Freud's Library and Appendix of Texts related to Antiquities', in Gamwell and Wells (eds), *Sigmund Freud and Art*, p. 188.

21. Nicholas Reeves in Gamwell and Wells (eds) *Sigmund Freud and Art*, p. 76.

22. Plutarch's *Isis and Osiris* is the other major source for these gods. Plutarch's *Moralia*, volume 5, records the only known narrative account of the Isis and Osiris myth.

23. 'The Claims of Psychoanalysis to Scientific Interest' (1913), S.E., vol. XIII, p. 177.

24. *Totem and Taboo*, S.E. vol XIII, p. 1.

25. *The Question of Lay Analysis* (1926), S.E., vol. XX, p. 214.

26. Jones, II, p. 351.

27. Edward W. Said, *Freud and the Non-European*, introduction by Christopher Bollas and a response by Jacqueline Rose, published in association with the Freud Museum London, Verso, London & New York, 2003, pp. 15–16.

28. Budge, *Amulets and Superstitions*, p. 138.

29. Budge, *Amulets and Superstitions*, p. 131.

30. Nicholas Reeves in Gamwell and Wells (eds) *Sigmund Freud and Art*, p. 63.

31. *The Ego and the Id* (1923), S.E., vol. XIX, pp. 34–37; p. 53.

32. E. A. Wallis Budge, *The Gods of the Egyptians, or Studies in Egyptian Mythology*, vol 1, Dover Publications, New York, (1904), 1969, p. 401.

33. An ancient baboon god called 'the Great White One' (*hedj wer*) was worshipped at Hermopolis Magna, a town later associated with the worship of Thoth. Patrick Boylan speculates on the origins of Thoth's connection with the ape, discounting the theory that apes displayed 'uneasiness and sadness during the time of the moon's invisibility' as well as 'the popular fancy which attributed peculiar knowledge and astuteness to the apes.' (Patrick Boylan, *Thoth: The Hermes of Egypt*, Oxford University Press, Oxford, 1922, p. 76, fns 1 and 2.) C. J. Bleeker points out

that 'whenever Thoth takes action and makes pronouncements, he appears in human form with the head of an ibis' but 'for domestic use the effigies of Thoth as a baboon were made'. (C. J. Bleeker, *Hathor and Thoth: Two Key Figures of the Ancient Egyptian Religion*, Leiden, Brill, 1973, pp. 108–113.

34. *Moses and Monotheism*, S.E., vol. XXIII, pp. 19–20.

35. Nicholas Reeves in Gamwell and Wells (eds), *Sigmund Freud and Art*, p. 65.

36. Freud kept thirty-six authentication documents from the Kunsthistorisches Museum that are preserved at the Freud Museum London, a small number in relation to his collection. The documents were prepared either by curators Dr Julius Banko or Dr Hans von Demel during the 1920s and 1930s.

37. Quoted in *Diary of Sigmund Freud, 1929–1939: A Record of the Final Decade*, p. 168.

38. Freud's *Mummy Portrait* from the Graf collection is documented in Paul Buberl, *Die Griechisch-Aegyptischen Mumienbildnisse der Sammlung Theodore Graf* (Greek-Egyptian Mummy Portraits in the Collection of Theodore Graf), Krystallverlag, Vienna, 1922. Titled *Alterer Mann* (Old Man) the *Portrait* (cat. no. 4946) discussed here is published as no. 53 in Buberl and no. 482 in Klaus Parlasca, *Repertorio d' arte dell'Egitto greco-romano*, (Inventory of Egyptian Graeco-Roman Art), L'Erma di Bretschneider, Rome, 1977, p. 88. *Mummy Portrait I* was bought prior to 1922, while *Mummy Portrait II* was bought 24 July 1931. See

Diary of Sigmund Freud, 1929–1939: A Record of the Final
Decade pp. 100 and 282.

39. *Moses and Monotheism*, S.E., vol. XXIII, p. 19.

40. Pfeiffer (ed.), *Sigmund Freud and Lou Andreas-Salomé,
Letters*, p. 27.

41. *The Freud Journal of Lou Andreas-Salomé*, p. 89.

42. *The Psychopathology of Everyday Life* (1901), S.E., vol. VI,
p. 167.

43. *The Psychopathology of Everyday Life* (1901), S.E., vol. VI,
pp. 169–170. Paragraph added 1907.

44. *The Psychopathology of Everyday Life* (1901), S.E., vol. VI,
pp. 169–170. Paragraph added 1907.

45. Ronald Clark, *Freud: The Man and the Cause*, Granada,
London, 1982, p. 220.

46. Masson (ed.), *Complete Letters of Freud to Fliess*, p. 113.

47. McGuire (ed.), *The Freud–Jung Letters: The Correspondence
Between Sigmund Freud and C. G. Jung*, p. 219.

48. David Bakan was told by Jewish scholar Chaim Bloch that
in Freud's library he saw 'a large collection of Judaica . . .
Among the books were a number of books on Kabbala in
German, and most importantly a copy of the French
translation of the *Zohar*.' Bakan notes these books are
absent from the extant Freud library. (David Bakan,
Sigmund Freud and the Jewish Mystical Tradition, Beacon Press,
Boston, 1975, p. xviii.) Freud owned both a German
translation and the Hebrew/Aramaic original of the
Babylonian Talmud that remain in his library today at the
Freud Museum London.

49. Jones, II, p. 392.
50. Quoted in a letter from Freud to Jones in Jones, II, p. 392.
51. I am grateful to Christian Huber, Sigmund Freud Museum Vienna, for locating and making available to me the original plans of Berggasse 19 showing both sets of Freud's rooms.
52. Freud (ed.), *Letters of Sigmund Freud*, pp. 378–379. In a letter to Julie Braun-Vogelstein, Braun's widow, Freud recalled visiting Adler at Berggasse 19. 'It strikes me as strange that this took place in the same rooms as those in which I have been living for the past thirty-six years.'
53. Sachs, *Freud, Master and Friend*, p. 51.
54. Jones, II, p. 51.
55. '"Civilized" Sexual Morality and Modern Nervous Illness' (1908), S.E., vol. IX, pp. 183–184.
56. Brabant, Falzeder and Giampieri-Deutsch (eds), *Correspondence of Sigmund Freud and Sándor Ferenczi*, vol. III, p. 78.
57. Sigmund Freud, *Unser Herz*, pp. 244–245.
58. Freud bought several museum publications including *Coins of Syracuse*, Set 24, British Museum, London, n.d.; *A Guide to the Babylonian and Assyrian Antiquities*, British Museum, London, 1900; *A Guide to the First and Second Egyptian Rooms*, 2nd ed., British Museum, London, 1904; *A Guide to the Third and Fourth Egyptian Rooms*, British Museum, London, 1904.
59. Russell Chamberlin, *Loot!: The Heritage of Plunder*, Thames and Hudson, London, 1983, p. 56. In 1820, Belzoni published his popular book *Narrative of the Operations and*

Recent Discoveries with the Pyramids, Temples, Tombs and Excavations in Egypt and Nubia.

60. Quoted in Chamberlin, *Loot!*, p. 61.

61. *Leonardo da Vinci and a Memory of his Childhood* (1910), S.E., vol. XI, p. 63.

62. McGuire (ed.), *The Freud–Jung Letters: The Correspondence Between Sigmund Freud and C. G. Jung*, p. 255; p. 260.

63. *Leonardo da Vinci and a Memory of his Childhood* (1910), S.E., vol. XI, p. 74; p. 75; p. 82; p. 88.

64. *Leonardo da Vinci and a Memory of his Childhood* (1910), S.E., vol. XI, Editor's Note, p. 61; p. 134.

65. *Moses and Monotheism* (1939), S.E., vol. XXIII, p. 7.

66. Freud to Arnold Zweig, 6 November 1934. Quoted in Gay, *Freud: A Life for Our Time*, p. 608.

67. *Moses and Monotheism* (1939), S.E., vol. XXIII, pp. 18–20.

68. *Moses and Monotheism* (1939), S.E., vol. XXIII, p. 21, fn 1; James H. Breasted, *History of Egypt from the Earliest Time to the Persian Conquest*, Hodder and Stoughton, London, 1906, p. 356. Freud marked the whole paragraph and underlined the word 'individual'. 'Akhenaten gradually developed ideals and purposes which make him the most remarkable of all the Pharaohs, and the first *individual* in human history.'

69. Cyril Aldred points out that Breasted was influenced by the pioneering research of Sir William Flinders Petrie after the latter's work at Tell el-Amarna in 1894. Flinders Petrie's admiration for Akhenaten was unreserved. He was 'the philosopher, moralist, religious reformer, art

innovator and idealist, almost anticipating the nineteenth century scientist and pacifist'. But Flinders Petrie and his followers were duped by the pharaoh's official propaganda. Recent historical assessments of the pharaoh are not so favourable. (Cyril Aldred, *Akhenaten: King of Egypt*, Thames and Hudson, London, 1988, p. 112.) Freud had several books by Flinders Petrie including his six-volume *A History of Egypt: From the Earliest Times to the XVI Dynasty*, Methuen, London, 1899–1905.

70. *Moses and Monotheism* (1939), S.E., vol. XXIII, p. 19.

71. *Moses and Monotheism* (1939), S.E., vol. XXIII, p. 28.

72. 'The Moses of Michelangelo' (1914), S.E., vol. XIII, pp. 215–217. There has been extensive debate on Freud's interpretation of the statue. Notable contributions include Rudy Bremer, 'Freud and Michelangelo's Moses', *American Imago*, no. 33, 1976, pp. 60–75; Harold Blum, 'Freud and the Figure of Moses: The Moses of Freud', *Journal of the American Psychoanalytical Association*, no. 39, 1991, pp. 513–35 and, recently, Malcolm Macmillan and Peter J. Swales, 'Observations from the Refuse Heap: Freud, Michelangelo's *Moses*, and Psychoanalysis', *American Imago*, vol. 60, no. 1, 2003, pp. 41–104.

73. *Moses and Monotheism* (1939), S.E., vol. XXIII, p. 127.

74. Matthias Seidel, 'The Valley of the Kings', in Regine Schulz and Matthias Seidel (eds), *Egypt: The World of the Pharoahs*, trans. Helen Atkins et al., Könemann, Cologne, 1998, p. 229.

75. Quoted in H. V. F. Winstone, *Howard Carter and the*

Discovery of the Tomb of Tutankhamun, Constable, London, 1991, p. 142.

76. Sachs, *Freud, Master and Friend*, p. 102.

77. Freud (ed.), *Letters of Sigmund Freud*, pp. 424–425.

78. Hilda C. Abraham and Ernst L. Freud (eds), *A Psychoanalytic Dialogue: The Letters of Sigmund Freud and Karl Abraham, 1907–1926*, trans. Bernard Marsh and Hilda C. Abraham, Hogarth Press and the Institute of Psychoanalysis, London, 1965, pp. 334–335.

CHAPTER 10: IDOLS

1. McGuire (ed.), *The Freud–Jung Letters: The Correspondence Between Sigmund Freud and C. G. Jung*, p. 218.

2. C. G. Jung, 'Psychological Aspects of the Mother Archetype' (1938), *Four Archetypes, Mother, Rebirth, Spirit, Trickster*, Arc, London, 1988, p. 30.

3. McGuire (ed.), *The Freud–Jung Letters: The Correspondence Between Sigmund Freud and C. G. Jung*, p. 133.

4. McGuire (ed.), *The Freud–Jung Letters: The Correspondence Between Sigmund Freud and C. G. Jung*, pp. 137–139.

5. McGuire (ed.), *The Freud–Jung Letters: The Correspondence Between Sigmund Freud and C. G. Jung*, p. 165.

6. McGuire (ed.), *The Freud–Jung Letters: The Correspondence Between Sigmund Freud and C. G. Jung*, p. 49. Though Ernest Jones writes that it was Jung who suggested Freud read *Gradiva* (Jones, II, p. 341), the Freud–Jung correspondence does not mention it. Freud writes '[i]t happened that in the group of men . . . who regarded it as a fact that the

essential riddles of dreaming have been solved by the
efforts of the author ... there was one who recalled that in
the work of fiction that had last caught his fancy there
were several dreams which had ... invited him to attempt
to apply to them the method of *The Interpretation of Dreams.*'
(*Dreams and Delusions in Jensen's 'Gradiva'*, (1907 [1906]),
S.E., vol. IX, pp. 7–10.) Later in the essay, Freud remarks
that 'the one ... who was interested in the dreams in
Gradiva' approached Jensen, asking if he knew about
psychoanalytic theories. (*Dreams and Delusions in Jensen's
'Gradiva'*, p. 91.) The man in question may have been a
member of the Vienna Psychoanalytic Society.

7. Quoted in Deirdre Bair, *Jung: A Biography*, Back Bay Books,
    Little, Brown and Company, New York & Boston, 2003,
    p. 115.
8. Bair, *Jung*, p. 47.
9. McGuire (ed.), *The Freud–Jung Letters: The Correspondence
    Between Sigmund Freud and C. G. Jung*, p. xvii–xviii.
10. *Dreams and Delusions in Jensen's 'Gradiva'* (1907 [1906]), S.E.,
    vol. IX, p. 71.
11. McGuire (ed.), *The Freud–Jung Letters: The Correspondence
    Between Sigmund Freud and C. G. Jung*, p. 51.
12. Masson (ed.), *Complete Letters of Freud to Fliess*, p. 423.
13. Freud, *Glory Reflected*, p. 112; p. 113
14. Gay, *Freud: A Life for Our Time*, p. 320.
15. *Dreams and Delusions in Jensen's 'Gradiva'* (1907 [1906]), S.E.,
    vol. IX, pp. 10–18.
16. *Dreams and Delusions in Jensen's 'Gradiva'* (1907 [1906]), S.E.,

vol. IX, p. 34.

17. *Dreams and Delusions in Jensen's 'Gradiva', (1907 [1906])*, S.E., vol. IX, p. 40.

18. 'Notes upon a Case of Obsessional Neurosis' (1909), S.E., vol. X, p. 176.

19. Masson (ed.), *Complete Letters of Freud to Fliess*, p. 440. The letter was written to Fliess on 8 May, two days after Freud's birthday. Freud's annual holidays were not until September (he went to Rome) and there is no record of him leaving Vienna in May, so it is likely he purchased the fresco there. The painted red numerals on the frames, 837 B and 837 A may refer to catalogue numbers in the (lost) 1914 catalogue Freud made of the collection. There are similar red numerals on other, but not all, antiquities.

20. Sigmund Freud, *Unser Herz*, pp. 157–166.

21. Johann Joachim Winckelmann, *A Critical Account of the Situation and Destruction of Herculaneum, Pompeii and Stabia* (1771). Quoted in Robert Etienne, *Pompeii: The Day a City Died*, trans. Caroline Palmer, Thames and Hudson, London & Harry Abrams, New York, 1994, p. 146.

22. Masson (ed.), *Complete Letters of Freud to Fliess*, p. 237.

23. Ovid, *Metamorphoses*, p. 187.

24. August Mau, *Pompeii: Its Life and Art*, trans. Francis W. Kelsey, Macmillan, New York, 1899, p. 345. Freud's copy was August Mau, *Pompeji in Leben und Kunst*, Illus., W. Engelmann, Leipzig, 1900.

25. 'The Moses of Michelangelo', S.E., vol. XIII, p. 211.

26. Archaeologist and Pompeian specialist Dr Pim Allison,

Australian National University, dates the frescoes as Second Style, i.e. 1st century B.C. to 1st century A.D. and suggests they may be Roman. (Email to the author, 19 June 2005.)

27. '"Civilized" Sexual Morality and Modern Nervous Illness', S.E., vol. IX, p. 182.

28. *Dreams and Delusions in Jensen's 'Gradiva'* (1907 [1906]), S.E., vol. IX, p. 24.

29. McGuire (ed.), *The Freud–Jung Letters: The Correspondence Between Sigmund Freud and C. G. Jung*, p. 52.

30. The art dealer was Felix Nanny, Türkenstrasse 92, Munich. (McGuire (ed.), *The Freud–Jung Letters: The Correspondence Between Sigmund Freud and C. G. Jung*, p. 52, fn 6.

31. Emmanuel Löwy's postcard to Freud is in on display at the Sigmund Freud Museum Vienna. Freud pasted the postcard onto cardboard to preserve it, so its date cannot be seen. Thanks to Christian Huber, Sigmund Freud Museum Vienna, for this information.

32. *Dreams and Delusions in Jensen's 'Gradiva'* (1907 [1906]), S.E., vol. IX, p. 95.

33. Freud, *Unser Herz*, p. 243.

34. *Dreams and Delusions in Jensen's 'Gradiva'* (1907 [1906]), S.E., vol. IX, p. 95. Freud continued to explore the role of the Horae in 'The Theme of the Three Caskets', published a year after the postscript to *Gradiva*, where he pointed out that while 'originally goddesses of the waters or the sky . . . it came about that [the Horae] became divine

representatives of the Seasons . . . guardians of the natural law and of the divine Order which causes the same thing to recur in Nature in an unalterable sequence'. ('The Theme of the Three Caskets' (1913), S.E., vol. XII, p. 297.)

35. Hesiod, *Theogony* and *Works and Days*, p. 29, line 901.

36. 'Your letter has reminded me of the fact that I am the same person who picked papyrus in Syracuse, fought with railway personnel in Naples, and bought antiquities in Rome.' Freud to Ferenczi, 2 October 1910. (Brabant, Falzeder and Giampieri-Deutsch (eds), *Correspondence of Sigmund Freud and Sándor Ferenczi*, vol. 1, p. 215.)

37. McGuire (ed.), *The Freud–Jung Letters: The Correspondence Between Sigmund Freud and C. G. Jung*, p. 122; p. 98.

38. C. G. Jung, *Memories, Dreams, Reflections*, recorded and edited by Aniela Jaffe, trans. Richard and Clara Winston, Fontana Press, London, 1995, pp. 178–181.

39. Freud, *Unser Herz*, p. 286.

40. C. G. Jung, *Memories, Dreams, Reflections*, p. 48.

41. C. G. Jung, *Memories, Dreams, Reflections*, p. 181.

42. The shopping trip took place when Freud and Jung visited Munich in late December 1910/early January 1911. (McGuire (ed.), *The Freud–Jung Letters: The Correspondence Between Sigmund Freud and C. G. Jung*, p. 386.)

43. McGuire (ed.), *The Freud–Jung Letters: The Correspondence Between Sigmund Freud and C. G. Jung*, pp. 251–252; p. 255.

44. McGuire (ed.), *The Freud–Jung Letters: The Correspondence Between Sigmund Freud and C. G. Jung*, p. 262; p. 216.

45. C. G. Jung, *Memories, Dreams, Reflections*, p. 178.

46. McGuire (ed.), *The Freud–Jung Letters: The Correspondence Between Sigmund Freud and C. G. Jung*, p. 218.

47. 'Psychoanalysis and Telepathy' (1941 [1921]), S.E., vol. XVIII, p. 193.

48. McGuire (ed.), *The Freud–Jung Letters: The Correspondence Between Sigmund Freud and C. G. Jung*, p. 429.

49. Brabant, Falzeder and Giampieri-Deutsch (eds), *Correspondence of Sigmund Freud and Sándor Ferenczi*, vol. 1, p. 80. Freud developed this view further in 'Psychoanalysis and Telepathy' (1941 [1921]), S.E., vol. XVIII, writing 'we must draw the inference that there is such a thing as thought-transference' (p. 184).

50. Brabant, Falzeder and Giampieri-Deutsch (eds), *Correspondence of Sigmund Freud and Sándor Ferenczi*, vol. 1, p. 523.

51. Freud (ed.), *Letters of Sigmund Freud*, p. 334.

52. Jones, III, p. 389.

53. Smiley Blanton, *Diary of My Analysis with Sigmund Freud*, biographical notes and comments by Margaret Gray Blanton, introduction by Iago Galdston, Hawthorn Books, New York, 1971, p. 88; p. 91.

54. McGuire (ed.), *The Freud–Jung Letters: The Correspondence Between Sigmund Freud and C. G. Jung*, p. 279; p. 282.

55. *Jahrbuch für psychoanalytische und psychopathologische Forschungen* (Yearbook of psychoanalytical and psychopathological Researches) was published between 1909–1914.

56. First published as *Wandlungen und Symbole der Libido* in *Jahrbuch für psychoanalytische und psychopathologische Forschungen*

then as *Psychology of the Unconscious: A Study of the Transformations and Symbolisms of the Libido; a contribution to the history of the evolution of thought*, trans. Beatrice M. Hinkle, Routledge and Kegan Paul, London, 1916. Rewritten as *Symbols of Transformation: An Analysis of the Prelude to a Case of Schizophrenia*, trans. R. F. C. Hull, Routledge and Kegan Paul, London, 1956.

57. C. G. Jung, *Psychology of the Unconscious*, p. 3.

58. McGuire (ed.), *The Freud–Jung Letters: The Correspondence Between Sigmund Freud and C. G. Jung*, p. 441. *Totem and Taboo* was published in four parts in *Imago* between 1912 and 1913, and published as a book in 1913 under its present title.

59. McGuire (ed.), *The Freud–Jung Letters: The Correspondence Between Sigmund Freud and C. G. Jung*, p. 459; p. 460.

60. McGuire (ed.), *The Freud–Jung Letters: The Correspondence Between Sigmund Freud and C. G. Jung*, p. 487; p. 502.

61. *Moses and Montheism*, (1939) S.E., vol. XXIII, p. 83.

62. McGuire (ed.), *The Freud–Jung Letters: The Correspondence Between Sigmund Freud and C. G. Jung*, p. 504; p. 487.

63. Christopher L. C. E. Witcombe, *Women in Prehistory: The Venus of Willendorf*, pp.1–5. http://witcombe.sbc. edu/willendorf/willendorfdiscovery.html

64. Similar *Female Figures* from the Orontes Valley and from the same period are in the Ashmolean Museum Oxford, cat. no. 256 (AN 1949.180) and especially cat. no. 257 (AN 1949.180). Like Freud's figure, it is unknown from which site in Syria they were recovered. For further

discussion of *Female Figure* see Jonathan Tubb in Gamwell
and Wells (eds) *Sigmund Freud and Art*, p. 36.

65. Roger Moorey, *Ancient Near Eastern Terracottas in the
Ashmolean Museum*, p. 2. www.ashmol.ox.ac.uk/ash/
amocats/anet/pdf-files/ANET-29Bronze2Syr-Catalogue-2.
pdf. The excavations took place in 1998.

66. Nicholas Reeves in Gamwell and Wells (eds) *Freud and
Art*, p. 47.

67. C. G. Jung, *Psychology of the Unconscious*, p. 144.

68. McGuire (ed.), *The Freud–Jung Letters: The Correspondence
Between Sigmund Freud and C. G. Jung*, p. 522.

69. C. G. Jung, *Psychology of the Unconscious*, p. 58.

70. C. G. Jung, *Memories, Dreams, Reflections*, pp. 180–181.
For Jones' account of the same incident see Jones, II,
pp. 145–147.

71. *Moses and Monotheism*, S.E., vol. XXIII, p. 23.

72. E. A. Wallis Budge, *The Gods of the Egyptians, or Studies in
Egyptian Mythology*, vol 2, p. 5.

73. McGuire (ed.), *The Freud–Jung Letters: The Correspondence
Between Sigmund Freud and C. G. Jung*, p. 534–535.

74. Freud (ed.), *Letters of Sigmund Freud*, p. 302.

75. 'On the History of the Psychoanalytical Movement'
(1914), S.E., vol. XIV, p. 43.

76. C. G. Jung, *Memories, Dreams, Reflections*, p. 194.

77. Louis Rose, *The Freudian Calling: Early Viennese Psychoanalysis
and the Pursuit of Cultural Science*, Wayne State University
Press, Detroit, 1998, p. 154.

78. Quoted in Bair, *Jung*, p. 537.

79. Jung, 'Psychological Aspects of the Mother Archetype',
    pp. 20–21.

CHAPTER 11: FAMILY, FRIENDS AND DEALERS

1. Jones, II, p.99.
2. Brabant, Falzeder and Giampieri-Deutsch (eds),
   Correspondence of Sigmund Freud and Sándor Ferenczi, vol. 2.
   pp. 13–14. The catalogue Freud made has been lost and is
   not referred to elsewhere.
3. Jones, III, p. 3.
4. Quoted in Elisabeth Young-Breuhl, *Anna Freud: A
   Biography*, Macmillan, London, 1988, p. 58.
5. Brabant, Falzeder and Giampieri-Deutsch (eds),
   Correspondence of Sigmund Freud and Sándor Ferenczi, vol. 2,
   p. 56.
6. Quoted in Young-Breuhl, *Anna Freud: A Biography*, p. 76.
7. Freud (ed.), *Letters of Sigmund Freud*, p. 301. This seems a
   better translation of the passage than the one that appears
   in *Correspondence of Sigmund Freud and Sándor Ferenczi*, vol. 1,
   p. 499, which reads 'My next company will be my little
   daughter.'
8. Jones, II, p. 99.
9. Freud, *Glory Reflected*, p. 59.
10. Elizabeth Ewing, *History of Twentieth Century Fashion*, Barnes
    and Noble, Totowa, New Jersey, 1986, p. 91.
11. Quoted in Joanne Entwistle, *The Fashioned Body: Fashion,
    Dress, and Modern Social Theory*, Polity Press, Malden, Mass.,
    2000, p. 118.

12. Ruth M. Reichmann, 'Tracht: Native Dress, Fashion or Costume?', *Indiana German Heritage Society Newsletter*, Fall 1996, vol. 12, issue 4, www.serve.com/shea/germusa/trachten.htm

13. Joanne Finkelstein, *After a Fashion*, Melbourne University Press, Carlton South, 1996, p. 41.

14. Susan Stanford Friedman (ed), *Analyzing Freud: Letters of H.D., Bryher and Their Circle*, New Directions, New York, 2002, p. 128.

15. 'Analysis of a Phobia in a Five-year-old Boy' (1909), S.E., vol. X, pp. 5–149.

16. Young-Breuhl, *Anna Freud*, pp. 76–77.

17. Paul Roazen, *Freud and his Followers*, Alfred A. Knopf, New York, 1975, p. 444.

18. Ferdinand Schmutzer's 1926 portrait of Freud was commissioned to celebrate his 70th birthday. Schmutzer (1870–1928) was professor of etching at Vienna Academy and a skilled etcher who produced popular rural and genre studies. Thanking the artist, Freud wrote, 'The etching is now to hand, and I have already seen it in Artaria's shop window. [Artaria & Co. was a Viennese music-publishing house that also published prints.] My family and colleagues react to it in one of two ways: either they admire it at first sight or they find it too severe, then, after looking at it for a long time, they admit that it looks more and more like me. I am deriving enormous pleasure from it and I feel compelled to thank you, for the trouble you have taken to reproduce my ugly face and to assure

you once more that only now do I feel secure for posterity. I may say that I fully expect the picture to appeal to a wider circle of people.' (Quoted in Harald Leupold-Löwenthal, Hans Lobner and Inge Scholz-Strasser (eds), *Sigmund Freud Museum* (English edition), Gingko Press, Corte Madera, California, 1995, p. 99.

19. E. A. Wallis Budge, *The Gods of the Egyptians, or Studies in Egyptian Mythology*, vol. 1, p. 451.

20. *New Larousse Encyclopedia of Mythology*, trans. Richard Aldington and Delano Ames, introduction by Robert Graves, Hamlyn, Twickenham, 1986, p. 108.

21. H.D. (Hilda Doolittle) *Tribute to Freud*, p. 187.

22. John Loring, *Tiffany's 20th Century: A Portrait of American Style*, Harry N. Abrams, New York, 1997, p. 26.

23. Alistair Duncan, *Louis Comfort Tiffany*, H. N. Abrams in association with the National Museum of American Art, Smithsonian Institution, New York, c.1992, p. 11.

24. H.D. (Hilda Doolittle) *Tribute to Freud*, p. 174.

25. Young-Breuhl, *Anna Freud*, p. 139.

26. Freud (ed.) *Letters of Sigmund Freud*, p. 301.

27. 'The Theme of the Three Caskets' (1913), S.E., vol. XII, p. 293; p. 297.

28. 'The Theme of the Three Caskets' (1913), S.E., vol. XII, p. 301.

29. Masson (ed.), *Complete Letters of Freud to Fliess*, p. 67.

30. Quoted in Gay, *Freud: A Life for Our Time*, p. 170.

31. Brabant, Falzeder and Giampieri-Deutsch (eds), *Correspondence of Sigmund Freud and Sándor Ferenczi*, vol. 3,

p. 124. On 30 April 1924, after another major operation, Freud wrote, 'Physically, I am still suffering in all kinds of places. The most painful is the stricture caused by the scar, which often makes it impossible to stick a cigar in my teeth, and which can only be counteracted mechanically by distention, by means of a clothespin.'

32. Jones, III, p. 94.

33. Max Schur, *Freud, Living and Dying*, Hogarth Press and the Institute of Psychoanalysis, London, 1972, p. 247.

34. *Civilization and its Discontents*, S.E., vol. XXI, p. 81.

35. Frank Riessman and David Carroll, 'A New View of Addiction: Simple and Complex', *Social Policy Magazine*, vol. 27, no. 2, Winter, 1996, http://www.selfhelpweb.org/addiction.html; Pfeiffer (ed.), *Sigmund Freud and Lou Andreas-Salomé: Letters*, p. 205; Freud (ed.), *Letters of Sigmund Freud*, p. 403.

36. Schur, *Freud, Living and Dying*, p.412.

37. Freud (ed.), *Letters of Sigmund Freud*, p. 424.

38. Ruitenbeek (ed.), *Freud As We Knew Him*, p. 359.

39. McGuire (ed.), *The Freud–Jung Letters: The Correspondence Between Sigmund Freud and C. G. Jung*, p. 393.

40. Madelon Sprengnether, *The Spectral Mother: Freud, Feminism and Psychoanalysis*, Cornell University Press, Ithaca & London, 1990, p. 127.

41. *Beyond the Pleasure Principle* (1920), S.E., vol. XVIII, p. 10; p. 63.

42. *Civilization and its Discontents*, S.E., vol. XXI, pp. 91-92.

43. 'On Transience' (1916), S.E., vol. XIV, p. 307.

44. Fang Jing Pei, *Treasures of the Chinese Scholar*, Weatherhill,

New York, 1997, p. 2.

45. Jane Portal in Gamwell and Wells (eds), *Sigmund Freud and Art*, p. 130.

46. Michael Sullivan, *An Introduction to Chinese Art*, Faber & Faber, London, 1971, p. 190.

47. Mae Anna Pang, Senior Curator, Asian Art, National Gallery of Victoria, email to the author, 3 August 2005.

48. According to Chinese astrologer Shelly Wu, 'two additional aspects worth noting are Freud's 6.30 pm birthtime which places him in the hours ruled by the scrutinizing and resourceful Rooster. His May birthmonth (known as the "5th moon" of the Chinese lunar year) is ruled by the sage Snake. The Snakes are the philosophical and deep spiritual advisers and psychiatrists of the Asian zodiac, known for flawless skin and flawless advice.' (Email to the author, 4 August 2005).

49. Carol Michaelson, *Gilded Dragons: Treasures from China's Golden Ages*, British Museum, London, 1999, p. 59.

50. Michael Molnar notes Marie Bonaparte gave Freud a Tang camel on 6 May 1933. Freud writes that a jade bowl and a camel came into the collection 5 September 1935. Freud does not specify which of the two Tang camels Bonaparte gave him. See *Diary of Sigmund Freud, 1929–1939: A Record of the Final Decade*, pp. 149; 189.

51. Jane Portal in Gamwell and Wells (eds), *Sigmund Freud and Art*, p. 127.

52. Freud (ed.), *Letters of Sigmund Freud*, p. 392.

53. H.D. (Hilda Doolittle) *Tribute to Freud*, p. 67.

54. Freud quotes from *Diary of Sigmund Freud, 1929–1939: A Record of the Final Decade*, pp. 114

55. Molnar also notes that Japanese translations were flooding in and Japanese psychologists coming to Europe to study. *Diary of Sigmund Freud, 1929–1939: A Record of the Final Decade*, p. xxi.

56. Quoted in *20 Maresfield Gardens: A Guide to the Freud Museum*, Serpent's Tail, London, 1998, p. 27.

57. *Diary of Sigmund Freud, 1929–1939: A Record of the Final Decade*, p. 70. In May 1930, Freud was staying at the sanatorium at Schloss Tegel, near Berlin, to be fitted for a new prosthesis.

58. *Diary of Sigmund Freud, 1929–1939: A Record of the Final Decade*, p. 75.

59. Alfred Bernhard-Walcher, 'Ein Stück aus Freuds Sammlung im Kunsthistoriches Museum Wien' (A Piece from Freud's Collection in the Art History Museum Vienna), in Marinelli (ed.), '*Meine . . . alten und dreckigen Götter': Aus Sigmund Freuds Sammlung*, ('My . . . Old and Grubby Gods': From Sigmund Freud's Collection), p. 155.

60. Ernest Lustig (Robert's son), telephone interview, Seminole, Florida, 23 September 2005.

61. Ernest Lustig (Robert's son), telephone interview, Seminole, Florida, 23 September 2005.

62. Lynn Gamwell, 'The Origins of Freud's Antiquities Collection', in Gamwell and Wells (eds), *Sigmund Freud and Art*, p. 29, fn 9.

63. *Diary of Sigmund Freud, 1929–1939: A Record of the Final*

Decade, pp. 198–199. On 30 October 1936, Freud records buying a 'new horse'. It maybe be imitation Tang or an archaic Greek horse.

64. Lynn Gamwell, 'The Origins of Freud's Antiquities Collection', in Gamwell and Wells (eds), *Sigmund Freud and Art*, p. 30, fn 16.

65. Pfeiffer (ed.), *Sigmund Freud and Lou Andreas-Salomé: Letters*, p. 202.

66. *Diary of Sigmund Freud, 1929–1939: A Record of the Final Decade*, p. 170; p. 176.

67. Freud (ed.), *Letters of Sigmund Freud*, p. 298.

CHAPTER 12: ANALYSIS AMONG THE RUINS

1. H.D. (Hilda Doolittle), *H.D. Collected Poems, 1912–1944*, ed. Louis L. Martz, New Directions, New York, 1986, p. 451.

2. H.D. (Hilda Doolittle), *Tribute to Freud*, p. 98.

3. H.D. (Hilda Doolittle), *Tribute to Freud*, p. 18. A differing view is offered by Margaret Gray Blanton, commenting on Freud's analysis of her husband, Dr Smiley Blanton. When Dr Blanton made notes on the sessions, Freud who knew about the notes, 'offered no objection whatever to any future use my husband might make of them. In such matters, Freud held the view that every individual was completely free to write as he wished about his personal experience, including analysis.' (Blanton, *Diary of My Analysis with Sigmund Freud*, p. 5.) For another account from the same period, 1934, see Joseph Wortis, *Fragments of an*

Analysis with Freud, McGraw-Hill, New York, 1975. Unlike the relationships with Blanton and H.D., Wortis and Freud seemed to irritate one another in equal measure.

4. The gift of the puppy, one of a litter from Freud's chow Lün, caused great consternation to H.D. and Bryher, who did not want the responsibility of the dog and did not know how to politely reject it. But the dog died soon after birth, solving the situation. Quotes are from Blanton, *Diary of My Analysis with Sigmund Freud*, p. 42; p. 31.

5. 'My Recollections of Sigmund Freud' in Gardiner (ed.), *The Wolf-Man and Sigmund Freud*, p. 150.

6. Robert P. Knight, 'A Visit with Freud', in Ruitenbeek (ed.), *Freud As We Knew Him*, p. 115.

7. Eileen Gregory, *H.D. and Hellenism, Classic Lines*, Cambridge University Press, Cambridge, 1997, p. 108.

8. H.D. (Hilda Doolittle), *Tribute to Freud*, p. 148.

9. 'A Note Upon The "Mystic Writing Pad"' (1925 [1924]), S.E., vol. XIX, pp. 227–232.

10. Imagism was an Anglo-American modernist poetry movement formulated by Ezra Pound around 1912. Its adherents included H.D. and Richard Aldington, though it was also to influence Marianne Moore and T. S. Eliot. Averse to the excesses of Romantic and Victorian poetry, Imagism was committed to precision in image and language and sought to relate the sculptural qualities of hardness and clarity to poetry. In 1912, Pound appended the name 'H.D. – Imagiste' to one of Doolittle's poems and she continued to publish, and to be known, by her initials.

Pound, Aldington and H.D. were united by their interest
in exploring classical Greek poetic models, especially
Sappho. Quoting Pound, Susan Stanford Friedman
describes 'the essence of the imagist task' as locating 'the
"image" that incarnated an "intellectual and emotional
complex in an instant of time" – or, to use T. S. Eliot's later
term, the "objective correlative" of subjective experience.'
(Susan Stanford Friedman, *Psyche Reborn: The Emergence of
H.D.*, Indiana University Press, Bloomington, 1981, p. 2.)

11. H.D. (Hilda Doolittle), *H.D. Collected Poems, 1912–1944*,
     p. 300.

12. H.D. (Hilda Doolittle), *Tribute to Freud*, p. 13.

13. Friedman (ed.), *Analyzing Freud*, p. 11. In her letter to
     Havelock Ellis, H.D. is quoting Bryher 'who says, in her
     witty way, "Sigmund Freud is sold on artists".'

14. Margaret Gray Blanton notes that, during the 1930s,
     Freud 'accepted as patients only those who planned to
     become professional analysts.' It was under these terms
     her husband, Dr Smiley Blanton, was accepted for analysis.
     (Blanton, *Diary of My Analysis with Sigmund Freud*, p. 5.)

15. Friedman (ed.), *Analyzing Freud*, p. 34. H.D. may be
     referring to either the *Mummy Bandages* or *Mummy Covering*.
     Her first visit was on 1 March when she mentions the
     Egyptian cloth. On 13 March 1933, Freud records that an
     'Egyptian fabric painting' came into the collection. (*Diary
     of Sigmund Freud, 1929–1939: A Record of the Final Decade*,
     p. 144.)

16. H.D. (Hilda Doolittle), *Tribute to Freud*, p. 119.

17. Friedman (ed.), *Analyzing Freud*, 'rather whimsically and ironically', p.11; remainder of quotes, p.34.

18. H.D. (Hilda Doolittle), *Tribute to Freud*, p. 17.

19. H.D. (Hilda Doolittle), *Tribute to Freud*, p. 13; p. 124; Friedman (ed.) *Analyzing Freud*, p. 34; p. 39.

20. Friedman (ed.), *Analyzing Freud*, Letter to Havelock Ellis, p. 45

21. Friedman (ed.), *Analyzing Freud*, p. 100; p. 44.

22. 'On Beginning the Treatment'(1913), S.E., vol. XII, p. 143.

23. H.D. (Hilda Doolittle), *Tribute to Freud*, p. 175.

24. Friedman (ed.), *Analyzing Freud*, p. 144

25. H.D. (Hilda Doolittle), *Tribute to Freud*, pp. 67–68.

26. H.D. (Hilda Doolittle), *Tribute to Freud*, pp. 146–147.

27. H.D. (Hilda Doolittle), *Tribute to Freud*, p. 68–69. Italics H.D.'s.

28. H.D. *Collected Poems*, p. 455.

29. H.D. (Hilda Doolittle), *Tribute to Freud*, p. 70; p. 187.

30. Friedman (ed.), *Analyzing Freud*, p. 331.

31. Evangeline Adams, *Astrology: Your Place Among the Stars*, Putnam, London (1940?), p. 8. H.D. received as gifts both Adams, *Astrology: Your Place Among the Stars*, Dodd Mead, New York, 1930, and *Astrology: Your Place in the Sun*, Dodd Mead, New York, 1927.

32. Friedman (ed.), *Analyzing Freud*, p. 203.

33. 'Dreams and Occultism' (1933[1932]), *New Introductory Lectures on Psychoanalysis*, S.E., vol. XXII, p. 34

34. H.D. (Hilda Doolittle), *Tribute to Freud*, p. 141.

35. Barbara Guest, *Herself Defined: The Poet H.D. and her World*,

Doubleday, Garden City, N.Y., 1984, pp. 207–208.

36. Friedman (ed.), *Analyzing Freud*, p. 100.

37. H.D. (Hilda Doolittle), *Tribute to Freud*, p. 67; p. 118; p. 67; p. 122.

38. H.D. (Hilda Doolittle), *Tribute to Freud*, p. 67; p. 124

39. H.D. (Hilda Doolittle), *Tribute to Freud*, p. 68.

40. Adalaide Morris, 'A Relay of Power and of Peace: H.D. and the Spirit of the Gift', in Susan Stanford Friedman and Rachel Blau du Plessis (eds), *Signets: Reading H.D.*, University of Wisconsin Press, Madison, 1990, p. 67.

41. Gregory, *H.D. and Hellenism*, p. 66.

42. H.D. (Hilda Doolittle), *Tribute to Freud*, p. 25.

43. H.D. *Collected Poems, 1912–1944*, p. 456.

44. Friedman (ed.), *Analyzing Freud*, p. 325.

45. H.D. (Hilda Doolittle), *Tribute to Freud*, p. 59.

46. H.D. (Hilda Doolittle), *Tribute to Freud*, p. 61; p. 84.

47. Friedman (ed.), *Analyzing Freud*, p. 303.

48. *Three Essays of the Theory of Sexuality* (1905), S.E., vol VII. p. 145 fn.

49. H.D. (Hilda Doolittle), *Bid Me to Live (A Madrigal)*, Dial Press, New York, 1960, p. 8.

50. H.D. (Hilda Doolittle), *Tribute to Freud*, p. 194.

51. H.D. (Hilda Doolittle), *Ion: A Play after Euripides*, Black Swan Books, Redding Ridge, CT, c.1986, p. 117; pp. 112–113.

CHAPTER 13: UNDER THE PROTECTION OF ATHENA

1. Freud (ed)., *Letters of Sigmund Freud*, p. 445.

2. Debórah Dwork and Robert Jan van Pelt, *Holocaust: A History*, John Murray, London, 2002, p. 95.

3. Adolf Hitler, *Mein Kampf*, p. 31.

4. Hamann, *Hitler's Vienna: A Dictator's Apprenticeship*, p. 71.

5. Engelman, *Sigmund Freud: Berggasse 19, Vienna*, p. 89.

6. Dwork and van Pelt, *Holocaust*, p. 123.

7. Jones, III, p. 151.

8. Schur, *Freud, Living and Dying*, p. 498.

9. Schur, *Freud, Living and Dying*, p. 499.

10. Paul Hofmann, *The Viennese: Splendour, Twilight and Exile*, p. 242.

11. Dwork and van Pelt, *Holocaust*, p. 124.

12. Paul Hofmann, *The Viennese*, p. 244.

13. Sigmund Freud and William Bullitt, *Thomas Woodrow Wilson, Twenty-eighth President of the United States: A Psychological Study*, Weidenfeld and Nicolson, London, 1967. Bullitt waited until Ellen Wilson, Woodrow Wilson's second wife, had died before publishing the book.

14. *Diary of Sigmund Freud, 1929–1939: A Record of the Final Decade*, p. 236.

15. For the fate of those books Freud chose to sell see Botting and Davies, 'Freud's Library and an Appendix of Texts Related to Antiquities', in Gamwell and Wells (eds), *Sigmund Freud and Art, His Personal Collection of Antiquities*, p. 186.

16. Quoted in *Diary of Sigmund Freud, 1929–1939: A Record of the Final Decade*, p. 236.

17. Arnold Werner, 'Edmund Engelman, Photographer of Freud's Home and Offices', *International Journal of Psychoanalysis*, vol. 83, 2002, p. 446.

18. For an overview on photography in Vienna see Monika Faber, '*Amateurs et Autres: Histoire de la Photographie (1887–1936)*', in *Vienne, 1880–1938: l'apocalypse joyeuse/sous la direction Jean Clair* ('Amateurs and Others: History of Photography in Vienna, 1880–1938: The Joyful Apocalypse'), Centre Georges Pompidou, Paris, c.1986, pp. 377–395.

19. Engelman, *Sigmund Freud*, p. 91; p. 93.

20. Susan Sontag, *On Photography*, Delta, New York, 1977, p. 133.

21. In November 1938, when Engelman escaped from Vienna, he could not risk taking the Freud negatives and gave them to Aichhorn for safekeeping. Then Engelman and his fiancée made their way to New York. After the war, Engelman returned to Vienna, trying to find his negatives only to learn that Aichhorn had died. Aichhorn's family had given the negatives to his secretary who, in turn, had given them to Anna Freud. Engelman then travelled to London and visited 20 Maresfield Gardens where he received the negatives from Anna. He was 'moved to see once more the beautiful pieces of art and furniture that I had last seen under such difficult circumstances.' (Engelman, *Sigmund Freud*, p. 102.)

22. Engelman, *Sigmund Freud*, pp. 96–97.

23. Quoted in Jones, III, p. 225.

24. Engelman, *Sigmund Freud*, p. 99.

25. Directly opposite the Belvedere Palace at 26 Prinz Eugengasse, the Rothschild Palace is now the embassy of Brazil. It was built in 1894 for Albert von Rothschild and in 1920 it was occupied by his son, Louis, until it was taken over by the Nazis in 1938. See also Pauline Prévost-Marcilhacy, *Les Rothschild: bâtisseurs et mécènes* (The Rothschilds: builders and patrons), Flammarion, Paris, 1996, pp. 358–359. I am grateful to Melanie Aspey, The Rothschild Archive, for information about the Rothschild Palace.

26. Immediately after the Anschluss, Louis' brothers, Alphonse and Eugene, managed to escape but Louis was stopped at Vienna airport by SS officers. After Louis was released, he made his way to America. See Derek A. Wilson, *Rothschild: A Story of Wealth and Power*, Andre Deutsch, London, 1988, pp. 370–371. In July 1999, the biggest auction ever held in Europe took place at Christie's London. It was the sale of Rothschild art treasures looted by the Nazis in 1938 that had been returned to the Rothschild family. The sale of paintings, furniture and ornaments raised £56.7 million, more than double its estimated value.

27. Engelman, *Sigmund Freud*, p. 99.

28. *The Complete Correspondence of Sigmund Freud and Ernest Jones, 1908–1939*, ed. R. Andrew Paskauskas, introduction by Riccardo Steiner, Belknap Press of Harvard University Press, Cambridge, Mass., 1993, p. 764.

29. Quoted in *Diary of Sigmund Freud, 1929–1939: A Record of*

the *Final Decade*, p. 237. The family did not leave together.
Minna and Dorothy Burlingham left first while Martin
and his family left on 14 May, Mathilde (Freud's eldest
daughter) and her husband Robert Hollitscher left on
24 May. Max Schur had developed appendicitis and was
forced to remain in Vienna for an operation, and left
shortly afterwards. Dr Josefine Stross, a pediatrician and a
friend of Anna's, accompanied Freud in Schur's place. The
Freuds were also accompanied by their chow, Lün, who
went into quarantine at Dover.

30. Quoted in *Diary of Sigmund Freud, 1929–1939: A Record of
   the Final Decade*, p. 237.

31. Freud (ed.), *Letters of Sigmund Freud*, p. 445–6.

32. Freud (ed.), *Letters of Sigmund Freud*, p. 447–8.

33. Salvador Dalí, *The Secret Life of Salvador Dalí*, trans. Haakon
   M. Chevalier, Vision, London, 1973, p. 23. Johann Rudolf
   Count Czernin was president of Vienna's Academy of
   Fine Arts from 1823–1827 and, from 1824, was in charge
   of the Habsburg collections. Vermeer's *The Artist's Studio* –
   to which Dalí refers – formerly in the Czernin collection
   is now in the Kunsthistorisches Museum. It was a
   favourite painting of Hitler's. Count Jaromir Czernin, who
   inherited *The Artist's Studio*, sold it to Hitler in 1940.
   During 1943–44 Hitler had the work hidden, with others
   from his personal collection, in the salt mines at Aussee
   where they were discovered by the American army in
   1945. *The Artist's Studio* was then presented it to the
   Kunsthistorisches Museum. The bulk of Johann Rudolf

Count Czernin's collection was acquired by the
Residenzgalerie Salzburg during the 1950s.

34. Quoted in Jones, III, p. 235.

35. André Breton, 'Interview with Professor Freud' in
Ruitenbeek (ed.), *Freud As We Knew Him*, p. 63.

36. André Breton, *Conversations: The Autobiography of Surrealism*,
trans. and introduction by Mark Polizzotti, Paragon
House, New York, 1993, p. 60.

37. André Breton, *Communicating Vessels*, trans. Mary Ann
Caws and Geoffrey T. Harris with notes and introduction
by Mary Ann Caws, University of Nebraska Press,
Lincoln and London, 1990, p. 22. Letter from Freud
quoted p. 152. Breton received three letters from Freud
on 13 December, 14 December and 26 December, 1932.
All are translated in full in this edition.

38. Dalí, *The Secret Life of Salvador Dalí*, p. 167. fn 1.

39. James, who was also a poet and an architect, had his own
reasons for visiting Freud. He wanted to undergo analysis
with Freud. Unconvinced, Freud told Zweig that he felt
'like making it not easy for [James], so as to test the
strength of his desire and to achieve a greater measure of
willing sacrifice. Psychoanalysis is like a woman who
wants to be won but knows she is little valued if she offers
no resistance. If your J. spends too much time in reflecting
he can go to someone else later, to [Ernest] Jones or to my
daughter.' Quoted in Jones, III, p. 235.

40. Zweig, *The World of Yesterday*, p. 286.

41. Quoted in William Rubin, *Dada, Surrealism and their*

Heritage, Museum of Modern Art, New York, 1968, p. 111.

42. Ovid, *Metamorphoses*, p. 87.

43. Lomas also links Dalí's interpretation of Narcissus with *The Double*, an essay by Freud's follower Otto Rank, where the 'deathly significance of the double is intimately connected with its narcissistic meaning'. Dawn Ades, *Dalí: The Centenary Retrospective*, Thames and Hudson, London, 2004, p. 270.

44. 'On Narcissism' (1914), S.E., vol. XIV, p. 88.

45. 'Leonardo da Vinci and a Memory of his Childhood', S.E., vol. XI, p. 100.

46. Dalí, *The Secret Life of Salvador Dalí*, pp. 24–25.

47. Quoted in Jones, III, p. 235.

48. Dalí, *The Secret Life of Salvador Dalí*, p. 397.

49. The picture did not belong to Freud. It was donated to the Freud Museum London in memory of its owner, writer Helene Eliat van de Velde (1894–1949). See *20 Maresfield Gardens: A Guide to the Freud Museum*, p. 28.

50. Dali, *The Secret Life of Salvador Dali*, p. 23.

51. Zweig, *The World of Yesterday*, p. 286.

52. *Diary of Sigmund Freud, 1929–1939: A Record of the Final Decade*, p. 247.

53. Quoted in *Diary of Sigmund Freud, 1929–1939: A Record of the Final Decade*, p. 247.

54. Quoted in *Diary of Sigmund Freud, 1929–1939: A Record of the Final Decade*, p. 247.

55. The house cost £6500 and required a loan of £4000 from

Barclays Bank. For further information about the house see 20 *Maresfield Gardens: A Guide to the Freud Museum*, pp. 5–8.

56. Quoted in *Diary of Sigmund Freud, 1929–1939: A Record of the Final Decade*, p. 248.

57. H.D. (Hilda Doolittle), *Tribute to Freud*, pp. 10–11.

58. Guest, *Herself Defined*, p. 246.

59. Jones, III, p. 232.

60. 'The Theme of the Three Caskets', S.E., vol. XII, p. 301.

61. Schur, *Freud, Living and Dying*, p. 527.

62. Schur, *Freud, Living and Dying*, p. 529.

63. Young-Breuhl, *Anna Freud: A Biography*, p. 246.

Bibliography

Hilda C. Abraham and Ernst L. Freud (eds), A *Psychoanalytic Dialogue: The Letters of Sigmund Freud and Karl Abraham, 1907–1926*, trans. Bernard Marsh and Hilda C. Abraham, Hogarth Press and the Institute of Psychoanalysis, London, 1965

Evangeline Adams, *Astrology: Your Place Among the Stars*, Putnam, London, (1940?)

Dawn Ades, *Dalí: The Centenary Retrospective*, Thames and Hudson, London, 2004

D. M. Amyx, *Corinthian Vase Painting of the Archaic Period*, 3 vols, University of California Press, Berkeley, 1988

Didier Anzieu, *Freud's Self Analysis*, trans. Peter Graham, Hogarth Press and the Institute of Psychoanalysis, London, 1986

Lisa Appignanesi and John Forrester, *Freud's Women: Family, Patients, Followers*, Basic Books, New York, 1992

Karl Baedeker, *Greece, Handbook for Travellers*, 10th edition, Karl
    Baedeker, Leipzig, 1894

Karl Baedeker, *Italy, Handbook for Travellers, Central Italy and Rome*,
    10th edition, Karl Baedeker, Leipzig, 1890

Karl Baedeker, *Italy, Handbook for Travellers, First Part: Northern Italy
including Leghorn, Florence, Ravenna and Routes through Switzerland and
Austria*, 11th edition, Karl Baedeker, Leipzig, 1899

Karl Baedeker, *Italy, Handbook for Travellers, Second Part: Central Italy
    and Rome*, 13th edition, Karl Baedeker, Leipzig, 1900

Karl Baedeker, *London and its Environs*, 14th edition, Karl Baedeker,
    Leipzig, 1905

Deirdre Bair, *Jung: A Biography*, Back Bay Books, Little, Brown and
    Company, New York & Boston, 2003

David Bakan, *Sigmund Freud and the Jewish Mystical Tradition*, Beacon
    Press, Boston, 1975

Honoré de Balzac, *Lost Illusions*, trans. Herbert Hunt, Penguin,
    London, 1971

Graeme Barker and Tom Rasmussen, *The Etruscans*, Blackwell,
    Oxford, 1998

Hortense Koller Becker, 'Carl Koller and Cocaine', *Psychoanalytic
    Quarterly*, vol. XXXII, 1963

Suzanne Cassirer Bernfeld, 'Freud and Archaeology', *American
    Imago*, vol. 8, 1951

Bruno Bettelheim, *Freud and Man's Soul*, Pimlico, London, 2001

Bruno Bettelheim, *Freud's Vienna and Other Essays*, Knopf, New
    York, 1990

Smiley Blanton, *Diary of My Analysis with Sigmund Freud*, biogra-
    phical notes and comments by Margaret Gray Blanton,
    introduction by Iago Galdston, Hawthorn Books, New York,
    1971

C. J. Bleeker, *Hathor and Thoth: Two Key Figures of the Ancient Egyptian Religion*, Brill, Leiden, 1973

Harold Blum, 'Freud and the Figure of Moses: The Moses of Freud', *Journal of the American Psychoanalytical Association*, vol. 39, 1991

Walter Boelich (ed.), *The Letters of Sigmund Freud to Eduard Silberstein, 1871–1881*, trans. Arnold Pomerans, Harvard University Press, Cambridge, 1990

Petr Bogatyrev, *Vampires in the Carpathians: Magical Acts, Rites, and Beliefs in Subcarpathian Rus'*, trans. Stephen Reynolds and Patricia A. Krafcik, East European Monographs, Columbia University Press, New York, 1998

Patrick Boylan, *Thoth: The Hermes of Egypt, a Study of Some Aspects of Theological Thought in Ancient Egypt*, Oxford University Press, Oxford, 1922

Eva Brabant, Ernst Falzeder and Patrizia Giampieri-Deutsch, under the supervision of Andre Haynal (eds), *Correspondence of Sigmund Freud and Sándor Ferenczi*, trans. Peter T. Hoffer, introduction by Andre Haynal, 3 vols, Belknap Press of Harvard University Press, Cambridge, Mass. & London, 1993–2000

André Breton, *Communicating Vessels*, trans. Mary Ann Caws and Geoffrey T. Harris with notes and introduction by Mary Ann Caws, University of Nebraska Press, Lincoln & London, 1990

André Breton, *Conversations: The Autobiography of Surrealism*, trans. and with an introduction by Mark Polizzotti, Paragon House, New York, 1993

Jane Brown, *Gardens of a Golden Afternoon: A Social History of Gardens and Gardening*, Penguin, Harmondsworth, 1985

Frederick Brown, *Zola: A Life*, Farrar, Straus, Giroux, New York, 1995

Paul Buberl, *Die griechisch-Aegyptischen Mumienbildnisse der Sammlung Theodore Graf* (Greek-Egyptian Mummy Portraits in the Collection of Theodore Graf), Krystallverlag, Vienna, 1922

E. A. Wallis Budge, *Amulets and Superstitions*, Oxford University Press, London, 1930

E. A. Wallis Budge, *The Gods of the Egyptians, or Studies in Egyptian Mythology*, vols 1 and 2, Dover Publications, New York, (1904), 1969

Jacob Burckhardt, *The Cicerone: Or, Art Guide to Painting in Italy*, trans. A. H. Clough, T. Werner Lawrie, London, 1917

Jacob Burckhardt, *The Civilization of the Period of the Renaissance in Italy*, trans. S. G. C. Middlemore, C. Kegan Paul, London, vol. 1, 1898

Jacob Burckhardt, *The Greeks and Greek Civilization*, trans. Sheila Stern, edited and with an introduction by Oswyn Murray, St Martin's Press, New York, 1998

Walter Burkert, *Greek Religion, Archaic and Classical*, trans. John Raffon, Basil Blackwell, Oxford, 1985

William M. Calder II and David A. Traill (eds), *Myth, Scandal and History: The Heinrich Schliemann Controversy and a First Edition of the Mycenean Diary*, Wayne State University Press, Detroit, 1986

Russell Chamberlin, *Loot!: The Heritage of Plunder*, Thames and Hudson, London, 1983

Jean-Martin Charcot and Paul Richer, *Demonaiques dans l'art* (1887), BM Israël, Amsterdam, 1972

Jean-Martin Charcot and Paul Richer, *Difformes and les malades dans l'art* (1889), BM Israël, Amsterdam, 1972

Kenneth Clark, *The Nude: A Study of Ideal Art*, Penguin, Harmondsworth, 1970

Ronald Clark, *Freud: The Man and the Cause*, Granada, London, 1982

Peter A. Clayton, *The Rediscovery of Ancient Egypt: Artists and Travellers in the Nineteenth Century*, Thames and Hudson, London, 1982

Robert J. Clements (ed), *Michelangelo: A Self-Portrait*, Prentice-Hall, Englewood Cliffs, 1963

Edward Crankshaw, *Vienna: The Image of a Culture in Decline*, Macmillan, London, 1976

James Stevens Curl, *Egyptomania: The Egyptian Revival, An Introductory Study to a Recurring Theme in the History of Taste*, Allen and Unwin, London & Boston, 1982

Gregory Curtis, *Disarmed: The Story of the Venus de Milo*, Knopf, New York, 2003

Anna Lucia D'Agata, 'Sigmund Freud and Aegean Archaeology. Mycenaean and Cypriote Material from his collection of Antiquities', *Studi Miceni ed Egeo-Anatolici*, Gruppo Editoriale Internazionale, Roma, 1994

Salvador Dalí, *The Secret Life of Salvador Dalí*, trans. Haakon M. Chevalier, Vision, London, 1973

Eve D'Ambra, *Art and Identity in the Roman World*, Weidenfeld and Nicolson, London, 1998

Georges Didi-Huberman, *Invention of Hysteria: Charcot and the Photographic Iconography of the Salpêtrière*, trans. Alisa Hartz, MIT Press, Cambridge, Mass., 2003

Leo Deuel, *Memoirs of Heinrich Schliemann: A Documentary Portrait Drawn from his Autobiographical Writings, Letters and Excavation Reports*, Hutchinson, London, 1978

Martin L. D'Ooge, *The Acropolis*, Macmillan, New York, 1908

Debórah Dwork and Robert Jan van Pelt, *Holocaust: A History*, John Murray, London, 2002

Lowell Edmunds, *Oedipus: The Ancient Legend and its Later Analogues*, Johns Hopkins University Press, Baltimore & London, 1985

Lowell Edmunds and Alan Dundas (eds), *Oedipus: A Folklore Legend*, New York, Garland, 1983

Stuart E. Eizenstat, *Imperfect Justice, Looted Assets, Slave Labor, and the Unfinished Business of World War II*, Public Affairs, New York, 2003

Edmund Engelman, *Berggasse 19, Sigmund Freud's Home and Offices, Vienna, 1938: The Photographs of Edmund Engelman*, introduction by Peter Gay, captions by Rita Ransohoff, Basic Books, New York, 1976

Edmund Engelman, *Sigmund Freud, Berggasse 19, Vienna*, introduction by Inge Scholz-Strasser, trans. Lonnie R. Johnson, Verlag Christian Brandstaetter, Vienna, 1998

John Elsner and Roger Cardinal (eds), *The Cultures of Collecting*, Reaktion, London, 1994

Robert Etienne, *Pompeii: The Day a City Died*, trans. Caroline Palmer, Thames and Hudson, London & Harry Abrams, New York, 1992

Monika Faber, 'Amateurs et Autres: Histoire de la Photographie (1887–1936)', in Jean Clair Paris (ed.), *Vienne, 1880-1938: l'apocalypse joyeuse*, Centre Georges Pompidou, Paris, c.1986

Paul Ferris, *Dr Freud*, Counterpoint, Washington, 1997

John Follain, 'Freud's Dream Girl', *Sunday Life*, 20 July, 2003

P. R. J. Ford, *Oriental Carpet Design: A Guide to Traditional Motifs, Patterns and Symbols*, Thames and Hudson, London, 1981

Michel Foucault, *Madness and Civilization: A History of Insanity in the Age of Reason*, trans. Richard Howard, Vintage, New York, 1973

Ernst L. Freud (ed.), *Letters of Sigmund Freud*, trans. Tania and James Stern, introduction by Steven Marcus, Basic Books, New York, 1975

Ernst Freud, Lucie Freud and Ilse Grubrich-Simitis (eds), *Sigmund Freud: His Life in Words and Pictures*, biographical sketch K. R. Eissler, trans. Christine Trollope, Norton, New York & London, 1998

Ernst L. Freud, 'Some Early Unpublished Letters of Freud', *International Journal of Psychoanalysis*, vol. L, 1969

The Freud Journal of Lou Andreas-Salomé, trans. and introduction by Stanley A. Leavy, Basic Books, New York, 1964

William McGuire (ed.), *The Freud—Jung Letters: The Correspondence between Sigmund Freud and C. J. Jung*, trans. Ralph Manheim and R. F. C Hull, Princeton University Press, Princeton, 1974

R. Andrew Paskauskas (ed.), *The Complete Correspondence of Sigmund Freud and Ernest Jones, 1908—1939*, introduction by Riccardo Steiner, Belknap Press of Harvard University Press, Cambridge, Mass., 1993

Martin Freud, *Glory Reflected: Sigmund Freud — Man and Father*, Angus and Robertson, London, 1957

Diary of Sigmund Freud, 1929—1939: A Record of the Final Decade, trans. and annotated with an introduction by Michael Molnar, Freud Museum Publications, London & Scribner, New York, 1992

Sigmund Freud, *The Standard Edition of the Complete Psychological Works of Sigmund Freud*, ed. and trans. James Strachey in collaboration with Anna Freud, 24 vols, (Hogarth Press, London, 1953—1974), Vintage, London, 2001

Sigmund Freud, *Unser Herz zeigt nach dem Süden. Reisebriefe 1895—1923* (Our Heart Points to the South: Travel Letters.

1895–1923), ed. Christfried Tögel in collaboration with Michael Molnar. Aufbau-Verlag, Berlin, 2002

Saul Friedländer, *Nazi Germany and the Jews*, Vol. 1: *The Years of Persecution, 1933–1939*, Weidenfeld & Nicolson, London, 1997

Susan Stanford Friedman (ed), *Analyzing Freud: Letters of H.D., Bryher, and Their Circle*, New Directions, New York, 2002

Susan Stanford Friedman, *Psyche Reborn: The Emergence of H.D.*, Indiana University Press, Bloomington, 1981

Susan Stanford Friedman and Rachel Blau du Plessis (eds), *Signets: Reading H.D.*, University of Wisconsin Press, Madison, 1990

Lynn Gamwell and Richard Wells (eds), *Sigmund Freud and Art: His Personal Collection of Antiquities*, State University of New York, Binghamton & Freud Museum, London, 1989

E. Gans-Ruedin, *Iranian Carpets: Art, Craft and History*, Thames and Hudson, London, 1978

Timothy Ganz, *Early Greek Myth: A Guide to Literary and Artistic Sources*, Viking Arkana, London, 1996

Muriel Gardiner (ed), *The Wolf-Man and Sigmund Freud*, Hogarth Press and the Institute of Psychoanalysis, London, 1972

Peter Gay, *Freud: A Life for Our Time*, W.W. Norton & Company, New York, 1998

Peter Gay, *A Godless Jew: Freud, Atheism and the Making of Psychoanalysis*, Yale University Press, New Haven & London, 1987

Adrian Goldsworthy, *The Punic Wars*, Cassell, London, 2000

E. H. Gombrich, *Art and Illusion: A Study in the Psychology of Pictorial Representation*, Phaidon, London, 1972

Eileen Gregory, *H.D. and Hellenism: Classic Lines*, Cambridge University Press, Cambridge, 1997

Barbara Guest, *Herself Defined: The Poet H.D. and her World*, Doubleday, Garden City, N.Y., 1984

Georges Guillain, *Jean-Martin Charcot, 1825–1893: His Life – His Work*, ed. and trans. Pearce Bailey, Paul Hoeber Inc., New York, 1959

Michael Grant, *Myths of the Greeks and Romans*, Phoenix, London, (1960) 2003

Robert Graves, *The White Goddess: A Historical Grammar of Poetic Myth*, Faber, London, 1961

Brigitte Hamann, *Hitler's Vienna: A Dictator's Apprenticeship*, trans. Thomas Thornton, Oxford University Press, Oxford & New York, 2000

Hesiod, *Theogony* and *Works and Days*, trans., introduction and notes by M. L. West, Oxford University Press, Oxford & New York, 1988

H.D., *Bid Me to Live (A Madrigal)*, Dial Press, New York, 1960

H.D., *Ion: A Play after Euripides*, Black Swan Books, Redding Ridge, Conn., c.1986

H.D., *Palimpsest*, preface by Harry T Moore, note on the text by Matthew J. Bruccoli, Southern Illinois University, Carbondale,1968

H.D., *Tribute to Freud*, Carcenet, Manchester, 1985

Howard Hibbard, *Michelangelo: Painter, Sculptor, Architect*, Octopus, London, 1979

Adolf Hitler, *Mein Kampf* (My Struggle), trans. and annotated by James Murphy, Hurst and Blackett, London, 1939

Paul Hofmann, *The Viennese: Splendour, Twilight and Exile*, Doubleday, New York, 1988

Homer, *The Odyssey*, trans. Walter Shewring, Oxford University Press, Oxford, 1980

Victor Hugo, *Notre-Dame of Paris*, Penguin Books, London, 1978

Wilma Abeles Iggers (ed.), *The Jews of Bohemia and Moravia: A Historical Reader*, trans. Wilma Abeles Iggers, Káĉa Poláĉková-Henley and Katharine Talbot, Wayne University State Press, Detroit, 1992

David Irwin (ed.), *Writings on Art*, Phaidon, London, 1972

T. G. H. James and W. V. Davies, *Egyptian Sculpture*, British Museum Publications, London, 1983

William M. Johnston, *The Austrian Mind: An Intellectual and Social History, 1848–1939*, University of California Press, Berkeley, 1972

Ernest Jones, *The Life and Work of Sigmund Freud*, 3 vols, Basic Books, New York, 1953–1957

C. G. Jung, *Four Archetypes: Mother, Rebirth, Spirit, Trickster*, Ark, London, 1988

C. G. Jung, *Memories, Dreams, Reflections*, recorded and ed. Aniela Jaffe, trans. Richard and Clara Winston, Fontana Press, London, 1995

C. G. Jung, *Psychology of the Unconscious: A Study of the Transformations and Symbolisms of the Libido; A Contribution to the History of the Evolution of Thought*, trans. Beatrice M. Hinkle, Routledge and Kegan Paul, London, 4th edition, (1916) 1944

C. G. Jung, *Symbols of Transformation*, trans. R. F. C. Hull, Princeton University Press, Princeton, 1990

Nikolaos Kaltsas, *Sculptures in the National Archeological Museum Athens*, J. Paul Getty Museum, Los Angeles, 2003

Vassos Karageorghis, *Ancient Art from Cyprus: The Cesnola Collection in the Metropolitan Museum of Art*, The Metropolitan Museum of Art, New York, 2000

Karl (Karolyi) Kerenyi, *Eleusis: Archetypal Image of Mother and Daughter*, trans. Ralph Manheim, Routledge and Kegan Paul, London, 1967

Karl (Karolyi) Kerényi, *Dionysos: Archetypal Image of the Indestructible Life*, trans. Ralph Manheim, Princeton University Press, Princeton, 1976

Francis King, *Florence: Literary Companion*, John Murray, London, 1991

Michael King (ed.), H.D., *Woman and Poet*, National Poetry Foundation, University of Orono, Maine, c.1986

H. D. F. Kitto, *The Greeks*, Penguin, Harmondsworth, (1957) 1985

J. G. Kohl, *Austria, Vienna, Prague, Hungary, Bohemia and Moravia*, Chapman and Hall, London, 1843

Udo Kultermann, *The History of Art History*, Abaris Books, [New York?], 1993

Eva Laible, '"Through Privation to Knowledge": Unknown Documents from Freud's University Years', *International Journal of Psychoanalysis*, vol. 74, 1993

Serge Lancel, *Hannibal*, trans. Antonia Nevill, Blackwell, Oxford, 1998

Manfred Leithe-Jasper and Rudolf Distelberger, *The Kunsthistorisches Museum Vienna: The Treasury and the Collection of Sculpture and the Decorative Arts*, Scala, Florence & Philip Wilson, London, 1982

Bernadette Letellier, 'A Short History of the Louvre's Department of Egyptian Antiquities', in Lawrence M. Berman (ed.), *Pharaohs: Treasures of Egyptian Art from the Louvre*, Cleveland University of Art & Oxford University Press, Cleveland, 1996

Harald Leupold-Löwenthal, Hans Lobner and Inge Scholz-Strasser (eds), *Sigmund Freud Museum*, English edition prepared by Thomas Roberts, Gingko Press, Corte Madera, California, 1995

John Loring, *Tiffany's 20th Century: A Portrait of American Style*, Harry N. Abrams, New York, 1997

William O. McCagg Jr, *A History of Habsburg Jews, 1670–1918*, Indiana University Press, Bloomington, 1989

Elizabeth McFadden, *The Glitter and the Gold: A Spirited Account of the Metropolitan Museum of Art's First Director, the Audacious and High-handed Luigi Palma di Cesnola*, Dial Press, New York, 1971

Malcolm Macmillan and Peter J. Swales, 'Observations from the Refuse Heap: Freud, Michelangelo's Moses, and Psychoanalysis', *American Imago*, vol. 60, no. 1, 2003

Charles Keith Maisels, *Early Civilizations of the Old World: The formative Histories of Egypt, the Levant, Mesopotamia, India and China*, Routledge, London, 1999

Emile Mâle, *The Gothic Image*, trans. Dora Nussey, Collins, London, 1961

Nanno Marinatos, *The Goddess and the Warrior: The Naked Goddess and Mistress of Animals in Early Greek Religion*, Routledge, London, New York, 2000

Lydia Marinelli (ed.), *'Meine . . . alten und dreckigen Götter'*, *Aus Sigmund Freuds Sammlung* ('My . . . Old and Grubby Gods', From Sigmund Freud's Collection), Strömfeld Verlag, Vienna, 1998

Louis L. Martz (ed.), *H.D. Collected Poems, 1912–1944*, New Directions, New York, 1986

Jeffrey Moussaieff Masson (ed.), *The Complete Letters of Sigmund Freud to Wilhelm Fliess, 1887–1904*, Harvard University Press, Cambridge, Mass. & London, 1985

August Mau, *Pompeii: Its Life and Art*, trans. Francis W. Kelsey, Macmillan, New York, 1899

Patrick Mauries, *Cabinets of Curiosities*, Thames and Hudson, London, 2002

Margaret Medley, *The Chinese Potter: A Practical History of Chinese Ceramics*, Phaidon, Oxford, 1976

Carol Michaelson, *Gilded Dragons: Treasures from China's Golden Ages*, British Museum, London, 1999

Domenico Monaco, *Illustrated Handbook to the National Museum in Naples*, 16th edition, Naples, 1911

Frederic Morton, *Thunder at Twilight: Vienna, 1913–1914*, Charles Scribner's Sons, New York, 1989

New Larousse Encyclopedia of Mythology, trans. Richard Aldington and Delano Ames, introduction by Robert Graves, Hamlyn, Twickenham, 1986

Martin P. Nilsson, *The Mycenaean Origin of Greek Mythology*, Cambridge University Press, Cambridge, 1972

Donald J. Olsen, *The City as a Work of Art: London, Paris, Vienna*, Yale University Press, New Haven & London, 1986

Walter Otto, *Dionysus, Myth and Cult*, trans. and introduction by Robert B. Palmer, Spring Publications, Dallas, 1981

Johannes Overbeck, *Pompeji in seinen Gebaeuden, Alterheumern und Kunstwerke dargestellt* (Pompeii as Seen in its Buildings, Antiquities and Art), 4th edition., W. Engelmann, Leipzig, 1884

Ovid, *Metamorphoses*, trans. and introduction by May M. Innes, Penguin, Harmondsworth, (1955) 1983

Camille Paglia, *Sexual Personae: Art and Decadence from Nerfertiti to Emily Dickinson*, Penguin, London, 1992

Erwin Panofsky, *Studies in Iconology: Humanistic Themes in the Art of the Renaissance*, Harper & Row, New York, 1962

Fang Jing Pei, *Treasures of the Chinese Scholar*, Weatherhill, New York, 1997

Ernst Pfeiffer (ed.), *Sigmund Freud and Lou Andreas-Salomé: Letters*, trans. William and Elaine Robson Scott, Hogarth Press and the Institute of Psychoanalysis, London, 1972

Lion Phillimore, *In the Carpathians*, Constable and Company, London, 1912

Picture Gallery of the Art History Museum Vienna, introduction by Friderike Klauner, Paul Hamlyn, London, 1971

Christopher Prendegast, *Paris and the Nineteenth Century*, Blackwell, Oxford, 1992

Tom Ramussen, 'Corinth and the Orientalising Phenomenon' in Tom Rasmussen and Nigel Spivey (eds), *Looking at Greek Vases*, Cambridge University Press, Cambridge, 1991

Rita Ransohoff, 'Sigmund Freud: Collector of Antiquities', *Archaeology*, April 1975

Donald Malcolm Reid, *Whose Pharoahs?: Archaeology, Museums and Egyptian National Identity from Napoleon to World War I*, University of California Press, Berkeley, 2002

Theodor Reik, *Listening with the Third Ear: The Inner Experiences of the Psychoanalyst*, Farrar, Strauss, New York, 1964

Theodor Reik, *The Search Within: The Inner Experiences of the Psychoanalyst*, Funk and Wagnalls, New York, 1956

Maurice Rheims, *Art on the Market: Thirty-five Centuries of Collecting from Midas to Paul Getty*, trans. David Pryce-Jones, Weidenfeld and Nicolson, London, 1959

Gisela M. A. Richter, *The Craft of Athenian Pottery*, Yale University Press, New Haven, 1923

G. M. A Richter, *The Engraved Gems of the Greeks, Etruscans and the Romans*, vol. 2, Phaidon, London, 1971,

John Paul Riquelme (ed.), *Bram Stoker, Dracula: Complete, Authoritative Text with Biographical, Historical and Cultural Contexts, Critical*

Essays and Essays from Contemporary Critical Perspectives, Palgrave, New York, c.2002

Ana-María Rizzuto, *Why Did Freud Reject God?: A Psychodynamic Interpretation*, Yale University Press, London & New Haven, 1998

Paul Roazen, *Freud and his Followers*, Alfred A. Knopf, New York, 1975

Louis Rose, *The Freudian Calling: Early Viennese Psychoanalysis and the Pursuit of Cultural Science*, Wayne State University Press, Detroit, 1998

Louis Rose, *The Survival of Images: Art Historians, Psychoanalysts and the Ancients*, Wayne State University Press, Detroit, 2001

Saul Rosenzweig, *Freud, Jung and Hall the King-maker: The Expedition to America, 1909*, Rana House Press, St Louis & Hogrefe and Hubor, Gottingen, 1992

Marsha L. Rozenblit, *The Jews of Vienna, 1867–1914: Assimilation and Identity*, State University of New York Press, Albany, 1983

Hendrik M Ruitenbeek (ed.), *Freud As We Knew Him*, Wayne State University Press, Detroit, 1973

Peter L. Rudnytsky, *Freud and Oedipus*, Columbia University Press, New York, 1987

Hanns Sachs, *Freud, Master and Friend*, Harvard University Press, Cambridge, 1945

Edward W. Said, *Culture and Imperialism*, Vintage, London, 1994

Edward W. Said, *Freud and the Non-European*, introduction by Christopher Bollas and a response by Jacqueline Rose, published in association with the Freud Museum London, Verso, London & New York, 2003

Helmut Satzinger, *Das Kunsthistorisches Museum in Wien, Die Aegyptisch-Orientalische Sammlung* (The Art History Museum in Vienna, The Egyptian-Oriental Collection) Kunsthistorisches Museum Wien und Verlag Philipp von Zabern, Mainz, 1994

Derek Sayer, *The Coasts of Bohemia: A Czech History*, Princeton University Press, Princeton, 1998

Arthur Schnitzler, *My Youth in Vienna*, Weidenfeld and Nicolson, London, 1971

Carl E. Schorske, *Fin-de-siècle Vienna: Politics and Culture*, Weidenfeld and Nicolson, London, 1980

Carl E. Schorske, *Thinking with History: Explorations in the Passage to Modernism*, Princeton University Press, Princeton, c.1998

Regine Schulz and Matthias Seidel (eds), *Egypt: The World of the Pharoahs*, trans. Helen Atkins et al., Könemann, Cologne, 1998

Max Schur, *Freud, Living and Dying*, London, Hogarth Press and the Institute of Psychoanalysis, 1972

James Shedel, *Art and Society: The New Movement in Vienna, 1897–1914*, Society for the Promotion of Science and Scholarship, Palo Alto, 1981

Peter Singer, *Pushing Time Away: My Grandfather and the Tragedy of Jewish Vienna*, Fourth Estate, Sydney, 2003

Madelon Sprengnether, *The Spectral Mother: Freud, Feminism and Psychoanalysis*, Cornell University Press, Ithaca & London, 1990

Nigel Spivey, *Etruscan Art*, Thames and Hudson, London, 1997

Susan Stewart, *On Longing: Narratives on the Miniature, the Gigantic, the Souvenir, the Collection*, Duke University Press, Durham, 1993

William H. Stiebing Jr, *Uncovering the Past: A History of Archeology*, Prometheus Books, Buffalo, 1993

Michael Sullivan, *An Introduction to Chinese Art*, Faber & Faber, London, 1971

Kasia Szpakowska, *Behind Closed Eyes: Dreams and Nightmares in Ancient Egypt*, Classical Press of Wales, Swansea, 2003

A. J. P. Taylor, *The Habsburg Monarchy: A History of the Austrian Empire, 1809–1918*, Hamish Hamilton, London, 1972

Christfried Tögel and Michael Schröter, 'Jacob Freud mit Familie in Leipzig (1859). Erzaehlung und Dokumente' (Jacob Freud with his Family in Leipzig. (1859) Anecdotes and Documents), *Luzifer-Amor*, vol. 33, 2004

Calvin Tomkins, *Merchants and Masterpieces: The Story of the Metropolitan Museum of Art*, Longmans, London & Harlow, 1970

David Traill, *Schliemann of Troy: Treasure and Deceit*, John Murray, London, 1995

Agnes Huszar Vardy, 'Viennese Coffeehouses: Legend and Reality', in S. B. Vardy and A. H. Vardy, *The Austro-Hungarian Mind*, Columbia University Press, Boulder, 1989

Giorgio Vasari, *Lives of the Artists*, vol. I, trans. George Bull, Penguin Books, London, 1985

Peter Vergo, *Vienna, 1900*, National Museum of Antiquities, Edinburgh, 1983

Allen M. Ward, Fritz M. Heichelheim and Cedric A. Yeo, *A History of the Roman People*, Prentice Hall, Upper Saddle River, New Jersey, c.2003

Derek A. Wilson, *Rothschild: A Story of Wealth and Power*, Andre Deutsch, London, 1988

Johann Joachim Winckelmann, *Reflections on the Imitation of Greek*

Works in Painting and Sculpture, trans. Elfriede Heyer and Roger C. Norton, Open Court, La Salle, Illinois, c.1987

Arnold Werner, 'Edmund Engelman: Photographer of Sigmund Freud's Home and Offices', *International Journal of Psychoanalysis*, vol. 83, 2002

Arnold Werner, 'Edmund Engelman, 1907–2000', *American Journal of Psychiatry*, no. 7, July 2004

Joseph Wortis, *Fragments of an Analysis with Freud*, McGraw-Hill, New York, c.1954

Yosef Hayim Yerushalmi, 'The Purloined Kiddush Cups: Reopening the Case on Freud's Jewish Identity', in *Sigmund Freud's Jewish Heritage*, State University of New York at Binghamton, New York, 1991. Published as a supplement to Lynn Gamwell and Richard Wells (eds), *Sigmund Freud and Art: His Personal Collection of Antiquities*, State University of New York, Binghamton & Freud Museum London, 1989

Elisabeth Young-Breuhl, *Anna Freud: A Biography*, Macmillan, London, 1988

Stefan Zweig, *Mental Healers: Franz Anton Mesmer, Mary Baker Eddy, Sigmund Freud*, Cassell, London, 1933

Stefan Zweig, *The World of Yesterday*, Cassell, Sydney, 1945

Index